Wissenschaftliche Untersuchungen
zum Neuen Testament · 2. Reihe

Herausgeber/Editor
Jörg Frey

Mitherausgeber / Associate Editors
Friedrich Avemarie · Judith Gundry-Volf
Martin Hengel · Otfried Hofius · Hans-Josef Klauck

177

Paul Foster

Community, Law and Mission in Matthew's Gospel

Mohr Siebeck

PAUL FOSTER, born 1966; 1999 B.A. of Divinity (Murdoch University); 2002 D.Phil. (Oxford University); currently Lecturer in New Testament Language, Literature and Theology at the University of Edinburgh.

ISBN 3-16-148291-3
ISSN 0340-9570 (Wissenschaftliche Untersuchungen zum Neuen Testament 2. Reihe)

Die Deutsche Bibliothek lists this publication in the Deutsche Nationalbibliographie; detailed bibliographic data is available in the Internet at *http://dnb.ddb.de*.

The book was printed by Druckpartner Rübelmann GmbH in Hemsbach on non-aging paper and bound by Buchbinderei Schaumann in Darmstadt.

Printed in Germany.

Preface

This book represents a minor revision of my doctoral thesis, of the same title. The thesis was submitted to the Faculty of Theology of the University of Oxford, and was examined on All Saints' Day, 2002. Prof. Jörg Frey, editor of *WUNT 2* was extremely efficient, helpful and supportive, in reading, recommending and commenting on the manuscript within three weeks of receiving it. This level of professionalism has also been exhibited by Dr Henning Ziebritzki, Mr Matthias Spitzner, and the whole editorial team at Mohr Siebeck.

I am also very much of aware of the contribution made by Profs. Christopher Rowland (Dean Ireland's Professor of the Exegesis of Holy Scripture, The Queen's College, Oxford) and Graham Stanton (Lady Margaret's Professor of Divinity, Fitzwilliam College, Cambridge) who served as the examiners of the thesis. Their comments were both incisive and constructive. Prof. Rowland also chaired the New Testament Graduate Seminar, providing an environment that was conducive to the presentation and testing of new ideas. Prof. Stanton also examined my Master of Studies thesis, which grew into the doctoral thesis. His support throughout my graduate research has always been highly valued and I wish him well at the present time. Alongside the fertile environment of the New Testament Graduate Seminar, participation in the Seminar on Judaism in the Greco-Roman World, chaired by Prof. Martin Goodman, during the period 1999-2003, allowed me to reflect more fully on the so-called 'Parting of the Ways' debate especially from the perspective of leading scholars of Judaism.

Above all, an enormous debt of gratitude is owed to Prof. Christopher Tuckett, supervisor of the doctoral thesis. It is impossible to speak highly enough of his scholarship, breadth of insight into the New Testament, his incisive mind, and of course his understanding of Q! Yet, it is his care and compassion that marks him out as a remarkable human being. I should also like to express my gratitude to the Theology Faculty of Murdoch University, Perth, Western Australia, where I first studied theology. In particular I am indebted to Prof. Bill Loader and Dr. John Dunnill, who are scholars of the highest calibre and taught me many courses in New Testament.

Along with the personal support I have received from individuals, there are a number of institutions that have supported this research financially. In particular I should like to thank the British government for an ORS award, the

Faculty of Theology of the University of Oxford for the fully funded Graduate Scholarship, and the Provost, Sir Alan Budd, and Fellows of the Queen's College for the Holwell Studentship. Not only did Queen's support me financially, but, moreover, it provided a rich environment for academic, spiritual, sporting and social pursuits. Without doubt it lived up to its motto: *Reginae erunt nutrices tuae* (Isaiah 49.23, Vulgate).

Finally I should like to thank the two ladies who mean the most to me in this world. First, my mother for her unstinting support and never failing love. Although I have too often failed to mention it, and probably been inarticulate on those occasions when I have tried, you are without doubt the best mother I could ever have been blessed with. Second, Miss Alexandra Wyles, who has brought me more happiness than I thought it was humanly possible for one person to know. Thank you for being utterly wonderful!

St Matthew's Day, 21 September 2003   Paul Foster

Table of Contents

Chapter 1

Introduction

1.1 Aims

This study seeks to make a contribution to Matthean scholarship by looking at the issues of the social location of the community, the role of the law within that community and its attitude towards the Gentile mission. Since the early nineteen nineties there has be a trend towards viewing the community behind the gospel as primarily a Jewish separatist group with the central belief that Jesus was the Messiah.[1] Some of the strongest advocates of this position have argued that the adherents to Matthew's teaching rejected contact with Gentiles and maintained a separate existence until the group faded away in late antiquity, perhaps under the influence of the spread of Islam. By focusing on the issues of the authority base of the community especially in relation to its attitude towards Torah, as well as the community's attitude to Gentiles as reflected in the text of the gospel, this study attempts to call into question some of these recent reconstructions. Instead, it is argued that at the time of the composition of the gospel the group had been decisively rejected by other parties in formative Judaism, and that the gospel was both a supersessionary document claiming many of the prerogatives of Judaism as its own, but also a pedagogical document encouraging and instructing the community with dominical authority, to continue and enlarge upon an outwardly focused Gentile mission.

There has been much debate in the last fifty years on each of the topics of community, law and mission in Matthew's gospel, yet it is important not to treat them as separate entities, but to see them as interrelated parts of an overarching whole. Obviously, these three areas of study do not form an exhaustive list in Matthean research. Christology,[2] ecclesiology[3] and

---

[1] For a full discussion of this trend, see the survey of recent research in chapter two.

[2] For studies on Matthean Christology see Kingsbury, *Matthew: Structure, Christology, Kingdom*, Verseput, 'The role and meaning of the "Son of God" title in Matthew's Gospel', 532-56.

[3] The works on Matthean ecclesiology are legion. For a recent treatment of the group from a sociological viewpoint see Crosby, *House of Disciples: Church, Economics and Justice in Matthew*. A slightly older, but highly valuable treatment is to be found in Schweizer, *Matthäus und seine Gemeinde*.

eschatology,[4] to name but three more possibilities, are topics which are also vital in gaining a comprehensive understanding of the theology and ethos of the communities for whom Matthew wrote. It must, however, be stressed that such aspects as these are not totally neglected in the present study. Yet, they are not given equal space as the three main topics under consideration, rather they are treated in an *ad hoc* manner when the major areas require reference to such discussions. In part, this is obviously a constraint of the limited space of this study, but it is not only a purely mechanical limitation. The decision to prescind from a detailed treatment of some of these other topics does allow this work to develop in a more focused manner in relation to its core interests. These three topics already cover a breadth of Matthean material and without a certain amount of selectivity the task at hand could become undifferentiated and lacking in clarity of thought.

More significantly, however, the issues of law and missionary orientation, in relation to Gentiles, offer potentially greater insight into assessing similarities and differences between formative rabbinic movements and the intended audience of the first gospel. In part, the obvious reason for the study of these categories is the fact that both groups had attitudes to Torah and proselytising that are recorded in extant literary sources. By contrast, although Judaism must have had a group structure perhaps based around synagogue meetings, it is not possible to reconstruct with any degree of certainty significant information about such structures in order make a meaningful comparison between the organisation of the two groups. On the other hand the interest of early rabbinic writings in Torah and halakhic issues does not need to be demonstrated, for even a cursory glance at Mishnaic and Talmudic sources demonstrates the fundamental centrality of correct understanding of the law. Similarly, although the attitude to proselytization is perhaps less well known, the extant Jewish material discusses this issue at some length. As Goodman's study clearly demonstrates, the attitude of the ancient sources is nearly uniformly opposed to a highly organised and active mission to Gentiles.[5] He does not argue that conversion to Judaism did not take place but rather that there was no strong impetus to engage in missionary activity. An even more extreme conclusion is drawn by Cohen, who unlike Goodman has perhaps polarised the evidence, but nonetheless portrays Judaism in antiquity as never being mission orientated and not interested in

---

[4] For a recent treatment of Matthean eschatology see Sim, *Apocalyptic Eschatology in the Gospel of Matthew.*

[5] Goodman, *Mission and Conversion: Proselytizing in the Religious History of the Roman Empire.*

proselytising after 135 C.E.[6] By its very nature, the Matthean promotion of a mission orientated outlook should signal substantial differences from formative Judaism. Therefore, the investigation of the topic of mission in the first gospel seeks not only to illuminate the question about who were the primary focus of such proselytising activity, but also demonstrates that such activity was in itself markedly different from normative Jewish praxis.

1.2 Intended readership

One of the assumptions of this study is that there did in fact exist during the last quarter of the first century C.E. a group of people living in reasonably close geographical proximity to one another who would have been the intended audience for the first gospel. This is not to assume that Matthew was necessarily writing for a single community or meeting of believers in Jesus. As Stanton has emphasized, the genre of a gospel is markedly different from that of an epistle, and consequently a larger audience than a single group of believers seems likely for such a literary work. Thus the answer he gives to his own question, "Is it likely that Matthew would have composed such an elaborate gospel for a relatively small group?" is a resounding 'no'.[7] Accepting the hypothesis of multiple communities does not call into question the validity of reading Matthew's gospel as a partially transparent document that reflects specific tensions and concerns that arose within a fairly focused cluster of groups that were the intended first readers of the gospel.

Until relatively recently such an assumption required little or no defence. However, Bauckham's recent work attempts to overturn this widespread consensus, and instead argues that the gospels should be seen as universal in scope and not focused on specific pastoral issues within single communities.[8] Turning to that issue, it is helpful to make a few remarks about Bauckham's thesis in relation to the other gospels before focusing on Matthew. First, if Bauckham's arguments are convincing they find their strongest support in relation to the gospel of Luke. More than any other of the canonical gospels Luke, in combination with its sequel,

---

[6] Cohen, 'Was Judaism in Antiquity a Missionary Religion?', in M. Mor (ed.), *Jewish Assimilation, Acculturation and Accommodation: Past Traditions, Current Issues and Future Prospects,* 14-21.

[7] Stanton, *Gospel,* 51.

[8] Bauckham (ed.), *The Gospels for all Christians: Rethinking the Gospel Audiences.*

gives the impression of promoting an empire wide vision for Christianity.[9]
Yet, despite this outward looking vision, this does not in itself exclude the
possibility that Luke was writing with a fairly well defined group of
Christians in mind, rather than hoping to launch his literary work as a
resource for the universal church even if such a conception existed at the
time of his writing. The gospel of Mark leaves little evidence by which to
decide if it was written for a specific liminal community, or whether its
message of suffering discipleship was aimed at a wider audience.[10] By
contrast, however, John's gospel appears so clearly addressed to a single
persecuted introverted community, that it seems to clearly defy
Bauckham's overall thesis. The story of the man born blind (Jn 9) and
especially the reference to the expulsion from the synagogue as a
consequence of confessing Jesus to be the messiah (ἐάν τις αὐτὸν
ὁμολογήσῃ Χριστόν, ἀποσυνάγωγος γένηται 9.22) is most naturally
understood as reflecting a specific situation.[11] Moreover, the other
references to being put out of the synagogue (ἀποσυνάγωγος 12.42; 16.2),
the ghetto mentality[12] that appears to develop in the latter part of the
farewell discourse (chapters 15-16) in comparison to the more open stance
in the preceding chapter, and the crisis occasioned by the death of the
beloved disciple (21.20-23),[13] are all important indicators that the fourth
gospel addressed a specific group or collection of closely related
communities and was not written for the benefit of the universal church.

---

[9] In broad terms, Wilson understands the purpose of Luke in this manner. Not only
does he reject a single community, instead preferring to speak of, "The communities for
whom Luke wrote…" (117), but also, and more significantly, sees universalism built in
to Lukan theology. He states, "Insofar as Luke provides a theoretical or theological
underpinning for this notion [the particularity of the law as a Jewish possession] it is to
be found in the notion that God is 'impartial' (οὐ προσωπολήμπτης Ac. 10.34) and makes
'no distinction' (οὐθὲν διέκρινεν Ac. 15.9) between Jews and Gentiles." (Wilson, *Luke
and the Law*, 104). See also Maddox, *The Purpose of Luke-Acts*, and Squires, *The Plan of
God in Luke-Acts*.

[10] See the following works for different perspectives on Markan discipleship and the
possibility of a community behind the gospel: Weeden, *Mark – Traditions in Conflict*;
Best, *Following Jesus: Discipleship in the Gospel of Mark*; Malbon, 'Texts and Contexts:
Interpreting the Disciples in Mark'; Shiner, *Follow Me! Disciples in Markan Rhetoric*.

[11] Martyn, *History and Theology in the Fourth Gospel*.

[12] The phrase is drawn from Ashton, who notes how in this material drawn from a
later strand of the compositional history of the gospel one can see a more inwardly
looking perspective. He states, "Suffice it to say that chapters 15-16 presuppose a very
different situation; the community has become a ghetto, and the commandment of faith in
chapter 14 has been replaced by a love commandment that is markedly less universal
than the 'love your enemies' of the Sermon on the Mount." (Ashton, *Understanding the
Fourth Gospel*, 200).

[13] For a discussion of the role of the beloved disciple in the fourth gospel see
Charlesworth, *The Beloved Disciple: Whose Witness Validates the Gospel of John?*

Turning to Matthew's gospel, first it needs to be noted that, like John, there are a number of texts that are most naturally understood as reflecting a specific situation or community outlook. Among these probably the most significant are the following. First, there is the description of a conspiratorial arrangement by the Jews to falsify the facts of the resurrection (28.11-15). That the author intended this to be understood as reflecting part of the contemporary situation can be seen from the reference καὶ διεφημίσθη ὁ λόγος οὗτος παρὰ Ἰουδαίοις μέχρι τῆς σήμερον [ἡμέρας] which not only demonstrates that this pericope is included because of its contemporary significance for readers, but also suggests that it is addressed to an audience where a number of Jews were still using this argument against those who are likely to read the first gospel. Second, the question of the temple tax (Matt 17.24-27) is most plausibly understood as providing a set of nascent believers with instruction to continue paying the *fiscus Iudaicus* in spite of the fact that their primary allegiance is no longer to their Jewish heritage.[14] Likewise, Carter sees this Matthean redactional pericope as addressing specific political concerns about the legitimacy of paying the post-70 Roman tax for the temple of Jupiter Capitolinus required of Jews, including Matthew's (largely) Christian-Jewish community.[15] Third, although well documented, the references either to 'their' or 'your synagogues' (Matt 4.23; 9.35; 10.17; 12.9; 13.54; 23.34) should not be underestimated as showing the boundary division between one community as opposed to the more dominant emergent Judaism. Coupled with these three important examples of information that seems to reflect quite a narrowly focused readership one could mention the teaching on church order (Matt 18.1-10), the instruction of the rabbis (Matt 23.1-7), the equality of status among Matthew's addressees (23.8-12) and a host of smaller redactional changes that all are more plausibly understood as the evangelist's endeavour to make the traditions he has received more relevant to a specific situation.[16]

---

[14] For a treatment of the history of the *fiscus Iudaicus* and its role in the formation of Judaism as a religious entity rather than an ethnic designation see Goodman, 'Nerva, the *Fiscus Judaicus* and Jewish Identity', 40-44.

[15] Carter argues that, "The central issue is the significance of paying the tax. It is argued that its payment, as paradoxical as it may seem, does not recognize Roman sovereignty but acknowledges God's reign. God displays sovereignty in providing the tax in the fish's mouth. Paying the tax con-tests and subverts Rome's claims and anticipates the establishment of God's reign in its fullness." Carter, 'Paying the Tax to Rome as Subversive Praxis: Matthew 17.24-27', 3-31.

[16] Here Sim is most helpful in his evaluation of Bauckham's argument. He notes, "Bauckham provides no hard evidence that the gospels were open-ended texts intended for an unspecified readership. He merely assumes that this was the case because the gospels, unlike the Pauline epistles, provide no definitive indication of their intended

While Bauckham's thesis has the value of causing one to reassess the basis for assuming that the gospels address specific group situations, the arguments he puts forward do not seem to undermine such a position. Stanton may well be correct in relation to Matthew that the evangelist was not writing for a single group of believers, but for a cluster of communities. What is important here, however, is not the number of communities, but whether the author had specific knowledge of these groups and tailored the message of his gospel to address specific concerns within these groups. The answer to this question can only come through reflection on the contents of the gospel and an assessment of whether redactional changes and the inclusion of other material is undertaken for literary purposes, or to specifically address the concerns of nascent communities about which the evangelist had personal knowledge. Certain texts, including those listed above, lend support to maintaining the assumption that Matthew's gospel falls into the second category since a significant number of the editorial asides and additional material strongly suggests specific communal concerns and situations.

1.3 Methodology

A number of approaches may be used in reading and interpreting the gospels. These are of course not mutually exclusive options, but rather can often reinforce each other in the endeavour of trying to understand the evangelists' central themes and concerns. Methods such as redaction criticism, social scientific approaches and literary criticism have all offered fresh and valid insights into the New Testament texts. Yet there has been a tendency at times for certain practioners of these methodologies either to over-exaggerate the applicability of these approaches, or to use them to fill in data where the evidence is simply lacking.

1.3.1 Redaction criticism

Although the actual term *Redaktionsgeschichte* is correctly traced back to Marxsen in the late nineteen fifties,[17] the method was being practiced a decade earlier by Bornkamm in his work on Matthew, but without the

---

readers. This explanation, however, is by no means the only one on offer. It is equally possible, perhaps more probable, that the lack of identification of the readers points to the proximity between the author and the Christian community for whom he was writing." Sim, 'The Gospels for All Christians? A Response to Richard Bauckham', 17.

[17] Marxsen, *Der Evangelist Markus: Studien zur Redactionsgeschichte des Evangeliums.*

formal label 'redaction criticism'.[18] The strength of this approach was the way in which it looked in detail at the theological concerns of the evangelists.[19] However, it was predicated upon a number of assumptions that were rarely stated. These include the belief that the correct solution to the synoptic problem has been found, that the changes the evangelists made to their sources reflect specific theological concerns which are represented in a consistent manner throughout the gospels, and that this retelling of the Jesus story is aimed at a specific community with certain pastoral or pedagogical needs.[20] Yet each of these assumptions has not gone unchallenged since the rise of redaction criticism.

First, the two source theory, positing Mark and Q as the primary sources for the other synoptic gospels, while remaining the consensus position in New Testament scholarship and being the position adopted in this study, has been re-examined in great detail with alternative solutions to the synoptic problem being proposed in its place.[21] Among the most popular alternatives are: (i) the Griesbach hypothesis, championed by Farmer and his followers, which calls into question the priority of Mark and the existence of Q;[22] (ii) Farrer's theory which while supporting the idea of Markan priority argues that Q did not exist but that Luke drew directly on Matthew's gospel[23] (this 'solution' to the synoptic problem has recently been vigorously defended by Mark Goodacre);[24] (iii) the similar theory of Matthean posteriority that reverses the dependence in the Farrer

---

[18] Bornkamm's first published work in this area appeared in 1948 with his influential essay, 'Die Sturmstillung in Matthäusevangelium'.

[19] The oft repeated charge that prior to the rise of redaction criticism the evangelists were simply seen as scissor and paste theologians, or people that threaded the beads of tradition onto the thin string of their own narrative, has always been a gross oversimplification and fails to take seriously the aims of earlier form and source critics. Their primary motivation was to look at an earlier stage of the use of the material prior to it being incorporated into the gospels. In this sense, their focus simply did not fall upon the evangelists as theologians in their own right.

[20] For an extended discussion of these issues particularly in relation to Matthew see Stanton, *Gospel*, 23-53.

[21] Specifically for a defence of the existence and plausibility of reconstructing the Q source see two of my own articles: P. Foster, 'In Defence of the Study of Q'; and 'Is it Possible to Dispense with Q?'

[22] This position came to prominence in the twentieth century with the appearance of Farmer's book, *The Synoptic Problem*. Numerous works have been published in support of Farmer's arguments including, Bellinzoni, *The Two-Source Hypothesis: A Critical Appraisal*, and more recently Dungan, *A History of the Synoptic Problem*. For a critical response see Tuckett, *The Revival of the Griesbach Theory*.

[23] See in particular, Farrer, 'On Dispensing with Q'; Goulder, *Luke: A New Paradigm*; 'Is Q a Juggernaut?'; and Goodacre, *The Case Against Q*; Shellard, *New Light on Luke*.

[24] Goodacre, *The Case Against Q*; and *The Synoptic Problem: A Way Through the Maze*.

theory stating it was Matthew who was dependent on Luke;[25] and (iv) multiple source theories[26] Yet none of these alternative theories in themselves would undermine the conception of redaction criticism, for it would simply mean that instead of looking at Matthew's modifications to Mark, the process would be inverted. What would be overturned are the findings of redaction critics who have used this approach based on the two-source theory.

The second assumption is perhaps the most important, for it undergirds the very practice of redaction criticism. It argues that the modification of source material reflects clear and consistent theological motivations on the part of the evangelists.[27] The first point to make in response to this is that 'the use of Christian tradition as it stands, without editorial shaping, may be just as much an indication of the evangelist's theological outlook.'[28] In other words, the very fact that an evangelist has incorporated source material without modification is plausibly an indication that he found the theological outlook of the predecessor's work congenial, and agreed with the views it expressed. While this point needs to be made, and ensures that the complete text of the gospel is considered when it is being examined for clues relating to the purpose of the evangelist in writing, it must be recognized that editorial alterations provide important examples of how traditions have been modified to bring them into closer accord with the beliefs of the author.[29] The second part of this assumption is that the evangelists present a clear theology that reflects a consistent portrayal of their own beliefs. However, such a degree of consistency should perhaps not be expected from the evangelists. Recent studies have called into question the consistency of Paul, who perhaps was the one New Testament figure who attempted to present his theological understandings in a

---

[25] The fullest argument for this case may be found in Huggins 'Matthean Posteriority', but see also Hengel, *The Four Gospels and the One Gospel of Jesus Christ*, 169-207.

[26] Vaganay, *Le problème synoptique: une hypothèse de travail*; Boismard, *Synopse des quatre évangiles en français*, Tome 2: Commentaire; 'The Multiple Stage Hypothesis'.

[27] For a discussion of this point of view see Perrin, *What is Redaction Criticism?*

[28] Smalley, 'Redaction Criticism', 188.

[29] A specific example of this process may be seen in the christological affirmation in Matt 16.16. The extended Petrine confession, Σὺ εἶ ὁ Χριστὸς ὁ υἱὸς τοῦ θεοῦ τοῦ ζῶντος, appears to reflect a more exalted understanding of Jesus than that contained in the Markan source (Mk 8.29). Perhaps some will see a tendency towards circularity here. Matthew is seen as being dependent on Mark, hence its extended christological is designated as being more developed, this is sometimes seen as supporting the notion that Mark must be prior to Matthew. The issue of the relevance of christological statements to the synoptic problem is investigated by Head, *Christology and the Synoptic Tradition*.

coherent manner.[30] If an author who was self-consciously using the epistolatory genre to communicate his beliefs to others could fail in this endeavour, it seems unfair to expect consistency and comprehensiveness from the evangelists, since they were primarily using narrative to tell the Jesus story, albeit that their telling of that story was intertwined with theological reflection. In this vein Stanton sounds a sober caution, "there is a real danger that the redaction critic's zeal to establish Matthew's theological emphases will gloss over some inconsistencies…The evangelist was rather less consistent than some of his modern students."[31] This salutary warning is in no way a denial of the unique concerns that the evangelist is communicating, but rather it recognizes that Matthew was not primarily writing a theological treatise, instead he was more concerned with didactical and pastoral issues.

The final assumption of redaction criticism, that of a specific situation being addressed by the evangelist, has been discussed at some length in the previous section. It was argued that despite recent efforts to see the gospels as being written with a universal audience in mind,[32] the very data contained in Matthew's gospel presses the reader to see that the evangelist at times reflected on the particular concerns of his audience, and that this group of people probably lived in relatively close geographical proximity.

While some recent studies have called each of these three assumptions of redaction criticism into question, and thus helpfully caused practitioners of this methodology to sharpen up their own thinking, none of these assumptions are seen as being fatally flawed. Specifically that: (i) the two source theory still appears the most plausible and efficient way to account for the literary relationships between the synoptic gospels; (ii) by producing holistic gospel accounts the evangelists were presenting their own theological outlooks; and, (iii) a number of key texts in the gospels suggest specific group situations are being addressed. In fact, taking into account the points made above, a careful use of redaction criticism still offers much that is of value in the study of the gospels and, moreover, will be used as an important tool in this monograph for studying Matthew's theological and pastoral concerns.

---

[30] For a discussion of this issue and the debate that has surrounded the issue of coherence in Paul's thought see Dunn, 'The Formal and Theological Coherence of Romans.'

[31] Stanton, *Gospel*, 41.

[32] Bauckham (ed.), *The Gospels for all Christians*.

1.3.2 Social Scientific criticism

Throughout the period of critical study of the New Testament scholars have not been unaware of the importance of social setting in determining the meaning of ancient texts. However, the goal of various social scientific approaches is wider than just integrating relevant cultural data into an overall interpretation of the text. Rather, as Elliott defines the purpose of this methodology, it highlights the interaction between social setting and the formation of the text.

> Social-scientific criticism, in its turn, studies the text both as a reflection of and a response to the social and cultural settings in which the text was produced. Its aim is the determination of the meaning(s) explicit and implicit in the text, meanings made possible and shaped by the social and cultural systems by both authors and intended audiences.[33]

Although there has been a proliferation of social scientific approaches, which makes it difficult to speak in general terms about the method, Elliott is surely correct to emphasize that at its base lies the conviction that text and context are more closely intertwined than had been previously been recognised.

This recognition of the interconnectivity of text and context has made a large impact on Matthean studies, yet Matthew was not the first gospel that has been scrutinized through the lens of the social scientific method. In his influential study, Esler applied sociological approaches to the narrative composition of Luke-Acts.[34] Adopting the insights of sociologists into contemporary sectarian movements Esler developed a typology and model which traced the development of the early Jesus movement from its location as a Jewish reform movement to a Christian sect.[35] This ground breaking work has been applied to the writings of the other evangelists. In relation to Matthean studies, a steady stream of material has continued to appear which assesses the beliefs and adherences of the community from the perspective of social scientific enquiry. Apart from numerous individual studies, the collection of essays edited by David Balch in the volume *Social History of the Matthean Community*[36] illustrates both the application of various forms of this methodology and their widespread use by a range of scholars who come to different conclusions on a number of issues. One of the issues that will be raised in this study will be the tendency in some reconstruction to privilege sociological theory over the more immediate exegetical evidence available for producing an

---

[33] Elliott, *Social Scientific Criticism of the New Testament*, 8.

[34] Esler, *Community and Gospel in Luke-Acts*.

[35] See especially chapter 3, 'Sectarian Strategies', 46-70.

[36] Balch (ed.), *Social History of the Matthean Community: Cross-Disciplinary Approaches*.

understanding of the theology and social location of the Matthean community.

An obvious apparent weakness of many of the recent reconstructions is the way that they are wedded to a particular geographical location. Most commonly in relation to the Gospel of Matthew, this is taken as being Antioch-on-the-Orontes.[37] This geographical location is usually assumed, rather than proved. Here Sim does better than most in discussing the evidence. Correctly tracing the first major attempt to locate the gospel in Antioch back to Streeter,[38] Sim fairly assesses the merits of the cumulative arguments Streeter put forward. The arguments concerning the stater and the half-shekel (Matt 17.24-27) are seen to be lacking in support from the evidence Streeter marshals. Moreover, a number of other arguments are ruled out as being spurious. Yet little thought appears to have been expended on explaining the implications, if such an identification is incorrect. Typically, the motivation seems to stem from placing the group, or groups, for whom Matthew wrote in a large urban centre where conflict with an entrenched synagogue based Judaism could readily take place.

However, there appears to be an even more fundamental weakness with the use of sociological approaches in accounting for the formation of early Christian communities. This weakness is the question of the applicability of social scientific criticism to the study of the communities behind the gospels. One factor that accentuates this problem, in comparison to its usage in Pauline Christianity,[39] is the very fact that we do not know with any certainty the geographical location of any of the gospel communities. It is not possible to know if they were written for disenfranchised rural populations suffering the ravishes of latifundalisation, or if in fact they

---

[37] Stark, in his essay 'Antioch as the Social Situation for Matthew's Gospel', provides a very stimulating analysis of many of the problems that could develop in a large urban centre in the ancient Mediterranean world and quite plausibly explains why the Christian faith was able to attract and revitalise the lives of many of the urban poor. However, despite the title of his paper, he fails to offer any reason for placing Matthew specifically in Antioch, rather than any other urban centre. The only reference to Matthew occurs in the final sentence of the paper when Stark appears to assume what he was trying to prove. In relation to the urban problems that were experienced in Antioch he states, "I leave it to those far more learned than I to detect how these urban facts of life are refracted through the lens of Matthew's Gospel." (Stark, 'Antioch as the Social Situation for Matthew's Gospel', 205).

[38] Streeter, *The Four Gospels*, 500-27.

[39] Not only do we know precise urban locations of many of Paul's nascent Christian communities which in turn allows the material remains of such cities to be assessed, but even texts such as 1 Cor 1.26 provide important insights into the societal make up of such communities. For an agenda setting a use of social scientific criticism in relation to Pauline Christianity see Meeks, *The First Urban Christians: The Social World of the Apostle Paul*.

were addressed to urban groups perhaps even resourced by wealthy patrons.

Yet, this is only part of the problem. Modern sociologists study New Religious Movements (NRM's) through a number of empirical observations. These include interviewing group members and those who have left the group, observing various rituals and liturgical forms, analysing national census figures, tracking group adherents to monitor their commitment span to the group,[40] ranking members on an orthodoxy index,[41] and so on. Yet when it comes to investigating the social location of the Matthean community (or those of the other gospels), the sole insight we have is a single document written by a member of the group for fellow group members.[42] The purpose of this document could be to promote the core values of the group, or perhaps to change some of the values held by the group. To decide between such alternatives requires detailed exegetical work before the insights of social scientific criticism can be integrated into the reconstruction of the purpose of the gospel. Thus, the task of investigating the communities behind the gospels should be seen for what it really is, an exegetical endeavour based upon the data contained in one ancient document.[43] Sociological theory may help to account for why a group acted in a certain manner, but it certainly does not provide a firm basis for filling in gaps in the gospel account. That is, if one is aware that Matthew's community is a sectarian group of some kind, it does not means that its values and behaviours followed those of similarly classed groups, unless there is evidence within the text to support such a conclusion. What social scientific criticism may helpfully do, however, is to highlight areas that could be fruitful for investigation, and which may have been overlooked without comparison to similar religious movements.

---

[40] Bainbridge, *The Sociology of Religious Movements*, esp. chap 1, 3-27.

[41] For a discussion of Orthodoxy indices see Stark and Glock, *American Piety: The Nature of Religious Commitment*.

[42] Actually the evidential base might be wider for some of the other gospel communities. If it is legitimate to count Luke-Acts as separate works there are two literary remains from that community, but the question remains as to whether either of these works give substantial insight into a community behind these documents. This appears to be less so the case for Acts than the Gospel. The case of the Johannine community (or, more accurately, cluster of communities) and its social location appears to be more secure. The evidence provided by the epistles in the Johannine corpus, make the knowledge of that community far more secure.

[43] The fact is explicitly stated by some of the practioners of social scientific criticism. Elliott observes, "social-scientific criticism is a *sub-discipline of exegesis* and is inseparably related to the other operations of the exegetical enterprise...Social-scientific criticism complements these other modes of critical analysis, all of which are designed to analyze specific features of the biblical texts." (Elliott, *Social Scientific Criticism of the New Testament*, 11).

Furthermore, it needs to be recognised that the gospel document itself, like all literature, does not offer a neutral assessment of the beliefs of the group, but is perspectival. It claims that the views it espouses are true, normative and binding upon community members in light of the understanding it advances in relation to the ministry and passion of Jesus. In part, this nullifies the applicability of social scientific criticism to biblical studies, since we do not have access to many of the cultural artefacts of the Matthean group apart from a single text, which may or may not reflect the position of a majority of group members. This is not to reject totally insights that might be gleaned from modern sociological studies into NRM's, instead it does seek to make clear that any such insights are limited in their scope and must always be checked against the actual data in the text. Moreover, the gospel text does not purport to describe the social location of the community directly; rather its focus is on the Jesus story (though admittedly this is retold to address the contemporary needs of its audience). Therefore, one must look for multiple references before claiming that some redactional comment reflects community practice, or else the level of transparency must be extremely high if an understanding of the community is to be read out of a single reference in the gospel. An example of this limitation may be seen in relation to the Matthean attitude to mission. Based on a couple of texts whose interpretation is disputed, Sim declares that the perspective of the writer of the first gospel in relation to Gentile mission is that it is only binding upon the community in the eschatological age.[44] By contrast Senior lists eighteen fairly secure references to positive attitudes to Gentiles and mission in the gospel.[45] In the latter case the multiple references and the level of transparency makes the case for a positive attitude to mission the more compelling.

However, there are positive benefits to be gained from the insights of social scientific understandings into marginalized religious groups, as long as such insights remain subservient to detailed and careful exegesis. Certainly Bryan Wilson's seven categories of sectarianism[46] have not only

---

[44] This is a major problem with Sim's dismissive attitude to the reality of the community participating in Gentile mission. His argument is based only on Matt 10.5b-6 and an extremely flimsy reinterpretation of Matt 24.14 which makes it the climax of an eschatological chain of events that he takes as meaning that only just prior to the end will the gospel go out to all the nations. Even here he only grudgingly admits that the Matthew community might have some role to play in non-Jewish evangelisation at this stage. (Sim, *The Gospel of Matthew and Christian Judaism*, 244).

[45] Senior, 'Between Two Worlds: Gentile and Jewish Christians in Matthew's Gospel', 14-16.

[46] Wilson lays out his definition of these seven sect types in *Magic and the Millennium: A Sociological Study of Religious Movements of Protest among Tribal and*

been influential, but have beneficially assisted in the categorisation of what one means when a nascent Christian group is depicted as sectarian as well as focusing investigation on those passages that might fruitfully reflect the features that are perhaps expected in different types of sectarian communities. However, what the sociological patterns of sectarianism do not allow is a naïve assumption that on the basis of a few similarities between ancient Christian communities and NRM's that it is possible simply to fill in the gaps in our knowledge by taking for granted that there is a one-to-one correspondence between a broad model based on modern groups and the situation that prevailed in first century communities. In fact Wilson himself warns careful readers of this fact when he states that,

> The processes of change in one movement may, then, illuminate patterns of development in another or in several others, and this we may usefully acknowledge without any commitment to a grand design of invariable and unilinear evolution. Obviously, every sect is in part idiosyncratic and unique, and where there are profound initial differences we must expect divergent developmental consequences. Again, each sect's distinctive history exhibits some purely adventitious and random features of which no general analytical scheme can take account.[47]

That Wilson feels obliged to make such salutary comments in relation to divergences between modern NRM's should lead one to be cautious in claiming that sociological models and insights can be easily obtained by comparing modern groups with the single partisan literary remain of the Matthean community.[48]

In fact many of these issues, although receiving a certain degree of clarification in later treatments, had already been anticipate in the classic study by Troeltsch.[49] Tackling the issues of state and society, Troeltsch noted the dissonance between modern and ancient conceptions. He noted that, "In our modern way of speech the State and Society are conceived as quite distinct from one each other, and the characteristic conception of Society only arises out of the contrast with the modern, formal

---

Third-World Peoples. He depicts the relationship between the seven sect types and deviance in the following way: "Concern with transcendence over evil and the search for salvation and consequent rejection of prevailing cultural values, goals, and norms, and whatever facilities are culturally provided for man's salvation, define religious deviance" (21).

[47] Wilson, *The Social Dimensions of Sectarianism: Sects and New Religious Movements in Contemporary Society*, 105-6.

[48] It is also worth noting that in conversation with Bryan Wilson, he expressed some disquiet over the misuse of the theories that he developed. In particular the tendency among biblical scholars to take the general patterns of sectarianism that he had described in his studies as invariable templates that all sectarians groups are assumed to fit regardless of the specific details and unique features exhibited in individual groups.

[49] Troeltsch, *The Social Teaching of the Christian Churches*.

constitutional conception of the State."[50] This awareness of the distance between ancient and modern forms of society informs Troeltsch's work in a sophisticated way that allows him to make meaningful comparisons without projecting modern behaviours onto ancient communities.

1.3.3 Literary criticism

The term 'literary criticism' when applied to biblical studies covers a number of approaches, not necessarily all complementary, that approach texts as autonomous entities that speak to a reader regardless of the original authorial intent for the text. Such approaches are by their very nature synchronic in perspective, and often attempt to read the text as a self contained world. This desire to read the biblical texts in an holistic manner was in part a reaction to the perceived tendency of redaction criticism to atomize the overall impact of a literary work by focusing on the editorial reworking of sources. Porter observes this phenomenon in respect to literary criticism being a response to redactional studies. He states,

> Redaction criticism, especially in its earlier forms (before having been influenced by literary criticism?), is often thought to have failed to see the whole text, concentrating more on seams or changes in the text rather than on what the text retains from its source, argued too much on the basis of word statistics, been wed to a particular kind of historical agenda, and been only concerned with a narrow range of 'theological' questions, often equated with reconstructions of early Christian communities.[51]

There is some truth in this perceived failure of redaction criticism, especially that it often failed to recognize that the evangelists were responsible for putting together their texts as whole documents and not only responsible for a few editorial comments and minor alterations.[52]

Obviously the weakness that literary criticism highlighted in some of the older forms of redaction criticism also reflects the strengths of literary criticism. Foremost among these strengths is the fact that this method deals with the macronarrative of a text. Thus, the literary work is viewed as a whole, with an overarching purpose to which all the parts contribute. Second, especially in relation to narrative accounts, there has been fruitful research in new areas such as character,[53] plot[54] and setting.[55] Third,

---

[50] Troeltsch, *The Social Teaching of the Christian Churches*, 31.

[51] Porter, 'Literary Approaches to the New Testament', 82.

[52] This has already been discussed at length in the treatment of redaction criticism above.

[53] For example see the following studies: Darr, *On Character Building*; Williams, *Other Followers of Jesus*; Kingsbury, 'The Figure of Jesus in Matthew's Story: A Literary-Critical Probe'.

literary criticism has served to emphasize the process of writing, reading and auditing literary documents in the ancient world. That many literary works were transmitted within a cultural where orality was the primary means for accessing texts has drawn attention to the performative nature of literature in the ancient Mediterranean world. Coupled with this is an appreciation of how a text works in communicating meaning and transforming and challenging the beliefs and values of the recipients of the text. As Porter states, this entails that "the interpreter must learn how it is that any given text, and thus how texts in general, work, that is how it is that they go about presenting their various features to the interpreter, and how it is that interpreters respond to them."[56] In essence this involves the branch of literary theory known as reader response criticism. In its most extreme form reader response theory is presented as saying that a text means what it means to a particular reader, and thus the reader is wholly determinative in creating meaning. Here the text has freed itself from the stricture of meaning whatever the author intended to communicate by his literary work.[57] By contrast, other approaches to reader response criticism argue that "there is a limit to the plausible readings set by the parameters of the text, with the gaps in the text providing places for subjectivity."[58] Such an approach does not cut a text totally free from original authorial intent.[59] However, most scholars who situate themselves within the historio-critical method wish to enquire after the meaning of a text within its original setting. Thus the focus is not placed on the reception of a text by a contemporary reader, but on the message conveyed by a text to its intended audience.[60]

Although some scholars may, however, be happy to employ the insights of literary criticism in a restricted manner, overall those who hold to a historical approach feel concerned that the objective balance of interpreting a text in line with its original intent may be lost. Here

---

[54] Especially on Matthew see: Kingsbury, *Matthew as Story*; Bauer, *The Structure of Matthew's Gospel*; Weavers, *Matthew's Missionary Discourse*.

[55] In relation to setting there is overlap with social scientific criticism, but at a literary critical level a treatment such as Scott, *Hear then the Parable*, which emphasizes settings such as agrarian society, or patron-client relationships as the know social backdrop to the fictive literary world of parables is an example where setting is utilised in primarily a literary, rather than social scientific manner.

[56] Porter, 'Literary Approaches to the New Testament', 115.

[57] This is how some critics define reader response criticism. For example see Fish, *Is there a Text in this Class?*

[58] Porter, 'Literary Approaches to the New Testament', 106.

[59] For a discussion of this methodological approach that still tries to set limits on the plausible readings of a text see Iser, *The Act of Reading*.

[60] For some of the difficulties attending the process of constructing the original audience of a text see the discussion in Beavis, *Mark's Audience*.

historical critics call into question the basic premise of many formulations of literary theory that state that a text is an autonomous world. By contrast, it is emphasized that any text is an inherently historical artefact, reflecting a specific linguistic community and adhering to certain conventions that operate within that circle. Porter warns of the possible danger of neglecting the original setting of a text. He states, "there may at best be incomplete understanding and at worst complete misunderstanding if the historical dimension is not duly considered."[61] Therefore, literary criticism does offer fresh insights into biblical texts, but its method must remain subservient to the historio-critical approach if links with origin intent and historical setting are to be valued. Moreover, within the community of faith, there is value ascribed to the history of interpretation for providing certain limitations on the types of interpretations that are plausible. In this regard the reception history of a text can also act as a control distinguishing between plausible and implausible acts of reading.

Looking at the three major methods of interpreting texts, redaction, social scientific and literary criticism, it becomes apparent that each of these approaches have strengths and weaknesses and hence a complementary outlook needs to be adopted when using this plurality of methods. Yet, this in itself raises the problem of how to discriminate between these competing approaches. Despite the limitations outlined above, this study gives precedence to the historical approach, especially as it is undertaken by redaction critics. This diachronic approach can of course lead to the danger of sifting sources, rather than concentrating on the overall message of the gospel. However, the very fact this danger is recognized means that with care it can also be avoided.

1.4 Scope

The decision to investigate the social setting of the community through the twin lenses of mission and law is not an arbitrary choice. While other aspects of Matthean theology, such as christology,[62] ecclesiology,[63] or even eschatology,[64] may have thrown light on the social setting of the group, the two issues under consideration have been chosen because they provide a

---

[61] Porter, 'Literary Approaches to the New Testament', 117.

[62] Müller, 'The Theological Interpretation of the Figure of Jesus in Matthew's Gospel', 157-73; Kingsbury, 'The Developing Conflict between Jesus and the Jewish Leaders in Matthew's Gospel: a literary-critical study', 57-83.

[63] Bornkamm 'The Stilling of the Storm in Matthew'; Bornkamm, 'The Authority to 'Bind' and 'Loose' in the Church in Matthew's Gospel', 37-50.

[64] Sim, *Apocalyptic Eschatology in the Gospel of Matthew*.

more ready and demonstrable comparison and contrast with known Jewish attitudes both prior to the fall of the temple and during the second century. Evidence is extremely sparse for the period that encompasses the most likely date of the composition of the first gospel (the last quarter of the first century C.E.), but if the Jewish attitudes to these issues are fairly uniform on either side of this period then it is not an unwarranted assumption to suppose that similar attitudes are most likely to have prevailed in the intervening years.

In relation to Torah understanding in Matthew's gospel, this monograph focuses on the most explicit statements that the evangelist provides about his understanding of the law for his group members. The material in Matt 5.17-48 provides two complementary treatments of the issue of the law. Firstly, it gives a partially abstract statement about the manner in which Matthew sees the law as having some kind of ongoing validity (vv. 17-20). Yet even here, as the reference to the scribes and the Pharisees shows, the evangelist wished to define his position in contradistinction from that of the perceived opponents of the community. Secondly, the antitheses (vv. 21-48) provide concrete examples of how one is to interpret the law. The stress falls upon Jesus' authority to redefine, or even, as it is argued in this study, to overturn certain halakhic stipulations. For this reason the antitheses will be analysed before the treatment of the programmatic statement on the law (5.17-20) instead of in the order these two units occur in the gospel. This reflects a conscious decision to allow Matthew's own commentary on his summary statements in the earlier verses to be given full weight. This process is quite different from Meier's treatment of 5.17-20 where he reorders material within that block in order to stress certain themes at the expense of others.[65] Rather, here the desired aim in this investigation is to listen carefully to the evangelist's own interpretation of those statements that have been so frequently exposed to such a range of opinions. Obviously, the antitheses do not offer a direct commentary on vv. 17-20, but they do illustrate how the Matthean attitude to the Torah was operative in six concrete cases. Any interpretation of 5.17-20 must at least show consistency with what Matthew presents in the

---

[65] Meier argues that "It seems advisable, therefore, to make an exception to the rule of following the given order, and to place 5.18 first in our treatment, since it offers the greatest possibilities for using objective 'controls' in discerning tradition and redaction." (Meier, *Law and History in Matthew's Gospel*, 45). This decision is based on the existence of a Lukan parallel (Lk 16.17), and also because it is seen as being of key exegetical importance because of its more stringent attitude to the upholding of the law. However, it is probably at least as plausible to suggest that one should not alter the internal order of this material and that the evangelist's own redactional comments in the other verses are equally important for determining his views as his alleged manipulation of the received tradition from Lk 16.17.

antithetical cases he considers. As a comparison, the antithetical statements contained in 4QMMT are also investigated as an illustration of how a group that considered itself still within Judaism used the antithetical form in Torah debate. While such a comparison shows a number of similarities, these should not be overplayed. The Matthean antitheses step outside the bounds drawn by the Qumranic example, for it is no longer Torah that functions as the highest source of authority, but Jesus' self-referential pronouncements. Obviously the role of the law in Matthew's gospel is not confined to the material in 5.17-48, however, this study focuses on the central discussion of Torah by the evangelist. Other passages dealing with the law are referred to throughout this discussion, but these are brought in to corroborate certain points, and are not treated in a systematic fashion. This decision is not primarily due to a limitation of space, but rather it realises that the material in 5.17-48 is the evangelist's most extended and heavily redacted treatment of the theme of the law. Therefore, it is likely that this passage may provide the best 'window' through which to see the issues confronting the Matthean community in relation to its understanding and interpretation of Torah.

The treatment on mission does, by the very nature of the dispersed references to Gentiles and missionary proclamation, encompass a wider range of texts scattered throughout the gospel. Yet it is this very recurrence of the theme of outreach to Gentile interspersed with so much other material in the gospel that gives it such a prominence in the gospel. This significance is further emphasized by the final pericope in the gospel issuing forth the climactic charge to take the gospel to all the nations. Such universalism, as opposed to the particularism that some have asserted is a unifying feature of both pre- and post-Temple destruction Judaism,[66] along with the Matthean group,[67] is found repeatedly in the final third of the

---

[66] Goodman argues that proselytization was not a widespread feature of first century C.E. Judaism. Further, he suggests that the impetus for Christian missionary activity is not to be traced back to some pre-existing Jewish practice. He states, "there is insufficient evidence that early Christians imitated or built upon the efforts by Jewish proselytizers. I hope I have said enough to show that proselytising is only an aspect of some religious groups at particular times, and that the Jews probably did not seek gentile proselytes in the first century CE." (Goodman, *Mission and* Conversion, 161). Thus he supports Jewish particularism, but rejects that the same outlook applied to Christianity.

[67] For Overman this particularism is not a totally rejection of Gentile converts, but there inclusion in the Matthean community is predicated upon a conversion experience that parallels that of Gentiles being included as full members in the synagogue environment. However, according to Overman, Matthew is not primarily interested in Gentiles rather the focus still lies primarily on winning Jewish converts. He asks, "Does Matthew mean that other Jews in the diaspora need to hear about Jesus-centered Judaism? Probably. Matthew would certainly have known about Jewish communities outside of Palestine and he would have believed that they, too, needed to embrace

gospel. Obviously, any attempt to explain the Matthean commitment to Gentile mission must grapple with the problematic statement in 10.5b-6, which appears to limit the scope of the evangelist's sphere of proselytising activity, and must be integrated within an holistic understanding of mission in the first gospel. However, it is not persuasive either to argue to the basis of 10.5b-6 that all the evangelist's positive statements about mission are neutralised by this single reference.[68] Any treatment must deal with both the negative outlook in chapter 10 as well as integrating the larger corpus of texts that call for the inclusion of Gentiles within the Matthean communities.

1.5 Summary

Therefore, the major aim of this investigation is to show that although the Matthean group originated in Judaism, nonetheless, by the time of the composition of the gospel the community functioned outside the confines of its original *locus operandi*. Specifically, that at the time of the writing of the gospel a major breach had occurred between the Matthean communities and the synagogues from which the original core of the evangelist's believers in Jesus had emerged. Consequently the group was now focusing its attention on recruiting new members from among gentiles, and the integration of recent non-Jewish converts created a number of tensions for long term traditionally Torah observant group members. Furthermore, in terms of methodology, the study seeks to demonstrate this through close study of the text of the gospel approached primarily in line with the historio-critical method using redaction criticism to highlight the key concerns of the evangelist. However, insights from both social scientific and literary approaches will be integrated; although at all times these will be subordinated to the historical approach.

Matthean Judaism in order to 'fulfill all righteousness.'" (Overman, *Church and Community in Crisis*: *The Gospel according to Matthew*, 406-7).

[68] Sim couples the statements in 10.5b-6 with a reinterpretation of 24.14, to attempt to blunt the clear implication of 28.19. He argues that the Gentile mission was not a present reality for the Matthean community, but on the basis of 24.14 was only an imperative in the eschatological age. Thus the injunction of 10.5b-6 still held force for Matthean adherents. Even if one were to accept Sim's reading of the mission being suspended until the eschatological age (a point that is far from certain), it still appears that Matthew views his community as living in such a period already, at least in an embryonic form. The Matthean redactional description in 27.51b-53 of the splitting of the rocks, the opening of the tombs and the reanimation of the dead saints, all are illustrations that the post-crucifixion era inaugurates a new age. (See Sim, *The Gospel of Matthew and Christian Judaism*, esp. 236-47).

Moreover, as has been mentioned, the scope of the discussion will be limited primarily to an exegetical investigation of those texts relating to mission,[69] as well as a focus on the central treatment of the law in Matthew's gospel (5.17-48). The issue of Torah observance and dissenting attitudes to its requirements will be set against the wider background of pre-destruction Judaism by a close comparison with the Halahkic Letter (4QMMT) and the series of antithetical statements contained in that document. In this way the study seeks to demonstrate that although the Matthean community used forms of argumentation common in Judaism and in spite of some of the debate revolving around the issue of Torah observance, the status of Jesus' authority above that of the law[70] and the decision to promote the ideal of mission among Gentile are marked departures from the various forms of Judaism that emerged after the destruction of the Temple.

---

[69] Specifically, the major texts that will be scrutinized in the chapter on mission are, Matt 10.5-23; 15.21-28; 21.43; 24.14; 26.13; 28.16-20. This approach has the advantage of focusing the discussion, by concentrating on the most relevant sayings. However, it can also result in a loss of the overall force that is conveyed by reading the gospel as a whole. Therefore, here it is proposed to concentrate on those texts that form the basis of the discussion, but also to look for their overall significance in the wider structure of the narrative.

[70] Byrskog, in his discussion of 1QpHab 7.1-8, highlights that "The Teacher [of Righteousness] was to the Qumranites much more than one teacher among many. The validated status made the Teacher and his teaching inseparable. The Qumranites did not subordinate the Teacher to the teaching. All teaching was to come from him." (*Jesus the Only Teacher*, 134-5). However, his authority is different to that of Jesus, since the Teacher had the authoritative interpretation of the Law, whereas the Matthean Jesus is view by the community as having authority to redefine or even overturn Torah.

Chapter 2

Recent Proposals concerning the Social Location of the Matthean Community

2.1 Introduction

The purpose of this chapter is to outline recent trends in the study of the Matthean community from the mid nineteen eighties onwards. The reason for this date is twofold. First, there are a number of excellent surveys of Matthean scholarship up until this period,[1] and second, it is from the mid eighties onwards that the use of sociological methods have made an impact on the study of the first gospel. Yet since nobody writes in a vacuum, a brief overview of critical scholarship on Matthew's gospel will be provided. This will take as its starting point the emergence of redactional approaches in the late nineteen forties up until the mid eighties when sociological methods started to be applied to the study of Matthew's gospel. This chapter will then interact with the work of five scholars who have made significant proposals concerning the nature of the Matthean community. These five, Stanton,[2] Saldarini,[3] Overman,[4] Sim,[5] and

---

[1] See in particular Stanton, 'The Origin and Purpose of Matthew's Gospel: Matthean Scholarship from 1945-1980'.

[2] Although Stanton's work appears in the volume *A Gospel for a New People* (1992), he acknowledges that this is, at least in part, a compilation of lectures and papers presented in the eighties (cf, preface xii). His work stands first in the list since he was the scholar who made the first concerted attempt to bring the insights of the social scientific methods to a study of the first gospel.

[3] Saldarini's work on Matthew came to its fruition in his 1994 monograph, *Matthew's Christian Jewish Community*. His first published specifically on this topic appeared in the Balch volume in 1991. However, much of the impetus for this work springs from his earlier study on Jewish religious groups, *Pharisees, Scribes and Sadducees in Palestinian Society* (1988).

[4] Overman's work is roughly contemporaneous with that of Saldarini. His main contributions are found in the two volumes *Matthew's Gospel and Formative Judaism* (1990) and *Church and Community in Crisis* (1996).

[5] Sim, once a research student of Stanton, in some ways represents the second generation of scholars who apply sociological methods to Matthew's gospel. His first major contribution to the debate appeared in a *JSNT* article 'The Gospel of Matthew and the Gentiles' (1995). After this his views find fullest expression in his two monographs,

Repschinski,[6] will be treated in this order because in general terms it reflects the chronology of the appearance of their first work on Matthew. However, since they continued to write on this topic there is much overlap and their work should not be seen as discrete stages in Matthean studies, but rather as part of the shared task of investigating the community of the first evangelist through the lens of sociological methodologies.

Yet scholars who apply the social scientific method to the first gospel have not always appreciated the difficulty of adopting sociological categories. This is especially apparent in relation to defining the Matthean group as sectarian. However, sociologists have been more aware of this problem and consequently have looked for a more nuanced and differentiated approach. Wilson in part tries to address this problem by presenting seven general typologies of sectarianism.[7] Similarly, Bainbridge notes that the

> problem is that defining *sect* as an intense schismatic group leaves one in an awkward position for speaking of groups that are schismatic but not intense, or intense but not schismatic. An alterative term has been proposed for moderate groups that arose through schism, *church movements*, and the example usually given is Reform Judaism. There are several ways an intense religious group can arise, but scholars generally restrict the term *sect* to groups within a religious tradition that also contain moderate groups.[8]

Even this definition is not really applicable to the social situation of the Matthean community. One is left to make the value judgment about whether emergent Judaism or the evangelist's group was the more moderate party.

However, before turning to an analysis of scholars who have applied sociological methods to the study of the first gospel, a brief treatment of the period preceding their work is provided. It is intended both to contextualise subsequent use of social scientific criticism, as well as providing an importance reference for comparison between more recent scholars and their predecessors.

Apocalyptic Eschatology in the Gospel of Matthew (1996) and *The Gospel of Matthew and Christian Judaism* (1998).

[6] Repschinski has tackled the issue of the setting of the community through a study of the controversy material. See *The Controversy Stories in the Gospel of Matthew* (2000).

[7] Wilson, *Magic and the Millennium*, 21.

[8] Bainbridge, *The Sociology of Religious Movements*, 23.

2.2 Matthean Studies from the late 1940's to the mid 1980's

This short section seeks only to give a brief overview of some of the most important developments in this period in order to locate the discussion of more recent trends. The starting point, the work of Bornkamm and the introduction of redaction criticism as a tool for studying the first gospel, is not just a convenient place to begin this survey: rather it is both a natural and highly significant juncture at which to commence.

Bornkamm's essay, 'Die Sturmstillung im Matthäusevangelium' marked the start of the redactional approach to the study of gospel pericopae. It also was Bornkamm's first attempt to discuss the social location of the Matthean community. The famous comment that Matt 8.23-27 is a "reference to the little ship of the Church",[9] is unpacked only slightly in this essay. At this stage Bornkamm only describes the Matthean community as a struggling and endangered entity. He states, "the story becomes a kerygmatic paradigm of the danger and glory of discipleship."[10] Reflection on the nature of the Matthean community found much fuller development in the article 'Enderwartung und Kirche im Matthäusevangelium.' There, Bornkamm argued that the group remained firmly within the synagogue environment, that it was responding to antinomian tendencies in some Christian groups, but the enlarged eschatological vision provided the community with an imperative to preach to all nations. The community is characterised in the following terms.

> That here [i.e., Matt 24.9] the picture of the Jewish-Christian congregation arises, which holds fast to the law and has not yet broken away from union with Judaism but rather stands in sharp contrast to a doctrine and mission set free from the law (which Matthew would regard as lawless) is crystal clear. This Jewish-Christian congregation shares the fate of the Jewish nation, the desecration of the Temple and the horrors of flight.[11]

While Bornkamm centres his discussion on the first evangelist's reaction to antinomian Christians, this is not seen as the only source of confrontation for the community. The second source of opposition comes from non-Christian Jews, who rejected the group's claims about the messiahship of Jesus. While the latter source of opposition is clearly evidenced within the gospel, the antinomian party remain shadowy opponents whom Matthew fails to name explicitly. Thus, at least initially,

---

[9] Bornkamm, 'The Stilling of the Storm in Matthew', 55.

[10] Bornkamm, 'The Stilling of the Storm in Matthew', 57.

[11] Bornkamm, 'End-Expectation and Church in Matthew', 22.

Bornkamm maintained that the conflict between the Matthean community and its opponents was, in large part, an inner Jewish struggle.[12]

However, Bornkamm modified his position in subsequent writing. The initial modification was to argue that there would have been considerable tension between the evangelist's community and emergent Judaism, even though the first group maintained its position in the synagogue.[13] Later, however, he went even further, suggesting that at the time of composition of the gospel, the Matthean group had in fact separated from the Jewish synagogue.[14] This progression of thought is helpful in showing the modifications that Bornkamm felt were necessary to account for the social location of the Matthean community. However, it also conveniently maps out the major options for describing the relationship between Matthew's community and Judaism that have been suggested by scholars writing from the beginning of the second half of the twentieth century onwards.

The early position of Bornkamm, that the community's struggle was *intra muros* in relation to the synagogue environment, has been supported by a number of scholars. Although Barth's primary thesis was to develop and defend the theory that Matthew was 'fighting on two fronts', in an incidental manner he supports the notion that the community was a 'conservative (Palestinian) congregation.'[15] While he never explicitly states that the group was still located in Jewish synagogues, its conservative attitude towards Torah,[16] and the conflict with the 'Rabbinate'[17] are taken to support the notion that such attitudes and tension are most naturally accounted for within the synagogue environment. However, Hummel is more explicit about the Matthean community existing within the sphere of synagogue life, albeit that its beliefs were developing a set of new understandings and creating a trajectory that was leading to separation from its current location. He states

Die äußere Zugehörigkeit zum jüdischen Synagogenverband war mit dem überwiegend judenchristlichen Charakter der Kirche des Matthäus gegeben. Solange

---

[12] Bornkamm states that, "The struggle with Israel is still a struggle within its walls." ('End-Expectation and Church in Matthew', 22).

[13] Bornkamm, 'Der Auferstandene und der Irdische', 171-91.

[14] Bornkamm, 'Die Binde- und Lösegewalt in der Kirche des Matthäus', 37-50.

[15] Barth, 'Matthew's Understanding of the Law', 65.

[16] "Matthew *generally* emphasises the abiding validity of the law and the prophets for the Church." Barth, 'Matthew's Understanding of the Law', 163.

[17] While talk of a 'Rabbinate' is obviously anachronistic, Barth contrasts the competing attitudes to the law in the following terms: "Matthew does not share the understanding of the law in the Rabbinate but rather opposes the Rabbinate face to face. But it would still not be correct to speak of a *lex nova* because the identity with the law of Sinai is so strongly emphasised." Barth, 'Matthew's Understanding of the Law', 159.

das Judentum nicht Maßnahmen zum endgültigen Ausschluß getroffen hatte, blieben die konvertierten Juden, die offensichtlich die Kirche des Matthäus prägten.[18]

Similarly, Davies suggested that at the time of the gospel's composition the community were still participating in synagogue life, even if the relationship with other factions had become strained. His reconstruction of a council of Jewish sages at Jamnia, and his insistence that the *Birkath ha Minim* was in large part directed against Christianity is overdrawn, and perhaps looks less convincing now than when it was first written.[19]

During this same period, a number of scholars adopted a different understanding of the Matthean community. While concurring that the group shared a common heritage with synagogue based Judaism, it was argued that by the time of the composition of the first gospel a definitive breach had already occurred between the Matthean party and their Jewish non-Christian opponents. This does not exclude the possibility that the adherents to the teaching of the first evangelist maintained a number of Jewish traditions and practices, rather it acknowledges that when the gospel was written, the group no longer participated in synagogue worship either having withdrawn, or having been excluded, from that religious milieu. Stendahl saw the community as being sharply differentiated from Judaism and incorporating Gentiles as group members. Furthermore, he suggested that the evangelist was a Jewish scribal figure by origin, who had become part of a Hellenistic community.[20] This *extra muros* perspective is also shared by Moule[21] and E. Schweizer,[22] with both seeing the Matthean community as a small marginal group being persecuted by synagogue opponents.

Some scholars have wished to suggest an even greater divide between the first evangelist and Judaism. Although never a majority position, it has been argued that Matthew was not Jewish, nor emerged from a Jewish background, but instead should be seen as a Gentile convert to Christianity. This point of view traces its origin back to Clark's seminal essay, which suggested that the favoured status of Gentiles in Matthew was not congruous with a Jewish author.[23] Similarly, in a detailed study, Strecker argues that some material that is usually identified as Jewish

---

[18] Hummel, *Die Auseinandersetzung zwischen Kirche und Judentum im Matthäusevangelium*, 159.

[19] Much of Davies reconstruction depends on his dating of the *Birkath ha Minim* so it is contemporary with Matthew's gospel, and his interpretation of the term הנוצרים (Nazoreans) which is taken as equivalent to 'Christians'. Davies, *The Setting of the Sermon on the Mount*, 276.

[20] See Stendahl, *The School of St. Matthew*, esp xiii.

[21] Moule, 'St. Matthew's Gospel: Some Neglected Features', 91-9.

[22] Schweizer, *Matthäus und seine Gemeinde*.

[23] Clark, 'The Gentile Bias in Matthew', 165-72

within the gospel may in fact have originated in Gentile circles, or it might represent earlier group tradition prior to the evangelist joining the community.[24] Trilling concurs with Strecker's reconstruction that the community had left its initial Jewish stage behind and was now an example of Gentile Christianity.[25] Meier is even more strident in his assessment, declaring there are statements in the gospel that no Jew could write (16.12 misunderstanding the doctrines of the Pharisees; 21.7 misconstruing the nature of Hebrew synonymous parallelism; 22.37 misquoting the Shema).[26] A slightly different perspective on the phenomenon of 'distance' from contemporary Judaism is provided by Hare. He argues that, "the Jewish disciples no longer 'belong' in the synagogue; it is an alien institution belonging to an alien people...for Luke the synagogue has always been a foreign institution, for Matthew it has become a foreign institution in which Christians of Jewish blood no longer belong."[27] Thus, the distance between Matthew and his Jewish opponents is not cultural, but reflects the passage of time and the fact that the community had been persecuted by Jewish opponents and ostracised from *their* synagogues. Hare's analysis is based on a detailed study of the references to persecution in Matthew's gospel, and he argues that hostility from Jewish opponents was experienced in the past for the evangelist's community. He states, "[t]here is no evidence of formal exclusion from the synagogues, but Matthew's description of the synagogue as an alien institution indicates that, whatever the cause, Christians are no longer members."[28] He then continues by suggesting that, although not formalised, the cause of the exclusion from the synagogues was "social ostracism and mutual hostility."[29]

These competing views for understanding the social setting of the Matthean adherents in relation to Judaism, were the major options until the mid 1980's. While the range of options has not changed, the application of social scientific criticism has led to much being written in support of the group existing within the bounds of synagogue based Judaism at the time of the composition of the gospel. The suggestions of more recent scholars are now considered in greater detail.

---

[24] Strecker, *Der Weg der Gerechtigkeit*, 15-35.

[25] Trilling, *Das wahre Israel. Studien zur Theologie des Matthäusevangeliums*.

[26] Meier, *Law and History in Matthew's Gospel*. See in particular his discussion of presuppositions in the introductory chapter. Section E addresses the question, 'Jewish or Gentile Redactor?' (14-22).

[27] Hare, *The Theme of Jewish Persecution*, 104-5.

[28] Hare, *The Theme of Jewish Persecution*, 125.

[29] Hare, *The Theme of Jewish Persecution*, 125.

2.3 G.N. Stanton: *A Gospel for a New People*

The approach Stanton adopts has much to commend it. Like many recent treatments of the Matthean community he also is indebted to insights gleaned from the social sciences. In particular he utilises the work of Lewis Coser[30] which although wider in its scope than focusing on group formation makes a number of pertinent observations that are directly applicable to the emergence of sectarian communities. Stanton uses the insights provided by Coser to illuminate the relationship between two situations of conflict between sects and parent bodies. These are the Dead Sea Scrolls community, as reflected primarily in the Damascus Document (CD), and the Matthean communities[31] as reflected in the first gospel.

Stanton tests three of the insights provided by Coser's research into social conflict against the documentary data of the Qumran and Matthean communities. The first point he investigates is that proximity of relationship may be an indicator of heightened intensity of conflict. This observation from the social sciences is seen to apply to the setting of both the groups under discussion. Stanton argues that this observation

> can readily be supported from the two writings we are comparing. In both there are claims that the 'new people' are the true people of God and the true interpreters of Scripture: their own history marks the fulfilment of the prophecies of Scripture. Both groups grudgingly acknowledge that at an earlier stage the parent group was acceptable – indeed it was a 'planting by God' (cf. CD 1.7; cf. Matt 15.13; 23.2).[32]

Therefore, the strident enmity that has arisen, with its concomitant violent reactions, reflects the degree to which the parent and emergent group were initially intertwined. The parent group feels betrayed and sees its core values as being undermined, whereas the offshoot party is striving to come to terms with its liminal status due to the parent body rejecting its claims to be the possessor of a new revelation. Primarily, it is the sharp invective that reflects the intensity of conflict. Stanton draws attention to

---

[30] Coser, *The Functions of Social Conflict.*

[31] Stanton correctly introduces the possibility that Matthew was not writing just for a single community, or group of believers in Jesus. Rather, the rapid dissemination of the first gospel, evidenced from the time of Ignatius onwards is strongly suggestive of the idea that the author had a circle of communities in view when he composed his account. Apart from the evidence of widespread use of Matthew in the second century, Stanton also offers a logistical argument for the gospel being composed with a wider audience in mind from the outset. He observes, "First century Christians met in houses; it would have been difficult for many more than 50 or so people to crowd into a quite substantial house. Is it likely that Matthew would have composed such an elaborate gospel for one relatively small group? Is it not much more likely that Matthew, like Luke, envisaged that his gospel would circulate widely?" (Stanton, *Gospel*, 50-1).

[32] Stanton, *Gospel*, 98.

the insults that are tossed back and forth between the Pharisees and the Matthean Jesus that the work of each other stems from demonic influences. The charge that Jesus casts out demons by Beelzebul 12.24 (cf., 9.34; 10.25), is answered by inverting the accusation and claiming that the punctilious purification insisted upon by the Pharisees results only in the creation of a dwelling place that is more congenial for unclean spirits (Matt 12.43-5).[33]

The second facet of Coser's model of social conflict, which Stanton sees as present in his investigation of sectarian communities, is the establishment of boundary issues that form the basis of dissent. While many beliefs and practices remain shared, the touchstone of orthodoxy is linked to a subset of key points of differing opinion. Yet such boundary issues are not only used for excluding those outside the group, they also function to define the beliefs required from those within the community.[34] In relation to the Qumran Community, as reflected in the Damascus Document, Stanton observes that erring or unfaithful community members are looked upon more severely than those who are outside the community. Yet perhaps here Stanton's bipartite model requires further modification since it appears that the sectarian outlook at Qumran differentiates between primarily three groups, although, admittedly the tripartite scheme is more fully apparent in the wider corpus of Qumranic texts. Firstly, there are those who are completely outside the ethnic boundaries of Israel; the only references to such people are usually hostile and see them more often than not as part of the oppressive Kittim who will be overthrown in the final eschatological war between the sons of light and the sons of darkness (1QM). Secondly, there are those members of wider Israel who have not accepted the distinctive practices or sectarian lifestyle of the community. The hope is that people from this group will become full adherents to sect,

---

[33] Here Stanton not only notes that Matthew intends his audience to see demonic spirits as representing scribes and Pharisees, but he also concurs with Gundry's assessment that the Pharisaic programme of righteousness is portrayed as creating fresh space for the work of unclean spirits. As Gundry states, "the period of the unclean spirit's absence ceases to be a period of temporary relief for a demoniac and becomes a figure of the apparent righteousness of the scribes and Pharisees; and the return of the unclean spirit with seven others worse than himself ceases to be repossession of a demoniac and comes to represent an outburst of multiplied evil on the part of the scribes and Pharisees." (Matt 12.43-45). (Gundry, *Matthew*, 246). Further, Stanton also sees the parable of the Tares as potentially making the same point by casting the Jewish leadership as conspiring with demonic forces by undermining the spread of the gospel. He states, "It is possible that a similar point is made in Matt 13.38: the "sons of the evil one" may include the Jewish religious leaders." (Stanton, *Gospel*, 100, n. 1).

[34] This point is made by Coser when he states, "Exclusion is attained through conflict with the outside and the maintenance of this exclusive standing requires the sect to be an internally cohesive conflict group." (*The Functions of Social Conflict*, 95).

and fully embrace its practices and beliefs. Finally, there are those who are already in the community, they have dedicated themselves to building the way of the Lord in the wilderness, they partake in the holy food, and view themselves as the core of Israel that will become the community of the last days.[35]

Similarly, Matthew may have a threefold division of humanity in mind, although the distinctions are often blurred and this results in a schema whereby a twofold division is often utilised. The more simplified split occurs in Matt 25.31-46 with the separation between the sheep and the goats at the final great assize. A similar duality can also be found in the parable of the Tares, Matt 13.36-43. However, alongside this pronounced twofold split Matthew also tends to have an underlying tripartite division consisting of: an in-group, his own community; an out-group, those who need evangelising; and, an opposing group, depicted as scribes and Pharisees, Jewish religious leaders and once as 'the Jews' (Matt 28.15).[36] Yet Stanton makes the important observation that even within the in-group, as is the case in CD, there is concern about recalcitrant or insincere adherents. Three passages are mentioned. In 7.19 unfruitful members will be cut down and burnt in a furnace, a similar fate awaits 'the Tares' in 13.42,[37] and the redactional alteration in 24.51 depicts the gruesome scene

---

[35] The community sees itself as a remnant, a new shoot from an existing plant, which is drawn both from Israel in general as well as from Aaronic, or priestly, origins. This is made explicit in CD 1.7-8 "he [God] visited them and caused to sprout from Israel and Aaron a shoot of the planting in order to possess his land and to become fat with the good things of the soil."

[36] The opposition in Matthew is a group that is consistently mentioned. Some of the references to Pharisees and Sadducees are most reasonably considered as historizing elements in the narrative, yet the concentration on these groups makes it apparent that such a focus was an important one for the Matthean community in its own contemporary situation. Similarly, the mission orientation of Matt 9.37-8, while placed on the lips of the historical Jesus, appears also to have contemporary significance for the group, especially as mission is a recurrent theme in the macronarrative.

[37] Although Stanton identifies this passage as reflecting inner turmoil and the existence of the community as a *corpus mixtum*, this reading of the passage is not accepted by all commentators. The parable falls into two discrete sections, the parable proper delivered to the crowds, 13.24-30, and its interpretation given privately to the disciples, 13.36-43. Suspending discussion of the original meaning of the parable (its authenticity as *ipsissima verba Jesu* is questioned despite the existence of a parallel in G.Thom 57), the Matthean interpretation seems to oppose Stanton's suggestion that it is reflecting an internal distinction in the community. Here Hagner discerns the evangelists meaning when he writes, "The field, explicitly identified as ὁ κόσμος, 'the world,' cannot have been understood as the Church by the evangelist or his readers. The identification of the field as the world does, however, point in itself to the worldwide mission of the Church and the spread of the gospel (cf. 24.14; 28.19)" (Hagner, *Matthew 1-13*, 393). The suggestion that the field represents the Church, and those who are in it may be

of the evil servant being hacked into pieces by a master who is enraged because of the mistreatment of the servants.[38] Stanton concludes his discussion on dissent in the two sectarian groups under consideration in both the Matthew's Gospel and CD, "the 'inner enemy' is rejected as vigorously as the 'outer enemy'. Both writings illustrate the hostility a group in conflict shows towards internal dissent."[39] Bainbridge supports the observation that marginalized groups, or those in conflict with a parent body, cannot tolerate internal dissent. In contrast to the commitment mechanisms[40] that function positively in New Religious Movements there are more intense consequences for creating dissent within the group or defecting from the community. As he observes,

> If the people who form a commune are already solidly connected to each other by bonds of love and friendship, each individual in their cohesive social group will be held in by such bonds. Defecting from the commune is tantamount to abandoning one's family and friends, a step not lightly taken.[41]

As a control mechanism, the threat of ostracism as a consequence of dissent is more severe for those who have invested most in converting to the sect. The new family and friendships may be removed, and there is a fear that what has been given up to enter such a group may not be recovered. From the perspective of the members who are not questioning the sect's values, such dissident members are seen as destructive quislings, and, having experienced the truth encapsulated in the group's teachings,

---

classified either as productive (wheat) or destructive (tares) members seen in Augustine's argument with the Donatists. The dispute arose over the role of traditors in the Church, who wished to return to their roles after vacillating in the face of persecution. Augustine opposed the more extreme position of the Donatists. In a popular writing, he determined if possible to win the ear of all classes by composing a rough poem, *Psalmus contra Partem Donati*, in the art of an Abecedarium, running the letters to U. Here he asserted that the tares should not be uprooted until the final judgment, and meanwhile should coexist within the church. Part of the dispute was more concerned with the validity of the sacraments administered by traditor bishops than with the actual fact of traditors themselves. However, the earliest extant reference is to be found in the writings of Hippolytus who reports the view of Callistus as being "Let the tares grow alongside the wheat; or in other words let sinners remain in the church" (*Haer* 9.12.22).

[38] The significant alteration is that the dismembered body will not be laid with the 'unbelievers' (Q 12.46), but with the 'hypocrites'. This later term is a Matthean favourite for characterising his opponents, and especially in relation to those practices that the evangelist views as superficial acts of piety, (Matt 6.2, 5, 16; 7.5; 15.7; 22.18; 23.13, 15, 23, 25, 27, 29).

[39] Stanton, *Gospel*, 102.

[40] Commitment mechanisms are basically the means by which members may express that their own beliefs are in line with the shared beliefs of the group, and thereby demonstrate their affiliation as a member of the religious community.

[41] Bainbridge, *The Sociology of Religious Movements*, 134-5).

their apostasy is worse than that of outsiders. This seems to be a fair reflection of the Matthean and Dead Sea Communities in their respective attitudes to those members in conflict with the group's beliefs and hierarchy (cf. Matt 7.21-23; 18.15-18; 24.11-13).

The final aspect of Coser's model of social conflict that Stanton considers is the issue of community cohesion and control. Obviously this is related to the issue of dissent in the previous paragraph, for dissent requires response or a mechanism to attempt to bring members back into line with the received teachings of the group. However, the positive motivation for cohesion is more significant since this was the force that attracted members to convert to the group initially and to adhere to a new set of values. Turning to the Community Rule (1QS) Stanton notes that the group does not appear to have been highly structured, instead it was an egalitarian entity, although, of necessity, authority patterns were beginning to develop.

> A sectarian community which perceives itself to be at odds with the parent body from which it has parted will have strong group cohesion and be much more likely to be egalitarian than to have a rigid internal structure. With the death of the charismatic leader, 'routinization of charisma' gradually takes place and eventually structures are developed.[42]

Both the Qumran and Matthean communities appear to be moving in the direction of creating authority structures in their groups, albeit in a rather undeveloped form in comparison to the parent bodies from which they have succeeded. In this sense, acceptance of the present powerless status of the community is legitimised as the correct form of existence for the group even if there is an expected reversal in the eschaton. While there is a theoretical ambivalence to authority structures, in practice there are some indicators of basic structures being developed. The tension between an anti-structural outlook (Matt 18.17-18; 23.8-12) contrasts with those passages that reflect the emergence of primitive structural systems (Matt 10.41-2; 16.19; 18.18; 23.34). Therefore, Stanton is able to see that on the basis of all three indicators, "Both the Damascus Document and Matthew's Gospel explain and sustain the separate identity of communities which have parted company painfully with parent bodies."[43]

Stanton's use of sociological theory resists the temptation to fill in gaps in our knowledge on the basis of what the sociological models tell us 'must' have happened. Rather, such models are seen as providing insight

---

[42] Stanton, *Gospel*, 103. Here Stanton is obviously dependent upon Weber's distinction between prophetic charisma and the routinization of such charisma after the leader's death. The model Weber proposes accounts for the emergence of more rigid structures and offices within a community (Weber, *The Sociology of Religion*).

[43] Stanton, *Gospel*, 106.

into what features to look for in the two narratives in order to better appreciate the conflict and emergence of both the Qumran and Matthean groups. Stanton appreciates the complementarity of rhetorical, literary and sociological approaches, and notes that when all three appear to support the same perspective they strengthen the overall understanding gained from the text. Specifically in regard to the last mentioned approach, Stanton sounds a significant, if too little heeded, warning.

> Sociological considerations based on comparisons with similar ancient societies will be more compelling than 'distant comparisons' with societies and groups in very different cultural, religious and historical settings. A healthy scepticism about claims of cross-cultural continuity is in order.[44]

The comparison between the Dead Sea and Matthean group is particularly apposite, for not only is there a relative temporal proximity, but more importantly both share the same religious heritage of Judaism, both are in conflict with the emergent or normative more powerful faction of the contemporary Judaism of their own day and both are seeking to legitimise and define their new pattern of existence in the newly experienced setting of alienation from the central religious institutions.

This sober approach that is fully cognizant of the limitations of the methodology is carried over into what Stanton claims can be known about the location and history of the community. While acknowledging the work of Overman in recognizing that many of the issues at stake for Matthew's community were also points of tension in other Jewish sects, Stanton also highlights an inconsistency in Overman's thesis. When Overman describes Matthew as having

> set the beliefs and life of his community over against those of formative Judaism in such a way that the people of his community would have to make a choice between the two. One could not support or be loyal to both. Lines of separation had been drawn, in a manner that appears to offer no way back.[45]

Stanton rightly criticises Overman for "not draw[ing] the conclusion to which most of his own perceptive observations point."[46] The conclusion to which Stanton alludes is that Matthew's community had already made the boundary-crossing journey over the line of separation. Overman offers no decisive way of telling on which side of the boundary the community was located, but he does importantly acknowledge that such beliefs and practice could have only one logical outcome, namely separation from the rival group. Stanton suggests that the gospel evidences a phase when the Matthean group had distanced itself significantly from synagogue based

---

[44] Stanton, *Gospel*, 108.

[45] Overman, *Matthew's Gospel and Formative Judaism*, 149.

[46] Stanton, *Gospel*, 123.

Judaism. Thus, the group is seen as *extra muros*, yet still defining itself over against Judaism. Those who wish to view the tension as *intra muros* are seen as ignoring some of the significant elements that appear to have been introduced during the final redaction of the gospel. It is in fact this exegetical concentration on a number of key texts in the gospel that leads to the conclusion that a decisive split had occurred, but the community was still defining itself in relationship to the synagogue opponents of its own day. Stanton explains the Jewishness of the text and the strident anti-Jewish polemic that both exist side by side in the following manner.

> The evangelist is probably not attacking real Jewish opponents: he is not engaged in direct polemic, but his gospel can be seen in a very broad sense as apology. It is not *tout court* the Christian answer to Judaism, but in many passages the evangelist writes with more than half an eye on known Jewish objections to Christian teaching. Contemporary Judaism is not simply ignored or set at a historical or theological distance: the evangelist develops a subtle dialectic and stresses equally strongly both continuity and discontinuity.[47]

Fundamental arguments that are seen to uphold this perspective are those texts that privilege Gentiles and promote mission to non-Jews, as well as those negative references to Judaism that although perhaps on a polemical level speak of the rejection of Israel nevertheless do not exclude the conversion of individual Jews.[48] Drawing on the observations of Schweizer,[49] Stanton focuses attention to two passages depicting persecution of members of the Matthean community. He states, "passages such as 23.34 and 10.23 which refer to persecution from town to town and, indeed, the 'death and crucifixion' of those disciples sent out by Jesus, confirm that the relationship between church and synagogue is definitely not *intra muros*."[50] Thus, Stanton's primary point is that the degree of persecution described mitigates against seeing the two parties in an *intra muros* conflict.

Similarly, the saying in Matt 23.34 which describes the fate of the prophets, wise men and scribes who have been sent, in the context of Matthew's gospel, to either the scribes and Pharisees (Matt 23.1-33) or more generally the inhabitants of Jerusalem (Matt 23.37-39), also suggests the necessity of seeing distance between the Matthean and synagogue

---

[47] Stanton, 'The Origins and Purpose of Matthew's Gospel', 1921.

[48] This position is in fact seen as a mediating position between those who assert that Matthew was a self conscious Christian-Jew who adhered to synagogue worship although this caused tension because of the messianism of Matthean believers, and other scholars who view Matthew as a Gentile with little awareness of the details of Jewish life. This latter position is represented by Strecker (*Der Weg der Gerechtigkeit*) and Meier (*Law and History in Matthew's Gospel*).

[49] Schweizer, 'Observance of the Law and Charismatic Activity in Matthew', 213-30.

[50] Stanton, 'The Origins and Purpose of Matthew's Gospel', 1915.

groups. Although the first evangelist takes this saying over from source material (Q 11.49), he modifies it in a very significant manner. As Tuckett notes the secondary character of Matthew's version seems apparent. He states,

> Luke has simply 'kill and persecute', whereas Matthew has in addition references to 'crucifying, flogging in your synagogues', and persecuting 'from city to city'. The reference to crucifying is clearly difficult, but the rest seem to be redactional additions by Matthew...the extra features here correspond with the parts of Matt. x which are peculiar to Matthew.[51]

Therefore, although Matthew takes over a saying that deals with the experience of suffering in the Q community, he intensifies the portrayal of that suffering.[52] Moreover, in this context, he introduces yet another reference to 'your synagogues' as the place where the messengers of his community have been subjected to such acts of brutality. The point Stanton makes is again seen to be valid. The intensity of the rejection and persecution portrayed by Matthew as being experienced by his group members, including death in some cases, is hardly consistent with a reconstruction of the social location of the evangelist's community that sees it still functioning within the bounds of the synagogue but involved in some kind of internal dispute or tension with the majority of synagogue attendees.

In conclusion, Stanton's work makes two extremely important contributions to studying the social history of the Matthean community. The first relates to his methodological usage of sociological theory. Such models are employed in a corroborative manner that allows observations from the social sciences to suggest possible directions of study and potential areas of investigation. However, the logical fallacy of assuming that all aspects of sectarian models are automatically present in the Matthean group is resisted. Instead, when exegetical evidence supports the existence of some aspect that is common to sectarian communities as being present in the evangelist's group, only then does Stanton proceed to employ the language and insights of the social sciences to penetrate more deeply into that aspect of the community's life. Secondly, Stanton is more persuasive in his treatment of texts that reflect a tension in Matthew's

---

[51] Tuckett, *The Revival of the Griesbach Hypothesis*, 158.

[52] Admittedly, the level of persecution in the Q version is not insignificant, with a reference to the prophets being killed. The reconstruction of the Q form offered by the IQP is ἀποστε()λῶ [(πρὸς)] (αὐτοὺς) προφήτας καὶ (σοφ)ους, [καὶ] ἐξ αὐτῶν ἀποκτεν(οῦσιν), see *The Critical Edition of Q*, 284. In comparison to this reconstruction, this already bleak prediction of the death of the prophets is made even more intense being coupled with crucifixion and scourging in the synagogue environment.

attitude towards Judaism. An important distinction is drawn in Matthew's methodology.

> The evangelist's juxtaposition of 'particularist' ('go only to the house of Israel') and universalist ('go to all nations') strands has baffled many modern readers, but as a 'foundation document' the gospel would have been read and listened to 'with awareness' by the original recipients. They would have known which parts of the story belonged to past history, and which parts were important for their on-going Christian community life.[53]

Therefore, the tensions between continuity and discontinuity that confronted the Matthean community are recognized as being reflected in the gospel narrative. Thus, Stanton understands the gospel to have been written for a collection of Christian communities that were struggling to come to terms with their alienation both from Jewish and Gentile worlds. The evangelist, through his writing of the gospel, is attempting to forge the identity of the new people of God. Yet this impacts on the group's understanding of Jesus in a way that Stanton does not fully develop. The claims made for Jesus and the authority he wields as the foundational figure in the group means that reconciliation between the Matthean and synagogue parties is impossible, since their respective authority bases are in conflict. No longer is Torah the ultimate source of authority for the evangelist and his adherents, rather the type of Messianic claims that they have advanced means that ultimate authority now resides in the one they portray as their vindicated and risen Lord. Dialogue with opponents is not the prime concern of the group, only conversion of those who do not accept its core values.

2.4 A.J. Saldarini, *Matthew's Christian-Jewish Community*

Saldarini[54] presents the Matthean group as a Christian-Jewish entity still operating within, and perceiving itself as part of, the world of Judaism. Saldarini's thesis has a number of methodological features that have been lacking in later reconstructions. First, he clearly presents the sociological theories that underpin his overall argument. Second, he treats more realistically those texts that speak positively concerning Gentiles. Third, his reconstruction is not linked to a specific temporal or geographical location. Fourth, and finally, his reconstruction supports the idea that although the Matthean community at the time of the writing of the gospel self-consciously perceived itself as part of Judaism, the gospel itself provides evidence that the community was entering a phase of

---

[53] Stanton, *Gospel*, 380.
[54] Saldarini, *Matthew's Christian-Jewish Community*.

redefinition and eventual alignment with the Gentile branch of Christianity.

Saldarini takes care to define what he intends by describing the adherents to the Matthean form of the Jesus teaching as either a 'group' or 'community'. Drawing upon the work of Muzafer Sherif, Saldarini adopts the following definition of the more generic term 'group'.

> Social psychologists define a group as 'a social unit that consists of a number of individuals who, at a given time, have role and status relations with one another, stabilized in some degree, and who possess a set of values or norms regulating the attitude and behaviour of individual members, at least in matters of consequence to them.' The author of Matthew is addressing a cohesive group which meets this definition.[55]

Adopting this sociological perspective, along with its definition of 'group', Saldarini sees the Matthean adherents as an aggregation of people who interact with one another in terms of certain shared beliefs and a loose group structure. Whereas the term 'group' is viewed as relatively neutral description, Saldarini argues that the label 'community' is too often used in relation to the Matthean group because of its positively laden and richly connotative associations. Further, Saldarini suggests that communities tend to be more egalitarian entities with a tighter structure, consequently they develop a more separate identity, which in turn makes the term 'community' a question begging label when one is trying to determine the relationship between the Matthean disciples and formative Judaism. Thus, he suggests, it is more appropriate to initially describe the Matthean adherents as a 'group' until evidence is forthcoming that they had in fact entered a phase of a more separate existence, in which case the term 'community' could be applied. He states, "Matthew and his associates have been called a 'group', the most general name available, because the designation 'community' implies to many people separation and independence from Judaism."[56]

Having decided to label the Matthean adherents as a 'group', Saldarini seeks to outline how this association engaged in the process of identity formation. Obviously, social conflict was one of the pressing factors that

---

[55] The definition that Saldarini uses is drawn from Sherif, *Group Conflict and Cooperation: Their Social Psychology*, 12. Saldarini's own comments are cited in *Matthew's Christian-Jewish Community*, 85-6.

[56] Saldarini does, however, nuance this understanding in his preceding remarks. He notes that at least insofar as the Matthean adherents are part of a wider Jewish community, they are in there own right a community, in some sense of that term. Yet, because of the perceived danger of the label 'community' being misconstrued in relation to Matthew's associates, it is deemed more appropriate to leave it to one side, and adopt the more neutral designation 'group'. (Saldarini, *Matthew's Christian-Jewish Community*, 87).

led that association to form a sub-group within the wider community of post-destruction Judaism. Therefore, basing his argument on the notion of exchange theory,[57] which sees that the incurred costs of rejecting a prior set of values must be compensated by the appropriation of a new set of beliefs perceived to be of greater worth.[58] Saldarini argues that the Matthean message appealed to group members because of its claim to be the true expression of renewed Judaism. This theory is applied to the Matthean group in the following manner.

> The members of Matthew's group combine a sharp critique of some community attitudes and practices with a deeply renewed sense of fundamental Jewish values, that is, divine rule (kingdom of God) and care (justice/righteousness), which has been communicated by God's emissary and son, Jesus. Their desire for a renewed relationship through Jesus and their conflict with the rest of the Jewish community combine to produce a strong sense of group identity, a complex web of social relationships, and a powerful set of transcendent goals and concerns.[59]

Thus, such an exchange allowed the adherents to compensate for their loss of social relationships not only by participation in a more cohesive group, but also through their belief that there would be a transcendent or otherworldly reward for enduring present deprivation.

From this perspective Saldarini proceeds to investigate what type of associations or social relationships best characterize the Matthean group. He suggests that two metaphors predominate in the depiction of the group dynamics. On the one hand there is the use of kinship and household terminology, with such language allowing for a multiplicity of relationships within the group to be described in terms of different familial bonds while at the same time reflecting the fact that these relationships were not fully formalized, but functioned at a fraternal level.[60] One may

---

[57] Stark and Bainbridge develop the use of exchange theory in relation to religious movements. They note that intangible compensators (i.e., future rewards) can be seen as substitutes for material reward among members of religious groups. (Stark and Bainbridge, *A Theory of Religion*, 36-7).

[58] A similar, but arguably less convincing, form of this notion of future rewards offsetting loss of present material benefits has been developed by Ian Smith in his application of Rational Choice theory, drawn from economic modelling, and applied to the churches to whom the book of Revelation is addressed. See, Smith, 'A Rational Choice Model of the Book of Revelation', 97-116.

[59] Saldarini, *Matthew's Christian-Jewish Community*, 89.

[60] The importance of brotherhood language is seen as being one of the strongest indicators of the significance of kinship terminology. This relationship is seen as defining both internal relations as well as differentiating the group from its opponents. Thus Saldarini asserts "The closeness of members within the group and with Jesus is reflected in Jesus' reference to the disciples as his brothers after the resurrection (28.10). Matthew's group, like all fledgling movements, sects, and interest groups, values unity and closeness among its members. Group identity and cohesion depends on common

perhaps fairly ask why the characterisation of the Matthean 'group' as a fraternity, is more acceptable than calling that entity a community. Perhaps, on the basis of the ἀδελφός language contained in Matt 18.15; 23.8, the notion of the group as a fraternity is seen as being justified from within the gospel itself. However, this very vivid use of familial language surely lands some weight to the case for referring to the Matthean adherents as a 'community'.

The other metaphor describing group interaction is that of discipleship including the ancient world understanding of the links between a teacher and pupil. However, the reference to ancient schools may conjure up incorrect notions of Matthew's assembly being modelled on Greek ἀκαδήμεια (cf., Ar. *Nu.* 1005; Epicr. 11.11; Ath 10.419d; Pl. *Ly.* 203a). The more likely context for understanding the teacher-pupil relationship for Jesus' ministry is the second temple or proto-Rabbinic master-disciple relationship. However, Saldarini rejects this model. He argues,

> In calling Jesus' followers 'disciples,' Matthew is following the Greek usage of Mark and, most likely, earlier Jesus traditions. He is using a Greek rather than Hebrew model for the relationship between Jesus and his associates....At the same time, Matthew is resisting the early rabbinic movement in the late first century, which also stressed master-disciple relations. He seeks to differentiate himself from it by insisting that only Jesus is master and teacher and that the terms and roles may *not* be replicated in the life of his group (23:8-10).[61]

Nonetheless, despite the correct recognition that Matthew is critiquing formalized hierarchies and deferential forms of address, it does not necessary follow that the actual model is being rejected. Rather, it is reformulated so that all group members are perceived as equals being guided by Jesus as the one teacher (23.10). At this level, Matthew wishes to stress the brotherhood of the community's discipleship in order to portray it as a more egalitarian entity than the system he is criticising. This same perspective permeates the woes that follow. Especially in the second woe (Matt 23.15), it is apparent that it is not the act of making proselytes that is criticized (for presumably Matthew's group was involved in similar activity), instead it is the outcome of that process that is the basis of objection. As is made clear in the clause, ποιεῖτε αὐτὸν υἱὸν γεέννης διπλότερον ὑμῶν, the problem that Matthew perceives with his opponents making converts is that they conform them to their own standard of behaviour rather than Matthean notions of 'righteousness'.[62]

---

perceptions of social reality, and on sharing positive contact." (Saldarini, *Matthew's Christian-Jewish Community*, 92).

[61] Saldarini, *Matthew's Christian-Jewish Community*, 95.

[62] At this juncture Keener correctly appreciates the nature of the rhetoric when he note that the opponents are characterized as "eager to proselytise, but their coverts

Saldarini does not suggest that the group maintained a permanent anti-Gentile outlook, nonetheless Gentiles are seen as being marginal characters in Matthew's presentation of the Jesus story. This is seen as being borne out at a literary critical level. In relation to Gentiles it is asserted that,

> They are not permanent characters in the narrative, but rather emerge briefly and then disappear without a continuing relationship with Jesus or his followers. In some stories, they symbolize the relationship of the later Matthean group with the non-Jewish world and offer hope that gentiles will also become members of Matthew's Christian-Jewish group. But they are so peripheral to the narrative and main characters that the thesis that the gospel is predominantly oriented toward a gentile mission or a gentile group is very unlikely.[63]

It is, however, equally true that the same comments could be made in terms of the relationship that Jesus exhibits towards most of the Jewish characters in the gospel, perhaps apart from the disciples, and even here only a subset of the twelve could be described as partially developed characters. Therefore, it seems unnecessary to understand such peripherality as implying lack of interest, for while the characters themselves may not be fully developed and quite correctly classified as flat, unidimensional or monochrome, this does not prove that as a class they are of little significance in terms of the overall narratival structure.

Saldarini notes the foregrounding of Gentiles in the overall narrative as a potential criticism of his argument. While he seeks to downplay the significance of these passages,[64] it may be asked why depth of characterisation and use of the title 'disciple' are more important indicators

---

simply mimic and accentuate their flaws." In this sense, Matthew may not be reacting against the Jewish model of teacher-disciple relationships, but rather rejecting the teaching that is given by the opponents. (Keener, *A Commentary on the Gospel of Matthew*, 547). This woe also raises the complex issue of the extent of Jewish proselytization in this period. While a number of scholars have assumed that there was an extensive Jewish mission among Gentiles, (see especially, Jeremias, *Jesus' Promise to the Nations*, 11-19), this idea has been rigorously challenged by Goodman in his *Mission and Conversion*.

[63] Saldarini, *Matthew's Christian-Jewish Community*, 68-9.

[64] Saldarini, however, wishes to downplay those passages where the Gentiles are given a degree of prominence in the story. While he observes that "Some gentiles have a special role in the foreground of Matthew's narrative," and follows this with a list of example such as the Magi, the centurion at the cross, the Canaanite woman and the centurion who has his servant healed, these are not seen as representing a new inclusive attitude towards Gentiles in the Matthean association of disciples. Rather it is asserted that, "The gentiles do not, however, become disciples, with all that that commitment implies. They are praised for their faith or partial recognition of Jesus. Matthew may be implying that they have some potential to be members of his group of believers-in-Jesus, but that they are not yet members, nor does the narrative imply that they will become so." (Saldarini, *Matthew's Christian-Jewish Community*, 82).

for determining the importance of Gentiles to the evangelist than their prominence in the narrative. Furthermore, the weight attributed to the fact that none of the Gentile characters is referred to as a disciple, leads to the conclusion that "the gentile characters are secondary to the members of Israel, and their story is partial and unfinished."[65] However, such observations do little to prove Saldarini's case. It is equally true that none of the women in Matthew's story are fully developed figures, neither are any called 'disciple', yet surely the implication of this is not that they were non-participants in the Matthean community.

More helpful are Saldarini's exegetical comments on references to the Gentiles. He correctly notes that there are no blanket affirmations of the chosenness of ἔθνοι and the corresponding rejection of Israel. Moreover, he observes that, "The Sermon on the Mount and other sections of Jesus' teaching contain standard stereotypes of gentiles common to Jews. These stereotypes remain as part of Matthew's world view despite his openness to non-Jews who respond to Jesus."[66] In this sense, the tension between positive and negative statements in regard to Gentiles is both acknowledged and taken seriously, and even though Saldarini comes to the conclusion that the group was Christian-Jewish, thereby seeing it as still Jewish in terms of its primary affiliation, there is a balanced recognition that the mildly pejorative comments in the Sermon on the Mount, and elsewhere, are not a programmatic rejection of all contact with Gentiles, but instead reflect entrenched and stereotypical Jewish caricatures. From this perspective, although not seeing it as a reality at the time of the composition of the gospel, Saldarini can see that the references to Gentile "leave an opening for subsequent loosening of boundaries to permit repentant gentiles who believe in Jesus to join the Matthean group."[67]

For Saldarini, the final commission in the Gospel (28.19-20) is given due literary weight and understood as a focal point in the narrative. Yet this charge is not seen as reflecting the contemporary reality whereby the community is involved actively in the proselytization of Gentiles, rather it is used in an inceptive transformational manner, whereby possible new directions are presented to the group. He states his understanding of the change to preach the gospel to the 'nations' in the following terms.

> Matthew's emphasis on bringing non-Jews into the community…(in contrast to the alleged hypocrisy of the leaders of the majority Jewish community) suggests that the community is moving toward a conversionist orientation that seeks to bring a mixed group of people into the community (21:43). For the author, that new community is still Jewish and will still adhere to the bulk of Jewish law and custom. The author still has a waning hope that other Jews will join him. However, the orientation of the

---

[65] Saldarini, *Matthew's Christian-Jewish Community*, 82.
[66] Saldarini, *Matthew's Christian-Jewish Community*, 76-7.
[67] Saldarini, *Matthew's Christian-Jewish Community*, 77.

Matthean community is changing from reformist to isolationist (vis-à-vis Jewish society), and is beginning to create a new community withdrawn from Judaism and the empire as well.[68]

The fundamental issue is whether the mission to Gentiles had already commenced in the Matthean community at the time of writing the gospel, or if the final charge was intended as a tractate to inaugurate such practice. As the citation makes clear, the latter is Saldarini's view. He sees the group members positioned on a cusp that marks a significant re-orientation in their thinking. The obvious question that needs to be addressed is how Saldarini can know with such certainty that the material in the gospel shows that the group's attitude was about to change, but at the time of writing they still had not altered their attitude.

Geographical location is not a major factor in Saldarini's reconstruction, although he does presuppose an urban setting. He feels conflict between Matthew's Christian-Jewish group and the Jewish community, centred in a local synagogue, could most easily arise in an area with a more concentrated population. This non-rural setting can be seen to be implied by the statement that "The author of Matthew...is most probably a Jew who, though expelled from the assembly of his city, still identifies himself as a member of the Jewish community and supports obedience to the Jewish law according to the interpretation of Jesus."[69] Thus while the locale of a city seems self-evident to Saldarini because of his underlying belief that conflict is more likely to arise in such a setting, there is no desire to link the gospel with Antioch or any other particular location. In fact Saldarini notes the social differentiation between Jews and Christians in Antioch by the time of the writing of Ignatius, no more than twenty to twenty-five years after the date he posits for the writing of the first gospel. However, such differences could be due to temporal, rather than geographical distance. In one of his endnotes, Saldarini refers to Schoedel's description of the social situation in Antioch as reflected in the Ignatian epistles. Schoedel discusses the Judaizers mentioned in Magnesians 9.1. He comes to the conclusion that such people were not Jewish Christians (and far less Christian-Jews), instead "they were interested in complex biblical exegesis akin to the sought of thing that is found in Hebrews and Barnabas and that in Ignatius's estimation it distracted the community from matters of more central importance

---

[68] Saldarini, 'The Gospel of Matthew and the Jewish-Christian Conflict', 59-60. It is worth noting that in this slightly earlier essay Saldarini does not maintain the distinction between 'group' and 'community', and rather, seems to be happy to allow the latter term to stand as his primary means of referring to Matthean adherents.

[69] Saldarini, *Matthew's Christian-Jewish Community*, 21.

(including solidarity under the bishop)."[70] In fact it may even be that because Saldarini is aware of the difficulty of placing a Christian-Jewish group in Antioch of the type he describes, that he avoids such a setting as a possible location for the Matthean group. Here he is far more attuned to the material contained in epistles of Ignatius and the cognitive dissonance of the perspective provided there in comparison with his understanding of the Matthean adherents. Obviously this is not to say that the Matthean community did not live within Antioch, since the use of the first gospel by Ignatius suggests some contact. However, Saldarini recognizes that there is little evidence to support what has become an almost axiomatic assumption in a number of reconstructions, namely that Antioch was the home of the Matthean group.[71]

Gentile mission is not an impossibility for the type of community Saldarini portrays. Although Saldarini argues that such a mission was not the present reality for the Matthean group at the time of the composition of the gospel, it is suggested that the evangelist was in fact providing a programmatic statement for a possible way forward. Stemming from its recently recognized liminal status within Judaism the group was then confronted with both coming to terms with this marginal existence and also with seeking a new outlet for its evangelistic activity. However, Saldarini suggests that the acceptance of non-Jews into the community could only be deemed appropriate if such converts submitted to the requirements of the law. He states, "Matthew seeks to incorporate non-Jewish believers-in-Jesus into his renewed Jesus-centred, but still Torah-observant Jewish community. Thus the nations, insofar as they are responsive to Jesus, are candidates for membership in Matthew's group."[72] Here Saldarini highlights that the primary entrance requirement centred on belief in Jesus, this is what marked the group off from the majority of Judaism and also this constituted the future basis for acceptance of Gentiles into his community. Nonetheless, belief in Jesus, as Saldarini understands it within the context of the Matthean community, was to be demonstrated by Gentile converts, at least in part, through the observance of Torah.

While Saldarini acknowledges that bringing Gentiles into the community reflects the fact that the community was being transformed from having an inward focus on reforming Judaism towards a conversionist orientation, he does not see this as having an immediate

---

[70] Schoedel, 'Ignatius and the Reception of Matthew in Antioch', 145.

[71] Meier, in his response to Schoedel, lists four texts that he sees as supplying clear proof of the dependence of Ignatius upon the Gospel of Matthew. (Meier, 'Matthew and Ignatius: A Response to William R. Schoedel', 178-86.

[72] Saldarini, *Matthew's Christian-Jewish Community*, 79.

impact on the law observant requirements of the group. However, the very act of calling for the formation of a mixed group appears to require some compromise of previously held values. Saldarini suggests that the fundamental requirement for entrance or inclusion into the Matthean group was belief in Jesus, albeit that this was demonstrated through Torah observance. Yet, this also obviously included some form of catechetical instruction so that new adherents to the group might observe Jesus' teachings, at least as it was understood by the wider membership of the group. Thus, as Matt 28.20 emphasizes, a fundamental part of proselytization was pedagogical activity, and the evangelist presents this as the charge of the risen Jesus, διδάσκοντες αὐτοὺς τηρεῖν πάντα ὅσα ἐνετειλάμην ὑμῖν. However, for Saldarini the need to compromise on Jewish Torah praxis lay in the future and had not been the experience of the community at the time of the composition of the gospel. Nonetheless, Saldarini suggests that such a compromise would be the outcome of the pathway that the group was following. To quote him at length:

> Matthew lost the battle for Judaism. Within Christianity his way of following Jesus died out for the most part during the following generation. His gospel was used by later Christians in order to make sense out of Christianity's relationship to Judaism, but fidelity to Torah in Matthew's sense was nonoperative and so 'fulfillment' of Torah was understood in a different way. From the viewpoint of deviance theory, Matthew's community or its successors were engulfed by their deviant role and adopted their deviance as a 'master status,' that is, as the set of values and characteristics that defined and controlled all other aspects of their lives. Within a short time, because of both rejection by the majority of the Jewish community and the dominance of non-Jewish believers-in-Jesus, most communities like Matthew's became sociologically Christian, that is, they lost their identification with Judaism and became a separate, competing group.[73]

The issue at stake in this reconstruction is not whether the community's reorientation towards Gentiles would result in it redefining itself as 'Christian' rather than a group in Judaism, for Saldarini acknowledges that this was shown to be the historical outcome. Instead, the question is whether this new self-understanding is actually reflected in the community at the time of the composition of the gospel, or as Saldarini contends was only a later development.

Despite Saldarini's insistence that at the time the evangelist wrote, Gentile converts were required to observe Torah, the brief references to Gentile mission do not support such a reading. In the Great Commission the twin entrance requirements for being made a disciple are baptism and observing Jesus' teachings. Here traditional Jewish boundary markers, circumcision,

---

[73] Saldarini, 'The Gospel of Matthew and the Jewish-Christian Conflict', 60-1.

food laws and Sabbath observance, are not mentioned.[74] While it might be argued that such items are included in Jesus' instruction, this does not appear to be exegetically defensible. The issue of circumcision does not arise in the gospel, Sabbath observance is subject to Jesus' higher authority (Matt 12.8), and while Matthew does not declare 'all foods clean' (Matt 15.11; cf., Mk 7.19c), neither does he place emphasis on his community members or prospective Gentile converts being required to embrace food laws.

Saldarini's understanding of the social background of the Matthean community has much to commend it. It recognizes the conflict between the Matthean group and formative Judaism in the post-destruction period, it outlines clearly the sociological presuppositions that underpin the reconstruction, it does not link the setting to a specific location, it takes seriously the positive statements about Gentiles, and, in particular, it sees that the Great Commission is offered to the Matthew's adherents not as an unrealised theoretical possibility, but as an important step challenging the community to engage actively in Gentile conversion. However, one is left wondering, in light of the positive references to Gentiles in the final third of the gospel, if the group had in fact not already commenced this missionary activity, and if the evangelist's purpose in writing was not at least in part an attempt to legitimise this mission by projecting it back into the ministry of Jesus and also by making it a command of the risen Lord to the post-Easter Church.

Further, contrary to Saldarini, there is no indication that non-Jewish converts were expected to observe Torah legislation. While it could be argued that this was self-apparent, such an argument from silence carries little force. It appears likely that the Matthean group knew of other Christian communities,[75] which had already included Gentiles, and as such

---

[74] This is not necessarily to follow Dunn in his assessment that ἔργα νόμου is to be understood are denoting those boundary marking activities that distinguished Jewish practice. Although in fairness to Dunn he does not suggest that works of the law is to be equated with circumcision, food laws and Sabbath, rather the phrase refers to keeping everything the law require, but these three distinctive elements became touchstones in the recognition of Jewish orthopraxy. As he states, "The phrase 'the works of the law,' does, of course, refer to all or whatever the law requires, covenantal nomism as a whole. But in a context where the relationship of Israel is at issue, certain laws would naturally come more into focus than others. We have instanced circumcision and food laws in particular." (*The Theology of the Apostle Paul*, 358). Moreover, discussing the pre-Pauline usage of the terminology in 4QMMT (מעשי התורה//ἔργα νόμου), Dunn concludes that Paul is objecting to such usage as that represented by the Qumran text. "MMT, in common with other strands of Second Temple Judaism, understood 'righteousness' and 'justification' in relationship to and as somehow dependent upon מעשי התורה/ἔργα νόμου." (Dunn, '4QMMT and Galatians,' 152).

[75] This appears even more likely on Saldarini's reckoning, since he places the Matthean community somewhere in 'Greater Syria', and illustrates the diversity and

they had already been required to confront the issue of what, if any, Torah requirements Gentiles would have to obey. It is somewhat surprising if Matthew's community was embarking on Gentile mission, but expecting converts to maintain the whole law, as Saldarini proposes, that one finds no obvious reflection of this in the pages of the gospel. Instead, although the group stressed its continuity with Jewish traditions, it nonetheless presented supersessionary claims for Jesus which made him the final source of authority within the community, and promoted the only entrance requirement as being baptism in the threefold name of Father, Son and Spirit.

2.5 J.A. Overman, *Matthew's Gospel and Formative Judaism*

Overman defines the Matthean community as being both sectarian and Jewish, or perhaps more frequently as 'Jewish Christian'. In relation to the description 'sectarian', he adopts the following generalized definition formulated by Blenkinsopp.

> We follow J. Blenkinsopp in taking the term *sectarian* to mean a group which is, or perceives itself to be, a minority in relation to the group it understands to be the 'parent body'. The sect is a minority in that it is subject to, and usually persecuted by, the group in power. The dissenting group is in opposition to the parent body and tends to claim more or less to be what the dominant body claims to be.[76]

Fundamental to this definition is the way it portrays the deviant group as being derivative upon an established group with whom there is a genetic relationship. The new group tends to be relatively weak in comparison the parent group, and this weakness is even reflected in the group being bereft of concepts adequate for self-definition. Consequently, in the struggle for definition, the nascent community draws upon some of the terminology of their perceived opponents, although this may involve a degree of subverting or caricaturing the way in which the original group employed such concepts. In effect, this results in a supersessionary claim, whereby the new group asserts that it is the legitimate inheritor of the common traditions, and therefore seeks to displace the established party. This aligns with those features that Blenkinsopp sees as prevalent in sectarian society. As he mentions, "At one stage of development a dissident group can simply exhibits separatist tendencies and therefore be more aptly designated a dissident group, a party, a school or something of the sort...a sect is not only a minority, and not only characterized by opposition to

---

spread of both Judaism and Christianity in this region. See Saldarini, *Matthew's Christian-Jewish Community*, 11-26.

[76] Overman, *Matthew's Gospel and Formative Judaism*, 8.

norms accepted by the parent-body, but also claims in a more or less exclusive way to be what the parent-body claimed to be."[77]

The description of sectarianism that is advanced by Overman is also dependent upon Bryan Wilson's study on contemporary marginal religious groups from a sociological perspective. Wilson draws attention to both the sense of displacement experienced by such groups in the context of the wider social order, as well as emphasizing the sense of alienation from those in authority.[78] Overman emphasizes the tendency for newly formed groups to denounce the enfranchised leadership, which is held responsible for the liminal status of group members, and further, for the newly formed marginal party to reject the organisational framework of wider society. For Wilson, such tendencies are seen as key indicators that the group is sectarian, and while the group in question may perhaps not admit to the term 'sect', it would at least recognize its own precarious position in the larger social order. Adopting these indicators, Overman labels the Dead Sea Community as sectarian.[79] Drawing primarily on the Damascus Document (CD) and the Community Rule (1QS) it is noted that the community rejects the established religio-political leadership based around the Jerusalem priesthood, and also that wider society is characterized as apostate because of its willing acceptance of this supposedly perverse form of authority. Therefore, the Qumran covenantors have both rejected the existing power structures, and removed themselves from wider society by forming a new community. In terms of Blenkinsopp's definition of sectarianism and the indicators of sectarian status noted by Wilson, Overman is correct in his assessment that the Dead Sea Community conforms to the broad pattern of a group alienated from wider society and rejecting the prevailing system.

In the same manner, Overman attempts to apply the same understanding of sectarianism to the Matthean community, as it existed in the period after the destruction of the Jerusalem Temple. However, the

---

[77] Blenkinsopp, 'Interpretation and the Tendency to Sectarianism: An Aspect of Second Temple History', 1.

[78] Wilson, *Magic and the Millennium*.

[79] It is perhaps best to nuance this presentation. Whereas Overman bases his assessment on later DSS such as CD and 1QS where the sectarian tendency are strongest, in earlier texts such as 4QMMT the community is trying to renew its position in society. Although it is unquestionably alienated in this early phase, it has not yet entered the stage in later texts where its polemic and rhetorical strategies are clearly world negating. In all likelihood it did not take the community long to move to this stage, presumably soon after the rejection of the Halakhic letter (4QpPs37 4.7-9) and the attack by the Wicked Priest (1QpHab 9.5f). However, this highly charged negative attitude towards all other groups within Judaism, and beyond, took some time to evolve and is best understood as recognition of the community's permanent liminality.

equation he wishes to draw is not as straightforward as it was in the case of the Qumran community. Firstly, the destruction of the Temple and the slaughter of the priests, according to Overman, meant that there was no existing leadership with whom to dissent. Secondly, during this post-70 C.E. period, wider society could not be described as a unified group, but rather was a collection of people attempting to come to terms with the trauma of the destruction. Thirdly, Overman suggests that the most appropriate model to depict the relationship between Matthew's group and his opponents is not that of deviation from an established parent body with its entrenched norms, but rather the scenario is that of competition between 'fraternal twins' who both seek self-legitimisation and self-definition. In this case the twins are seen as being the Matthean group and formative rabbinic Judaism. Thus Overman advances the opinion, "Nowhere is the shared matrix of Christianity and emergent rabbinic Judaism more evident than in Matthew's Gospel. These two movements are fraternal twins. They developed and defined themselves in light of one another."[80] From this perspective, it becomes apparent that it is inappropriate to represent the Christian movement in its Matthean form as seeking to supplant a coherent, established, and autocratic leadership. Such a body simply did not exist in the aftermath of the 70 C.E. destruction, and it would be many decades (if not centuries) before rabbinic Judaism developed into a movement with a substantial power base. Rather, there was competition between developing parties, for the right to claim ownership of the relics and ruins of the heritage and traditions that surrounded a temple-based form of Judaism.

Thus, Overman notes that these two competing groups attempted to claim the leadership of Judaism in different ways. For the Matthean group the way forward lay in a reinterpretation of such religio-cultural artefacts in light of its Messianic and prophetic foundational figure. Alternatively, for emergent Judaism the way forward was based on a need to intensify accurate understanding, study and observance of the halakah. These paths were both legitimate responses, both drew on the same stock of traditions, both involved reinterpretation, but the two were ultimately incompatible with each other. The resultant tension that arose from the respective claims to be the legitimate interpreter of Jewish tradition forms the crux of the antagonism that developed between these two embryonic religious movements. According to Overman, the centrality of Torah interpretation in religious debate prior to the fall of Jerusalem was in fact intensified after its collapse. He thus contends that the law and its interpretation became the fundamental authority issue confronting Jewish religious groups in post-70 C.E. Judea and Galilee. He argues,

---

[80] Overman, *Matthew's Gospel and Formative Judaism*, 160.

This privileged position and reputation became all the more crucial in the post-70 period following the destruction of the temple. The law now emerged as the central symbol for post-70 Judaism. Who was recognized as the authoritative interpreters had a great deal to do with who emerged as the accepted and established movement.[81]

Obviously the importance of the law in rabbinic Judaism can legitimately be extrapolated back, *mutatis mutandis*, from the Mishnaic period to the formative era, since the centrality of Torah forms the basis of the group's self-understanding and moreover, its rationale for being. Further, the importance of the law is not a totally new factor, from the time of the Deuteronomistic Historian onwards there was a continuous tradition within Judaism of renewal movements that saw such revivification of the national cult arising from more exact observance of the law.

In relation to the programmatic statement in Matt 5.17-20 dealing with the evangelist's attitude towards the law, Overman states that it should be taken at face value, which for him means that it gives explicit support for fulfilling all the requirements of the law. As he comments, "Although this passage is the subject of lively controversy, it is unambiguous and does indeed command obedience to the whole Torah. Of course, we would not expect anything less from a faithful, apparently well trained, late-first century Palestinian Jew."[82] Yet, despite Overman's comment to the contrary, the passage is not unambiguous and the issue is further complicated by the series of antitheses that follow, since these six statements exhibit a more complex attitude to the law than that of straightforward, unnuanced observance of its stipulations. Thus as Meier suggests, the saying on the law cannot be understood apart from the antitheses that follow, or for that matter apart from the wider gospel context. He observes, "This programmatic statement on the Law is then illustrated by six antitheses (5.21-48), which are introduced by 5.20 (and in a broader sense, by the whole of 5.17-20)."[83] Yet, since Overman does not recognize the interplay between the Torah statement and the antitheses, he interprets the programmatic comment of 5.17-20 as unambiguously upholding observance of the Torah.

When Overman states that Matthew is portraying his community as the correct upholders and interpreters of Torah tradition, it does not automatically follow, as he assumes, that this means that the group had a conservative attitude to the law. Of course it is partially correct to assert that,

One senses that Matthew sees himself and his community as the guardians of the right understanding of the law and the prophets. His interpretation and that of Jesus

---

[81] Overman, *Matthew's Gospel and Formative Judaism*, 69.
[82] Overman, *Church and Community in Crisis*, 1996, 78.
[83] Meier, *Law and History in Matthew's Gospel*, 43.

reflected in the gospel is not radical, dismissive or *de novo* where the law and Israel's traditions are concerned. To the contrary, they fulfil and embody those laws and traditions.[84]

While Matthew's claims of continuity and correct fulfilment are self-evident, one cannot assume that this automatically leads to the conclusion that Overman suggests, specifically that this implies a conservative approach to such traditions. This can only be established by considering the manner in which the antitheses deal with specific halakhic issues, and the authority base that Matthew draws upon to resolve such disputes. Overman adopts a fairly standard line arguing that the antitheses do not revoke the law; instead they intensify its demands by calling for a higher standard of righteousness. Unsurprisingly his discussion focuses on three of the six statements, dealing with murder, adultery and love of enemies. He comes to the conclusion that "What Matthew is trying to accomplish in 5.21ff....is the connection that exists between characteristics and attitudes on the one hand and behaviour community well-being on the other." Thus the antitheses are seen as providing concrete examples of how the law should function for this Jewish community of believers in Jesus, and the answer Overman provides is that its full force still stands, yet its values must be internalised and the outcome must be a higher standard of ethical behaviour.

However, the evidence Overman ignores, in fact goes against his reading of the text. The third and fifth antitheses, dealing with divorce and *lex talionis* respectively, do not neatly align with this pattern. It may be argued that they do reflect a more humane and merciful application of Torah that neither allows divorce to be a matter of personal convenience nor injustice to be avenged with direct retribution. However, both of these new attitudes do in fact involve removing a permission given in Torah casuistic rulings. In relation to the divorce command Overman only offers the cursory assessment that "Matthew was very much a part of the first-century debate about divorce in Palestine. Hillel and Shammai also debated this issue (*b. Git.* 9.10)."[85] He does not, however, explain where in the spectrum of halakhic debate the Matthean attitude falls, or whether other participants in such a debate would see it as an abrogation of the law. Further, the issue of retribution, despite Overman purportedly discussing 5.38-48, is not treated.[86] In that section his focus is exclusively on the love command. Yet as Meier realises,

---

[84] Overman, *Church and Community in Crisis*, 81.

[85] Overman, *Church and Community in Crisis*, 82.

[86] In his commentary on these verses (see *Church and Community in Crisis*, 84-7), Overman simply states that non-retaliation was forced on Matthew because of the colonial setting of the Roman empire, and this is part of the reason the love command

In the fifth antithesis, Jesus revokes the *jus talionis* of Ex 21:24, Lev 24:20, and Dt 19:21. This is perhaps the clearest and least disputable case of annulment in the antitheses. Probably one cannot even speak of a *permission* being annulled. Such introductory phrases as Dt 19:21a ('and your eye shall show no pity') indicate an obligatory command rather than a permission.[87]

Whether or not Meier is correct in his assessment that this is the clearest instance of annulment, nonetheless, he cogently demonstrates that readings of the text, such as Overman proposes, do not hold.

Even more telling is Overman's non-treatment of the antithesis dealing with oaths. Again we have a ruling placed on the lips of the historical Jesus that runs directly counter to the Pentateuchal legislation. The use of oaths, or vows, is explicitly commanded as a means of safeguarding the truth, (cf., Ex 22.6-7, 10; Num 5.19-22; Deut 6.13; 10.20). Matthew is not simply calling for care in the use of oaths out of respect for the divine name, rather he calls into question the whole process of swearing a vow because he views it as being fundamentally opposed to the sanctity of the divine name. Overman may be correct that this is related to the Matthean desire to avoid courts and legal proceedings,[88] but nonetheless, it calls into question the legitimacy of oaths even in those circumstances where one was obliged to use them in accordance with Mosaic ordinances.

Similarly, there are aspects of Overman's treatment of chapter 28, in particular the interpretation of the term Ἰουδαῖοι in v. 15 and his understanding of the function of the Great Commission (vv. 16-20), that raise a number of exegetical questions. First, turning to the reference to the Jews. Overman rightly questions the assumption that the use of this term can be seen as evidence for arguing that the author of the first gospel was himself a Gentile.[89] However, the importance of this usage is obscured by

---

comes to the fore. However, there is no explanation about the ruling of the fifth antithesis in relation to Torah stipulations.

[87] Meier, *Law and History in Matthew's Gospel*, 157.

[88] The concern to avoid involvement with judicial authorities does appear as a primary concern in the antitheses (cf., 5.22, 25-6, 33-4, 38-9, 41). Overman sees this primarily in terms of Roman legal institutions in the Eastern Mediterranean. He states, "Matthew repeatedly urges his audience to avoid courts at all costs. The courts and other military venues were where the Matthean community ran the clear risk of encountering the imperial presence and the punishment that they could dole out for any form of deviance." (Overman, *Church and Community in Crisis*, 85). However, the reference to the ἀγγαρεύσω apart, there seems to by little to connect the discussion of courts in the antitheses with imperial institutions. It is more natural to take the reference as relating to Jewish institutions and internal disputes. In part Overman recognizes this point, but sees the doling out of justice that resulted from internal Jewish disputes to be within the hands of Roman officials.

[89] Although not representing the totality of his argument, this view can be traced back to Clark ('The Gentile Bias in Matthew', 165-72). In this important paper Clark set

Overman since he reduces the discussion to the somewhat peripheral issue of the ethnic identity of the author of the gospel. Simply because Matthew is identified as being a Jew, this does not mean, contrary to Overman, that Ἰουδαῖοι is being used as a self-reference that denotes the group's conformity with wider Judaism. It is worth quoting Overman in full to see how he arrives at his conclusion. He states in reference to Ἰουδαῖοι that

> [w]hile the meaning of the term is far from absolute, it does not suggest that Matthew was a Gentile and is here slandering Jews. Rather, this term is used here, as in many inscriptions and in Josephus, as a circumlocution for all Jews, or, more precisely, themselves. That is, Matthew's use of the term 'Jews' here in 28:15 really says something like 'The rumor has circulated among all of us [*Ioudaios*] until this day.'[90]

While agreeing with the observation that the term does not establish Matthew's ethnic identity as being Gentile,[91] it does not automatically follow that it is a self-denoting or reflexive reference. Overman suggests that the term has been utilised in this context because Matthew has concerns about what those outside his community are thinking. Yet it needs to be asked whether the gospel was likely to be used in such a way so that it would have been heard or read by those outside the community. Since an external audience appears unlikely, it seems far more plausible to see it as a document with a pastoral focus. Therefore, the reference to Ἰουδαῖοι has the function of denoting the behaviour of those Jews who oppose the Matthean community for group members who are either themselves not ethnically Jewish, or to those who no longer hold their 'Jewishness' as their primary allegience.

Overman, however, links his understanding of the term Ἰουδαῖοι to his interpretation of the Great Commission. He argues that the missionary charge was given as a theoretical pedagogical incentive to the group. It did not denote the present reality, for the community was still comprised of

---

forth for the first time in the modern era the view that Matthew himself was a Gentile, primarily seeing that such a conclusion was warranted because of the repeated manner in which the evangelist privileges Gentiles while consigning Jews to a bleak eternal future. Although this position has never been a majority position, it has nevertheless continued to attract small numbers of scholars. One of the more significant contributions that sought to provide additional evidence for identifying Matthew as non-Jewish is the work of Strecker, *Der Weg der Gerechtigkeit.*

[90] Overman, *Church and Community in Crisis*, 401.

[91] In fact, in fairness to both Clark and Strecker, this reference by itself does not form the basis for seeing Matthew as a Gentile. Rather, it is only seen as being a piece of corroborative evidence in a wider thesis of non-Jewish authorship, that is seen as supported more strongly by the gospel's generally positive attitude towards gentiles and the notion that they are seen as the privileged new people of God who displace the Jews from their previous position of priority in the soteriological plan.

ethnic, or 'Matthean-Jews'. Thus, for Overman the commission is more concerned with eschatology than with evangelistic outreach. He suggests that Matthew was trying to explain the delay of the parousia by relating that event to the worldwide proclamation of the gospel. It is stated that,

> Matthew's position of Matthean Judaism being open to other people and other races is related to his view of the end. If others hear about the message of Matthean Judaism, then the end will come. Both 24:14 and 28:20 suggest that. Mission, despite the modest interest in it in Matthew's church, is related to Matthew's view of history. The era or age will draw to a close and the age that promises a better life for Matthean Jews will draw near if the mission to the rest of the world is engaged.[92]

Thus, mission is not an end in itself, and the evangelist is not primarily concerned with the welfare of Gentiles, but according to Overman mission is an expedient that can precipitate an eschatological reversal of fortunes for the community by bringing to an end its present experience of alienation and the sense of marginalization in society. However, it needs to be asked whether this is really a plausible reading in terms of the Matthean Jesus' emphasis on repentance and evangelism both for Jews and non-Jews alike. Rather, Gundry's assessment appears more astute when he acknowledges that a number of themes coalesce in 28.16-20, but the one that is paramount is mission to all the nations. As he sees, "To include Gentiles as well as Jews, therefore, the present commission expands the earlier commission (cf. Matthew's bringing Gentile women into the genealogy of Jesus, the descent of Abraham, through whose seed God promised that all the nations of the world should be blessed."[93]

The strength of Overman's treatment comes primarily from its clarification of the situation after the destruction of the temple as being one where a number of competing groups struggled to come to terms with the removal of the authority structures that had previously been present. The Matthean group cannot be understood as a deviant movement that had split away from a parent group that still had existing power structures. Both the Matthean group and its opponents were relatively fragile entities in the aftermath of the events of 70 C.E. However, Overman is not necessarily correct to see that the Matthean group was a strict Torah observant party that functioned exclusively within 'Judaism' and only upheld mission as a kind of trigger that precipitated the eschaton. The group's attitude to both law and mission are more complex than Overman suggests. Torah is both upheld by the community's foundational figure, yet at the same time it is reinterpreted and even superseded by the interpretations Jesus offers. Also, mission is not upheld simply as a means of inaugurating eschatological events, but is seen as part of the inclusive

---

[92] Overman, *Church and Community in Crisis*, 411.
[93] Gundry, *Matthew*, 595.

vision for the community that is commanded by Jesus himself. Thus, while Overman helpfully presents some of the shared values between the Matthean group and formative Judaism, he perhaps has a tendency to downplay the degree of separation that emerges between these two competing outlooks.

2.6 D.C. Sim, *The Gospel of Matthew and Christian Judaism*

Like Overman and Saldarini, Sim locates the Matthean community within the orbit of formative Judaism. In fact for Sim the adherents to the teaching of the first evangelist are far more tightly bound to wider Judaism than is suggested by other scholars who see this group as part of post-destruction Judaism.[94] To arrive at this determination of the social location of the Matthean community Sim argues that, by its general nature, the material contained in the gospel suggests such a reconstruction. He states, "The definitive evidence that Matthew's group was still within the orbit of Judaism comes not from the witness of a few Gospel passages but from the general perspective from which the evangelist writes. That is to say, Matthew writes from a thoroughly Jewish outlook and he constantly affirms the basic and distinctive tenets of Judaism."[95] Moreover, he argues that the label he applies to the community, namely that of 'Christian Judaism', emphasizes the distinctively Jewish character of the group and further, that the noun Judaism nominates the primary religious affiliation. Here Sim acknowledges his debt to Saldarini for the understanding that the group was first and foremost a Jewish entity. However, by contrast, he distances himself from Overman's nomenclature of the group as being 'Matthean Judaism', since such a label is seen as being too restrictive. Thus he argues, "Although Overman's name correctly places the evangelist and his readers within the Jewish religion, it fails to note that they were representatives of a broader religious movement that both preceded and

---

[94] This is in contrast to Bornkamm, in his earliest phase, Hummel and Saldarini. Whereas, *mutatis mutandis*, these three scholars saw Matthew's group as still identifying themselves as a 'Jewish' entity, nonetheless, they acknowledge the strength of the discord between the evangelist and his opponents. As has been noted, Saldarini sees that such a tension must inevitably lead to a separation, although he argues that this still remains in the future for the Matthean adherents. Thus at the time of composition Saldarini argues that the gospel reflects "a fluid social situation with imprecise boundaries, ongoing conflict, and unresolved tensions." (Saldarini, *Matthew's Christian-Jewish Community*, 9). Yet, for Saldarini, it was not until the second century that a decisive break took place.

[95] Sim, *The Gospel of Matthew and Christian Judaism*, 5.

succeeded them. This movement was Christian Judaism, not Matthean Judaism."[96]

While Sim is particularly strong in his portrayal of the Jewish aspect and affiliation of the group, it is not as clear what the qualifier 'Christian' adds to the descriptive label. His *via negativa*, whereby he states what the term 'Christian' does not mean for his study, is not instructive in showing why it is necessarily joined to the appellation 'Jewish'. His statement portraying what is not intended is presented in the following manner.

> [T]he use of the term 'Christian Jew(ish)' in this book is slightly different from its usage in some earlier studies. Scholars have employed this term in reference to both the Matthean and Johannine communities. According to their usage, these groups were Christian Jews when they were still attached to the synagogue, but when they fell into conflict with other Jews and left the synagogue they became Jewish Christians. The implication is that with their departure from the local Jewish assembly their religious affiliation changed from Judaism to Christianity. This is a simplistic view of the situation...The evangelist's Christian Jewish group remained within Judaism, but as a sectarian movement in opposition to the more powerful parent body.[97]

From this perspective Sim maintains that non-participation in synagogue life, be that due to self-imposed withdrawal or forced ostracism, is not in itself sufficient ground for describing the community as no longer being Jewish. At a fundamental level this is of course correct. The apparently self-enforced or voluntary separation of the Qumran covenanters from Temple based religion did not result in their denial of their own Jewishness, in fact it was asserted more strongly, with the Dead Sea Scrolls Community declaring that it was the only faction that was worthy of the description of true Israel.[98] However, the corollary of Sim's argument, which he implicitly assumes, does not necessarily hold. Simply because separation from the synagogue environment does not automatically imply rejection of Jewish identity it does not follow that all groups that ceased to operate within the locale of the synagogue continued to claim allegiance to their Jewish origins. Rather, in all likelihood, the traumatic period following the breach with synagogue led to a period of

---

[96] Sim, *The Gospel of Matthew and Christian Judaism*, 26.

[97] Sim, *The Gospel of Matthew and Christian Judaism*, 26-7.

[98] In the case of the Qumran community its existence is represented sometimes as voluntary separation, while at other times, at least in the case of the Teacher of Righteousness, the desert life is seen as due to imposed exile. Thus according to the Pesher on Ps 37, the Wicked Priest, 'pursued the Teacher of Righteousness to the house of his exile, that he might swallow him with venomous fury' (2.15). By contrast, communal life is seen as a voluntary association for the majority of group members: 'And when these become members of the community in Israel according to all these rules, they shall separate from the habitation of ungodly man and go into the wilderness to prepare the way of Him' (1QS 8.12).

redefinition, and responses differed from group to group. The answer of the Johannine community, with its focus on the anointed paraclete inspired didactic activity[99] coupled with a radical ethic of intra-group love,[100] was not the way forward for the Matthean community.

Sim's answer to the function of the label Christian in the title 'Christian-Judaism' is at best a partial response. Initially he prescinds from the use of Christianity to describe the Matthean group, seeing it as only appropriately applied to the emergent Gentile Christian faction. As he states, "In view of the fact that one party made a concerted effort to remain within Judaism, it seems incongruous to describe both groups under the umbrella term "Christianity"."[101] The term 'Christianity' is understood as an anachronism during the first century, and Sim suggests nothing would be lost if it were dropped altogether since the term is inherently ambiguous. Sim does not consider the term Judaism to be equally ambiguous. Yet, it could be suggested that it is similarly precarious to label groups as Jewish, particularly in the period after 70 C.E. when the essence of Judaism was redefined due to the removal of Temple based worship and the cultic accoutrements that accompanied such a system. Sim opts for 'Christian Judaism' as being appropriate as long one acknowledges that common acceptance of Jesus does not entail seeing Gentile and law observant followers as part of the same religious tradition. Yet the fact that both groups not only share the same foundational figure, but also utilise many of the same traditions,[102] should lead one to look for links, and not just areas of discontinuity.

---

[99] In the farewell discourses, an important role is attributed to the Spirit in terms of a didactic function within the group. The Spirit not only reminds the community of the words of Jesus, but moreover, brings out new teaching in the community. As Nissen states, "The paraclete will provide continuing guidance even about matters concerning which Jesus left no instruction." (Nissen, 'Community and Ethics in the Gospel of John', 206).

[100] Smith summarises the role of the love ethic for the group. "Love among the members of the community establishes its unity. This unity, the realisation and manifestation of love, is the basis of the community's witness to the truth of Jesus as well as its very existence." (Smith, *Johannine-Christianity*, 219).

[101] Sim, *The Gospel of Matthew and Christian Judaism*, 24.

[102] Regardless of which solution to the synoptic problem one adopts, the borrowings by the evangelists suggest that, *mutatis mutandis*, the gospel writer did not feel constrained to jettison the whole contents of the Jesus tradition as espoused by alternative communities. Taking Markan priority as the most likely explanation of the synoptic relationship, it then becomes incumbent upon Sim to explain how, on the basis of his reconstruction of an exclusivist law-observant community of the first gospel, this group not only came to posses a copy of the Markan gospel, but felt happy to incorporate much of its material into its own gospel. The distance may not be as great as Sim suggests.

Although not brought out in his treatment of the social history of the Matthean community, Sim does find another reason why the first evangelist's adherents should be known not just as Jews, but more specifically as Christian Jews. His monograph dealing with apocalyptic eschatology in Matthew reveals not only that such motifs had their origin in Judaism, but that the type of apocalyptic vision to which the Matthean groups subscribed had become significantly centred on the future role of Jesus as Messiah so as to be differentiated from other expressions of eschatological messianism. The identification of Jesus as Son of Man is a tradition that Sim sees Matthew sharing with both the Markan and Q communities. From this perspective he states,

> Matthew adopts from Mark the view that Jesus was both the authoritative Son of Man and the suffering/resurrected Son of Man. From Q the evangelist took over a number of traditions which speak of the rejection (not suffering) of the Son of Man during his mission. Matthew's adoption of this material serves many christological and theological purposes, but one of these is to identify the coming Son of Man with the rejected but vindicated Jesus of Nazareth.[103]

Sim, however, does not see this as creating close links with Gentile Christianity; rather it is the strident manner in which apocalyptic symbols are used in Matthew's gospel that demonstrates both the distance from the Gentile branch of the wider movement and the experience of liminality in relation to wider Judaism. Thus, it is this sense of alienation, according to Sim, from Judaism, Gentile authorities and Gentile Christianity that created the upsurge of interest in apocalyptic eschatology. Therefore, he contends that, "the complex social setting of the Matthean community as reconstructed here is more than sufficient to explain its embracement of apocalypticism and its recourse to apocalyptic eschatology."[104] By its very nature, adherence to an apocalyptic worldview reflects a group which feels sociologically marginalized, and consequently portrays itself as persecuted yet looks for a future vindication.

Drawing on the sociological theory of sectarianism postulated by Coser, Sim adopts one of his fundamental assertions to 'prove' that the community remained self-consciously Jewish. Coser suggested that the level of intensity and the ferocity of polemic that exists between dissenting groups is in direct correlation to the proximity between the parties.[105] Following this perspective, Sim proffers the following observation, "It is now well recognized that polemical and stereotypical language such as we find in Matthew does not reflect distance between the two parties. On the contrary, it reflects both physical and ideological proximity between the

---

[103] Sim, *Apocalyptic Eschatology in the Gospel of Matthew*, 94.

[104] Sim, *Apocalyptic Eschatology in the Gospel of Matthew*, 220.

[105] Coser, *The Functions of Social Conflict*, 67-72.

disputing groups, since its very purpose is to distance one party from the other."[106] Nonetheless, Sim does concede that the sharpness of the polemic does reflect at least a partial physical separation in that the Matthean group was no longer part of the community that met in the official place of Jewish worship, the synagogue.

In part, such a separation allows Sim to cast those adherents to the teaching of the first evangelist as deviant in nature. From its own perspective this recently ostracised community faced the challenge of defining and asserting its own identity in opposition to its adversaries who remained within the sphere of synagogue life. Sim argues that this status of being a deviant community in the eyes of their synagogue opponents resulted in the need for the group to present itself in a positive light and correspondingly to demonise the synagogue community from which it had emerged. Furthermore, he argues that, "the evangelist's community had parted company with the official place of Jewish worship, in this case the synagogue, and perceived itself to be a rival and superior institution."[107] It is this combination of conflict and identity formation which, according to Sim, accounts for both the group's life outside the synagogue while at the same time explaining its desire to hold firm its Jewish identity by claiming correct interpretation of Jewish traditions. This results in an understanding of the Matthean community as existing in a religious ghetto of exclusivist messianic Judaism.

Perhaps the major weakness in Sim's treatment of the Matthean community stems from the overplaying of the sense of alienation experienced by the community and its subsequent recourse to an apocalyptic eschatology as the ideological vehicle for dealing with such ostracism. This results in the inability of Sim to integrate the positive statements in the gospel about Gentiles and any possibility of mission to incorporate them into the Matthean ἐκκλησία. While he suggests that the incorporation of Gentiles into the community remained a theoretical possibility, the stridently anti-Gentile nature of the group meant that only full adherence to the ceremonial law, including circumcision, would entail acceptance within the group. However, for Sim, this anti-Gentile stance of the Matthean group is not simply a result of its Jewish orientation, but also stems from the experience of persecution at the hands of Gentiles in the period after the destruction of Jerusalem. Again Sim relates this to Matthew's scheme of apocalyptic eschatology. It is argued that 24.4-14 provides a timetable for the unfolding events that lead to the end. Sim seeks to demonstrate that the Matthean community was part way through this catalogue and that its present corresponds to the description in vv. 11-

---

[106] Sim, *Apocalyptic Eschatology in the Gospel of Matthew*, 186.
[107] Sim, *Apocalyptic Eschatology in the Gospel of Matthew*, 186.

12, which depict the rising up of ψευδοπροφῆται and the increase of ἀνομία. Moreover, it is argued that the editorial addition of τῶν ἐθνῶν (Matt 24.9) to the Markan account, which contains the simpler description that 'you will be hated by all' (Mk 13.13), demonstrates that the community of the first gospel was living through a period of Gentile persecution.[108] Supposedly, this placed the Matthean community in a particularly invidious position, for the members were susceptible to persecution both because of their Jewish allegiance (in the aftermath of the revolt) and also because of their Christianity (according to Sim the Neronian persecution and the death of Jesus himself demonstrate this possibility).[109] Thus Sim concludes,

> [I]t is clear that Matthew and his church had good reason to be fearful of the Gentile world. Not only could they be attacked by Gentile mobs for being Jews, but they could also be persecuted by Gentile authorities for being Christians as well. In the light of its extremely precarious and vulnerable situation, it is quite understandable that this community was critical of the surrounding Gentile society and adopted a policy of avoiding and shunning it.[110]

Yet one is left wondering about the validity of this reconstruction, not least because of the interest in Gentiles in the first gospel. The theory of non-contact with the Gentile world, which is developed by Sim, appears to result from two approaches to texts that utilise ἔθνος terminology. First, the texts that may be considered to make explicitly negative statements concerning Gentiles are transformed into a programmatic commentary on Matthean portrayal of community relationships with the non-Jewish world. Second, positive references to the ἔθνη essentially ignored (Matt 12.21; 21.43; 24.14; 25.32; 28.19).

Also ignored are those texts in the final third of the Matthean account that appears to privilege those not originally part of the Kingdom. Those who are referred to favourably are described by the evangelist in a variety of terms: as being in second (or even last) place in the salvific plan; at some points are even referred to explicitly as 'the Gentiles'; or even as the 'nations'. This displacement of the initial recipients of the covenant is mentioned in a number of places. Even as early in the narrative as Jesus' encounter with the centurion (Matt 8.5-13) the geographical horizon is

---

[108] An aspect of the experience of persecution that Sim does not discuss is that directed at the community by Jews. Although Hare's major claim that "[t]he mission to the synagogues and the attendant persecution of missionaries belong for Matthew essentially to the past" may be debated, it is hard to deny the reality of persecution from Matthew's Jewish opponents if one wishes to take the statements in the gospel as a fair reflection of the evangelists understanding of the tensions between the two parties. (Hare, *The Theme of Jewish Persecution*, 170).

[109] Sim, 'The Gospel of Matthew and the Gentiles', 39.

[110] Sim, 'The Gospel of Matthew and the Gentiles', 39.

widened for the inclusion of those who will partake in the eschatological banquet. While the sons of the Kingdom are cast out into the darkness, the chance to recline with the patriarchs is extent to the group described in the following manner; πολλοὶ ἀπὸ ἀνατολῶν καὶ δυσμῶν ἥξουσιν (Matt 8.12). Sim does make brief mention of this passage in two places. First, he catalogues it as part of the evidence used by commentators who argue that Matthew does have a favourable attitude to the Gentiles.[111] Second, he later dismisses such an interpretation in the following manner. Discussing both this passage and the interaction with the Canaanite woman in 15.21-28, Sim excludes these passages from the discussion by stating, "The cure of a Gentile, like the healing of the centurion's servant in 8.5-13, is therefore an aberration in the context of Jesus' mission, and its significance resides in the fact that Jesus could at time show mercy and compassion to Gentiles who expressed great faith in his power."[112] While there is certainly some reticence to heal in the story of the Canaanite woman, in the story of the centurion it is the Gentile who shows more sensitivity to purity issues (8.8) than Jesus. While not too much should be claimed for the picture of many coming from east and west as pre-empting the Great Commission,[113] the confidence of an inclusive eschatological scenario mitigates against accepting the portrayal of the Matthean community as having withdrawn behind the veneer of an inwardly focussed apocalyptic eschatology as a means of coping with a sense of alienation and insecurity. Unlike the Johannine community, the Matthean adherents had not withdrawn into a ghetto existence centred on only love of fellow members.

Another important sequence of material which privileges later recipients over those to whom salvific priority was initially given is the triad of parables contained in Matt 21.28-22.14. One major branch of the textual tradition of the parable of the Two Sons attributes obedience to the sibling who is called second despite his initial refusal. There are strong reasons to see this form as the Matthean version of the parable since the

---

[111] For the full list of material presented by Sim as having been used by commentators to support a favourable attitude to Gentiles in Matthew's gospel see, *The Gospel of Matthew and Christian Judaism*, 217.

[112] Sim, *The Gospel of Matthew and Christian Judaism*, 224.

[113] Hill presents what is likely the correct understanding of Matt 8.12 in that he sees the logion drawing upon the Isaianic hope of a renewed and valid form of worship in Zion for all the nations. He suggests, "The 'many' from the east and the west are the Gentile believers who will enjoy the messianic banquet, which often symbolizes the joys of the future kingdom (cf. 22.1-14; 25.10; 26.19). The verse reveals an interest in thee ultimate salvation of the Gentiles, but it cannot be used to establish Matthew's insistence on a Gentile mission before the end. It refers to the eschatological pilgrimage of Gentile to God's holy mountain (Is 25.6)." (Hill, *The Gospel of Matthew*, 159).

structuralism aligns more closely to the following two pericope.[114] The second parable in this triadic sequence is particularly germane to the Matthean view of both the Jewish leadership and his perception of the Gentiles. The Matthean redactional saying in v 43 is highly significant, both in terms of what it states about the respective relationships between the initial tenants and their loss of control of the kingdom, and also the transfer of responsibility to ἔθνει. It is worth quoting Hagner's understanding of what this parabolic transfer denoted.

> This setting aside of the privilege of Israel as the unique people of God in favor of another people, namely, the church, is of course nothing short of revolutionary. The singular ἔθνος, which means 'people' or 'nation,' inevitably alludes to the eventual mission to the Gentiles, the ἔθνοι, plural of the same word (cf. 12:21; 24:14; 28:19)...To be sure, as several have pointed out, it is not *necessary* to interpret the ἔθνος as meaning the church. But given the total context of the Gospel, this is the most natural interpretation of the passage.[115]

Despite the importance of this verse in the debate concerning Matthew's attitude to the Gentiles, and the vast amount of secondary literature it has generated, Sim virtually ignores this redactional saying. He mentions this verse only three times in his monograph. Firstly, he cites Stanton's use of the verse as evidence that the evangelist and his communities no longer considered themselves as members of Judaism, but instead as being a separate entity.[116] The second time Sim mentions the verse he puts forward the argument that the term ἔθνος should not be translated as nation, but 'a people.' Thus it is suggested,

> The people who are given the kingdom of God, the new tenants and the legitimate leaders of the Jewish people, are either the Matthean community alone or Christian Judaism in general. This pericope in no way suggests that the evangelist's community has broken with Judaism; rather, it details God's rejection of the Jewish leadership, and it demonstrates that Matthew's Christian Jewish group claimed (albeit unsuccessfully) a leadership role within the Jewish community and within the Jewish religion.[117]

However, Sim's argument is questionable both linguistically and hermeneutically. The decision to translate ἔθνος as 'a people' in reference to the Matthean community as a distinctly Jewish entity is problematic. In Jewish literature the term גוים is consistently used to denote foreigner, and in the LXX this term is uniformly rendered by ἔθνος or the plural ἔθνη. The third time Sim mentions 21.43, he notes that it is "of particular

---

[114] For a defence of the Codex Vaticanus reading representing the Matthean structure see Foster 'A Tale of Two Sons', 26-37.

[115] Hagner, *Matthew 14-28*, 623.

[116] Sim, *The Gospel of Matthew and Christian Judaism*, 2.

[117] Sim, *The Gospel of Matthew and Christian Judaism*, 149.

importance" for the view that "the nation represents the Christian Church which is composed of both Jews and Gentiles",[118] but he simply refers readers back to his earlier discussion of the text, and rejection of such an interpretation.[119]

The third parable in this sequence, the story of the royal wedding banquet (Matt 22.1-14), also portrays a reversal of fortunes. Those who are originally privileged with an invitation to the feast, because of their refusal to accept this generous summons, are not only displaced, but because of the maltreatment of the king's servants (v6) find themselves the subject of royal retribution resulting in the destruction of their city and their own death (v7). This parable is a passage to which Sim devotes a considerable amount of space. He sees, in line with the majority of critical scholarship, that 22.7 is an explicit reference to the destruction of Jerusalem.[120] This is an important marker for dating the gospel in the post-destruction period, although the citation of the first gospel by Ignatius means that the *terminus post quem non* may be around 110 C.E.[121] This allows Sim to insert the Matthean community in the window of time at Antioch after the initial Gentile mission in Acts 13-14 instigated by the Antiochean church and the resurgence of Pauline Christianity in the same locale which had taken place by the time of Ignatius, circa 110 C.E. However, Sim's reading of this parable is somewhat forced in that he sees it as offering evidence that the community was still involved in "open-ended mission to the Jews."[122] Specifically he sees this narrative as part of a web of evidence where the continuing Jewish mission is clearly depicted.

> Matthew has conveniently provided us with a history of the Jewish mission as conducted by his community. The earlier phases are described in the allegory of the wedding feast in Matthew 22:1-10. The first invitation to the feast is met with blank refusal (v. 3), while the second results in shameful treatment and murder of the king's servants who delivered the invitation (vv. 4-6). In response to this act, the king who holds the feast sends his troops to destroy the city of the murderers (v. 7).[123]

According to Sim, this parable does appear to evidence an initial 'mission' to a group that proved to be non-receptive. However, it is hard to envisage how it can be read as the first phase of a mission history to this recalcitrant

---

[118] Sim, *The Gospel of Matthew and Christian Judaism*, 217.

[119] In a footnote, Sim simply states, "This interpretation of 21:43 was discussed and criticised in chapter 3." (Sim, *The Gospel of Matthew and Christian Judaism*, 217, n. 3).

[120] This verse is described by Sim in his treatment of the dating of the Matthean narrative as, "his [i.e. Matthew's] explicit allusion in 22:7 to the destruction of Jerusalem." (Sim, *The Gospel of Matthew and Christian Judaism*, 33).

[121] Sim does not interact with the current debate about the dating of Ignatius' martyrdom, and hence the date of the writing of his epistles.

[122] Sim, *The Gospel of Matthew and Christian Judaism*, 158.

[123] Sim, *The Gospel of Matthew and Christian Judaism*, 159.

group when the parable depicts them as not only having their city destroyed, but consequently, they are themselves obliterated. Such a group no longer would appear to be a very productive mission field.

Without doubt it is Sim's treatment of Matt 28.16-20 that raises the most questions. Initially leaving aside the issue of whether the mission was inclusive or exclusive of Jews, it can hardly be denied, as Sim agrees, that it is widening the sphere of outreach. "There is no doubt that 28.19 accepts without question the validity of the Gentile mission; it is no less an authority than the risen Christ who instigates it."[124] This statement coheres with the perspective of other interpreters such as Davies and Allison who state, "The resurrection marks the end of the exclusive focus on Israel. The Jewish mission is now world mission."[125] However, Sim does not allow the full impact of his opening statement to stand, for he immediately qualifies it with the following explanation that undermines what he had previously stated. "But accepting the legitimacy of the Gentile mission does not necessarily mean that the Matthean community had any active involvement in it."[126] This seems a bewildering interpretation. Throughout the gospel there has been a movement away from those privileged with the initial offer of the kingdom and a subsequent rise in the claims made on behalf of those originally excluded. Even in 24.19 there is an explicit statement of the need to proclaim the gospel ἐν ὅλῃ οἰκουμένῃ εἰς μαρτύριον πᾶσιν τοῖς ἔθνεσιν in order to precipitate the end. It seems a somewhat strange interpretation if the climax of the Matthean narrative, with its final exhortation to take the gospel to all the nations, is in fact something in which the community must not participate. Such a reading, while perhaps within the realms of theoretical possibility, seems unnatural. More compelling is the reading suggested by Luz. He understands Matt 28.16-20

---

[124] Sim, *The Gospel of Matthew and Christian Judaism*, 243.

[125] Davies and Allison also wish to address the issue of whether this charge incorporated or excluded the Jews. In seeking to understand the meaning of πάντα τὰ ἔθνα they come to the conclusion that it does in fact involve Israel, thereby being universal in the fullest sense. They suggest six reasons to support such a conclusion that are worth quoting in full. "(i) In Matthew ἔθνα certainly can mean those outside Israel (4.15; 6.32; 10.5-6, 18; 15.24; 20.19). But it can also have comprehensive meaning (24.9, 14; 25.32). When this last is the case the qualifier πᾶς is used; and because πᾶς is used in 28.19, here to the expression has universal sense. (ii) There is no explicit abrogation of the Jewish mission. (iii) In Dan 7.14, which lies behind our verses, the phrase includes Israel. (iv) It is historically implausible that, in Matthew's time and place, there were no longer Christian missionaries to Jews. (v) Inclusion of the Jews harmonizes with the universalism of the rest of the passage. (vi) The comparable πάντα τὰ ἔθνα of Lk 24.47 must include Jews." (*Matthew*, vol 3, 684). While not all of these points are of equal weight, their cumulative strength means that the author is not envisaging the cessation of mission to Jews.

[126] Sim, *The Gospel of Matthew and Christian Judaism*, 243.

as a programmatic statement placed on the lips of the historical Jesus that now encourages the community to become actively engaged in Gentile mission. He argues,

> At this juncture the author of the gospel of Matthew now offered clear instructions in the name of the risen Lord: 'Make all heathens (nations) my disciples' (28:19)...the decision to take up the Gentile mission marked a great step on the part of this Jewish-Christian community toward the Gentile-Christian Great Church, which at that time already existed independently of Israel.[127]

Perhaps at the time the evangelist wrote such a mission was only in its embryonic stage, but it is presented as the way forward. Contrary to Sim, the fact that such an affirmation is given by the risen Christ supposedly about fifty to sixty years prior to the penning of the gospel is not problematic. This is because the purpose of the gospel was to change behaviour in the community, or, perhaps, to encourage a fuller compliance, not to explain a prior lack of fulfilment. Thus, Sim's failure to integrate a plausible reading of the Great Commission into his overall understanding is another reason to question his portrait of the social setting of the Matthean community.

In conclusion, Sim's reconstruction of the history and social relationships with wider Judaism is neither compelling nor balanced. The texts in the gospel that Sim reads as supporting his thesis are not only open to different interpretation, but these alternative understandings have more to support them both in terms of the plain sense of the text and in relation to the wider Matthean macronarrative. Moreover, Sim ignores or gives a cursory treatment of too much of the material in the gospel that appears to point in the opposite direction to which he is arguing. As has already been mentioned, it is the treatment of the climactic Great Commission that raises many questions about Sim's overall thesis. Beaton, likewise, has detected this as a fundamental flaw in his overall argument. He notes that,

> One may also question Sim's treatment of 28:19, a text which would seemingly indicate participation in a Gentile mission. In my opinion, he fudges on this one when he suggests that only 28:19 and possibly 24:4-14, may allude to Gentile

---

[127] Luz in fact argues that one of the major contributing factors that led to this reorientation was not only the failure of a mission among synagogue based Jews, but more fundamentally the integration and acceptance of the teaching of the Mark gospel by the Matthean evangelist. Obviously some of the statement contained in Mark were too radical for the Matthew (notably Mk 7.19c), however, the acceptance of the majority of the Markan material reveals a general acceptance of the message it advanced, and the portrait of Jesus it provided. Thus, according to Luz, with the assistance of the Markan account Matthew came to the realization that the dominically sanctioned way forward for his community was to embrace Gentile outreach, (*The Theology of the Gospel of Matthew*, 20).

mission, but labels this evidence ambiguous and asserts that the Matthean community would have been non-participants.[128]

Not only does this reflect Sim's strategy (presumably unconscious) of underplaying texts most naturally read as favourable towards the Gentiles, but it also reveals little literary critical sensitivity to ancient texts that often conclude on a high note with a pastoral charge to encourage the original auditors to modify their behaviour in accord with the message of the text. Therefore, although a stimulating presentation of the life, praxis and core beliefs of the community, Sim's reconstruction is one sided and is driven by a preconceived notion of the relationship between that group and its Jewish neighbours.

2.7 Boris Repschinski: *The Controversy Stories in the Gospel of Matthew*

Repshinski does not focus on the whole of the gospel narrative, but rather seeks to gain an important insight into the relationship between the Matthean community and formative Judaism through the controversy stories. Therefore, in regard to methodology and approach, his work is similar to the present study in that both seek to elucidate the relationship between the evangelist's adherents and the form of Judaism with which it was in dispute by focusing on a particular aspect of the gospel. For Repschinski that aspect is the controversy stories, and he approaches the study of the controversy stories primarily as a redaction critical endeavour. However, in the final chapter, where he tries to locate the social location of the community, Repschinski integrates the findings of his redactional study with reflections on the sociology of leadership. In response to Dunn's question, "Are Matthew and his community outside the walls of Judaism, or did they regard themselves as inside?",[129] Repschinski suggests, "A conceivable answer to this question is that both alternatives could be correct."[130] From this perspective it is argued that "It seems probable, then, that Matthew's community saw itself within Judaism, yet at odds with the leaders of the Judaism it encountered."[131] However, he suggests that the stance of other Jewish groups towards the Matthean group resulted in a different understanding of the community's status *vis-à-vis* Judaism. He states,

---

[128] Beaton, review of D.C. Sim, *The Gospel of Matthew and Christian* Judaism, 246.

[129] Dunn, *The Parting of the Ways*, 152.

[130] Repschinski, *The Controversy Stories*, 344.

[131] Repschinski, *The Controversy Stories*, 346.

As both Judaism and Christianity were in a formative stage, and thus transitional, it can no longer be established with certainty whether Matthew's claim to Jewishness was acknowledged by other Jewish groups. It is probable that Matthew did not want to part company with Judaism; but perhaps formative Judaism had already parted company with Matthew.[132]

Although not explicitly utilising the language of the social sciences, Repschinski highlights a number of important issues in relation to group formation. These issues include: the importance of perspective; the fluidity, or transitional nature of group values at a formative stage; and, the problem of determining when two groups have actually 'parted company'. In essence he sees that the controversy stories, as presented in their Matthean redactional form, were intended to delegitimize "the Pharisees from their place of prominence"[133] and consequently to establish the Matthean community's claim to the leadership of Judaism. Yet Repschinski acknowledges that the Gentile mission remains problematic for his reconstruction. He notes this tension in the following manner. "If it is right to interpret the Matthean group in terms of a Jewish sect, the mission to gentiles breaks the pattern of a supposedly tightly inward looking group."[134] This tension is not resolved, but rather, is just noted. It is therefore appropriate to look at how Respchinski develops his argument in order to appreciate how he arrives at this somewhat uncomfortable tension.

Repschinski first surveys redactional approaches to Matthew's gospel. He comes to the conclusion that such a method is ultimately indecisive for determining the relationship between the Matthean group and emergent Judaism. He states

The issue of a Jewish or Gentile audience for the gospel of Matthew shows the limitations of redaction criticism quite clearly. While the method can approximate themes and topics in the gospel, it needs to be amplified with a methodology that helps in reconstructing the social setting of the gospel. Redaction criticism needs, by its very nature, to stay close to the text in the examination of older and newer material that make up the present text. But the reconstruction of a community needs other tools as well...the most influential studies concerning themselves with the social situation of the gospel have tried to incorporate into their investigation the help of, for want of a better term, sociological aids.[135]

Repschinski is perhaps overstating the limitations of redaction criticism, for it needs to be recognized that this approach enabled scholars to understand that the evangelists were not mechanical editors, but were skilled authors in their own right, and further, that the very manner in

---

[132] Repschinski, *The Controversy Stories*, 347.

[133] Repschinski, *The Controversy Stories*, 346.

[134] Repschinski, *The Controversy Stories*, 348.

[135] Repschinski, *The Controversy Stories*, 49-50.

which they compiled, expanded and commented upon source material was often an important indicator of the pedagogical and pastoral issues confronting their respective communities. That redaction criticism has not provided a definitive answer in regard to the social relationship between the Matthean group and the Judaism with which it was in conflict is perhaps more of a reflection of the narrowness of the evidential base than an inherent weakness in the methodology itself.

Having described this supposed weakness in redaction criticism, Repschinski turns his attention to social scientific approaches that view Matthew's community as a sectarian Jewish group.[136] At this point Repschinski draws on the work of Neusner, and his understanding of the shift that occurred after 70 C.E. from temple based worship towards smaller localized associations and groupings with a concomitant emphasis on Torah observance.[137] This period is viewed as a time of great fluidity during which competing groups came into conflict as they tried to promote their claims for continuity with temple based Judaism and battled to attract adherents.[138] From this perspective the social situation of the communities that adhered to the teaching of the first evangelist is described in the following manner. "[T]he Matthean group can be imagined as a Jewish group in opposition to the Pharisaic/rabbinic movement, just as other groups might have been in conflict with this 'fledgling coalition of forces' before it outmanoeuvred its competitors."[139] Like Overman, Repschinski

---

[136] Actually Repschinski's subheading on page fifty is entitled 'Sociological Approaches: Matthew's Community as a Sectarian Jewish Writing'. One assumes that he has had a simple lapse in concentration here. Surely he does not mean Matthew's community is a 'writing', be it sectarian or otherwise. It appears more likely that the heading was either meant to read 'Matthew's Gospel as a Sectarian Jewish Writing' or 'Matthew's Community as a Sectarian Jewish Group'. Either of these titles fairly represents what is being said in the section that follows his heading.

[137] Neusner, "The Formation of Rabbinic Judaism, 3-42.

[138] There is a danger that such a portrait of post 70 C.E. Judaism can be cast as too rigid an antithesis to pre-destruction Judaism. This can result in the anachronistic assumption that prior to the Roman levelling of the temple, religion in Judea was both monolithic and uniform. Apart from Josephus' classic description of the different sects, the development of the Jesus movement itself witnesses a further pluriformity in Jewish religion in the period from the thirties onwards. Moreover, although Freyne is correct in his assessment that, "The fact that the Galileans may not have followed Pharisaic regulations concerning the half shekel offering and do not appear to have been too scrupulous in regard to tithing cannot be interpreted as a total lack of interest in the temple", (Freyne, *Galilee*, 393), it does at least provide corroborative evidence that religious life was practiced in different ways while the temple was in existence.

[139] Repschinski, *The Controversy Stories in the Gospel of Matthew*, 50. The words in quotation marks are draw from Sim, *Apocalyptic Eschatology in the Gospel of Matthew*, 183-4.

draws upon Blenkinsopp's definition of sectarianism,[140] thereby highlighting the derivative nature of a new religious movement on the parent group. However, the same criticism that was made in respect to Overman's argument needs to be reiterated in this context, namely, that it appears inaccurate to characterise the Matthean group as being a splinter movement from a parent body, especially since Overman, Repschinski, and the majority of scholars understand rabbinic Judaism to be itself emerging and coalescing in this period. Thus, it is inappropriate to represent the opposition group as a fully established parent group. Rather, these two competing parties were both attempting to make continuity claims in the aftermath of the destruction of temple-based Judaism. It does, however, appear that by the time the first gospel was composed emergent Judaism had more effectively established its power base, and this resulted in the marginalization of the Matthean group. Repschinski suggests that as a consequence of such competition, which had materialized itself in acts of overt persecution, the Matthean group had begun to engage in proselytizing activity directed towards Gentiles. This understanding of the social setting does not make the anachronistic assumption that the Matthean group was derivative upon emergent Judaism in the way that a number of modern sects have emerged from already defined and established religious groups.[141]

Apart from this supposed deviation from a parent group, Repschinski also draws attention to the invective of polemical language as an indicator in social conflict theory of the sectarian nature of a group. Drawing on Coser's insights,[142] Repschinski states, "Rather than an indication of historical distance, polemics is the sign of the ideological proximity of two groups at odds with one another over the same issues. The more acrimonious the debate the closer the two groups are."[143] However, caution again seems to be required. Proximity may be found through competition over potential converts, as a result of geographical location, or even claims to be the authentic representative of a religious tradition. While each of these options is theoretical possible, only on the basis of the evidence available within the text can any one of the possibilities be put forward as the basis for the type of relationship that generated such antagonism between the two parties.

---

[140] For details see section 5, page 46, in this chapter.

[141] The problem of defining groups as sectarian has been recognized by sociologists, but often this difficulty is not appreciated in regard to the relationship between emergent Judaism and the early Christian movement. Wilson in part tries to address this problem by presenting seven general typologies of sectarianism (see Wilson, *Magic and the Millennium*, 21). See also Bainbridge, *The Sociology of Religious Movements*, 23.

[142] Coser, *The Functions of Social Conflict*, 67-72.

[143] Repschinski, *The Controversy* Stories, 53.

Curiously, however, Repschinski appears to undermine his own reading of the insights provided by social scientific criticism. Having rehearsed the standard textual and sociological arguments for the Matthean group as a sect within Judaism,[144] Repschinski asserts that ultimately these methods are inconclusive. He states, "The limits of such a sociological approach to the question of Matthew's place *intra* or *extra muros* of Judaism are quite obvious. We have only the gospel of Matthew to make any judgment."[145] Yet here the limitation is not seen as a lack of evidence from the Matthean side of the debate, but rather the fact that it is impossible to know how the opponents were reacting to this splinter group. While this would obviously provide a valuable resource into gauging the reciprocity of the polemic it is questionable whether in fact such literature is needed in order to glean sociological insights into the self-perception of such new religious movements. As practitioners of the sociology of religious movements appreciate, it is usually through the new group defining itself against alterative movements that the sectarian nature of that party emerges. As Stark and Bainbridge note in their definitions of 'cult' and 'sect', it is as a consequence of deviance and schism that such new movements are formed.

> A *sect* movement is a deviant religious organization with traditional beliefs and practices. A *cult* movement is a deviant religious organization with traditional beliefs and practices. ...these refer to deviance, which some readers might mistake as a synonym for bad, so we should also define it. *Deviance* is departure from the norms of a culture in such a way as to incur the imposition of extraordinary costs from those who maintain the culture. Finally, we suggested that sects arise through schism, so we need a definition of that as well. A *schism* is the division of the social structure of an organization into two or more independent parts.[146]

---

[144] The textual arguments include the role of scribes in the Matthean group and the competition with scribes and rabbis in the opposing group (13.52; 23.7-8, 34). Two of the important sociological arguments are the "delegitimation of the parent body" by claiming that the new movement preserves correct tradition and orthodoxy, and secondly the intensity of polemical language as an indicator of close relationship. (Repschinski, *The Controversy Stories*, 53-4).

[145] Repschinski, *The Controversy Stories*, 55.

[146] Stark and Bainbridge, *A Theory of Religion*, 328. However, in his more recent book Bainbridge attempts to get away from some of the pejorative overtones that have been attached to the terms 'sect' and 'cult' by referring to such groups as different religious organizations. This approach is refreshing since it removes many of the value laden terms from the debate and allows legitimacy to be found in the variant expressions of the religious group under study. Furthermore, in an equally nuanced manner Bainbridge asserts, "we will view religion not as a set of distinct organizations arranged in conceptual boxes, but as dynamic systems of beliefs, practices, socio-economic structures and human beings." (Bainbridge, *The Sociology of Religious Movements*, 24-5).

Furthermore, it is through the literature and statements of the new group that the causes and experience of such schism are most clearly seen, since, having incurred the cost of their deviance, they are most keenly aware of the need to account for and justify such separation.

Thus Repschinski's assessment, that the sociological method is limited in relation to studying the Matthean community because it does not have access to the perspective of formative Judaism, may be questioned. While admittedly, access to the documents reflecting the perspective of the opponents would provide a more complete picture they are not primary evidence in determining the self-perception of the evangelist's adherents. In fact, such data, if available, would be more beneficial for establishing the relationship of formative Judaism to the wider religious world of which it too was a part. Repschinski argues that,

> It is unclear how the movement of formative Judaism reacted to Matthew's claims. It is conceivable that Matthew was still debating when his conversation partners had already left him. The theory of the Matthean community as a Jewish sect offers some insight into the self-perception of the community. However, no converse evidence of how the parent body saw the Matthean community is available. Without evidence from the other side of the debate the riddle will probably never be solved with any certainty.[147]

While the first two statements are self-evidently correct, it is debatable whether this leads to the conclusion. While evidence from the opponents may provide a more objective account of the conflict, it is not necessarily needed to assess the Matthean community's self-understanding of itself as either part of, or separate from, Judaism. This caveat reads as an attempt by Repschinski to prove that his study of the controversy stories, (which through a mirror reading give insight into the perspectives of the opposing party), does in fact provide what both redaction and social scientific criticism were lacking, namely an appreciation of the perspective of the competing group thereby providing the missing part of the puzzle.

This methodological overview leads Repschinski into a detailed study of the controversy stories. These are seen as revealing the particular issues confronting the evangelist's community specifically in respect to the conflict with Jewish leaders, which was a live issue for the group in its contemporary situation. This detailed study of the controversy stories is aimed a answering the specific question that is the very focus of Repschinski's investigation, namely: "Was the Matthean community *intra* or *extra muros* of Judaism?"[148]

Undoubtedly, the most significant aspect of the study lies in the detailed and comprehensive analysis of the seventeen individual pericopae that are

---

[147] Repschinski, *The Controversy Stories*, 55.
[148] Repschinski, *The Controversy Stories*, 61.

classified as *Streitgespräche* or controversy stories.[149] Here Repschinski uses a combination of the methods of redaction, form and, social scientific criticism to exegete the text and to draw conclusions concerning the relationship between the Matthean group and the emergent Judaism with whom he engages in such fierce polemic. His detailed analysis of individual pericopae means that it is not possible to interact with each of the texts that are treated, instead, a brief overview of the approach to Matt 12.1-8 is provided as representative of Repschinski's work. This choice is not arbitrary. Instead it focuses on a pericope where the issues of authority and law come clearly to the surface. This allows significant interaction between the study Repschinski has undertaken and those areas which are under investigation in this study.

Source critically, it is correctly noted that after a significant interruption Matthew resumes the Mark controversy cycle (Mk 2.1-3.6) that he broke off from at the end of Matt 9.17. While this may have resulted in destroying the careful structure of the five Markan conflict accounts with their increasing polemic,[150] it does allow the first evangelist to focus attention to the issue of Sabbath observance in a more detailed manner. However, Repschinski fails to discuss the significance of inserting these two stories after the sayings of 11.25-30. All he notes is that the material that precedes chapter 12 draws attention to christological issues. He states, "In the midst of the negative appraisal by crowds and cities Jesus than makes a declaration of his identity and the nature of his own teaching: He is the Son of the Father, the revealer of the Father, and his yoke is easy (11.25-30)."[151] Yet no connection is made between this observation and the way it may have shaped the audience's response to the controversy material that follows. Within the macrostructure of Matthew's gospel, the two Sabbath controversy stories are preceded by the thanksgiving in 11.25-27 and the declaration of relief and rest from burdens in vv. 28-30. Although a number of commentators have suggested that 11.28-30 contains certain verbal points of contact with Sir 51, Stanton is correct to

---

[149] The seventeen pericopae under investigation are Matt 9.2-8, 10-13, 14-17; 12.1-8, 9-14, 22-37, 38-45; 15.3-9; 16.1-4; 19.3-9; 21.23-27; 22.15-22, 23-33, 34-40, 41-46; and Matt 13.53-58; 21.14-17. The first group of fifteen represent those pericopae that Bultmann classified *Streitgespräche* or controversy dialogues, whereas the final two were described as biographical apothegms, but having a close relationship to the wider set of controversy stories, (Bultmann, *The History of the Synoptic Tradition*, 11-61.

[150] For a discussion of the literary structure of this unit see in particular Dewey, *Markan Public Debate*, and Kiilunen, *Die Vollmacht im Widerstreit*. The debate concerning whether this unit constitutes a pre-Markan collection is helpfully summarized in Guelich, *Mark 1-8:26*, 82-3. Guelich's own assessment is that "Mark's redactional effort appears limited to the 'seam' of 2:1-2." (83), and that the rest of the material is traditional with no obvious major redactional insertions being discernable.

[151] Repschinski, *The Controversy Stories*, 93.

claim that it is more appropriate to read this material in the light of the gospel itself.[152] Specifically, there are important links with the Sabbath controversies that follow. As Yang observes in relation to the referents in 11.25 of σοφῶν καὶ συνετῶν,

> 'The wise and understanding' in the present Matthean co-text most likely represent the opponents of Jesus in the Gospel, and may refer to the Pharisees and scribes in particular, who are, on the one hand, well instructed in terms of the Torah (cf. 23.2), and who are, on the other hand, the most outstanding opponents of Jesus throughout the Gospel as well as the immediately following opponents in ch. 12.[153]

Thus, by juxtaposing the material of 11.25-30 with the ensuing Sabbath controversies the evangelist may be intending a contrast between Jesus' attitude to the law (and by implication his own attitude to Torah), with the more demanding understanding of the Pharisees.[154]

In terms of the first of these Sabbath controversies Repschinski notes the important redactional reshaping introduced in this pericope.[155] He suggests quite reasonably that this development of the Markan pericope sheds light on the *Sitz im Leben* of the Matthean community, which is to be understood as

---

[152] In fact as Stanton recognizes, "the verbal links between Matt 11.25-30 are in fact quite slender. Only two words, 'toil' and 'yoke', and one phrase, 'find rest', from these three Matthean verses are found anywhere in Sirach." (Stanton, *Gospel*, 329).

[153] Yang, *Jesus and the Sabbath in Matthew's Gospel*, 155.

[154] However, it should be noted that observance of the law would have been understood by Matthew's opponents as promoting correct ethical behaviour. For this reason, it is inappropriate to create a false dichotomy between Jewish legalism and Jesus' ethical concern for the human plight. Thus the true rest envisioned in 11.28 is illustrative of the qualitative superiority of Jesus in relation to the Mosaic system. Therefore, the transition to the two Sabbath controversies in 12.1-14 is not as abrupt as sometimes imagined, rather the discussion of rest prepares for the debates that arise in the immediately following material. Also the controversies serve as an illustration of Jesus' less burdensome attitude to the law in contrast to his Pharisaic opponents. Hagner is keen to point out that the twin sabbath controversy incidents are examples of Jesus' more lenient attitude to the sabbath in marked comparison to his opponents. "The evangelist makes the connection by means of the assertion that about the time Jesus made the previous remarks, these illustrative examples occurred. Jesus' view of the sabbath in this and the following pericope is seen to be more lenient than that of the Pharisees." (Hagner, *Matthew 1-13*, 328).

[155] The seven significant alterations can be summarized as: (1) a tighter temporal link with the preceding material; (2) the threefold answer structure; (3) reformulation of the objection to focus on Sabbath observance not lawlessness; (4) creating a closer parallelism between the plight of David's men and the disciples; (5) introduction of the argument based on priestly sacrifice on the Sabbath; (6) the scriptural appeal to Hos 6.6; (7) Providing a christological focus (although not explicitly stated, apparently at least partially through the excision of Mk 2.27). (Repschinski, *The Controversy Stories*, 106-7).

reflecting the ongoing struggle of the community with its opponents.[156] Describing the harsher rebuttal of the Pharisees that occurs in Matthew's version of the controversy, Repschinski sees the following community situation standing behind this reworking of the material.

> The rebuttal of the Pharisees is not just an argument concerning the Sabbath practice of the disciples, but it becomes an exposition of pharisaic hypocrisy and pretension that makes the christological conclusion of the pericope considerably more pointed. This leads to the conclusion that the Matthean community was, in fact, under attack for its Sabbath practice from more conservative Jewish quarters that were identified with the Pharisees. In such a struggle the identification of the disciple with the priests in the temple raises the question whether Matthew actually saw the disciples of Jesus as the replacement of the priestly class which had become meaningless after the temple was destroyed.[157]

This conclusion clearly makes some significant points, most importantly that the question of Sabbath observance was a live issue for the group. However, it does not automatically follow that the 'struggle', as Repschinski describes it, was necessarily ongoing in the sense that it represented an *intra muros* conflict. It is at least equally conceivable that Matthew was writing a pastoral justification for members of his community who perhaps were questioning whether their stance on Sabbath, which may have been one of the significant issues leading to a separation that had taken place, was in fact justifiable. When this alternative to Repschinski's reconstruction is coupled with the well known references to 'their' or 'your synagogues' (Matt 4.23; 9.35; 10.17; 13.54; 23.34), it becomes more plausible to read this Sabbath controversy as an attempt to legitimise the community's life outside the synagogue walls, as it came to terms with the need to define itself in respect to its primary allegiance to Jesus. In the case of Matt 12.1-8, Repschinski is correct that christological themes come to the fore, but primarily they are used to claim a new authority base for the community and its own understanding of Sabbath.

Despite Repschinski's attempt to use the controversy stories to establish that the Matthean community was still in an *intra muros* relationship with Judaism at the time of the composition of the gospel, in a candid comment contained in his conclusion the following concession is made. He comments,

---

[156] Here Repschinski makes the important point that, "As Matthew inserts a new argument into the controversy, and as he heightens the aspect of conflict between the Pharisees and Jesus, he solves some of the Markan puzzle. Obviously the story is not primarily a historical reminiscence any more, if it ever was such in Mark. The Matthean development shows that the *Sitz im Leben* of this story was, for Matthew, very much within the life of the community." (Repschinski, *The Controversy Stories*, 104).

[157] Repschinski, *The Controversy Stories*, 104.

> The controversy stories are only one possible window into the richly complex story of Jesus and his community in Matthew's gospel. They place this story firmly within the Jewish tradition and witness to the claim of Matthean Christianity within the community of Jewish groups. However, Matthew's community is probably more complex than its analysis as a Jewish sect allows.[158]

Here Repschinski acknowledges the discord that is produced if one simply tries to account for the first evangelist and his community perceiving themselves as solely Jewish. The conclusions that are drawn from his close study of the controversy stories are balanced. The decision to refer to the religion of the group as Matthean Christianity is significant,[159] for it is an acknowledgment of where the primary allegiance and authority base of the group is to be located. Further, Repschinski takes seriously the comments about Gentile mission. Thus he notes that "If it is right to interpret the Matthean group in terms of a Jewish sect, the mission to gentiles breaks the pattern of a supposedly tightly inward looking group."[160] Finally, Repschinski observes that the appropriation of the gospel as early as the time of Ignatius evidences the disappearance of any residual Christian-Jewish group, and shows how easily this document could be taken up by Gentile Christians and read as a universal tractate for the whole church.[161]

Although this review has highlighted some areas of weakness in Repschinski's work and emphasized areas where its perspective is at odds with the present study, it needs to be stressed that overall his study of the controversy narratives is a thorough and balanced treatment. The limitations of the evidence are recognized, the exegetical investigations are detailed and quite often bring fresh perspectives to heavily quarried pericopae and the final conclusions are not overstated. However, despite the detailed analysis of individual units there seems little to necessitate the conclusion that it is more natural to read "the Matthean controversy stories

---

[158] Repschinski, *The Controversy Stories*, 347.

[159] Especially in contrast to the approach adopted by Sim which denies that the Matthean community ever had contact with the Gentile world or non-Jewish branch of the church, the decision to describe the adherents to the first evangelist's community as Matthean Christians both recognizes that there were distinctions from other Christian communities, but nonetheless, the group derived its self identity from its beliefs in Jesus. This contrasts favourably with "Sim's thesis [which] has shock value" and as Senior further notes, states that "Matthew's Jewish-Christian community was indistinguishable in Gentile eyes from the rest of the Jewish community and, therefore, shared in the Jewish community's sufferings at the hands of the Gentiles." (Senior, 'Between Two Worlds', 10).

[160] Repschinski, *The Controversy Stories*, 348.

[161] Repschinski, *The Controversy Stories*, 349.

as reflections of a struggle *intra muros* of Judaism."[162] Repschinski ends his study by mentioning three possible areas for further investigation. Interestingly, each of these areas, even on his own reading, calls into question the general conclusion that he tentatively advances. Firstly, it is noted that Matthew's primary source is Mark.[163] He concurs with Luz's assessment that Matthew is a "Neufassung des Markusevangeliums und nicht eine Neufassung von Q."[164] He then observes that, "it still seems significant that Matthew choose to draw extensively on a gentile writing."[165] The implication being that Matthew's attitude to Gentiles cannot have been totally negative, nor is it likely that his community had no contact with the Gentile branch of the Jesus movement. Thus Matthean Christians are seen as potentially more open to non-Jews than those parties that are known to have defined themselves self-consciously as Jewish.

Secondly, the Gentile mission is recognized as a challenge to understanding the Matthean group as existing within the walls of Judaism. Goodman has convincingly argued that mission was not to any great extent a major concern of second temple and post-destruction Judaism.[166] While Repschinski notes "how little of the gentile mission of 28.19 seems to retroject into the narrative",[167] he also recognizes that the great commission is indeed a pivotal or climactic text within the gospel, and consequently needs to be taken seriously as part of Matthew's overall theology. The tension between the prior material and commission is depicted in the following manner.

> The Gentile mission never becomes a matter of controversy, nor does Matthew ever spell out its concrete practicality for a law-abiding community. It is introduced only at the end of the gospel as the mandate of the risen Christ, and it comes as somewhat

---

[162] This is in fact the title of Repschinski's concluding chapter. However, in the actual discussion he constantly qualifies this assertion and ultimately asserts that the evidence of the controversy stories is inconclusive by itself, but nonetheless feels that this is the more natural way to read the material. Illustrating the indeterminate nature of the evidence he quotes a question asked by done and offers his own answer. "James Dunn's formulation of the issue reveals the problem precisely. He asks: 'Are Matthew and his community outside the walls of Judaism, or did they still regard themselves as inside?' A conceivable answer to this question is that both alternatives could be correct." (*The Controversy Stories*, 343-4, quoting Dunn, 'The Question of Anti-Semitism', 152).

[163] In his study Repschinski adopts the majority viewpoint of the two-source hypothesis, and thereby sees Mark as the primary source, Q material integrated into this framework, and the overall narrative given its shape and distinctive Matthean flavour through the redactional contribution of the evangelist.

[164] Luz, *Matthäus*, 1-7, 58.

[165] Repschinski, *The Controversy Stories*, 349.

[166] Goodman, *Mission and Conversion*.

[167] Repschinski, *The Controversy Stories*, 348.

of a surprise. But if Matthew's community took this mandate seriously, this perhaps alienated it further from the Judaism of its time.[168]

Therefore, a certain incongruity is recognized between arguing for Matthew's community as a group within Judaism, yet at the same time participating in Gentile mission. As an aside, one suspects it is the irreconcilability of these two features that leads Sim to deny the reality of Gentile proselytization by Matthean Jews (as he characterizes adherents of the group), instead he can only suggest that while they accepted the theoretical legitimacy of Gentile mission, they only participated in converting fellow Jews.[169]

The third area that Repschinski marks out for further study is the role and portrayal of Peter in Matthew's gospel. While this is the least developed of the three areas, it is noted that although Peter is prominent in Mark's account, this characterization is heightened by Matthew.[170] While it is not suggested that Matthew had direct access to the traditions in Acts that associated Peter with Gentile mission, Repschinski observes that, "It is curious, to say the least, that Peter would become a figure on which the gentile community of Mark as well as the Jewish community of Matthew focused."[171] Thus, throughout the concluding remarks made by Reschinski there is a backing away, or nuancing of the claim that Matthew's community still perceived itself as Jewish. In effect his overall conclusion appears to be that Matthew's community was *intra muros* in relation to Judaism, but that this was a very strange group within Judaism. Not only did it stand in opposition to the leadership of emergent rabbinic Judaism, but it promoted Gentile mission, used a Gentile source as a major component of its own programmatic gospel, attributed a greater status to Peter who was know to associate openly with Gentiles, and even placed on the lips of Jesus a charter to engage actively in mission to non-Jews. Repschinski, commendably, does not shy away from this evidence, but it does become increasingly difficult to support his reading of the controversy stories when one attempts to integrate it with the wider evidence of the narrative and what is know about early Christianity and the reception of Matthew's gospel.

---

[168] Repschinski, *The Controversy Stories*, 345.

[169] Sim, *The Gospel of Matthew and Christian Judaism*, 44.

[170] The one reference that Repschinski cites is 16.18-19, however, instances could obviously be multiplied to support this case, (Matt 10.2; 14.28-31; 15.15; 17.24; 18.21; 26.35).

[171] Repschinski, *The Controversy Stories*, 348.

2.8 Conclusions

This overview has traced developments in the understanding of the social location of the Matthean community from the beginning of the second half of the twentieth century onwards. While the period before the application of social scientific criticism was treated in a less detailed manner,[172] it provided important background for locating the context of subsequent developments. However, from the mid 1980s onwards, social scientific approaches have been regularly applied to investigations of the Matthean community. On the whole, these appear to have moved the assessment of the social location of the group firmly in the direction of seeing it as a deviant movement operating within the orbit of Judaism.[173] Initially, this endpoint was not the outcome of social scientific criticism when applied to the first gospel. Stanton, drawing upon the work of Coser, saw the group as having emerged from a situation of bitter conflict with its parent group and then looking for a new way forward in relation to Gentile mission.[174] By contrast, Saldarini suggests that at the time of the writing of the gospel the Matthean group inhabited two worlds, "Just as Matthew's group lives as part of the Jewish community, albeit as a deviant group, so it is also part of the network of Christian communities dotting the shores of the Mediterranean Sea in the late first century."[175] However, although seeing the group still within Judaism at the time of the composition of the gospel, he sees that it is on a trajectory that will lead it out of the Jewish world it inhabited. Overman locates the community more securely in the Jewish environment. He characterizes formative rabbinic Judaism and Matthean Judaism as fraternal twins competing for the religio-social remains of post-destruction Judaism.[176] However, Overman interprets the mission charge of Matt 28.19 as something that does not reflect a concern about Gentiles, but rather speaks of the Matthean view of eschatology.[177]

Sim is even more radical in his description of the Matthean community as a Jewish group with an anti-Gentile outlook. The group not only had no contact with the Gentile world at the time when the gospel was written, but remained anti-Gentile throughout its history. It finally ceased to exist

---

[172] Another reason for the less detailed coverage of this period is the existence of a number of surveys that analyse developments in Matthean studies in this period in detail.

[173] This, in broad terms, is the assessment of Saldarini, Overman, Sim and Repschinski, although each formulation has slightly different features.

[174] Stanton, *Gospel*, 157-62.

[175] Saldarini, *Matthew's Christian-Jewish Community*, 202.

[176] Overman, *Matthew's Gospel and Formative Judaism*, 160.

[177] "The era or age will draw to a close and the age that promises a better life for Matthean Jews will draw near if the mission to the rest of the world is engaged." (Overman, *Church and Community in Crisis*, 411).

perhaps in the third or fourth centuries, or maybe even as late as the
seventh century when it would have been swept away by the spread of
Islam.[178] However, until its demise it remained a Jewish group upholding
Torah and other traditions. Moreover, Gentile mission was not practiced by
the group, but formed part of its eschatological horizon.[179] Repschinski
also places the community within the world of Judaism. He sees the
Matthean controversy stories as an attempt to displace the Pharisaic
leadership.[180] This is aimed at a Jewish community, and seeks to advance
their own claims to be the legitimate interpreters of Judaism. Here the
outlook is remarkably similar to that of Overman. However, unlike
Overman, Repschinski does not see Gentile mission as simply advocated
by Matthew to herald in the eschatological age. Rather, it is seen as being
valued in its own right by the evangelist. This leads Repschinski to note a
tension that is not resolved in his study. He sees the group sociologically
as an inward looking Jewish sect, but at the same time engaging in Gentile
mission for its own sake.[181] Thus Repschinski, who adopts the new
consensus that the Matthean group is a Jewish entity, sees that a tension is
created when one looks at the data in the gospel. He realises that when the
issue of mission is considered the most obvious reading of texts like the
Great Commission do not align easily with a view of the community being
a deviant group within wider Judaism. He leaves this tension unresolved.
However, perhaps the most natural thing to do at this juncture would be to
question the new consensus.

This is precisely what this study shall now do. First by looking at the
issue of law through the eyes of both the Qumran[182] and Matthean
groups,[183] different approaches to reinterpreting Torah traditions will be
assessed. The issue of mission in Matthew's gospel will then be assessed.
The Great Commission and the treatment of Matthew's attitude to the
Gentiles is perhaps the weak point in most reconstructions of the Matthean
community that attempt to locate the group in a Jewish context.[184] It will

---

[178] "Its disappearance from the stage of history can possibly attributed to the success
of Islam which swept through the region in the seventh century." (Sim, *The Gospel of
Matthew and Christian Judaism*, 297).

[179] Sim, *The Gospel of Matthew and Christian Judaism*, 244.

[180] Repschinski, *The Controversy Stories*, 346.

[181] Repschinski, *The Controversy Stories*, 348.

[182] See the discussion of 4QMMT and other Qumran texts in chapter 3.

[183] The issue of the law in relation to the Matthean community is taken up in chapters
4 and 5.

[184] This weakness is perhaps most apparent in Repschinski's treatment of the Great
Commission. Although he recognizes a tension with the reconstruction he proposes, he
does not attempt to offer a solution. By contrast Sim and Overman can only deal with
mission by pushing it onto the Matthean eschatological horizon.

be argued that the attitude towards Gentile mission more naturally reflects a community that had stepped outside the bounds of Judaism.[185]

---

[185] In chapter 6 a detailed study will be provided of those texts that offer a perspective on the issue of mission among the Gentiles.

Chapter 3

4QMMT and Halakhic Debate

3.1 Introduction

The purpose of this chapter is twofold: first, it locates the antithetical debate of Matt 5.21-48 against the wider background of Judaism; second, it seeks to illustrate how dissident groups in Judaism interacted with their opponents. In relation to the first aim, the Halakhic letter from Qumran (4QMMT) is particularly important since it is the only example of Jewish antithetical debate that precedes Matthew's gospel. Admittedly, later examples exist, particularly in the Mishnah where the whole debating procedure involves putting forward the competing rulings of different rabbis.[1] However, the debates of the Mishnah are presented in a more discursive or scholastic tone. Acknowledging this difference leads to the second aim of this chapter, and the reason for choosing 4QMMT as an appropriate example for comparison with the six antitheses in Matthew's gospel. Whereas the debates enshrined in the Mishnah report competing viewpoints from within the world of rabbinic Judaism, both 4QMMT and the Matthean examples reflect disputes between one group, which has a sense of being disenfranchised from the rest of Judaism, and its perceived opponents.

Schiffman notes the significance of the Halakhic letter as a foundational document which "demonstrates quite clearly that the root cause that led to the sectarian schism consists of a series of disagreements about sacrificial law and ritual purity."[2] The letter clearly reflects an early period in the sect's development, before they considered themselves

---

[1] As has often been noted, although the positions of various named rabbis are listed, usually the position that is supported by the redactors of the Mishnah is simply attributed to an unnamed authority, or, more commonly, a generalised group such as 'the sages'. An example is to be found in *m. Ber* 5.4 'When a man has before him many kinds [of food], R. Judah says: If there is among them one of the seven kinds, he must say the benediction over that one. But the Sages say: He may say the Benediction over which of them he will.' Examples such as this could be multiplied. It is interesting that while the polemical tone that characterises Matt 5.21-48 and 4QMMT is absent, like those examples, the authoritative ruling is frequently put last. In this way the position that is presented as correct closes the debate.

[2] Schiffman, *Reclaiming the Dead Sea Scrolls*, 83.

persecuted and ostracised. Instead, they could reflect on their withdrawal as a self-imposed separation. Moreover, as 4QMMT evidences, the writer of the letter still hoped that other pious Jews might recognize the truth of the group's halakhic claims. As the writer states,

7   we have separated ourselves from the multitude of the people [and from all their impurity]
8   and from being involved with these matters and participating with [them] in these things...
10   [And] we have [written] to you so that you may study (carefully) the book of Moses and the books of the Prophets and (the writings of) David [and the] [events of] ages past.   4QMMT d (+e) (=4Q397 14-21)[3]

Although the bitterness that characterises some of the later Qumran documents is not present at this stage,[4] the letter clearly shows that right interpretation of Torah stands at the centre of the decision to have a segregated existence, with the goal being to live in a state of higher purity. Since the issue of law observance and the interpretation of Torah also stands behind many of the attempts to reconstruct the social location of the Matthean community, it is appropriate to make a comparison with the Qumran community operating in the milieu of second temple Judaism trying to confront related issues.[5]

3.2 Torah and Sectarian Dissent

The issue of the law is a central theme in Matthew's gospel, with Matt 5.17-20 forming a programmatic statement on Jesus' attitude to the Torah. The evangelist exegetes the meaning of this affirmation of the validity of the law by means of the six antithetical formulations that follow (5.21-48). No doubt Matthew intended his audience to see a harmony between these two neighbouring sections of the macronarrative, and for this reason some scholars reject the view that the antitheses can set aside the law.[6] However,

---

[3] This quotation and those that follow are taken from Qimron and Strugnell, *DJD X, Qumran Cave 4, V,* '2. The Composite Text', 43-63.

[4] As Strugnell notes, "The language used to describe the later sect and the language that shows its sectarian, dualistic, and apocalyptic nature is missing in MMT." ('MMT: Second Thoughts on a Forthcoming Edition', 71).

[5] Obviously there are important differences between the social location of the two groups. With the temple still standing, the Qumran community had visions of a renewed cult adhering to its own Torah interpretations centred around the Temple (11QT).

[6] Davies and Allison correctly see 5.17-20 as the introduction or preamble to the six formulations contained in 5.21-48, however, they reject any sense of abrogation. Commenting on the relationship between these two sections they state, "As introduction or preamble to 5.21-48 it [5.17-20] is intended to prevent the readers of the First Gospel from making two

Sim summarises the opposing viewpoint (not his own). He states, "Needless to say, a good many scholars have viewed these statements as true antitheses, whereby Jesus contrasts his teachings with the demands of the Torah and in some cases annuls its commandments."[7] In part, this divergence of opinion reflects a failure to consider the social function of 5.21-48 alongside its theological interpretation. Matthew utilises antithetical halakhic arguments not only to present alternative legal stances, but also to advance authority claims for his own community. As a recently formed entity, the evangelist's group bases its identity on the authoritative declarations of its founder.[8] Fundamentally, what is at issue is not the alternative legal viewpoint, but the authority ascribed to the one who speaks for the community.

Matthew, however, is not the first Jewish sectarian to employ antithetical halakhic debate to claim superior understanding of the law in direct opposition to other groups operating within Judaism. The Dead Sea party also distinguished its position from that of their opponents by using the same literary form. In the recently published document 4QMMT, there is a series of about 24 individual halakhot in which the community distinguishes its position in opposition to that of other sects operating during the Maccabean era. Baumgarten appears correct in his assessment that the text represents,

> a letter written by a leader of the Qumran group, early in the history of its existence, explaining why its members chose to secede from 'official' Judaism...An ideological section concludes the letter, in which the author explains that for those reasons he and his friends have elected to secede from 'official' Judaism. That is, because they have been unable to change the practices of 'official' Judaism on these matters, they would rather reject the whole.[9]

Although the publication of 4QMMT came too late to be incorporated into Stanton's work on Matthew, nonetheless he was attuned to its

---

errors. First, it plainly states that the six subsequent paragraphs are not to be interpreted as they have been so often by so many – as 'antitheses', 'antitheses' that, in at least two or three instances, set aside the Torah." (Davies and Allison, *Matthew,* vol 1, 481). However, the situation is not so simple. While Matthew wishes to claim continuity with the law, some of the antithetical counterproposals that he places on the lips of Jesus stand in fundamental opposition to the traditional legal rulings contained in the Torah.

[7] Sim continues by noting the disagreement that exists between such scholars over the issue of precisely which statements reject the law. "There is little agreement, however, on which of these six teachings constitute a breach of the law or even their precise number. Estimates differ from author to author, but as many as three of the six antitheses have been cited as deliberate annulments of the written law." Sim, *The Gospel of Matthew and Christian Judaism,* 129

[8] Scholars such as Saldarini would question this reconstruction of the social setting of the Matthean Community (*Matthew's Christian-Jewish Community,*). See the discussion in the previous chapter.

[9] Baumgarten, *The Flourishing of Jewish Sects in the Maccabean Era: An Interpretation.*

potential significance for providing important comparisons between the social settings of the Qumran and Matthean groups. In relation to this Dead Sea document he notes, "As is usually the case with a sectarian community, its halakah was more strict than that of its opponents. (We may note Matt 5.20 and the antitheses in 5.21-48 as a significant parallel.)"[10] However, the parallels are even stronger than Stanton imagined. Not only do both documents contain a series of antithetical halakah, but likewise they understand the performance of the legal rulings, as interpreted by the respective groups, as pertaining to righteousness. In the concluding line of the hortatory epilogue of 4QMMT, the Qumran apologist assures his addressees that the outcome of walking according to the interpretation presented in the legal antitheses is that לך לצדקה ונחשבה (it will be reckoned to you as righteousness),[11] with obvious echoes of Gen 15.6 and Ps 106.31.[12]

Similarly in the thematic prologue to the Matthean antitheses the notion of δικαιοσύνη is prominent, with the meaning of abounding righteousness being illustrated in the series of antithetical statements that follows. For the Qumran community the 'righteousness' they sought is most naturally understood as a right relationship with God brought about by observing the interpretation of Torah as promoted by the group. Moreover, as a point of contact, it should be noted that the Matthean evangelist advocates a 'righteousness' that is based on observance of the group's values, which surpasses the standards set by opponents (5.20), and which in turn is linked to the community's understanding of the kingdom (6.33). A sharp distinction should not be drawn between seeking the kingdom[13] and seeking righteousness.[14] For the author of the first gospel these ideas are inextricably bound together, and the way to achieve the goal of the

---

[10] Stanton, *Gospel*, 93.

[11] Qimron's translation is totally inadequate at this point. He renders this phrase as 'And this will be counted a virtuous deed of yours, since you will be doing what is righteous.' This fails to mention the direct parallel with both Gen 15.6; Ps 106.31. Instead he suggests, "The entire concluding phrase is perhaps informed by Deut 6.24-25." (Qimron, and Strugnell, *DJD X, Qumran Cave 4, V,* 63).

[12] In an unpublished paper delivered at Oxford on the 3rd of March 2000, C.A. Evans argued that the primary parallel was Ps 106.31, where the zealousness of Phineas becomes a paradigmatic example of how the law is to be upheld through earnestly carrying out its requirements.

[13] For a discussion of the textual problem that surrounds the words τοῦ θεοῦ, which are bracketed in the NA[27] text, see Metzger, *A Textual Commentary*, 15-16. Although not coming down decisively in favour of omitting the words, it is noted that the committee felt it was more likely that these words were not original.

[14] Davies and Allison, *Matthew*, 661.

kingdom is by living in accord with the community's understanding of righteousness.[15]

Yet at an even more fundamental level, the issue of dispute between the opposing groups (both in the Qumranic and Matthean settings) is not so much alternative halakhic positions, but the right to be considered the authoritative interpreter of Torah tradition. In relation to the social setting of Matthean community, Loader observes, "The status of his [Jesus'] antithetical statement is, however, not a second opinion, but an authoritative declaration made on his own God given authority."[16] This is an obvious contrast to halakhic debate in the Mishnah. Correspondingly, in 4QMMT the writer of the letter does not enter into debate with his opponents but simply declares the true interpretation of the law for the benefit of the addressees. Yet, despite these similarities between the two documents, Matt 5.21-48 differs markedly from the Qumran text in an important respect. Whereas the Halakhic letter is conciliatory in tone seeking to reconcile the recipients, the Matthean antitheses are addressed primarily to members of evangelist's own community. They deride the alternative viewpoint and do not seek to heal a breach with their adversaries. Rather, they reflect the more developed separatist outlook of the Matthean community. Such a social situation still lay in the future for the Qumran group when 4QMMT was written. However, the more intense polemic and separatist attitudes come to the fore in some of the pesharim.[17]

Thus the antitheses of Matt 5.21-48 form an inwardly focused tractate with polemical, pedagogical and pastoral intent for group members. To appreciate the function of antithetical argument in the gospel, this study will investigate how such debate operated in wider Judaism by first studying its application in the Halakhic letter. Then this form of argumentation will be studied in detail as it is utilised by the Matthean redactor to subvert the opposing positions of his adversaries, thereby making an exclusive claim for the centrality of Jesus as the legitimate interpreter of Torah.

---

[15] The phrase καὶ τὴν δικαιοσύνην αὐτοῦ used in 6.33 raises the grammatical question concerning the reference of the genitive pronoun. The reference could either be to the righteousness of the kingdom, or to the righteousness of God. Przyblylski argues that it denotes God's righteousness (*Righteousness in Matthew*, 89-91). However, it is far from certain that the evangelist would have distinguished between these possibilities, even if he had noticed the ambiguity in his phrase.

[16] Loader, *Jesus' Attitude Towards the Law*, 173.

[17] See in particular 1QpHab and 4QpPs37.

3.3 The Form and Purpose of 4QMMT

The text of 4QMMT is partially preserved in six fragments discovered in cave four at Qumran. The reconstructed composite text published by Qimron and Strugnell[18] consists of three main sections. Section A, the calendric material, is the most problematic part of the reconstruction. This is due to the fact that it is preserved in fragmentary form in only one of the texts, 4Q394. It has been questioned whether this description of the 364-day calendar paralleling the horological system in *Jubilees* is actually part of the original Halakhic letter. Apart from the obvious form critical and substantive differences from the rest of the document, Strugnell adduces strong textual arguments for its secondary nature. He observes, "In manuscript 4Q394 the presence of the 364-day calendar-list is certain since it is preserved directly before the first line of section B (the legal section). However, in the second manuscript of the work, 4Q395, which also gives the start of section B, enough uninscribed leather is preserved before section B to make it highly probable that no text ever stood before it."[19] However, whilst there may be valid concerns about the authenticity of the calendric material in its present context, section B, the halakhic material, and section C, the hortatory epilogue, form the major components of the text and their originality is not questioned.

This discussion is important in relation to the antitheses in Matthew's gospel. When it is recognized that the Halakhic letter probably consisted of a non-extant incipit or introduction, the antitheses, and an appeal to the recipients to change their Torah practices, an important parallel can be see with the Matthean discussion. After presenting the differing interpretations in the antitheses, like the Halakhic letter,[20] the opponents remain clearly in view (Matt 6.1-6), and alternative standards of righteousness are commented upon. However, unlike 4QMMT,[21] the evangelist shows a more hostile attitude towards the opponents, since there is no appeal seeking rapprochement. The opponents are vilified, being labelled twice as hypocrites (Matt 6.2, 5), and repeatedly criticised for their public displays

---

[18] Qimron and Strugnell, (eds.), *DJD* X.

[19] Strugnell, 'MMT: Second Thoughts on a Forthcoming Edition', 61.

[20] Although Strugnell raises the issue of whether the competing group can be described as adversaries at the time when MMT was written. He notes that a minimalist reading would simply conclude that the document "was sent by a priestly faction that was later to evolve, under the influence of the Teacher of Righteousness, into the Qumran sect." ('MMT: Second Thoughts on a Forthcoming Edition', 72). Yet, regardless of whether the opposing group is described as another faction or opponents, it is obvious that the polemic of the antitheses in Matt 5.21-48, and the characterisation of the 'hypocrites' in Matt 6.1-6 is a more strident treatment of those who dissent from the authorial position, than that reflected in 4QMMT.

[21] See the hortatory epilogue, lines 112-17.

of religious piety. This is an indication that the evangelist is using a known form of Jewish literary debate, but intensifies the polemic by neither interacting with alternative viewpoints in a scholastic manner (as in Mishnaic debates), nor does he make an appeal to the opposing group to fall into line with his own group's practices, rather they are dismissed as 'hypocrites' and seen as unable to appreciate true righteousness (Matt 6.1). Thus, although using the form of Jewish debate, Matthew shows considerable distance from the idea of trying to convince those with opposing views to consent to his understanding. This does not appear to be part of his agenda. Rather, he presents his opponents as being outside of the requirements of righteousness, they are neither seekers of the kingdom nor the righteousness that attends it. This creates a distance between the two groups, and Matthew does not make an offer of reconciliation to the opposing party.

3.3.1 The Halakah of the Qumran Community

Forming the bulk of the text is the central legal section comprising a sequence of 24 halakhot[22] that contrast a selection of the nomistic positions held by the author and his adherents, in contrast to the views being opposed. The final part of the text, section C, the hortatory epilogue, is the most instructive about the self-perceived purpose of the legal positions in section B. In lines 114-116, the author exhorts the recipients to

> 28 Consider all these things and ask Him that He strengthen
> 29 your will and remove from you the plans of evil and the device of Belial
> 30 so that you may rejoice at the end of time, finding that some of our practices are
>   correct   4QMMT d (+e+f) (=4Q398 14-17 ii)

In this sense, the rhetorical function of the letter appears to be primarily deliberative, that is seeking to persuade the addressee of the correctness of the author's positions,[23] rather than forensic, that is seeking to undermine the opposing viewpoints in a juridical sense.

---

[22] The precise number of individual legal precepts is unclear. This is due to the fact that some of the rulings at the beginning of section B are fragmentary, while others run together in a manner that makes it hard to determine if they are separate precepts or parts of the same ruling. Qimron speaks of more than twenty halakhic statements, Schiffman (*Reclaiming the Dead Sea Scrolls*, 84) enumerates them as being twenty-two and on my own count there are twenty-four statements although some are not recoverable beyond a few words.

[23] Although admittedly not coming out of an Hellenistic environment, 4QMMT appears to contain the three modes of rhetorical persuasion as described by Aristotle. "The first kind depends on the personal character of the speaker [ethos]; the second on putting the audience into a certain frame of mind [pathos]; the third on the proof, or apparent proof, provided by the words of the speech itself [logic]." (*Rhetoric* 1.2). Each of these elements is present to some degree in the Halakhic letter. In lines 92-94, the author describes his own group as a

This conciliatory tone that pervades the hortatory epilogue calls for explanation, especially in light of the antagonistic and hostile nature of the disputation as portrayed in most of the other sectarian scrolls that describe the relationship of the community with its opponents. A highly plausible suggestion is that 4QMMT comes from an early date in the community's history, reflecting a period when debate with those who held opposing points of view could occur without persecution. Apart from the more restrained tone of 4QMMT, there is other evidence that points to its being an early, or even foundational document of the nascent Dead Sea community. The pesher on Psalm 37 describes the Wicked Priest as 'the person who spies on the Righteous One [and wants] to kill him because of the precepts of the law which he sent him' (4Q171 iv 7-9). It is feasible that 'the precepts of the law' in question are in fact those contained in 4QMMT, and its epistolatory form suggests that the scroll is in fact a copy of the original letter. Identifying the Wicked Priest as Jonathan, Qimron dates MMT (the autograph rather than the fragments found in cave 4) to around 150 B.C.E. and concludes,

> It stands to reason that the schism in MMT occurred a short time before the composition of the document. The palaeography may also imply such an early date, as does the contrast of MMT with the prohibition of dispute with opponents found in 1QS 9.16-17.[24]

Furthermore, Schiffman agrees that the letter stems from the immediate aftermath of a dispute over legal issues that led to the author's group removing itself from Temple worship. While one may not wish to concur with Schiffman's assessment that the Qumran community was Sadducean in origin,[25] his study has allowed for a greater recognition of the priestly origins of the group and the foundational role of the halakhic letter. This document evidences a genuine attempt to heal the breach between the author's party and the 'you' group addressed in the text.

The ideological aim of the halakhic material is described in lines 95-96, namely that the 'you' group may correctly 'understand the book of Moses [and the words of the pro]phets and of David and the annals of each generation.' In this sense the Teacher of Righteousness has not presented himself as a new authority source within Judaism above the law, but rather as the correct interpreter of that Mosaic tradition. As the series of halakah evidences, the disagreements centre on purity and ritual issues, with primary concern revolving around the sanctity of Jerusalem and correct observance of

---

segregated community pursuing purity and honesty; this corresponds with the Aristotelian notion of the integrity of the orator. There is also the conciliatory appeal in lines 114-118 that serves to place the recipients in the correct frame of mind. Finally, the bulk of the work is devoted to legal 'proofs' furnished to demonstrate the logic of the group's halakhic stance.

[24] Qimron, 'Miqsat Ma'ase Ha-Torah', 84.

[25] Schiffman, 'The *Temple Scroll* and the Nature of its Law', 54.

regulations pertaining to offerings and acts of purification. This coheres with the centrality of the role of priests in the Qumran community, and the theory that the origins of the movement arise out of the disenfranchisement of a priestly group during the Antiochean crisis and the subsequent installation of the Hasmonean priests.[26]

An initial observation needs to be made about the structure of the rulings in the legal section. While a few of the halakhot are explicitly antithetical in form, contrasting two opposing viewpoints, the majority are antithetical only by implication. That is, they present only the viewpoint of the author explicitly. However, in the majority of cases the alternative positive is patently clear. An example of the explicit antithetical form is presented in lines 12-16, which relates to the thank offering.

> 9   [And concerning the cereal-offering] of the sacrifice
> 10   of well-being which they (the opponents) leave over from one day to the following one: but [it is written]
> 11   that the cereal-offer[ing is to be ea]ten after the suet and the flesh (are sacrificed), on the day when they are sacri[ficed (i.e. before sunset).
>
> 4QMMT a (+b̲) (=4Q394 3-7 i)

This ruling describes the praxis that the Qumran group finds offensive, specifically, reserving part of the cereal offering until the following day. Such a practice is not attributed to the addressees, but to a third group (the 'they' party), whose legal positions the author wishes to demonstrate as false to the recipients of the letter. Yadin in his work on 11QT 20.12-13 draws attention to a parallel ruling in that context, 'it (the cereal offering) should be eaten on the same day before sunset.' He notes a rabbinic ruling that opposes the Qumran position, 'Cereal offering...shall be eaten during the day and the night up to midnight' (*m. Zebah* 6.1)[27]. In this case it is possible to see the two alternative positions placed alongside one another in antithetical fashion, with the 'you' group being urged to come down in favour of the author's viewpoint.[28]

---

[26] It does need to be acknowledged that a minimalist approach questions this conflation of material contained in different scrolls. See Strugnell, 'MMT: Second Thoughts on a Forthcoming Edition', 70-3.

[27] Yadin, *The Temple Scroll*, 89.

[28] As Qimron describes, it is easy to see how the debate could have arisen since the Levitical material does not stipulate a time for consuming the cereal component of the thank-offering. 'Now the flesh of the sacrifice of his thanksgiving offering for peace shall be eaten on the day when it is offered; none of it shall be left over until morning' (Lev 7.15). Thus Qimron notes the difference in hermeneutical understanding, "the rabbis interpreted the word *yom* as including also part of the following night, according to their general rule that in sacrificial matters night follows day, and in accordance with the second statement in the biblical source...What was the view of the sect as reflected in MMT? The word *yom* in both the biblical source and in the expression *bayom zobahem* is taken to mean the same day (ie

In contrast to those halakhic rulings that give an explicit statement of the alternative point of view of the opponents, there is a far more numerous collection of precepts that simply state the group's interpretation. This form is illustrated by the halakah referring to flowing liquids.

> 55 And concerning liquid streams: we are of the opinion that they are not
> 56 pure, and that these streams do not act as a separative between impure
> 57 and pure (liquids). For the liquid of streams and (that) of (the vessel) which
> receives them are alike, (being) a single liquid. (4QMMT 55-58)
>
> 4QMMT a (+c+ց) (=4Q394 8 iv)

Thus, although there is no reference to the practice of the 'they' group, by implication it can be seen that the opponents viewed a flowing stream as an effective separation between pure and impure. Moreover, pouring a liquid from a clean container into an unclean vessel did not render the initial container impure. Thus, the manner in which the issue is raised without stating explicitly the divergent view nonetheless evidences the positions of both the author and his opponents. The sectarian understanding is stated concisely and without recourse to a supporting authority. However, this abbreviated structure is still antithetical in that it implies a rejected legal position, followed by the opposing understanding of the issue, presented by a writer representing a group.

Elam[29] has rightly questioned the generalization made by Sussman that, "all the halakhot in the Dead Sea scrolls which are at variance with Pharisaic halakha are stricter than the corresponding rulings."[30] However, while there are some inconsistencies on either side, as Elam demonstrates, it is still more natural to read the Qumran ruling as advancing a stricter interpretation. In relation to flowing liquids, a significant parallel is preserved in *m. Yad* 4.7.

> The Sadducees say: We protest against you, O Pharisees, for you pronounce clean unbroken streams (of liquid poured from a clean vessel into an unclean vessel).

Here, the position espoused by the Halakhic letter corresponds with that of the Sadducees, as it is portrayed by their Pharisaic opponents in the

---

before sunset)." (Qimron, and Strugnell, (eds.), *DJD X*, p150). Obviously, the sect suggested that the stipulation of Lev 7.15b was achieved by also consuming the cereal offering before sunset.

[29] Elam, 'Some Remarks on 4QMMT and the Rabbinic Tradition' 99-128.

[30] Sussman, 'The History of the Halakha and the Dead Sea scrolls', 197. However, Sussman correctly appreciates that the divergent rulings in MMT bear witness to a complex tradition and transmission process in the development of Pharisaic halakah. He states, "In contrast to Geiger, the Pharisaic halakha is not a late development, opposed to the 'early' Sadducean halakha. It is now evident that both halakhic systems existed side by side and grappled with each other from ancient times" (197).

Mishnah. While it would be somewhat facile to identify the 'they' group with the Pharisees on the basis of this later rabbinic dispute, 4QMMT does evidence that the same controversy that is portrayed in the Mishnah was already a source of disagreement between two groups that existed in the second century B.C.E.. Furthermore, the ruling concerning flowing liquids does not stem directly from biblical legislation concerning purity, nor does it formally state its authority source for this position. Rather, the Qumranic position is presented as being inherently correct. Thus as Strugnell perceives, in the halakhic section, "the laws are a written collection of pronouncements ascribed to the 'we' –community, not to God, or to the angels, or to Moses as the source."[31] Yet, despite this observation, the concern of the halakhic epistle remains correct performance of the law even in relation to those matters not directly addressed in the biblical corpus.

3.3.2 The Purpose and Setting of the Halakhic Letter

The data provided by 4QMMT is extremely valuable for at least three reasons. Firstly, it bears witness to one type of such legal debate during the second temple period. Secondly, it reveals the types of positions adopted by two groups that led to their schism. Finally, it gives insight into the nature and theological basis of sectarian communities during this era. Qimron notes, "MMT contains the largest surviving corpus of early controversial halakhot, though such halakhot also appear in other sources, both sectarian and rabbinic."[32] The function of this series of legal precepts as a division marker between the author's adherents and the 'they' group needs to be stressed. What differentiates the Qumran sectarians from their adversaries is specifically those positions taken in relation to the issues outlined in section B of the letter.

Yet, the harsh polemical tone of later DSS is missing from this letter. Thus, as has already been suggested, this letter was a foundational document for the party that at the time of the letter's composition had only recently withdrawn from Temple worship and was seeking to enact an alliance with the 'you' group. Qimron identifies these addressees in the following manner: "the identity of the 'you' group may be established from the epilogue, in which the addressee is referred to as the leader of Israel. It appears that he was one of the Hasmonean kings. The pesher on Ps 37 indicates that this addressee may have been the famous Wicked Priest."[33] Therefore, if this plausible reconstruction is correct, 4QMMT

---

[31] Strugnell, 'MMT: Second Thoughts on a Forthcoming Edition', 64.

[32] Qimron, and Strugnell, (eds.), *DJD X*, 176.

[33] Qimron, and Strugnell, (eds.), *DJD X*, 175.

preserves the earliest literary remains of sectarian writing from Qumran, and importantly portrays the period before the group underwent persecution by the Hasmonean king to whom the infamous title 'the Wicked Priest' was to be attached.

Schiffman is even more precise in his reconstruction of the 'you' group, separately defining the usages of the singular and plural forms of the second person pronoun. He states, "the plural sections are addressed to the priests of the Jerusalem Temple, and the singular to the Hasmonean ruler."[34] The emphasis in 4QMMT on purity issues and temple administration likewise suggests that the Qumran group was originally composed of a priestly party disenfranchised during the Antiochean crisis, or during the aftermath of the Hasmonean wars. Their withdrawal centred upon a number of halakhic points. They hoped that by presenting their position to the temple priests and the Hasmonean ruler (probably Jonathan), they would gain a sympathetic hearing and a restoration of their status in the temple, along with cultic practice being administered in accord with their interpretations.

None of these desired outcomes were to materialize. Instead the group found itself ostracized permanently, persecuted by the one whom they had hoped would champion their cause, driven to a more marginalized existence and forced into a more inwardly looking sectarian society. Thus, while the halakhic precepts may lack the 'hard edge' of later polemical sectarian writings, they reflect an important stage in the self-definition of what was to become the Dead Sea Scrolls community,[35] prior to its overtly antagonistic attitude towards its opponents which came about as a consequence of an attack by the Wicked Priest. This appears to have led to the exile of the Teacher of Righteousness.[36]

3.4 Conclusions

Authority issues are the central concern of both 4QMMT and the Matthean antitheses. However, the sense in which authority functions in both groups is markedly different even though the aim of producing a higher standard of righteousness is similar. For the group that adhered to the rulings in the Halakhic letter Torah remains authoritative, but it must be observed in line

---

[34] Schiffman, *Reclaiming the Dead Sea Scrolls,* 86.

[35] VanderKam notes that the editors of 4QMMT (Strugnell and Qimron) understand the purpose of the letter in the following terms. "The purpose of the letter was to spell out the differences between the two parties and to summon the opponents to amendment of life." VanderKam, *The Dead Sea Scrolls Today*, 60.

[36] See 1QpHab 11.2-8.

with that community's interpretation. By contrast, the authority base of the Matthean community shows greater distance from that of the group's opponents. While the positions that Matthew interacts with come with the authority of 'the ancients' or the rulings of Torah ('you have heard that it was said'), these no longer form the basis of authority for the evangelist. The authoritative countermanding 'I' shows that the group's stance on the issues discussed stem from the pronouncements of the community's foundational figure. This is not simply a claim that the group has the right interpretation of Torah, but this constitutes a higher claim, namely the right to re-interpret the law thereby making its authority subservient to that of Jesus.

Furthermore, the lack of reconciliation in the Matthean antitheses stands in noticeable opposition to the conciliatory tone of 4QMMT.[37] In this sense, the antitheses in the Halakhic letter share far more in common with the rabbinic Torah disputes contained in the Mishnah. In the rabbinic corpus opposing positions are openly discussed without acrimony, but always in pursuit of finding the legitimate, or valid, understanding of the Torah. The goal is a shared one, and even rejected positions are cherished for the service they have provided in coming to a correct understanding of Torah. While 4QMMT may not be quite so congenial to the opposing positions, its lack of hostility towards those whom it seeks to convince, shows that it is far closer to inhabiting the thought world of rabbinic Judaism than that of Matthew's gospel.

By contrast, the evangelist is hostile to his opponents and their understandings of the law. He shows little interest in winning them over to his position, he rejects their manner of Torah observance, which admittedly may be caricatured for the sake of his own polemical goal (Matt 23),[38] and presents a different basis for authority. Such antagonism illustrates a different stage in the respective development of the two communities. These are major differences that not only reflect a different attitude between the Matthean and Qumran groups at the time of writing the respective documents in question, but more importantly suggest that the Matthean group stood at greater distance from their synagogue based

---

[37] As VanderKam notes in relation to the tone of the dispute in the Halakhic letter and the way in which it presents its competing viewpoints, "All this is done in a surprisingly friendly manner." *The Dead Sea Scrolls Today*, 60.

[38] Although Newport sees Matt 23.2-31 as a pre-existing source reflecting an *intra muros* situation (unlike most of the rest of the gospel which he views as being reflective of a later *extra muros* setting), he nevertheless recognizes the heightened polemic towards opponents. This he sees primarily as "reflect[ing] the animosity felt by one who was within synagogal Judaism towards what he considered to be a complacent and hypocritical leadership." (Newport, *The Sources and Sitz im Leben of Matthew 23*, 134). He does not consider the option that a different attitude towards Torah is in effect.

opponents than the author of 4QMMT and his adherents did in relation to the Temple based Judaism of their day.[39]

---

[39] See Stanton, *A Gospel for a New People*, 85-107, for a discussion of sectarian perspectives provided by comparing Matthew with the Damascus Document (CD).

Chapter 4

The Matthean Antitheses (Matt 5.21-48)

4.1 Introduction

The series of six antitheses in Matthew's gospel differ in tone and subject matter from the twenty-four halakot in MMT. They are cast in a more consistent and explicitly antithetical framework, and reflect a heightened polemic. Their purpose is not to effect reconciliation, but to establish the authority source of the positions advanced by the evangelist. Since the antithetical form was an accepted literary vehicle for engaging in dispute, the evangelist has turned to this genre to present his alternative interpretations. Yet it needs to be noted from the outset that for Matthew the antitheses have an ethical function in their provision of instruction for the community. This presents a different emphasis in comparison with the legal orientation of halakhic argument in later rabbinic texts, although the rabbis would have felt that the Jewish ethical base could only be established through correct observance of Torah.[1] The Qumran text, while aligning more closely with the later rabbinic examples, also stresses the moral necessity of obeying its legal rulings.[2] Therefore, its purpose lies somewhere between the rabbinic Torah debates and the Matthean desire to claim an ethical standard of behaviour that surpasses the conduct of his adversaries. It is through the genre of the antitheses that the Matthean redactor seeks to present a clearly differentiated position between Jesus and Moses, the authority figures in the two conflicting communities. Moreover, the evangelist also draws a distinction between his community and their opponents, who are labelled as scribes and Pharisees (5.20).

In terms of their position in the Matthean macronarrative, this sequence of six antitheses constitutes an interpretative explanation of the programmatic statement in 5.17-20 concerning the law. Thus for Luz, the antitheses serve as an exposition of Jesus' 'fulfilling' of the Torah. He states,

---

[1] The formulation of very specific regulations of how to obey the law should not be seen as an end in itself, rather it reflects a desire to take Torah seriously as the ordinances of God and to apply its rulings to every aspect of life.

[2] See the appeal in the hortatory epilogue, which calls on the addressees to walk 'uprightly' in respect to the requirements of the Torah.

They demonstrate how the Son of God fulfils in complete sovereignty God's word of law and prophets in putting his word over against Moses. Matthew has indicated this already through the localizing of Jesus' first proclamation of the gospel 'on the mountain.' Now 5:17-48 makes clear that this does not mean that a second Moses abolishes the Torah of the first Moses. Instead, Jesus' proclamation of the will of God is the 'door' to the Old Testament.[3]

While Luz is correct to draw out the significance of Jesus on the mountain as a direct Mosaic allusion, he does not define in a satisfying manner the relationship between the old dispensation and the new, nor between the first lawgiver and the new teacher who is claiming the authority to speak God's words.

However, focusing on the important transitional statement in 5.20, Allison is more explicit in outlining his proposal for the relationship between the legal statement (5.17-20) and the antitheses (5.21-48). He suggests,

Not only does 5:17-20 rebut in advance a wrong interpretation of 5:21-48, it also supplies the reader with a clue as to the right interpretation. 5:20, in announcing that the righteousness of Jesus' followers must exceed that of the scribes and the Pharisees, anticipates that Jesus' words in the subsequent paragraphs will, in their moral stringency, exceed those of the Torah.[4]

Advancing this perspective, Allison argues that the Mosaic law and Jesus' teaching cannot be construed as standing in opposition. Rather, the new didactical imperatives demand far more from their adherents, and yet no tension exists with the Sinai prescriptions since Jesus simply brings out their true intent. While the first two antitheses fit Allison's thesis (and possible the sixth which deals with love of neighbours), the others pose greater problems for his position. In relation to the fourth antithesis dealing with oaths, there is a repealing of certain Torah directives that call for oaths to be used in certain situations as statements of surety (cf, Exod 22.6-7, 10; Num 5.19-22; Deut 6.13; 10.20).

Nonetheless, Allison is correct to emphasize the importance of δικαιοσύνη in understanding the series of antitheses. Not only do the references to this term in 5.20 and 6.1 form a literary *inclusio* about the series, but also as the context makes clear, the antitheses are intended as a hermeneutical guide to show how the community's righteousness is to exceed that of the scribes and Pharisees. Thus as Müller observes, "the realization of such righteousness as conforms to God's will...is a manifestation of the Law's true significance."[5] Since the antitheses are set

---

[3] Luz, *Matthew 1-7*, 279.

[4] Allison, *The New Moses*, 182-183.

[5] Müller, 'The Theological Interpretation of the Figure of Jesus in the Gospel of Matthew', 170.

in a framework of δικαιοσύνη terminology, and function as an exposition of the programmatic legal statements in 5.17-19, each antithesis will be studied individually to ascertain how it has redefined traditional Torah material. Such an approach contrasts with attempts that first seek to determine the notoriously difficult statements in vv. 17-19.[6] Rather, this study utilises Matthew's own commentary on the 5.17-19 as the principal means for understanding the role of the law in the Matthean gospel. Moreover, at a literary level, it is important to see if there are any structural or thematic indicators that account for the ordering of the antitheses. In this vein, what Gourgues has said concerning the beatitudes applies equally well to the antitheses, "Considérées du point de vue de leur signification, les béatitudes, telles qu'elles se présentent dans le texte final Mt 5.3-12, ne font pas que se suivre selon une order plus ou moins arbitraire."[7] Thus it is necessary to study both the Matthean ordering and redaction of the antitheses to appreciate the hermeneutical commentary on the role of the law in the evangelist's community.

4.2 The Antithesis on Murder (Matt 5.21-26)

The first antithesis, dealing with murder, is the longest of the six statements presented in this list. It contains the fullest form of the introductory formula (although v. 33 of necessity prefixes the resumptive πάλιν to the identical phrase), and in vv. 23-26 two loosely related examples are attached that illustrate how anger can be overcome through acts of reconciliation. In terms of sources, only vv. 25-26 have a synoptic parallel with the Q material contained in Lk 12.57-59. The parallel to vv. 23-24 from Mk 11.25, cited by Aland,[8] is a parallel only in terms of a similar concept, and in no way can be considered as a source for the Matthean material. This means that the opening four verses (vv. 21-24) are either to be ascribed to independent Matthean tradition, or must be treated as a redactional composition, or have come about through a combination of traditional material and redactional reworking. Diversity of opinion exists between scholars. Hagner ascribes at least vv. 21-22 to a source, "The antithesis proper is without parallel in the Gospels and is thus from

---

[6] Specifically, this study contrasts with that of Meier, who first looks for consistency in the legal material of vv. 17-20. When he has established a salvation history perspective on the law, which he sees as limited to the pre-resurrection era, he then proceeds to treat the antitheses as the 'conformation' of this basic thesis. (*Law and History in Matthew's Gospel*).

[7] Gourgues, 'Sur l'articulation des béatitudes matthéennes (Mt 5:3-12): une proposition', 340.

[8] Aland, (ed.), *Synopsis Quattuor Evangeliorum*, 79.

Matthew's own source rather than from Mark or Q."[9] However, Gundry comes to the opposite conclusion seeing 5.21-24 as Matthean on the basis of diction. Specifically in relation to vv. 21-22 he argues, "the parallelism evident in the present saying characterizes his [Matthew's] literary style. We justly conclude that Matthew composed this antithesis."[10] However, an intermediate position appears more defensible, whereby the evangelist combines items of source material with his own redactional concerns. It is therefore necessary to separate source and redactional elements to appreciate the specific concerns of the evangelist in the newly shaped text.

4.2.1 Verse 21

In their present form, the introductory formula that commences each of the antitheses may rightly be seen as stemming from Matthean composition. Not only do such formulae impose a structured framework on the final form of 5.21-48, but more importantly they are not attested in any of the parallel source material. Admittedly, in the final antithesis there is the vestige of a counterproposal in the Q source ἀλλά ὑμῖν λέγω τοῖς ἀκούσιν (Q 6.27a), however it is questionable whether one can conclude from the adversative ἀλλά that the original saying stood in opposition to a statement preserving the formulaic opening to the sixth antithesis (Matt 5.43a), and thus construe from this a source for the antithetical introductions.[11] Yet, Lambrecht suggests that this material from Q may have acted as a trigger for the Matthean compositional technique. He states, "It is possible that something like an antithetical introduction already existed in Q (cf. Lk 6.27)."[12] However, if this earlier formula existed, it is no longer recoverable, since the evangelist has reshaped his source material in such a manner to create a highly ordered six-fold antithetical scheme, with his own introductory formulations.[13] The passive verb form ἐρρέθη is most commonly understood to have God as its implied subject. This is the most likely explanation, for as Davies and Allison note, "In both Jewish and Christian writings, 'it (was) said (by God)' is common for introducing OT quotations."[14] Moreover, Betz notes "the use of the passive form in

---

[9] Hagner, *Matthew 1-13*, 114.

[10] Gundry, *Matthew*, 85.

[11] This is not to exclude the possibility that the adversative ἀλλά may have at one stage stood in contrast to something, however, whatever that something may have been is now irrecoverable.

[12] Lambrecht, *The Sermon on the Mount*, 98.

[13] For a discussion of this point see Suggs, 'The Antitheses as Redactional Products', 93-107.

[14] Davies and Allison, *Matthew*, vol 1, 510-511.

formula quotations where the subject is then explicitly stated as 'the Lord'."[15]

After the opening Matthean introductory formula the thesis is presented, to which the subsequent antithesis in v. 22 will respond. The thesis is in fact a combination of two elements, the apodictic ruling οὐ φονεύσεις (Ex 20.13; Dt 5.17 LXX) and the casuistic prescription that ὃς δ' ἂν φονεύσῃ, ἔνοχος ἔστιν τῇ κρίσει The repetition of ἔνοχος ἔστιν τῇ κρίσει suggests, as Luz observes, that "verse 22a is closely connected with 21b...Thus there is no reason to separate v. 22 from its connection with the thesis."[16] For this reason it is most likely that v. 21b was part of Matthew's source material connected with the antithesis of 22a. However, the evangelist recast this material by attaching the formulaic opening, and placing it at the head of a redactional series of six antitheses.

4.2.2 Verse 22

The unity of this verse is debated. It consists of three antithetical statements, which in itself is unique in the Matthean series, although these three statements are linked in terms of their structure depicting an offence with its corresponding punishment. As was argued above, the verbal linkage between 21b and 22a speaks for the combination of these elements in the tradition. However, the final two components of v. 22 are often seen as secondary additions to this tradition. Bultmann tentatively suggests that v. 22b is an insertion. He argues,

> if v22b be original, κρίσις must be understood differently in v22a from v21 so as to contrive a climax: κρίσις , συνέδριον, γέεννα. But in fact the Sanhedrin was not an example of something higher than a local court. Neither can one see why a term of abuse should be more harshly punished than anger.[17]

Likewise, Davies and Allison suggest that the final component is not part of the original tradition. "The line might be redactional and added to give 5.22 a triadic structure."[18] Therefore, the presence of Matthean vocabulary, the change from a generalized act of anger to two specific offences and the overloading of the antithesis so that it now has three elements contrasting the single thesis, all support the notion that at least v. 22c, if not also v. 22b, are redactional additions.[19]

---

[15] Betz, *The Sermon on the Mount*, 215, note 125.

[16] Luz, *Matthew 1-7*, 281.

[17] Bultmann, *History of the Synoptic Tradition,* 134.

[18] Davies and Allison, *Matthew,* vol 1, 514.

[19] In opposition to this conclusion, the unity of v. 22 is defended by Luz, on the basis of its thematic intensification of punishment. He notes that the triple antithetical form is 'singular', but he sees this as an oral device employed by the historical Jesus. He

Such a reconstruction leads to an examination of the evangelist's motivation for these twin additions. The reference to συνέδριον is instructive. Within the gospel material nearly all references to the Sanhedrin occur in the context of Jesus' trial.[20] Outside of this specific context the Sanhedrin is mentioned only in three places: Jn 11.47, a passage which a number of scholars understand as a displaced scene from the trial of Jesus;[21] in Mk 13.9//Matt 10.17; and in our present passage Matt 5.32. With the second example (Mk 13.9//Matt 10.17), Matthew transfers this saying from its Markan setting to utilise it as part of his missionary discourse. Gundry links this verse with the historical situation of a Matthean Gentile mission. "Thus the mission that began with a limitation to Israel expands to include Gentiles. The expansion takes place because of rejection by Jewish courts and synagogues."[22] Proleptically, in 5.22, the consequence of calling a brother ῥακά[23] leads to judgement before the Sanhedrin. Thus Matthew has Jesus invert the accusations made by the opponents of the community. It is not members of the community who are liable to punishment by the Sanhedrin and the prospect of the Gehenna of fire. Rather, even those who insult the group with the apparently tame insults of ῥακά and μωρέ will find themselves liable to Sanhedrin justice and Gehenna fire.

---

contends, "In my opinion, v. 22 is an original unit which cannot be further dissected. The variation of πᾶς ὁ to ὃς δ' ἄν was required stylistically. Verse 22b,c furthermore contains a rhetorically extremely effective intensification of the punishment. It seems to me that this unified piece of tradition has its origin with Jesus." (Luz, *Matthew 1-7*, 281).

[20] The references to Jesus before the Sanhedrin in the context of the Passion story are to be found at Matt 26.59; Mk 14.55; 15.1; Lk 22.66.

[21] Although Brown argues for a nuanced understanding, he observes, "this session of the Sanhedrin, which according to Johannine chronology took place several weeks before the Passover (xi 55, xii 1), is not attested in the synoptic tradition. This fact, plus certain seeming inaccuracies about the role of the Pharisees in the Sanhedrin and the term of office of the high priest, has led many critics to regard xi 43-53 as a theological construction based upon material borrowed from the synoptics." (Brown, *The Gospel according to John I-XII*, 441).

[22] Gundry, *Matthew* 192.

[23] The exact sense of ῥακά is hard to determine with any certainty, although it appears to stand in some type of parallelism with μωρέ. Yet it is hard to determine whether this is synonymous parallelism (denoting an equal sense for these two terms), or step parallelism (whereby μωρε denotes an intensification in the name calling). Luz notes the lexical problems surrounding this term and comments, "ῥακά is most probably a transcription of the Aramaic word ריקא, a frequently used, relatively harmless word which probably had the meaning of 'hollow head'." (Luz, 282). Jeremias (TDNT vol 7, 975) notes that the vocalisation ῥακά (instead of ῥεκά) is likely to come from the Syriac raqa' and supports the hypothesis of a Syrian setting for Matthew's community (cf. 4.24).

4.2.3 Verses 23-24

After the threefold antithesis, Matthew's first example depicts how to avoid hostilities among brothers. The ethic of this parable is to illustrate the disjunction that can exist between cultic punctiliousness and an unforgiving attitude. Although the illustration presupposes the existence of both Temple and its altar, this is not anachronistic since the evangelist places the story on the lips of Jesus at a time when the Temple was still in operation.[24] Moreover, the source material used here may well come from a time when offerings were still able to be presented in the Temple.[25] Also in this material there is a marked shift in the use of pronouns from the foregoing section, the change being from the third person to the second. Hagner suggests, "this may be accounted for by the illustrative nature of the material and its character as personal application."[26] Alternatively, this grammatical inconsistency may reflect the existence of a seam in the tradition. Regardless of the correct explanation, it is important to note that whereas the antithesis of vv. 21-22 has both a polemical and pastoral intent, criticising those who taunt the Matthean community while consoling the group that they are not in fact the ones liable to Sanhedrin and Gehenna, in vv. 23-24 the focus is pedagogical instructing the community how to conduct its own internal relationships.

The fact that the parable focuses on individual responsibilities is obvious from the repeated use of second person singular forms. So, like the antithetical formulation in vv. 21-22, the emphasis falls on individual relationships. Guelich is correct in his assessment of the contextual link the example story of vv. 23-24 makes with the immediately preceding material.

---

[24] Stanton correctly allows for a degree of sophistication on the part of the original hearers of the gospel story, whereby the audience was able to discern between historicized aspects within the narrative and those aspects that directly addressed their own situation. In relation to the awareness of the original recipients he observes, "They would have known instinctively which parts of the story belonged to past history, and which parts were important for their ongoing community life. For example, they would have known it was both impossible and inappropriate for them to offer gifts at the temple altar (5.23-4)." (Stanton, *Gospel*, 380).

[25] Davies and Allison concur with this assessment and list three points in support of the conjecture. "5:23-4 would appear to be pre-Matthean, and possibly even dominical. For (1) the continuing existence of the sacrificial system in Jerusalem may be presupposed, and this suggests composition before A.D. 70 (while Matthew was composed later); (2) the elevation of brotherly reconciliation above sacrifice is consistent with Jesus' strong emphasis on loving one's neighbour; and (3) 5.23-4 is also perfectly in accord with the fifth clause of the Lord's Prayer, which puts forgiveness of others before God's forgiveness of oneself." (Davies and Allison, *Matthew,* vol 1, 516).

[26] Hagner, *Matthew 1-13,* 117.

Within the context of the first Antithesis, the parable, by focussing primarily on the need for reconciliation and restored relationships, has gone beneath the specifics in 5:22 and interpreted the demand for what it is, namely, a demand for restored relationships in which anger and invectives have no place. [27]

So Matthew, while creating a tripartite series of antitheses in v. 22 that focus on the tensions between his community and their opponents, is able to return to the intention of the primitive antithetical statement in 22a, by presenting a parable that calls for rapprochement between alienated individuals.

4.2.4 Verses 25-26

With the second example the evangelist returns to the judicial setting, with a clear link established to vv. 21-22 by the use of κρίσις/κριτής language. The material contained here in the Matthean narrative is drawn from Q, with the parallel occurring in Lk 12.58-59. Davies and Allison note how the change of context has realigned the emphasis of this parable. "Originally the parable probably gained its meaning from its eschatological context in the preaching of Jesus (cf. Lk 12.49-57)... In Matthew, this eschatological urgency has obviously receded to some extent and homiletical or common sense paraenetic motives have come forward."[28] However, apart from the change of context, Matthew also appears to have reworked the opening part of the source for his own redactional purposes. As Guelich suggests, "This difference may well reflect the difference in setting, with 5.25 being materially related to the basic theme of 5.23-24."[29] Whereas Matthew retains the Q designation of two of the characters, ἀντίδικος and κριτής, he replaces the reference to the ἄρχοντα with κριτής, making the narrative more uniform, and instead of the more technical Roman office of πράκτωρ he utilises the more general term ὑπηρέτης. Perhaps Matthew has refashioned the source material to better conform the roles of the characters to the offices of the adversaries engaged in the legal examinations experienced by the community.[30] This

---

[27] Guelich, *The Sermon on the Mount*, 190.

[28] Davies and Allison, *Matthew*, vol 1, 519.

[29] Guelich, *The Sermon on the Mount*, 191.

[30] However, Guelich, since he does not consider the possibility of Matthean redactional work reflecting his communal situation, arrives at the opposite conclusion. It is possible that Luke has introduced terminology that is judicially and technically specific to the Roman context. Thus he states, "Both Matthew and Luke note the judge (κριτής) as the one before whom the case opens. Luke 12:58 uses the more technical Roman judicial language (cf. ἄρχοντα =magistrate in 12:58a) with "bailiff" (πράκτορι) rather than the less precise *assistant* (ὑπηρέτης) of Matthew. Similar Greek usage of *assistant* in a court setting (Bauer, s.v.) makes allegorical usage (Strecker, *Weg.*, 159,

possibility is of course speculative and should not be pressed too far. However, this line of interpretation is supported to some degree by Luz, who emphasizes the reality of legal persecution for those in the Matthean group. He states, "Guards (court offices, as administrators of torture?) and trials were...familiar to the community of Matthew living in Syria."[31]

Once again it is possible to discern a piece of Matthean redaction that has been shaped to function at two levels. This second story stems from Q material, and may be authentic Jesus material, enshrining a call to avoid legal trials because of the eschatological urgency that it describes in its original context.[32] Thus while it sits comfortably on the lips of the historical Jesus, as the parable now stands it reflects the conflict situation that existed between the Matthean community and its adversaries, serving to issue a plea not to provoke legal hostilities. Moreover, at an individual level there is a call to enact reconciliation with any potentially litigious ἀντίδικος. This tension reflects a social situation where the evangelist's community, which had recently broken with its synagogue origins, is urging those still inside the synagogues to make the same decisive boundary-crossing journey. However, to those who remained faithful to their Jewish faith in its synagogue context, members of the evangelist's community had become apostates and traitors and thus were liable to reprisal. Such persecution acted as a salutary warning to others considering defecting from the synagogue community.

4.3 The Antithesis on Adultery (Matt 5.27-30)

This pericope consists of two components, the antithetical formulation of vv. 27-28, and the ensuing twin proverbial applications concerning the eye (v. 29) and the hand (v. 30). Here, as Meier notes, this antithesis functions to demonstrate that the Matthean Jesus "hardly revokes the letter of the Law prohibiting adultery; he simply states that lustful glances and a lustful

---

n.6) in Matthew quite untenable. Luke rather than Matthew, has most likely made the modification in any case." (Guelich, *The Sermon on the Mount,* 191-2). Contrary to Guelich, the use of ὑπηρέτης can be accounted for by suggesting it more accurately represents the social setting of the Matthean community.

[31] Luz, *Matthew 1-7,* 290.

[32] Davies and Allison are sympathetic to taking this material as authentic Jesus tradition. They observe, "Nothing stands in the way of tracing 5.25-6=Lk 12.58-9 to Jesus. (1) The conditions reflected, especially the role of the κριτής, point to Jewish territory; (2) the urgent eschatological orientation of the parable is consistent with Jesus' outlook; and (3) there is no good reason for doubting the passage's unity." (Davies and Allison, *Matthew,* vol 1, 519).

heart are just as bad."[33] Betz presents the ethical inference that underlies this material. He states, "the original intent of the prohibition calls for more than a simple compliance in the literal sense; it calls as well for the removal of the root cause through the control of one's erotic desires."[34] In this sense the second antithesis functions to exegete the principle of v. 20, showing how the righteousness practised in the community is to exceed that of its scribal and Pharisaic opponents.

4.3.1 Verse 27

The two elements that constitute this verse, the introductory formula and the traditional Torah based proposition, both occur is a more abbreviated form compared with the first antithesis. The formulaic opening drops the reference τοῖς ἀρχαίοις, most probably simply for stylistic reasons. Also in contrast to the initial antithesis, here the sparse apodictic command of Exod 20.14//Dt 5.18 (LXX) is quoted without appending the corresponding penalty outlined in case law (cf. Lev 20.10; Dt 22.22). This staccato presentation of the thesis allows the evangelist to focus fuller attention on the following antithetical formulation. Yet, while it is possible to speak in technical terms of an antithetical statement, as Davies and Allison correctly note, "there is no 'antithesis'. That is Jesus does not do away with the Torah injunction against adultery."[35] However, instead the tension stems from the implicit claim made by the Matthean Jesus to be the legitimate and authoritative interpreter of the Jewish law. Obviously this claim is supported by the evangelist and his community, but is rejected by their opponents. In this sense although the dominical pronouncement is aligned with Torah intent, implicitly the source of dispute arises because of the insistence that Jesus is entitled to arbitrate on these issues in a manner that places him above the law.

4.3.2 Verse 28

Jesus' pronouncement broadens the understanding of what constitutes adultery, by encapsulating not only physical acts but also inward thought. Yet, as Luz notes, the idea is not necessarily original on the part of Jesus. "it fits into the intensified interpretation of the sixth commandment which we can observe in connection with the concept of purity in Judaism at the time."[36] Close parallels exist in rabbinic literature. The *Mekilta* of R.

---

[33] Meier, *Law and History in Matthew's Gospel*, 136-7.

[34] Betz, *The Sermon on the Mount*, 231.

[35] Davies and Allison, *Matthew*, vol 1, 522.

[36] Luz, *Matthew 1-7*, 296.

Simeon III states "He is not to commit adultery...either by the eye or by the heart", also in *Pesiq. R.* 24.2 a similar ruling occurs, "Even he who visualises himself in the act of adultery is called an adulterer." Intensification of rules governing sexual relations are also present in the writings of the Qumran community. The Damascus Document in its regulation on marriage for those who live outside the actual Qumran site states, "If they dwell in camps according to the rule of the land and take wives and beget children, let them walk according to the word of the law, and according to the regulation of binding vows" (CD 7.6-8). Thus, while no DSS speaks of marriage at Qumran, for those living in the 'camps' the Torah stipulations are intensified by making marriage also subject to the binding vows, presumably required as part of one's adherence to the community.[37]

In this sense Jesus' declaration stands at one with that strain of Jewish thinking which sought to interiorize and deepen the understanding of what it meant to commit adultery. The equation between action and thought in effect puts punishment beyond the realm of casuistic law and locates it at the great assize when the intent of the heart might be assessed. This insight accounts for Guelich's conclusion that, "Jesus not only countered the Old Testament Law with its definition of adultery as an overt physical act between a man and a married woman, but he also countered the casuistic, judicial way in which one perceived the law."[38] Although there is a danger in Guelich's statement of caricaturing Judaism as an external legal code, nonetheless, the attitude of an internal ethic, presented in v. 28, subverts the Torah as an instrument of dealing with adultery. Therefore, the transition to the following sayings with their focus on eschatological fire becomes apposite. For only at the consummation of the age will the inner thoughts of the heart be known.

4.3.3 Verse 29-30

These twin sayings function like the two parables in the previous antithesis, in that they provide examples of the implication of Jesus' radical ethic. Here Matthew utilises material from his Markan source (Mk

---

[37] While their own writings do not bear testimony to marital practice Josephus discusses Essene marriage in two passages, *Jewish War* 2.120; 2.160-161. In the second passage Josephus speaks of the branch of Essenes who practice marriage (presumably those living in camps). He describes their attitude to sexuality in the following manner, "they give their wives, however, a three years' probation, and only marry them after they have by three period of purification given proof of their fecundity. They have no intercourse with them during pregnancy, thus showing their motive in marriage is not self indulgence but procreation of children."

[38] Guelich, *The Sermon on the Mount,* 194.

9.43, 47). The fact that Matthew reproduces these sayings in Matt 18.8-9 in an even closer parallel form has led some to propose that the material in 5.29-30 draws upon a doublet contained in Matthew's special source material.[39] However, on the basis of the Matthean compositional technique in the previous antithesis where he appends pedagogical material to the basic antithetical form, it is more likely that the joining of these two verses is due to redactional activity rather than the existence of a doublet that preserved these sayings in an alternative sequence.

The proverbial sayings present the seriousness of 'thought-adultery' by metaphorically presenting self-mutilation as a more preferable option than the consequent eternal annihilation. Gundry draws out some of the irony in the 'eye' saying. He notes, "σκανδαλίζει means 'trap' or 'cause to stumble', yet eyesight is supposed to keep one from falling into a trap or stumbling!"[40] Yet the use of hyperbole or overstatement reinforces the seriousness with which the Matthean Jesus treats lustful thoughts. Thus Sanders perceives this as a literary device for Matthew, "hyperbole...is a special form of concreteness."[41]

The tradition Matthew utilises from the Markan source (Mk 9.43-47) preserves three statements recommending mutilation of the hand (v. 43), the foot (v. 45) and the eye (v. 47). In Matt 18.8-9, the first evangelist preserves this ordering, although the πούς reference has been collapsed into the 'hand' saying making it a subsidiary rather than an independent injunction in v. 8, then in 18.9 the 'eye' saying is reproduced in close correspondence to the Markan form. By contrast in 5.29-30 the 'eye' saying is presented prior to the 'hand' saying and the reference to ὁ πούς has been totally deleted. This is not surprising. The subject of visual adultery naturally engenders the idea of punishing the eye, hence the redactional move of this saying to first place. However, the specific reference to ὁ ὀφθαλμός σου ὁ δεξιός is more difficult to explain. The adjective δεξιός used in relation to the eye is unique to this Matthean context, and while it may be natural to think of the right hand being a greater loss for most people than the left, there seems little to distinguish between the two eyes. It is best therefore to concur with the explanation of Davies and Allison that the reference, "'Right' is perhaps inserted to enhance the parallelism with the 'right hand' in 5.30."[42]

---

[39] For this proposal cf., Klostermann, *Matthäusevangelium*, 45. and Dupont, *Béatitudes*, 1:121-23.

[40] Gundry, *Matthew*, 88.

[41] Sanders and Davies, *Studying the Synoptic Gospels*, 178.

[42] However, Davies and Allison note references where the putting out of a right eye is a prescribed punishment. "For 'right eye' see 1 Sam 11.2 ('gouge out all your right eyes")"; Zech 11.17 ("May the sword smite his arm and his right eye')." (Davies and Allison, *Matthew,* vol 1, 524).

For Matthew, these radical acts of self-discipline encapsulate the quest for a higher form of righteousness. While the OT did not attempt to police 'thought adultery', for the Jesus of the first gospel, the consequences of imaginary acts of lust are treated as seriously, if not more so, than the physical acts they visualise. Here then, the desire is to demonstrate that the righteousness practised by the community's opponents is greatly exceeded by the interpretation of the law announced by Jesus, as demonstrated through the actual behaviour of members of evangelist's group. Behind this debate stands the implicit claim that Jesus is the legitimate and authorized interpreter of Torah for the Matthean community.

4.4 The Antithesis on Divorce (Matt 5.31-32)

The divorce antithesis is the shortest in this series of six Matthean formulations. It contains no parabolic or proverbial appendix that might serve as an example or pedagogical application. In this sense, in terms of form, it is the purest[43] of the six statements paralleling closely a number of the rulings in 4QMMT, which simply present the opposing viewpoint and the group's ruling in stark opposition.[44] Yet, despite the simplicity of form, a greater complexity arises in trying to determine the attitude of the redactor towards the law at this point. Specifically, has the evangelist undermined the law by removing the Torah's permission for a bill of divorce to be issued, or does he in fact, like the previous two antitheses, argue for a higher form of righteousness that can justifiably be derived from the intent of the Torah?

For Meier, it is the first option that describes Matthew's purpose, and the divorce saying represents a fundamental attack on the ongoing validity of the law within the evangelist's community. Ultimately, Meier's interpretation depends on his reading of the exceptive clause παρεκτὸς λόγου πορνείας which is unique to Matthew's gospel. He understands πορνεία as specifically designating incestuous Gentile marriages that were confronting the community because of their non-Jewish mission. Since Meier sees this clause as calling for the dissolution of marriages that were never divinely sanctioned, he argues that the clause in no way allows

---

[43] By describing this statement as the purest in form of the six Matthean antitheses, no claim is being advanced for its temporal priority. Simply the observation is drawn that it is closest in structure to the Qumranic antitheses of 4QMMT.

[44] Minear finds these features of the third antithesis so disturbingly different that he questions the authenticity of the pericope in its present Matthean location. He suggests, "The first step is to separate the third [antithesis] vv. 31-32) from the rest, because its form is so different, it deals with a different sort of problem, and it is on a level of thinking different from the others." (Minear, *Matthew: The Teacher's Gospel*, 49).

divorce of legitimate marriage in any circumstance. Thus he understands this antithesis to suspend part of the Mosaic Law. He proposes that, "what is being excluded by the *parektos logou porneias* clause is the lax practice of maintaining incestuous unions in the case of proselytes. Seen in this light Mt 5.32 is just as much an abrogation of the Mosaic Law on divorce in Dt 24.1 as is Lk 16.18."[45] However, opposing this viewpoint is the position adopted by Luz. Like the previous two formulations he sees this ruling on divorce still allowing for the dissolution of legitimate marriages (*contra* Meier), but nonetheless, in line with the call of 5.20 for a more exacting standard of righteousness, the grounds on which such divorce can be obtained are narrowed. Thus the law still holds force, but in a more specifically focused manner. As Luz himself puts the issue,

> How can one still speak of 'fulfillment of the law' in the sense of 5:17-19 with this antithesis formed by Matthew himself? Our text gives an answer only implicitly: with the possibility for πορνεία, a case is left in which one writes a bill of divorce in the sense of Deut 24.1.[46]

It is because Luz understands πορνεία in a broader sense than Meier, that he is able to understand the concessive clause allowing for divorce in line with the Mosaic permission, albeit in an even more restrictive, higher righteousness, sense. To decide on which of these reconstructions better suits the Matthean intent it is necessary to turn to the text.

4.4.1 Verse 31

This verse has no synoptic parallels and is best understood as a Matthean creation, formed to introduce the saying on divorce that has been taken over from the tradition. Bultmann arrives at this conclusion, seeing the antithetical formulation as due to redactional activity. He states, "In Matt. 5[31f.] the saying about divorce appears as an antithesis to the legal saying in Deut. 24[1.], while in Lk. 16[18.] (Q) and Mk. 10[11f.] it does not appear in antithesis, and this is doubtless the original version."[47] Like the two preceding antitheses this verse comprises of a formulaic opening, here in its briefest form, and a Torah reference, here to Deut 24.1. However, it should be noted that the Torah reference differs from the previous antitheses in two ways: firstly, it does not stem from the Decalogue; and secondly, it does not represent a direct citation of scripture.[48] The clause to

---

[45] Meier, *Law and History*, 150.

[46] Luz, *Matthew 1-7*, 301-302.

[47] Bultmann, *History of the Synoptic Tradition*, 135.

[48] Yet it must be noted that although v21 cited an apodictic ruling from the Decalogue it also combined this with a casuistic principle from Lev 24.17 that was not a

which Matt 5.31b alludes stands at the end of Deut 24.1, וְשִׁלְּחָהּ מִבֵּיתוֹ
וְכָתַב לָהּ סֵפֶר כְּרִיתֻת וְנָתַן בְּיָדָהּ. However, prior to regulating for a bill
of divorce, the text stipulates that such a course of action can only be
undertaken if the wife 'finds no favour in his [the husband's] eyes *because*
he has found some unseemliness (עֶרְוַת דָּבָר).' Scholars treat the meaning
of עֶרְוַת דָּבָר differently, but as it forms part of Deut 24.1, and that
appears to be the text that is in the evangelist's mind when formulating this
antithesis, it is likely that the Matthean understanding of the Hebrew
phrase will help explain the sense of the exceptive clause, παρεκτὸς λόγου
πορνείας. As is discussed in the appendix, the most likely sense here is an
act of sexual impropriety outside of the marriage union.[49]

4.4.2 Verse 32

Whereas the preceding verse represented a purely Matthean creation, the
evangelist clearly develops source material at this point. Tuckett observes,
"Matthew also has a parallel to the divorce saying of Lk 16.18 in Matt
5.32. The close proximity of the parallels to Lk 16.16,17,18 within Matt 5,
in vv. 17, 18, 32, thus add additional weight to the argument that these
verses belonged together in Q."[50] Kloppenborg concurs with this
assessment of Matt 5.32 as belonging to Q, and he argues that it is
relocated in Matthew's gospel to suit the intentions of the redactor. "Q
16.18//Matt 5.32, presumably transferred to the Sermon on the Mount by
Matthew and used in his antithesis on adultery and divorce (there is
scarcely any reason for Luke to move this saying from its Matthaean
position to its present Lukan location)."[51] Nonetheless, the question is
somewhat confused by the existence of the Markan parallel in Mk 10.11-
12, which Matthew clearly draws upon as his source in 19.9f. However,
there are sufficient differences in detail[52] to posit two separate forms of a
tradition (presumably going back to the historical Jesus), rather than to
postulate that both Lk 16.18 and Matt 5.32 have independently used Mk
10.11-12. As Davies and Allison state the case for two forms, "we thus
appear to have two slightly different traditions. In Mark the husband

---

direct quotation. Thus Matthew's handling of the text in v31 is not necessarily greatly
different to the earlier antitheses.

[49] For an extended argument in support of this option, see the excursus, 109-113.

[50] Tuckett, *Q and the History of Early Christianity*, 407.

[51] Kloppenborg, *The Formation of Q*, 79.

[52] In particular, Matt 5.32 and Lk 16.18 share the phrase πᾶς ὁ ἀπολύων τὴν γυναῖκα
αὐτοῦ, whereas Matt 19.9 and Mk 10.11 introduce Jesus' ruling on divorce as ὃς ἂν
ἀπολύσῃ τὴν γυναῖκα αὐτοῦ. These alternative linguistic formulations suggest two
possible underlying traditions.

causes the woman to commit adultery (because she, it is assumed, will remarry). Which of these two formulations is the more original cannot be determined (*pace* Guelich, pp. 200-2, who favours Mark)."[53]

Apparently in v. 32, the Matthean redactor introduces the following changes into the source material: (1) the prefacing of the Q saying by the adversative antithetical formulation ἐγὼ δὲ λέγω ὑμῖν ὅτι; (2) the deletion of the phrase καὶ γαμῶν ἑτέραν μοιχεύει; (3) the introduction of the exceptive clause with its consequence of causing the wife to commit adultery; and (4) the rewording of the final clause. The introductory declaration calls into question the legal ruling of v. 31, yet without necessarily denying the validity of Torah. Guelich understands its function in the following manner,

> Yet even 5:32a, set within the context of the Law, maintains the 'new' element of Jesus' teaching on divorce in comparison with Judaism. First, although 5:32a does not redefine adultery as do Lk 16:18a and Mark 10:11, it does maintain the focus on man's role in the act of adultery by assigning to him the responsibility for the wife's adultery. This assignment of guilt to the husband does not contradict or set aside the Law, but it goes beyond the Law in its extension of responsibility to the husband.[54]

While noting Guelich's anachronistic use of Judaism, viewed as a monolithic entity rather than a diverse collection of religious expression, it is possible to agree with his main thrust, namely that although the Law is not set aside in the divorce antithesis, its demands are again heightened.

Matthew's exceptive clause, παρεκτὸς λόγου πορνείας, is a redactional insertion[55] that reflects the communal attitudes and traditions of the evangelist's audience. As Luz comments, "Thus, in the Matthean community Jesus' prohibition of divorce was promulgated, unless there was a case of adultery. With this, it took up the basic Jewish conviction: unchastity is an abomination which desecrates the land of Israel."[56] It is in this context of traditional Jewish morality that the formulation of the antithesis reflects the origins of the community in a Jewish milieu. Moreover, the exceptive clause interprets the ruling of Deut 24.1 to define when divorce is permissible. For, as Davies and Allison argue, "the phrase appears to be based on the 'erwat dabar of Deut 24.1 (the LXX has ἄσχημον πρᾶγμα)."[57]

---

[53] Davies and Allison, *Matthew,* vol 1, 528.

[54] Guelich, *The Sermon on the Mount,* 202.

[55] A similar redactional addition is made with a variant form of the exceptive clause in Matt 19. 9, μὴ ἐπὶ πορνείᾳ.

[56] Luz, *Matthew 1-7,* 306.

[57] Davies and Allison, *Matthew,* vol 1, 528.

4.4.2.1 Excursus: The Meaning of עֶרְוַת דָּבָר

The exact meaning of the phrase עֶרְוַת דָּבָר is hard to determine since it occurs in the extant literature only twice, at Deut 23.15 and here at Deut 24.1. In BDB, the suggested translations of the feminine noun עֶרְוָה are 'nakedness' or 'pudenda', and specifically in relation to the construct chain עֶרְוַת דָּבָר BDB proposes the following options, '2. דָּבָר עֶרְוַת *nakedness of a thing*, i.e., prob. *Indecency, improper behaviour* Dt 23.15, 24.1.'[58] As the reference in Deut 23.15 (LXX 23.14) makes clear, the phrase is not exclusively used to denote sexual intercourse or fornication, for in that context it refers to the need for proper latrines outside the camp (cf. 11QT 46.13-16),[59] and the concomitant requirement to bury or cover human excrement. The 'nakedness of a thing' appears to refer here to human bodily functions in a general sense and not specifically to sexual transgression of the marriage relationship. However, in the context of Deut 24.1 the use of עֶרְוַת דָּבָר denotes some aspect of dissolving the marital bond, yet there is little indication as to precisely what might be this 'nakedness of a thing', which allows or provides evidence for divorce.

Versional evidence also illustrates a certain hesitation in rendering the sense of this phrase. In the LXX the generalized ἄσχημον πρᾶγμα is utilised for the translational equivalent. Yet this is still ambiguous, for as Betz realizes, 'The LXX translators took the expression in a more general sense as ἄσχημον πρᾶγμα, the Greek perhaps pointing to a legal matter as grounds for divorce; at least this is suggested by the story of Susanna where it clearly refers to adultery.'[60] BAGD supports the use of this Greek term ἀσχήμων as denoting an improper revealing of private parts. 'The word is applied esp. to sexual life... Hence τὰ ἀ. (it is probably unnecessary to supply μέλη) the *unpresentable*, i.e., *private parts*.'[61] Also LSJ notes the term is used euphemistically in the LXX 'for αἰδοῖν',[62] here also connoting 'private parts' or 'pudenda'. Thus on the basis of the LXX, and other usages of ἀσχήμων, it would appear that the Greek translators understood דָּבָר עֶרְוַת as referring to revealing one's private parts outside the marriage union, thus it functioned euphemistically as a designation for adultery or sexual irregularity.

However, in the Vulgate, Jerome appears to understand the Hebrew in Deut 24.1 not so much as referring to sexual indiscretion but rather to cultic impurity. He renders the verse in the following manner.

---

[58] BDB, *A Hebrew English Lexicon of the Old Testament,* Oxford: OUP, 1903.

[59] Commenting on the ruling in the Temple Scroll, VanderKam notes, 'The Temple Scroll offers legislation on the same subject [toilet habits] but in connection with the holy city of the sanctuary. "You shall make for them latrines outside the city where they shall go out, north-west of the city. These shall be roofed houses with holes in them into which the filth shall go down. It shall be far enough not to be visible from the city (at) three thousand cubits" (46.13-16). It has often been noted that, as the sabbath limit for a journey was two thousand cubits, the Essenes had to plan carefully so as not to defile the seventh day.' (VanderKam, *The Dead Sea Scrolls Today,* 86-87).

[60] Betz, *The Sermon on the Mount,* 231, also cf., note 384.

[61] BAGD, 119.

[62] LSJ, *A Greek English Lexicon,* 267.

> Si acceperit homo uxorem, et habuerit eam, et non invenerit gratiam ante oculos eius propter aliquam foeditatem: scribet libellium repudii, et dabit in manu illius, et dimittet eam de domo sua. (Vg. Deut 24.1)

The important phrase for the discussion is aliquam foeditatem (=for any reason of impurity), appears to envisage a wider frame of permission for divorce, not only on the basis of adultery, but also because of ritual impurity. This reading may superficially lend some support to Meier's thesis that the Matthean exceptive clause was legislating against incestuous gentile marriages.[63] However, it needs to be recognized that a possible rendering of the Vulgate translation of a Hebrew text that may lie behind the Greek of the exceptive clause is hardly a chain of possibilities that inspires great confidence.

In rabbinic literature the problematic nature of Deut 24.1 is also attested by the two competing interpretations characterized in Mishnaic debate. Guelich presents the opposing viewpoints in the following manner.

> On the one side, Rabbi Hillel and his followers took the phrase in a broader sense concentrating on *dbr* (a 'matter,' a 'case'). This larger umbrella covered such diverse actions as speaking disrespectfully of one's husband and burning his food (Str-B 1.314-17). On the other side, Rabbi Shammai and followers took the phrase in a narrower sense, concentrating on the term '*rwh* ('indecency'). This smaller umbrella covered primarily behavior contrary to the moral customs of the day, including not only adultery but appearing on the street with hair down, uncovered arms, or a slit in the sides of a skirt (Str-B 1.315).[64]

However, Betz claims that Matthew's text represents more faithfully the Shammaiite school of thought, which primarily 'took Deut 24.1 as implying adultery.'[65] This seems defensible on the basis of the Mishnaic evidence that limits divorce to those provable cases of unchastity.[66]

Therefore, the evidence for determining the meaning of עֶרְוַת דָּבָר is not totally uniform. On one side, the LXX rendering ἄσχημον πρᾶγμα, the usage in *Sus* 63 that explicitly refers to adultery and the viewpoint of Shammai give weight to understanding the phrase to depict an improper breach of sexual relations thus fracturing the marriage union. Alternatively, the Vg., which may allude to cultic pollution, and Hillel who promoted divorce on the grounds of 'the shame of any thing', suggest that the phrase allowed divorce under a wider range of circumstances. Therefore, the cumulative evidence reveals that Deut 24.1 was ambiguous and could be interpreted in a variety of ways. However, there appears to have been a slightly stronger tendency towards the first

---

[63] It must be stated that Meier does not employ the Vulgate rendering of the Hebrew to support his argument. Rather, he tries to derive the reference to incestuous gentile marriages from the usage of πορνεία in 1 Cor 5:1 and the apostolic decree (Ac 15:28-9), as well the perceived social problem in the Matthean community of trying to integrate Gentile converts who were already in marriages of closer blood relationship than allowed by the Jewish law.

[64] Guelich, *The Sermon on the Mount,* 203.

[65] Betz, *The Sermon on the Mount,* 247.

[66] The Mishnaic evidence is as follows, *m. Git.* 9.10, (translation of Danby, Mishnah, 321): 'the School of Shammai say: A man may not divorce his wife unless he has found some unchastity in her, for it is written, *Because he hath found in her* indecency *in anything.*'

possibility, namely that this was a reference to sexual transgression as the basis of a divorce case.[67]

As the excursus on עֶרְוַת דָּבָר argues, the evidence favours the possibility that in the context of Deut 24.1 the term refers to those illegitimate sexual acts performed by the wife with a partner other than her husband, i.e., unchastity. Meier's conclusion, that all the clause excludes is "the lax practice of maintaining incestuous unions in the case of proselytes",[68] and therefore that 5.32 can be read as an abrogation of Torah, cannot be sustained. There is no explicit (or implicit) connection in the text with the issue of incestuous marriages and his lexical argument draws upon a narrow range of πορνεία usage, thus making the conclusion dubious. Therefore, while in some texts πορνεία can denote incestuous marriages (cf. 1 Cor 5.1), there is no reason to understand the term as being limited to this meaning in the present Matthean context.

The final clause of the divorce antithesis, καὶ ὃς ἐὰν ἀπολελυμένην γαμήσῃ μοιχᾶται, envisages and condemns the involvement of a third party who marries the divorced woman. The import of the argument appears to stem from the woman's status as one guilty of πορνεία. Implicitly, this verdict of guilt in relation to sexual impropriety excludes remarriage as a possibility for such a woman within the community. As Davies and Allison suggest

---

[67] Meier's protest that 'the LXX never translates "erwa as *porneia*"', (143), hardly seems perspicacious. Not only is עֶרְוָה a rare word, but also as has already been shown, as is the case in Deut 23.15 (LXX 23.14), it can be used in contexts that have no relation to sexual or marital matters. Rather, it is a euphemistic term employed to avoid direct reference to things involving nakedness or impurity, and the LXX follows this euphemistic usage with its translation ἄσχημον πρᾶγμα. However, since Matthew wished to make his position clear to the readers of the gospel narrative, it is no surprise that he used the more direct and explicit term.

[68] Meier, *Law and History*, 150. Meier notes that this theory can be traced back to Baltensweiler ('Die Ehebuchsklauseln bei Matthäus. Zu Matth. 5,32; 19,9,' 340-56). Baltensweiler proposes two contexts from which to view the exceptive clause. (1) Marriage practice in the ancient Mediterranean world; and (2) NT references to πορνεία. However, the meaning of the exceptive clause in a Jewish context, and specifically in relation to Deut 24.1 is not taken as a primary frame of reference. Helpfully, Hill gives a clear summary of this position. "Baltensweiler (*TZ*, XV, 1959, 340-56) argues that *porneia* indicates a marriage contracted within prohibited degrees of kinship (Lev 18.16-8; cf. Ac. 15.28-9)…Such marriages were contracted among pagans and tolerated by Jews in the case of proselytes: they would have become a problem for the legalist Jewish Christian circles, and Matthew might have been prepared to permit divorce in such cases. In doing so, he was not far from the absolute prohibition; in fact he would be maintaining the sanctity of marriage by condemning illicit unions." (Hill, *The Gospel of Matthew*, 125).

If a woman has been divorced because of πορνεία, then she is an adulteress and it would be clearly wrong to marry her. If, on the other hand, the cause for her divorce was something else, then she was according to 5.32a, unlawfully divorced (as πορνεία is the only valid reason for divorce); therefore she cannot be free to marry another.[69]

Thus while Matthew does not seek to rule out the possibility of divorce (although he limits the occasions on which it can be obtained), he appears, in his quest for a higher righteousness, to make the Torah permission for remarriage a logical impossibility. This should not however, be read as an intentional portrayal of Jesus abrogating the divorce law, to do so is to fail to recognise the logical consequence of the antithetical statement.[70] By seeking a narrower attitude to the divorce legislation promulgated in Deut 24.1 the Matthean redactor wished to portray his Jesus as upholding the true spirit of the law. However, while not wishing to present Jesus as opposing the law in this antithesis, unwittingly the evangelist may have created a logical conundrum, whereby the possibility of remarriage allowed by the Torah is no longer an option consistent with the narrow grounds upon which divorce may take place within the Matthean community.

4.5 The Antithesis on Oaths (Matt 5.33-37)

For Bultmann, this fourth antithesis constitutes part of his proposed series of three traditional antitheses, comprising of the first, second and fourth statements in Matthew's sixfold list.[71] In relation to those three supposedly traditional formulations (vv. 21f., 27f., 33-37), he argues,

---

[69] Davies and Allison, *Matthew,* vol 1, 532.

[70] Thus, contrary to Meier, at this point the evangelist is not directly trying to attack the validity of the law. Instead, his call for a higher form of righteousness is not logically consistent with the broader basis for divorce in Deut 24.1. If the evangelist intended this as an attack on the validity of Torah itself, his meaning was quite opaque. However, it is the presentation of Jesus as interpreter of the law and the one who brings the higher righteousness that comes to the fore.

[71] Bultmann summarises his position on the tradition history of the antitheses in the following statement. "Thus the older formulation $5^{21f., 27f., 33-37}$ has given rise to the analogous formulations, in which unattached dominical sayings have found a home. The motive for the formulation is clear: the antithetical form commends itself by its catechetical character." (Bultmann, *History of the Synoptic Tradition,* 136). The influence of Bultmann's proposed division, although now waning, has been enormous creating the standard reference to the first, second and fourth antitheses as traditional, and the third, fifth and sixth as redactional or secondary. However, as is recognized by a number of scholars, and as is suggested here, the division between tradition and redaction is far more complex. Thus it is argued that it is possible to detect the evangelist's

for these passages the antithesis was plainly never an isolated saying, for it is only intelligible in relation to the thesis, and does not have the form of a mashal. Finally, in distinction from the secondary formulations, these three passages are alike in putting the thesis in the form of a prohibition (οὐ φονεύσεις, οὐ μοιχευσεις, οὐκ ἐπιορκήσεις), and this prohibition is not abolished, but surpassed.[72]

Specifically in relation to the fourth antithesis dealing with oaths it is possible to question both of Bultmann's points. Namely, it is not obvious that the antithesis was never an isolated saying, nor does it appear certain that the prohibition against oaths simply surpasses the law, and does not in fact abolish Torah legislation.

Firstly, in relation to the assertion that the antithetical statement of v. 34 could never have stood in isolation from the thesis of v. 33, it needs to be noted that while there is no gospel parallel to this material, the saying in James 5.12 that is related to Mt 5.34f. does in fact stand without the foregoing thesis. No literary dependence between James and Matthew is being suggested here, only the observation is being drawn that a saying like Matt 5.34 could, and in fact does, exist without the contrasting thesis. The relationship between the saying in James and its Matthean counterpart is complex, and is probably best understood in the cautious manner proposed by the Jesus Seminar, "Fellows of the Seminar concluded that the surviving pronouncements on the subject of oaths probably mask something Jesus said on the subject...The parallel in James suggests that fragments of vv. 34-35 and 37 may be original with Jesus, while the balance of the formulations in 5.33-37 are the work of Matthew."[73] Moreover, the composite nature of Matt 5.33-37 has been recognized by a number of scholars, primarily on the basis of the catalogue of prohibited forms of oath in 34b-6, which appear redundant after the total prohibition of v. 34a.[74]

---

editorial work not only in the secondary antitheses, but also in those formulations that Bultmann classified as traditional.

[72] Bultmann, *History of the Synoptic Tradition,* 135.

[73] Funk, Hoover, and the Jesus Seminar, *The Five Gospels*, 143.

[74] Davies and Allison also see a tension between the ὅρκους of v33b, which they take to mean vow and not an oath, and the command of 33a, 'Do not make a false oath.' On this basis they suggest, "When to all these observations we add that the subtraction of 33b and 34b-6, leaves a perfectly coherent piece, it is inviting to conclude that the original unit consisted only of 5.(33a), 34a + 37." (Davies and Allison, *Matthew,* vol 1, 533). It needs to be noted that their reference to 5.33a appears not to include the opening formula, but only the command οὐκ ἐπιορκήσεις, more correctly designated as 5.33aβ. However, the bracketing of this element shows that they consider its place in the original unit as being questionable. On balance, it appears more likely that the evangelist is responsible for all of v33, and he then developed an independent logion, of the kind attested by James 5.12, to form the expanded antithesis of 5.34-37.

Bultmann's second claim, that the antithesis does not abolish the law, is rejected by a number of commentators who see it presenting a real abrogation of the use of oaths as prescribed in the OT. Discussing the fourth antithesis Meier notes that it does revoke definitively the OT institution of oaths, and this cannot be understood simply as the removal of permission, as was the case with the ruling on divorce. Rather, as Meier states,

> in a few cases a vow or oath was specifically commanded or imposed by the Law. In these cases, the command of the Torah is directly revoked (e.g., the oath imposed on a neighbor who was supposed to safeguard a man's goods, when those goods are stolen or lost, Ex 22:6-7, 10; the oath imposed on a woman suspected of adultery Num:19-22; cf. also the general unconditional commands in Dt 6:13; 10:20).[75]

Thus, there appears to be a clear sense in which the Matthean Jesus, on the basis of his own authoritative reinterpretation of Torah, categorically rejects the religio-judicial institution of oaths. Luz, who views the prohibition as having its origin with Jesus, argues, "Jesus in v. 34 articulates a fundamental and unrestricted (ὅλως) prohibition of oaths. Probably he was the first person to draw from the critical attitude towards oaths which was widespread in antiquity the consequence of a fundamental prohibition."[76] However, despite the natural reading of v. 34a as a total ban on oaths, Guelich holds that the statement only redefines the practice of swearing and cannot be read as the rejection of the institution. Therefore he contends, "the demand of the antithesis *transcends* the demand of the premise...the rejection of swearing is set against perjury. In other words the 'Law' is transcended by the counter-demand."[77] This assessment is dubious, since it fails to give due weight to the radical nature of Jesus' demand, instead the conclusion seems to be driven by the desire to have the so-called traditional antitheses (the first, second and fourth) present a Jesus who upholds the law, albeit in a more ethicized sense, whereas only in the later redactional formulations is the new element of contradiction or abrogation introduced. The evidence and tradition history appear more complex. Ultimately, Guelich's reconstruction suffers because it is not

---

[75] Meier, Law and History, 150. From this evidence Meier notes the contrast with the divorce law that regulated for an acknowledged negative situation. In opposition, oaths are positively assessed in Torah writings, and their use is explicitly commanded in certain cases.

[76] Luz, *Matthew 1-7*, 313-14. While Luz is more than likely correct in his assessment, Josephus reports a similar attitude on the part of the Essenes *(Bell.* 2.135). However, the extant material from Qumran demonstrates that group members were required to use an oath as part of the entrance rite into the community (1QS 5.7-9). On this basis it appears best to speak of an aversion towards oaths at Qumran and not a total prohibition.

[77] Guelich, 'The Antitheses of Matthew V. 21-48: Tradition and/or Redaction?' 450.

supported by the data, since the fourth antithesis is most naturally read as an authoritative rejection of oaths by Jesus.

4.5.1 Verse 33

Matthew's preference for triadic structures is reflected here with the resumptive πάλιν creating a division that makes a split between the first and last three statements in the sixfold antithetical table. As Wiefel comments, "Die vierte Antithese schließt sich redaktionell durch πάλιν an die drei vorausgehenden an, ist jedoch formal und inhaltlich von ihnen deutlich geschieden."[78] This division is further supported by the restatement of the full form of the introductory formula, which is used to open both series of three antitheses (cf. v. 21). This provides further evidence of the careful literary structuring of 5.21-48 in the final stage of its composition, with the formulaic openings to each of the six antitheses being part of the framework created by the Matthean redactor.

After the introductory formula, as Hagner notes, "the evangelist presents *not* a quotation from the OT, as in the first two antitheses, but a crystallization of OT teaching on the subject (cf. Lev 19.12; Num 30.2; Deut 23.21-23; cf. Zech 8.17)."[79] The first part of the Matthean scriptural pastiche, οὐκ ἐπιορκήσεις, is most closely paralleled by the ruling in Lev 19.12a, וְלֹא תִשָּׁבְעוּ בִשְׁמִי לַשָּׁקֶר. Interestingly, the LXX rendering, καὶ οὐκ ὀμεῖσθε τῷ ὀνόματί μου ἐπ᾽ ἀδίκῳ, prohibits swearing in God's name when it is linked with unrighteousness. The plea in v. 20 that calls for a righteousness exceeding that of the community's opponents may partially explain Matthew's rejection of oaths, since they can be associated with unrighteousness. It is significant that in the final antithesis the redactor explicitly makes use of this δίκαιος/ἄδικος contrast (5.45). Yet this interpretation, although interesting, should not be pressed, since Matthew does not develop this point explicitly and it is hard to demonstrate that the evangelist was drawing upon the LXX. More plausibly, Saldarini sees the rejection of oaths as reflecting the conflict situation of the evangelist's community. He observes, "Matthew disagrees with a group which stresses the fulfilment of vows."[80] Moreover, within the gospel this negative critique of oaths and vows recurs, not only in the closely related woe contained in Matt 23.16-22, but also at a number of other points. The same attitude is present in the rejection of the Korban vow in Matt 15.3-6

---

[78] Wiefel, *Das Evangelium nach Matthäus,*Theologischer Handkommentar zum Neuen Testament, 113.

[79] Hagner, *Matthew 1-13,* 127.

[80] Saldarini, *Matthew's Christian-Jewish Community,* 156.

(although Matthew avoids using this Aramaic term), and strikingly the issue is intrinsically present in the trial narrative, where in contrast to both the false oaths brought against Jesus,[81] when adjured to speak under oath he replies with integrity but without a vow.[82]

The second part of the scriptural reference recalls the charges of Num 30.2 and Deut 23.21-23, which states that vows should be honoured because they are made to God, and he is the one who requires their fulfilment. However, the language is most closely paralleled in Ps 50.14, 'but you shall pay your vows to the Most High.' Gundry explains how this citation has been utilised to fit the Matthean context. He states,

> By substituting oaths for vows in the quotation of Ps 50:14, Matthew assimilates the passage to the topic of oaths. The ensuing prohibition of swearing confirms this shift in terminology, and the association of vowing and swearing in Num 30:3 shows how easy Matthew found the shift.[83]

Thus, with this compressed and composite citation, Matthew is able both to succinctly encapsulate the sense of the OT teaching on this topic, yet by not employing lengthy verbatim quotations he focuses the hearers' attention on the authoritative counterproposal issued by Jesus.

4.5.2 Verse 34a

As in verses 22, 28 and 32, Jesus' antithetical proposal opens with the declaration ἐγὼ δὲ λέγω ὑμῖν, but does not continue as did the three previous antitheses with the phrase ὅτι πᾶς ὁ... In fact this new abbreviated form becomes the fixed pattern in the final three antitheses (cf., vv. 34, 39, 44). This is not merely a stylistic alteration. Rather, the emphasis changes from being a commentary on the actions of a hypothetical third party, instead becoming a direct appeal to the audience to conform to the imperative of the antithesis. Davies and Allison mention this alteration in passing, but do not comment on the heightened impact it

---

[81] Also compare Peter's misuse of swearing (Matt 26.72, 74).

[82] Approaching the use of oaths in Matthew's gospel from the perspective that she describes as speech-act theory, Brant comments on this critique of oaths in the gospel as a literary device that underscores the power of God in contrast to the evil intent of oaths. Thus Brant states, "The oaths of Matthew's narrative set into motion events that are ordained by God. The oaths all have evil or wrong-headed intent, but God's plan works out anyway. The power of evil is real in that it can bring about Jesus' death, but its ultimate goal is thwarted by God's plan of redemption through that death. Jesus' warning that oaths are from evil must be placed in the context of the eschaton. Evil becomes impotent. Oaths are from evil and the effect they wrought is evil but evil is disarmed. The oaths lead to death, but death has no dominion." (Brant, 'Infelicitous Oaths in the Gospel of Matthew', 19-20).

[83] Gundry, *Matthew*, 92.

creates for the audience.[84] The command made to the community is the absolute μὴ ὀμόσαι ὅλως, which is most naturally read as a total prohibition against oaths. France gives one of the most direct assessments of the antithesis that gives due weight to its reversal of the law. He correctly sees that "the elaborate system of oaths and vows is undercut by the simple principle, 'Do not swear at all', with the implication that the legislation of the Old Testament 'comes from evil' (5.33-37)."[85] The absolute statement forbidding the use of vows has been seen by some scholars as standing in tension with the following list of specific oath forms that are not to be used by community members. Yet this exclusive contrast between the general command and the specific examples may be creating a false dichotomy between the two statements. Whereas v. 34a may preserve pre-Matthean tradition, the series that follows is perhaps the redactor's way of spelling out part of the range of that absolute prohibition.[86] The reference to heaven and earth in this sequence may also be part of the tradition (cf., James 5.12).

4.5.3 Verse 34b-36

This material is helpfully split into two sections by Davies and Allison, namely vv. 34b-35 and v. 36. The first section is unified both in terms of theme and structure. Thematically the three parallel clauses all debar the use of circumlocutions for the divine name as a valid oath form. The three excluded forms all reflect the Jewish notion of the ineffability of the Tetragrammaton, and the concomitant need to find a suitable replacement when making an oath, (cf., *m. Sebu.* 4.13; *m. Ned.* 1.3; *m. Sanh.* 3.2; Str-B 1, 332-4).[87] Structurally, the triadic arrangement is formed by the exact parallelism that exists between the three clauses. The three objects that are ruled out as possible referents for oath formulae are heaven, earth and Jerusalem. Likewise, James 5.12 has a threefold prohibitory list comprising of heaven, earth and any other oath, (μήτε τὸν οὐρανὸν μήτε

---

[84] Davies and Allsion state, "Here the introduction, as in 5.39 and 44, prefaces an imperative (contrast 5.22, 28, 32)." (Davies and Allison, *Matthew,* vol 1, 535).

[85] France, *Matthew,* 193.

[86] Luz argues that 34b-35 is secondary to the opening half of 34. He states, "The expansions from the Old Testament of the three substitute swearing formulas in vv. 34f. are secondary. Since they are beautifully symmetrical, they have been formulated in one process." (Luz, *Matthew 1-7,* 313).

[87] This use is summarised by Davies and Allison. "According to Deut 6.13 and 10.20 oaths should be in God's name. But by the first century that name could no longer be pronounced. So one of the unstated assumptions behind 5,34b-6 is that God's name itself could not be named and that, therefore, when one takes an oath, a substitute for God's name must be used." (Davies and Allison, *Matthew,* vol 1, 536).

τὴν γῆν μήτε ἄλλον τινὰ ὅρκον). In comparison, Matthew's list contains the specific reference to Jerusalem instead of the generalized reference to any other oath. Moreover, in the Matthean sequence each element is suffixed by an explanatory comment showing how that oath impinges upon the divine realm. Hagner understands the rejection of these oath forms in the following manner,

> All oath taking implicates God, is in effect to swear by his name, and thus all oath taking is to be understood as possessing an absolute character. But whereas this might well have served the point Jesus wanted to make, i.e., the necessity of an absolute integrity, he goes further to the quite shocking initial statement that oath taking is altogether unnecessary, and since it serves no purpose, should be avoided. Therein lies the real antithesis.[88]

Thus, these triple examples of improper oaths do not serve to limit the general principle of v. 34a, rather they show that all oath forms are to be equally rejected. It is therefore not necessary to read vv. 34b-36 as creating a tension with the absolute prohibition of v. 34a, instead they portray the consistency with which oaths are to be rejected by the evangelist's community.

The statement in v. 36 likewise rejects another alternative oath form, however, it differs both in style and content from the three preceding oaths. The content no longer concerns the impingement on the divine realm, but upon human powerlessness. The structure partially follows the 'μήτε ἐν...+ reason' form used in vv. 34b-35, but differs in the first element by the addition of the genitive form of the second person singular pronoun followed by the verb, while the reason is no longer a positive statement about God's realm but a negative comment concerning human impotence. Furthermore, Luz note a change in tone. He states, "The tone of this verse is one of wisdomlike resignation, similarly to Matt 6.27, 34."[89] These factors have led Davies and Allison to question the authenticity of this verse in its present context, instead they suggest it is post-Matthean addition to the gospel.[90]

---

[88] Hagner, *Matthew 1-13*, 128.

[89] Luz, *Matthew 1-7*, 317.

[90] While Davies and Allison are not explicit in stating that this verse was a post-Matthean addition, this is the clear implication of two of their statements. First, they note in relation to the threefold pattern of 34b-35 that, "The neat triadic structure of these perfectly parallel clauses argues for 5.36 being a late addition, for 5.36 breaks the pattern of 5.34b-35." (536-37). While they clearly take 5.36 as being later than 5.34b-35, at this point it is not certain who made the addition. If 5.34b-35 were considered Matthean source material, it would be conceivable that they were referring to 5.36 as an addition to the tradition by the evangelist himself. However, this possibility is ruled out, since they state in relation to v. 36, "Because this verse destroys the triadic structure of the qualifications in 5.34-6, and because Matthew loves triads, 5.36 is not likely to be

The prohibition relating to swearing by one's own head is not, however, totally foreign to the context, although it admittedly introduces a new nuance to those types of oaths explicitly rejected by the evangelist. Also, it is not correct to state that it breaks the foregoing triadic structure, since its content marks it off from that material. Moreover, this example also fits the Jewish setting of oaths, as swearing by one's head is attested in *m. Sanh.* 3.2. Thus, while introducing a new aspect into the type of oaths forbidden by the absolute prohibition of v. 34a, it is possible to see the redactor both developing the threefold structure already attested in the James parallel and attaching the originally independent logion of v. 36. This results in the creation of a sequence that parodies the oath taking practices of the opponents of the Matthean community. It is no longer possible to tell if community members had been pressed to take oaths using such forms in their persecution by synagogue authorities. However, after the decisive break with nascent Judaism the group is instructed to reject all forms of oaths and vows, and to use in their place simple affirmations of integrity.

4.5.4 Verse 37

In the final verse of the fourth antithetical statement, the Matthean Jesus offers his alternative to oaths and vows, either a ναὶ, ναί or οὖ, οὖ This imperative is again addressed to a second person group, in the historical setting the disciples of Jesus, but in the narratival world of Matthew the

---

assigned to his hand. This is consistent with word statistics" (537). The clear conclusion of their argument is that they consider 5.34b-35, in its present form, to be Matthean as can be detected from its developed triadic structure, further, since v. 36 breaks this structure, it is therefore both late and non-Matthean, thus it is a post gospel addition. This is obviously the correct conclusion, since they cite other commentators who hold this view as corroborative evidence. While concurring with a number of their observations, the conclusion implied by Davies and Allison does not necessarily follow. The parallel in James 5.12 shows that the triadic structure of rejected oaths may well be pre-Matthean, although the evangelist has here recast and expanded this triple structure thereby enlarging the unit so that each prohibited oath has a corresponding reason for its rejection. Moreover, while the language of v. 36 may not be strictly Matthean, (Davies and Allison note, "Only κεφαλή (Mt 12; Mk 8; Lk 7) and ἡ (Mt 60; Mk: 33; Lk: 45) might be considered Matthean favourites. μέλας is a synoptic *hapax legomenon.*)" (537, n. 40), it is at least as feasible that when Matthew redacted the existing triadic structure, as evidenced by the James parallel, at the same time he combined an additional saying (v. 36) from another source, which was thematically related by its exclusion of another type of vow. In its favour, this reconstruction is supported by the textual evidence of all extant mss, since nowhere in the tradition is v. 36 omitted. Obviously Davies and Allison's proposal would be greatly enhanced if v. 36 was missing is any strand of the textual tradition. This, however, is not the case.

auditors of the gospel. The alternative of simple affirmations or negations creates an obvious dichotomy with those whose praxis involved swearing by heaven, earth, Jerusalem or even the very hairs of their head. After the redactional development of the primitive threefold form attested by Jas 5.12, in v. 37a the evangelist is much more closely aligned with the material in James. Gundry comments on this coincidence between the two form of the tradition stating,

> Back in close parallel with the dominical tradition, Matthew characteristically inserts λόγος (16,2 – not in Jas 5:12). The definite article with λόγος replaces the definite article with the first ναί (cf. James). This replacement favors a change of meaning from 'let your yes be yes and [your] no [be] no' (so James; cf. Philo *Spec.* 2.1 §4) to 'let your word be 'yes, yes, no, no.'[91]

Obviously, for Matthew these double responses should not be construed as alternative forms of oath taking, instead they are emphatic declarations of the integrity of the speaker's statements. The intention is to stress the absolute nature of the rejection of oaths by Jesus, and not to present a new dominically instituted utterance paralleling the practice of the synagogue opponents.

The second part of the verse, with its use of περισσόν, recalls the use of this terminology in 5.20, there entailing a call for abounding righteousness. Here however, the connotation is negative. Matthew is rejecting any formulation that goes beyond the simple responses cited in the first part of the verse. In this final redactional comment in the fourth antithesis,[92] Matthew states that despite surface references to God in oath taking, such uses of the divine name (or circumlocutions in its stead), are in fact ἐκ τοῦ πονηροῦ. The use of the definite article before πονηρός is in all likelihood an allusion to the devil, rather than to either some abstract personification of evil, or to an evil person (cf. Matt 13.19, 38).[93] This association between vows and the Evil One, coupled with the absolute prohibition of v. 34a, provides a strong case for seeing an abrogation of Torah legislation in this antithesis by the Matthean Jesus. This categorical rejection of the religio-legal institution of swearing

---

[91] Gundry, *Matthew*, 92-93.

[92] The use of typically Matthean vocabulary in this clause, (περισσεύω/περισσός, Matt: 7; Mk: 2; Lk: 13 and πονηρός Matt: 26; Mk: 2; Lk: 13), as well as the fact that the concluding statement deviates from the parallel tradition in Jas 5.12, all make a strong case for the identification of v. 37b as a redactional product.

[93] Betz wishes to associate these prohibited oaths with magical formulations, and thus sees this clause suggesting that oaths originated in the demonic realm. In a note he comments, "Overtones of demonic evil cannot be denied, because 'oath' was understood since Hesiod to be a demonic being. See Hirsel, *Eid*, 142-49." (Betz, *The Sermon on the Mount*, 271, n. 598.). While the passage does link oaths with evil, contrary to Betz, there is no apparent reason to see the use in Hesoid providing the background to this association.

oaths is made on the basis of Jesus' authoritative counterproposal. While such a declaration held sway in the Matthean community, the use of oaths remained commonplace among the Torah observant group. Thus the critique of oath taking and the citation of specifically forbidden forms is intended to call into question the practice of the synagogue opponents, and further, to associate their actions with the evil one.

4.6 The Antithesis on Retribution (Matt 5.38-42)

In this fifth antithetical formulation Jesus is portrayed as speaking against the law of retribution (*lex talionis*), legislated by the conditions described in three different passages, Ex 21.24; Lev 24.20; and Deut 19.21. Although the Exodus and Deuteronomy references have five elements in common (life for life, eye for eye, tooth for tooth, hand for hand, foot for foot), the ruling in Leviticus parallels the other two prescriptions in terms of the eye and tooth sayings. Thus it appears that Matthew has presented the thesis in terms of the most readily recognizable form of Pentateuchal legislation, but once again, this highly abbreviated form ensures that the accent falls more fully on the counterproposal that follows, rather than upon the primary thesis that is being rejected.

Guelich, however, makes a compelling case that Deut 19.21 is the text foremost in the evangelist's thinking, since it likewise involves a judicial setting, shares common terminology with Matt 5.38-39a (ἀντιστῆναι and τὸν πονηρόν), and finally the case similarly involves a false accuser.[94] Thus in the antithetical series another reference to courtroom settings is to be found. This coheres with both the first antithesis, which spoke of being liable to courts and sanhedrins, as well as the preceding statement, where the use of oaths most naturally suggests a juridical background. Such allusions may reflect the experience of the community's recent past, prior to their split with the synagogue. However, the setting and background material from Deut 19.15-21 are carefully chosen and crafted in such a manner that they fit both the

---

[94] It is helpful to quote the parallels that Guelich adduces between Deut 19.15-21 (LXX) and Matt 5.38-39a to fully appreciate the strength of his argument. "First, the setting of Deut 19:16 involved the hypothetical trial of a false witness, a most appropriate and hardly coincidental sequel to the previous Antithesis. Second, the false witness had accused (ἀντήστε) his brother in court (19:18). Third, the penalty was based upon the *lex talionis* principle by assigning to the false accuser the same penalty that would have been incurred by the accused. And fourth, the reason given for such action was to remove the *evil one* (τὸν πονηρόν) from the community. All four elements found in Deut 19:16-21 constitute the premise and antithesis of 5:38, 39a. Furthermore, the judicial setting extends to the next two commands of 5:39b, 40 (cf. Luke 6:29)." (Guelich, *The Sermon on the Mount,* 220)

community's recent turmoil and reflect the Matthean presentation of the trial of Jesus. The opening statement in Deut 19.15, 'One witness shall not rise up against a man for any iniquity,' recalls the false testimony brought against Jesus, as does the critiques of oaths in the previous antithesis. Moreover, the use of ἀγγαρεύσω (v. 41) which perhaps occurs in the context of a traditional saying,[95] may also function in the Matthean narrative as a literary allusion to the passion story. As Gundry suggests, "ἀγγαρεῦσαι probably anticipates the story of Simon of Cyrene, whom Roman soldiers requisitioned to carry Jesus' cross (27.32)." [96] This may well imply that while the evangelist has shaped traditional material to address the contemporary situation of his community, he also wishes them to recognise points of contact between what they experience and Jesus' own experience of suffering.

At a source critical level, Matthew appears to have created the antithetical formulation of vv. 38-39a, but appended to this redactional creation the four traditional sayings that explain the meaning of Jesus' alternative proposal in v. 39a. Three of these four sayings have Lukan parallels and may correctly be classified as Q material. However, Davies and Allison also wish to view v. 41 (unparalleled in Luke) as part of Q, but dropped by Luke in accordance with his favourable portrayal of Roman authorities.[97] However, this may be incorrect since Matthew alone has the reference to being press-ganged for service (Matt 5.41). Moreover, if this saying was part of Q it would appear to overload the number of examples (Luke's version already has two pairs of balanced double sayings). Thus, it appears more accurate to speak only of those verses that are paralleled in Luke as stemming from the Q source, and to see v. 41 as either an independent tradition or a redactional creation that Matthew has combined with the Q material. This redactional process is reflected in the composition of the fourth antithesis where the independent saying concerning swearing by the hairs of one's head (5.36) was attached to the underlying common source attested in Jas 5.12.

---

[95] Davies and Allison suggest that this verse does not originate with Matthew. They argue, "The appearance of *mille* is especially appropriate in 5.41 given the context - Roman requisitioning;...the vocabulary does not move us to claim redactional composition; further Luke may have omitted 5.41 because of his general tendency to exonerate the Romans." (Davies and Allison, *Matthew,* vol 1, 546-47). The view that v. 41 represents authentic Jesus tradition is also supported by the Jesus Seminar. "Among the things Jesus almost certainly said is the trio of 'case parodies' in Matt 5:39-41, with parallels in Luke 6:29. These cleverly worded aphorisms provided essential clues to what Jesus really said. And the consensus among the Fellows of the Seminar was exceptionally high." (Funk, Hoover, and the Jesus Seminar, *The Five Gospels,* 144).

[96] Gundry, *Matthew,* 94.

[97] See the reference in note 98. (Davies and Allison, *Matthew,* vol 1, 546-47).

4.6.1 Verse 38

The introductory formula to the second antithesis in the second group of three, ἠκούσατε ὅτι ἐρρέθη, parallels exactly the form used to commence the second antithesis in the first triad. This reflects the careful structuring of the entire antithetical sequence by the final redactor of this material. As was the case with the third and fourth antitheses, the compressed citation of scripture that follows the introductory formula, serves to present an accurate summary of the intent of Torah legislation, rather than to provide a lengthy verbatim quotation. This allows attention to be focussed on the Jesuanic antithesis that follows. The reference ὀφθαλμὸν ἀντί ὀφθαλμοῦ καὶ ὀδόντα ἀντὶ ὀδόντος is contained in three Pentateuchal passages (Ex 21.24; Lev 24.20; Deut 19.21), but the conjunction καὶ is not present in the LXX of these passages, nor is there a conjunctive *waw* in the MT of these verses.

4.6.2 Verse 39a

Following the slightly modified antithetical form used in the second triad of antitheses, the first five words ἐγὼ δὲ λέγω ὑμῖν μὴ..., reproduce the formula used by the Matthean Jesus in the previous antithesis. The new imperative stated by Jesus is an unequivocal rejection of retributive justice and a plea for passivity, μὴ ἀντιστῆαι τῷ πονηρῷ. As Meier correctly observes,

> This is perhaps the clearest and least disputable case of annulment in the antitheses. Probably one cannot even speak of *permission* being annulled. Such introductory phrases as Dt 19:21a ('and you shall show no pity') indicate an obligatory command rather than a permission. The same note of obligation in seeing strict justice done is clear throughout the context of the three passages cited.[98]

---

[98] Meier, *Law and History*, 157. Guelich concurs that this is a fundamental rejection of Torah judicial stipulations. He states, "The fifth Antithesis strikes at the very basis of legal justice. The Law's explicit basis for such justice, the *lex talionis*, stands over and against Jesus' demand of not seeking vindication from the evil one in court. In other words the implication of this Antithesis..., set aside rather than supersede the Old Testament Law." (Guelich, *The Sermon on the Mount*, 224). Further, these sentiments are echoed by Hagner and Luz in their respective commentaries. However, in contrast, Davies and Allison reject any contradiction here between the OT and the NT. They arrive at this conclusion by suggesting that Jesus' radical ethic is limited to individual application and does not entail the rejection of institutional practice. Thus they argue, "While in the Pentateuch the *lex talionis* belongs to the judicial process, this is not the sphere of application in Matthew. Jesus, to repeat, does not overthrow the principle of equivalent compensation on an institutional level – that question is just not addressed – but declares it illegitimate for his followers to apply it to their private disputes." (Davies

While the general sense is clear, precisely who or what τῷ πονηρῷ designates is open to interpretation. Lexically, there appear to be three major options: (i) to take it as a reference to Satan = 'the evil one' (cf. 5.37), this option has the strength that it fits with the most likely reading of the usage in the preceding verse; (ii) to understand a reference to evil in general, i.e. 'Do not resist evil', perhaps reflecting a usage similar to that in 1 Thess 5.15; (iii) to see it denoting the specific person against whom the law of retribution could be brought, i.e. 'Do not resist the evil person', in its favour, this option reflects the background material from Deut 19.19-21. Further, in support of the final alternative being the sense intended by the evangelist, is the way in which the sequence of attached sayings exemplifies the behaviour of passive non-resistance towards specific individuals who are unjust oppressors. Thus Hare entertains the possibility that the opponents denoted in 5.39 may have been, "personal enemies or religious opponents."[99]

4.6.3 Verse 39b-41

Matthew follows this antithetical statement with three specific example that each portray how the evil person is not to be resisted, namely, by turning the other cheek (v. 39b), not withholding one's own possessions (v. 40), and going the extra mile (v. 41). These are not simply admonitions to suffer injustice, although taken at face value they call for an attitude whereby the oppressed invite further oppression and deprivation. Yet, taken at a deeper level, Luz sees them as a critique of those powers that seek to debase humanity. He feels that such actions are "the expression of a protest against any kind of spiralling force which dehumanises the human being... In them is to be found a gentle protest and an element of provocative contrast to the force which rules the world."[100] Although these sayings have been recast in a Matthean context, it is still likely that they reflect this subversive element, whereby the aggression enacted by the adversaries of the community is to be overcome by the non-violent reaction of group members. That at least is the ideal that Matthew presents in the gospel.

The first illustrative saying is linked to the preceding antithesis by the conjunction ἀλλά, which in all likelihood is redactional. The Matthean form of the saying (cf. Lk 6.29a), presents a slightly fuller form, as well as changes in vocabulary, ῥαπίζω and στρέφω for Luke's τύπτω and παρέχω

---

and Allison, *Matthew,* vol 1, 542). However, it is difficult to see where this distinction is reflected in the text.

[99] Hare, *The Theme of Jewish Persecution,* 122.

[100] Luz, *Matthew 1-7,* 328.

respectively. It is hard to determine the word combination that better reflects the source. For Gundry, it is Matthew who has altered the original form as preserved in Luke. Therefore he suggests, "Matthew replaces τύπτοντί (so Luke) with its synonym ῥαπίζω and παρέχε (so Luke) with στρέφον."[101] However, Davies and Allison come to precisely to the opposite conclusion, "Matthew's ῥαπίζω and στρέψον (both in Did. 1.4) probably reproduce Q, Luke's τύπτω (Mt: 2; Mk: 1; Lk: 4; Acts: 5) and παρέχω (Mt: 1; Mk: 1; Lk: 4; Acts: 5) being redactional. If so, Luke would preserve Q except in his choice of verbs."[102] While these divergent reconstructions show that the range of evidence is too narrow to arrive at any firm conclusion, the word statistics do reflect some interesting (if not decisive) trends. First the term ῥαπίζω is rare in the NT occurring on only two occasions, but both of these are in Matthew (5.39; 26.67), although the cognate noun occurs three times (Mk 14.65; Jn 18.22; 19.3). It is not possible to decide whether the two occurrences in Matthew show significant redactional intent. Matt 26.67 is the evangelists reworking of Mk 14.65, but the modification of the noun form into a verbal construction is probably due to stylistic reworking, and hence, not theologically significant. The fact that Matthew has not introduced ῥαπίζω into the context of 26.67, but only modified the form may lend slight support to it being present in the source behind 5.39. Nonetheless caution seems best in this case. In relation to the term στρέψω, it occurs 6 times in Matthew and 8 times in Luke (3 times in Acts). It is interesting that on each occasion it occurs in Luke's gospel the form is identical στραφείς (2nd aorist passive participle). By contrast Matthew shows great variety in the forms he employs (5.39; 7.6; 9.22; 16.23; 18.3; 27.3). None of these six Matthean usages has a Lukan parallel which shares the verb στρέψω, and in fact only 5.39 and 9.22 have Lukan parallels (Lk 6.29 and 8.48) This makes it extremely difficult to determine if Matthew has a consistent attitude to this term. Yet, whereas Luke is always uniform in his usage, Matthew seems less concerned about the verb στρέψω, and this may support Davies and Allison's contention that the first evangelist has preserved both verbs as contained in Q. However, the evidence is far from conclusive and no firm decision can be advanced.[103]

---

[101] Gundry, *Matthew*, 95.

[102] Davies and Allison, *Matthew,* vol 1, 543.

[103] Luz notes that the evidence of second century sources does not assist the determination of the wording of Q. He states, "The numerous variants in the Apostolic Fathers and in the Apologists hardly help in this reconstruction" (Luz, *Matthew 1-7,* 323). Parallels are contained in *Didache* 1.3-5; Ignatius, *Pol.* 2.1; *2 Clem.* 13.4; Polycarp, *Phil.* 12.3; Justin, *Apol.* 1.15.9-13; 16.1f.; *Dial.* 96.3.

However, while certainty, is not possible in relation to the verb forms, the addition of the specific δεξιάν is almost certainly an addition due to the hand of Matthew, with this same term being a redactional addition in the second antithesis (5.29-30). Jeremias argues that this addition is highly significant since he views the act of striking the right cheek as a symbolic (as well as a real) insult given to the disciples by those who accuse them of being heretics. Thus he suggests, that this is not "reaction to a general insult, but...outrage suffered as a consequence of following the suffering saviour."[104] However, this reconstruction is problematic. If, as is suggested, this saying has a dominical origin, it is hard to see why the disciples of the historical Jesus would be treated as worthy of humiliating blows. Moreover, the identification of members of the Matthean community as 'heretics' is difficult to glean from the redactional addition of δεξιάν. Rather, all that can be stated with certainty is that in terms of the pastoral needs of his community, Matthew saw this traditional saying as giving meaning to the new ethic of not using retributive justice.

The second appended saying is also paralleled by Lk 6.29, but with significant differences both in vocabulary and structure. Perhaps the only area of commonality, apart from the conceptual coincidence, is the use of the two clothing terms, ὁ χιτών and τὸ ἱμάτιον, although their order is reversed in the two accounts. Again, it is not possible to determine with any significant degree of probability which order is original. However, the introductory phrase καὶ τῷ θέλοντί σοι κριθῆναι is almost certainly Matthean redaction since it again brings to the fore the evangelist's concern to avoid legal disputes (5.25-6), and once again places an antithesis in the context of a court setting (5.25, 31, 33). Thus reflecting the tone of 5.25, the follower of Jesus is entreated to placate the one who is both opponent and oppressor. In relation to the subject matter of vv. 25-26, Overman notes, "These verses may also apply to reconciliation between a community member and someone outside the community who wishes to initiate legal proceedings against the member. In vv. 25-26 the aim of this reconciliation is to avoid being brought into court, which is not an institution that served the Matthean community well."[105] This theme is seen to re-emerge in the present antithesis through the presence of judicial terminology in this clause. Thus, the first evangelist recasts the tradition in order to portray that stage of the community's life when some form of

---

[104] Jeremias, *The Sermon on the Mount*, 29.

[105] Overman, *Matthew's Gospel and Formative Judaism: The Social World of the Matthean Community*, 96. Since the court scene is also apparent in the fifth antithesis, Overman likewise sees the issue of reconciliation rather than litigation emerging in vv38-42. He argues that this suggests a pattern of reconciliation in order to avoid the judicial consequences of trial before courts.

quasi-legal prosecution had been a real threat. Rather than becoming embroiled in such judicial controversies, a conciliatory attitude is presented as the effective means of countering such overt hostilities.

The third specific saying on the theme of passive non-resistance is unique to Matthew's account. Its opening clause, καὶ ὅστις σε, parallels the introduction to v. 39b, and thus may an indicator that it is due to redactional reworking. However, there is also the possibility that the saying was attached at the pre-redactional stage. It is also possible that both elements are possible: a traditional saying that has undergone editorial reshaping. However, the similarities between 5.39b and 41 definitely point to redactional activity.[106] While the saying reflects the Roman practice of requisitioning goods or transportation (ἀγγαρεύσω),[107] within the macronarrative it also anticipates the incident when Simon the Cyrene is press-ganged to carry the cross. Once again a striking example is utilised to illustrate that community members are to subvert the violent overtures of their adversaries through non-resistance.

4.6.4 Verse 42

As a conclusion to the fifth antithesis, Matthew moves from the three specific examples cited, to express the general principle that underpins these situationally based illustrations. Yet, as Davies and Allison observe, the connection with the foregoing material is somewhat loose. They state,

> Mt 5.42=Lk 6.30 was originally no doubt isolated. It does not really fit the present context well, which is about revenge and love of enemies; and in 5.42 the disciple is no longer a victim. Furthermore, there is an independent variant in Gos. Thom. 95, and it is bound to nothing before or after: 'If you have money do not lend at interest, but give to the one who will not be able to give it back.'[108]

Therefore, Matthew has allowed the saying to stand in its present context because he found it already associated with the two examples in Q 6.29, although he has supplemented the source with the logion about going the extra mile, thereby creating a triad of specific examples that illustrate the antithetical statement of v. 39a, which calls for non-opposition.

As a whole, the fifth antithesis rejects the *lex talionis* as a principle that can be operative in this new community. Obviously, for many members this

---

[106] As Davies and Allison suggest, " the parallelism between 5.39b and 41 could well be in part due to Matthew: ὅστις + σέ + verb + object + verb introducing command is the construction in both places." (Davies and Allison, *Matthew*, vol 1, 547).

[107] See Horsley, *New Documents Illustrating Early Christianity,* vol I, for documentation of the practice of requisitioning, and ἀγγαρεύσω as a technical term to describe this acquisition of transportation and supplies for travelling Roman officials.

[108] Davies and Allison, *Matthew,* vol 1, 547.

marked a decisive change in attitude to that inherited from their Jewish background. The linking of this abrogation with judicial language and a court setting, both in terms of the subject matter of the antithesis and the reference in v. 40, may reflect the recent experience of the community. In place of the misuse of Torah legislation that has been directed at the evangelist's group, Matthew calls for a different standard of justice, as exemplified in vv. 39b-42. Guelich correctly paraphrases the sentiments of the antithesis in v. 39a as "you shall not oppose an evil person in court," and he concludes, "As an apodictic command, the antithesis categorically prohibits legal retaliation against an offending party."[109] While at a theological level this might be part of the desire to demonstrate a new ethic and a higher righteousness, at a functional level it may be motivated by a concern to extricate the community from the judicial authority exercised by their synagogue opponents.

4.7 The Antithesis on Love of Enemies (Matt 5.43-48)

The final antithesis is linked thematically to the preceding formulation, in that it calls upon its hearers to display a radical attitude towards adversaries and enemies that does not respond either with retaliation or hatred. Schottroff observes, "the command to love enemies is an appeal to take up a missionary attitude towards one's persecutors."[110] In the aftermath of its breach with Jewish synagogues, and in the process of engaging in the first tentative stages of Gentile evangelization, the evangelist's group viewed itself as persecuted, but presented as its ideological goal the desire not to respond in like measure. For the evangelist's community such persecution primarily appears to have emerged through conflict with Jewish authorities (5.25; 10.17), but there is also concern about the reception that will be received when the group engages more actively in mission to the Gentiles (10.18).[111]

---

[109] Guelich, *The Sermon on the Mount*, 220.

[110] Schotroff, 'Non-Violence and the Love of One's Enemies', 23. However, Schotroff notes that such a radical ethic can stimulate provocation from one's adversaries. "The challenge may not have pleased their enemies at all. Hence it is only partly true to say that love of enemies is the central content of Christian proclamation. It is certainly also a *means* for mission and conversion." (93).

[111] This does not necessitate accepting Hare's thesis that the Jewish mission had come to an end for the Matthean community, and at the time of the writing of the gospel the community was only proselytising Gentiles. (See Hare, *The Theme of Jewish Persecution of Christians*, esp. 167-171). However, persecution from the Jewish group that opposed the Matthean community does seem to be one of the factors that led to a more positive attitude towards engaging in Gentile mission.

Many of the themes in this final antithesis are anticipated earlier in chap. 5, especially in the concluding beatitude. In that final extended blessing, (5.11-12), there is a marked shift from the general third person form of address, to the striking second person language spoken directly to community members. Although this composition draws upon Q material (Matt 5.11-12//Lk 6.22-23), the final beatitude has correctly been recognized as both containing traditional material and editorial reworking,[112] primarily because of its high proportion of Mattheanisms. Moreover, Meier notes the disparity between the shorter form of 5.10,[113] also dealing with persecution and the extended treated treatment of the same topic in 5.11-12.[114] However, this double treatment of the topic with the forthright address directly to the community corresponds with the literary function of the final antithesis (5.43-48). While Matthew had already made the switch to second person plural forms at the beginning of the second triad of antithetical statements rather than presenting third person examples (cf. 5.34), the terminological similarities between the final beatitude and the closing antithesis reveal that the evangelist is again treating the theme of persecution. This threat had been very real for the group, resulting in their exclusion from the synagogue and their liminal existence outside of their familiar religious environment.

The similarities between the beatitude and the antithesis are: (i) the use of persecution language in both contexts, διώκω, 5.11, 12 and 5.44; (ii) continued use of πονηρός, 5.11//5.44; (iii) the references to οὐράνος, 5.12//5.45; and (iv) the mention of reward, μισθός, 5.12//5.46. In the final antithesis the addition of διώκω and οὐράνος is redactional, while the correspondence in the use of πονηρός and μισθός is due to the use of Q tradition that used such language to described an earlier persecution

---

[112] The redactional process appears to involve a number of stages. The initial stage is probably due to Q, whereby the extended format paralleled in Lk is introduced in order to address the *Sitz im Leben* of persecution in the Q community. Matthew then utilised this material since it readily aligned with the situation of his own community, but reworked this material by including typically Matthean expressions.

[113] This verse is usually seen as a redactional creation. See Bultmann, *History of the Synoptic Tradition*, 110.

[114] Meier comes to the following conclusions regarding the compositional history that resulted in the attachment of 5.11-12 to 5.10. He comments, "the short Matthean beatitude on persecution for justice's sake (5.10) collides awkwardly with the longer Q beatitude on persecution that follows immediately and ends the whole series (5.11-12). Indeed, so gauche is the succession of the two beatitudes on persecution that is difficult to imagine the literarily skillful Matthew going out of his way to manufacture a second beatitude on persecution to stand ungainly alongside another that was already disproportionately long. The juxtaposition is much more likely the result of two different traditions of beatitudes than an inept *creatio ex nihilo* by Matthew." (Meier, *A Marginal Jew*, Vol. 2, 334-35).

experienced by that community. Thus in terms of content there are important points of contact between the final beatitude and the closing antithesis in the Matthean narrative. This connection is not surprising, since Matthew has taken up the Q source in the final antithesis, which he broke off from following at the end of his list of beatitudes. Thus in Luke, the love of enemies command (Q 6.27) followed on directly from the intervening final woe, which reflects the language of the closing Q beatitude (6.22-23). Yet Matthew has developed the language of ostracism and hatred that originally depicted the experience of the Q community, and has transformed it into a heightened description of persecution, thereby reflecting the recent turmoil in his own group. In particular, the exclusion of his group from the synagogue meetings (Matt 4.23; 9.35; 10.17; 12.9; 13.54; 23.34) of his Jewish opponents has caused the feelings of bitterness that the evangelist speaks out against in the charge to 'love your enemies.'

4.7.1 Verse 43

As with all the antitheses, both the opening formula and the primary thesis are unparalleled in the gospel tradition. However, there is perhaps some deviation in the closely structured usage of introductory formulae that has been present up to this point, which consisted of the careful paralleling of the formulae in the two triads of antitheses. Whereas here one might have expected the introductory formula to read 'Ἐρρέθη δέ, thus producing an exact correspondence between the third statements in both triads of antitheses,[115] Matthew opts for the slightly fuller 'Ηκούσατε ὅτι ἐρρέθη, found also in the second (5.27) and fifth (v. 38) antithetical statements. Here the evangelist has formed the introductory formula and primary thesis in order to introduce the climactic antithesis which is shaped out of material that originally followed on from the concluding beatitude.

---

[115] Such a parallelism is expected on the basis of the matching of formulae previously seen between corresponding elements in the first and second triads. Thus, there is a parallelism between the first and fourth elements, the second and fifth, but the pattern breaks down with the third and sixth element, where in the sixth antithesis the evangelist reverts the form used in the second and fifth antithetical formulations.

First:'Ηκούσατε ὅτι ἐρρέθη τοῖς ἀρχαίοις   Fourth:'Ηκούσατε ὅτι ἐρρέθη τοῖς ἀρχαίοις
Second:'Ηκούσατε ὅτι ἐρρέθη   Fifth: 'Ηκούσατε ὅτι ἐρρέθη
Third: 'Ερρέθη δέ,   Sixth: 'Ηκούσατε ὅτι ἐρρέθη

While the breaking of an otherwise highly organized pattern is somewhat unusual, it may simple reflect Matthew's preference for the 'Ηκούσατε ὅτι ἐρρέθη form over the highly abbreviated 'Ερρέθη δέ. Moreover, while certainty is of course impossible, it may be the case that the verb of hearing, ἀκούω, is important in the context of persecution referred to in this final antithesis. It is possible to speculate that the community had 'heard' firsthand their adversaries reject them as neighbours and instead command hatred of those now ostracised from the synagogue.

The thesis that Jesus comments upon in the following verse consists of two imperatives. The first, ἀγαπήσεις τὸν πλησίον σου, derives from the apodictic Torah command of Lev 19.18 וְאָהַבְתָּ לְרֵעֲךָ כָּמוֹךָ (MT). The final element, 'as yourself' may have been dropped for two reasons. Firstly, it is extraneous to the basic command and as has already been seen, Matthew prefers to keep the statement of the legal precept under discussion to a minimum. Secondly, the simple ἀγαπήσεις τὸν πλησίον σου allows for a parallelism to be developed with the second imperative, which could not be formulated so as to contain the 'as yourself' reference. In the opening imperative Matthew's text parallels exactly the LXX, of course without the final ὡς σεαυτόν.

The second imperative, καὶ μισήσεις τὸν ἐχθρὸν σου, is more problematic since it is not contained in the OT. While similar sentiments may be found in certain texts (Deut 7.2; 20.16; 23.4,7; 30.7; Ps 26.5; 137.7-9; 139.19-22), the closest parallel in Jewish tradition is to be found in the 1QS 1.10-11, which in relation to those outside the group commands members 'to hate all the sons of darkness, each according to his guilt at the time of God's vengeance.' This loose parallel in no way evidences a reaction from the evangelist that can be construed as responding to Essene teaching.[116] Rather, it appears that Matthew has stated what was for him the obvious corollary of the halakhic understanding of love of neighbours, namely hatred of enemies, and it is this implication that he rejects. Whether this corollary was one drawn by Matthew in light of his community's experience at the hands of its adversaries, or reflected the wider hermeneutical understanding of Lev 19.18 circulating in formative Judaism, is hard to determine. For McNeile it is the latter option that appears most likely. However, while he states in relation to this imperative to hate enemies, "the remainder of the verse is an inference which the Rabbis might draw from such a passage as Dt. xxviii. 4-7,"[117] he offers no evidence from the rabbinic material to support his conclusion.

---

[116] This statement is made in contrast to certain reconstructions that view the Qumran community as the unidentified addressees of the Matthean polemic. (See Davies, *The Setting of the Sermon on the Mount*, 245-48 and O. Seitz, 'Love Your Enemies', 39-54).

[117] McNeile's comments suggest that his statement may be sustained at least from Talmudic evidence. He states, "The teaching of the Talmud, as a whole, hardly goes beyond the present verse: it enjoins patience under injuries, kind treatment of others in order to receive the equivalent, love of proselytes and those who are well disposed to the Law; but of love to enemies it says nothing." (McNeile, *The Gospel according to St. Matthew*, 71). However, it needs to be noted that neither does it say anything concerning hatred of enemies. Therefore McNeile's argument from silence is a non-argument.

4.7.2 Verse 44

This verse consists of three elements, Jesus' authoritative speech marker, ἐγὼ δὲ λέγω ὑμῖν (cf., 5.22, 28, 32, 34, 39), the command to love enemies and the injunction to pray for persecutors. The first element, which introduces the alternative ruling agrees with the form used in the five previous antitheses, but is unique in that it is the only time this formula has a partial parallel in the source material. The Lukan version of the saying opens with the phrase, ᾽Αλλὰ ὑμῖν λέγω τοῖς ἀκούουσιν (Lk 6.27). On this basis Dupont,[118] Manson[119] and Davies,[120] have suggested that this reflects traces of an original antithetical formula that lay behind the Q tradition. However, the sixfold repetition of this formula, five of which appear certainly redactional, speaks against this proposal.[121] Even the more circumspect proposal of Guelich seems to miss the most natural explanation that the antithetical formulation is a creation of the first evangelist. He puts forward the following idea,

> rather than being the vestigial remains of the antithetical format, this phrase found by Matthew in the Q tradition may well have served as the catalyst for his introducing the Antitheses whose introductory formulas reflect a certain catch-word similarity.[122]

Yet the most likely explanation remains that here the expression is redactional, as elsewhere in the antitheses, and this partial parallel that exists here is purely coincidental.

The next two elements, love of enemies and prayer for persecutors, both stand in opposition to the second imperative in v. 43, 'hate your enemies.' Matthew has cited this received tradition in a manner that puts it on an equal footing with the quotation from Lev 19.18. While the initial counterproposal is drawn directly from the source shared with Luke (Lk 6.27), the second counterproposal replaces the three statements from Lk 6.27b-28. However, the Matthean command, προσεύχεσθε ὑπὲρ τῶν

---

[118] J. Dupont, *Les Béatitudes: Le problème litteraire. Les deux version du Sermon sur la Montangne et des Beatitudes*. 189-91. Yet his position appears weakened by the fact that he sees the adversative ἀλλά of 6.27 as being the product of Lukan redaction. This appears to remove the antithetical force that he wishes to ascribe to the underlying tradition.

[119] Manson, *The Sayings of Jesus*, 161.

[120] See Davies, *The Setting of the Sermon on the Mount*, 388.

[121] It does, however, need to be noted that Matthew is capable of taking up an element from a source and repeating it elsewhere in his narrative. An example of this is the insult γεννήματα ἐχιδνῶν that Matt takes over from Q (Matt 3.7/Lk 3.7), but reproduces independently on two separate occasions (Matt 12.34; 23.33). However, the antithetical formulae are not simply repeated at unrelated points throughout the narrative, but are carefully structured to contribute to the literary flow of 5.21-48. thus it seems best to see all six introductory formulae as stemming from the evangelist.

[122] Guelich, *The Sermon on the Mount*, 225.

διωκόντων ὑμᾶς, utilises the term προσεύχεσθε although it is now co-ordinated with a new referent, 'persecutors'. It is interesting to note that the singular references to τὸν πλησίον σου and τὸν ἐχθρὸν σου, have been transformed into the plural for both the subject and the object of the twin commands in v44, τοὺς ἐχθροὺς ὑμῶν and τῶν διωκόντων ὑμᾶς. While the plural 'your' represents historically the disciples and in terms of reader response considerations the Matthean community, it is appropriate to ask about the identity of the plural enemies and persecutors of the struggling and marginal community of the first evangelist. Betz answers the question by considering the wider narrative of the Sermon on the Mount. He states, "they must be the same as those described in SM/Matt 5.11, 12, that is, fellow Jews for whom the Christian community represented 'heresy'."[123]

It is problematic to determine whether this sixth antithesis suspends or deepens the law. Clearly, the double pronouncement in v. 44 directly opposes the statement in v. 43 to hate one's enemies. Yet although this imperative is countermanded in Jesus' antithetical utterance, the difficulty arises since v. 43b is not part of Torah legislation. For Meier this is the clinching observation that categorically demonstrates the Law is not here abrogated. Therefore he comes to the following conclusion, "No matter what its origin, the last part of vs. 43 is not a citation of written Torah. Consequently, Jesus' prohibition of hatred of enemies cannot be considered a revocation of the letter of the Torah."[124] While the logic of Meier's argument may initially appear correct, the situation is not as straightforward as he suggests. It has already been observed that in the series of antitheses Matthew does not always cite Torah legislation exactly, rather a tendency has been recognized whereby he abbreviates, summarises and even crystallizes its rulings. In the latter part of v. 43 he presents a statement as though it were part of the received tradition, or at least an obvious implication or formal corollary of the initial injunction that is itself undoubtedly drawn from the Torah. While the command ἀγαπήσεις τὸν πλησίον σου is intensified, upheld and given wider application, it is equally true that the imperative μισήσεις τὸν ἐχθρὸν σου, presented as authoritative tradition, is rejected, revoked and replaced. Thus here, Matthew clearly attacks an attitude which he presents as being embedded

---

[123] Betz, *The Sermon on the Mount*, 313. However, in line with his theory that the Sermon on the Mount circulated as an essentially complete unit prior to its incorporation into the Matthean macronarrative, he sees it addressing the experience of persecution of the putative group that stood behind the documents composition. While disagreeing with his reconstruction of the tradition history of SM, it is natural to see it addressing the communal experience of alienation from the Jewish parent group. Yet, since the Sermon is demonstrably a Matthean redaction product, it is more appropriate to identify the persecuted party as the community of the first evangelist.

[124] Meier, Law and History, 139.

in Torah tradition. Therefore, like the preceding two formulations, this antithetical statement is intended to be read as an obvious rejection of the tradition presented as law in the opening thesis of v. 43.[125]

4.7.3 Verse 45

Promise of filial relationship with God is based upon embracing the radical ethic that Jesus calls for in v. 44. Here is an example of the tendency that Saldarini describes whereby, "the Matthean group's relationship with the Father further illuminates its self-perception."[126] There is a partial parallel to this verse in Lk 6.35b, καὶ ἔσεσθε υἱοὶ ὑψίστου ὅτι αὐτὸς χρηστός ἐπὶ τοὺς ἀχαρίστους καὶ πονηρούς, however, the wide divergence makes it difficult to determine the original form, and in all likelihood the source has undergone independent modification by both redactors.[127] The examples of divine provision of sun and rain serve as pedagogical motivation for the community to be loving towards opponents in the same manner that this illustration portrays God blessing even those who can be characterized as evil or unrighteous. Like the antithetical statement of v. 44, this saying rejects any distinction between groups that are to be loved or hated. All alike are to be loved by the community. They are called to be encompassing in their attitude of love and prayerfulness both for adversaries and community members. In this context the connection with the seventh beatitude (5.9), 'Blessed are the peacemakers, for they shall be called sons of God,' forms a thematic link with this logion and reflects the call for a conciliatory attitude, which the evangelist portrays as resulting in the promise of an eschatological relationship with God.

---

[125] While reaching the somewhat facile conclusion that the Law is not revoked since μισήσεις τὸν ἐχθρόν σου is not, properly speaking, Torah, even Meier concedes that there is a strong note of repealing tradition in this final antithesis. He states, "One must admit, though, that of the three antitheses we have just examined No. 6 comes closest to revocation, since it is opposed to a number of passages in the OT where hatred of enemies is approved." (Meier, Law and History, 139).

[126] Saldarini, *Matthew's Christian-Jewish Community,* 93.

[127] While Fitzmyer argues that Luke preserves the more original form, he also detects redactional activity on the part of the third evangelist. He states, "*sons of the Most High.* Matt 5:45 has, 'sons of your Father in heaven.' Since the latter phrase is also found in the Matthean Our Father (6.9; cf. 7.21), it probably reveals that Matthew has changed the original form of "Q." The Lucan phrase echoes the OT *huioi hypsistou* (Ps 82.6). The singular of this title has been applied to Jesus in 1.32." (Fitzmyer, *The Gospel According to Luke I-IX,* 640). Alternatively, Luz argues that Matthew has the more original form. "In v. 45 Matthew, who speaks in concrete pictures, deserves priority to Luke, who formulated theologically." (Luz, *Matthew 1-7,* 339). On balance, although certainty is impossible, Fitzmyer appears to present the more convincing argument, but it is likely that both evangelists have introduced changes to the source material.

4.7.4 Verse 46-47

This unit offers the second reason for obeying the radical demand issued by Jesus to love enemies and to pray for persecutors (5.44), namely that such indiscriminate love that is the hallmark of the transformative power operative in the group leads to eschatological reward and, moreover, is a sign of their abounding righteousness.[128] In contrast to the promise of filial relationship given in v. 45, which Guelich describes as the positive basis for obeying the command of v. 44, he argues that Matthew now follows "with a negative basis consisting of two rhetorical questions (5.46-47)."[129] While this polarization between positive and negative arguments may be a little too strong, it does reflect the change in tone between the two motivational statements that were combined by the redactor. The material in v. 45 emphasized the relationship with the Father that stood as the cornerstone of the community's self-perception, and this had become a necessary replacement for the other relationships that had been lost. Stanton appreciates this sociological dimension perhaps better than most other scholars. Describing the phenomenon of alienation experienced by the community, he writes,

> The evangelist and his readers have parted company with other strands of first century Judaism especially Pharisaism (21:43). They perceive themselves to be under threat of persecution from their opponents (5.10-12; 10.17f.; 21.41-5; 22.6f.; 23.31-5), a somewhat beleaguered minority at odds with the parent body, and to a certain extent, with the Gentile world (5.47; 6.7, 32; 10.18, 22; 18.7; 24.9).[130]

However, in response to this ghetto mentality that had developed among those groups of Christians for whom he wrote, the evangelist calls for a wider and more inclusive attitude.

Structurally verses 46 and 47 are aligned, with each comprising of a conditional clause followed by two rhetorical questions. Betz comments on this arrangement stating, "the argument here is *a contrario*, taking the form of a carefully composed *isocolon*. The two parts each consist of a conditional clause, a rhetorical question introduced by τίνα/τί ('whom/who'), and a second rhetorical question introduced by οὐχι ('not')."[131] This saying has already been linked in the source with the

---

[128] Davies and Allison present the logic of these verses in the following manner: "if disciples love only those who love them, they are hardly doing anything out of the ordinary, much less surpassing the righteousness of the scribes and the Pharisees." (Davies and Allison, *Matthew*, vol 1, 549).

[129] Guelich, *The Sermon on the Mount*, 231.

[130] Stanton, *Gospel*, 94.

[131] Betz, *The Sermon on the Mount*, 318.

material that forms Jesus' antithetical response, (Q 6.32 following on closely from Q 6.27), probably on the basis of the catchword 'love'. However, the community is called upon to have more than an internally focused love. Matthew's first question, τίνα μισθὸν ἔχετε, is a redactional alteration[132] of Luke's ποία ὑμῖν χάρις ἐστίν. Therefore, the first evangelist links the practice of love of enemies to eschatological reward. Pastorally, this promise functions to assure group members that even though they are now marginalized and deprived, it is by holding to the core values of the community that they will receive a reversal of fortunes in the eschaton. The second rhetorical question presents tax gathers as a manifest example of self-interest and loving only those who respond will respond with love. [133] However, in the wider narrative Matthew can speak positively of οἱ τελῶναι (Matt 9.10-11; 11.18-19; 21.31-32), presenting them as intimate associates of Jesus.

In v. 47, the parallel saying reinforces the point, and as Hagner notes in this context "ἀσπάσησθε, 'salute,' 'greet,' in parallelism with 'love,' means something like 'wish peace and blessing upon,' or 'show favour towards' (the only other use of the word in Matthew occurs in 10.12)."[134] It is possible to speculate that while community members continued to greet one another, after their alienation from the synagogue they refused to greet those who had formerly been their compatriots.[135] Matthew associates this negative picture of restrictive greetings with the Gentiles, οὐχὶ καὶ οἱ ἐθνικοὶ τὸ αὐτὸ ποιεῖτε; This reference to Gentiles, in a manner that is not wholly positive, has led some to suggest that Matthew had not yet come to view them as members of his community. Putting forward this proposal, Sim argues that the outsider status of Gentiles is confirmed in the gospel and specifically in relation to 5.47 he states, "As it stands the Matthean text reflects a rather unfavourable attitude towards Gentiles."[136] Yet this conclusion does not take into account the way in which other sayings about tax collectors in the first gospel can portray these characters as friends of

---

[132] The use of μισθός as a Matthean alteration is supported by his preference for the term, Matt: 10; Mk: 1; Lk: 3. Also the same combination of μισθός and ἔχετε in Matt 6.1 appears readctional.

[133] Davies and Allison argue that τελῶναι stood in the tradition and that Luke was responsible for the change to his more favoured term ἁμαρτωλοί. "Luke has probably turned 'too collectors' (Mt: 8; Mk: 3; Lk: 10) into 'sinners' (Mt: 5; Mk: 6; Lk: 17)." (Davies and Allison, *Matthew*, vol 1, 457-58).

[134] Hagner, *Matthew 1-13,* 135.

[135] Betz suggests that it is possible to read the term 'brother' as fellow Jew. He observes, "the term occurs in SM/Matt 5:22, 23, 24, 47; 7:3, 4, 5, although unspecified...The juxtaposition with 'pagans' (vs47) suggests the meaning of fellow Jew." (Betz, *The Sermon on the Mount*, 319, n. 959).

[136] Sim, *The Gospel of Matthew and Christian Judaism,* 227.

Jesus (Matt 9.10; 10.3; 11.19[137]) and recipients of the kingdom (Matt 21.31, 32). Likewise, here Matthew presents a caricature of Gentile behaviour for literary impact, so that he might call the community to an elevated standard in their practice. This concern is exemplified by the τί περισσὸν ποιεῖτε clause, which precedes the reference to Gentiles. In fact on the basis of the association between tax gathers and Gentiles (Matt 5.46-47; 18.17), Hummel comes to the opposite conclusion to Sim, understanding the future call of the Gentiles by the Matthean community already to have been anticipated in the ministry of the historical Jesus by his positive attitude to οἱ τελῶναι.[138]

Furthermore, the first rhetorical question in v. 47 uses the term περισσόν, which picks up the language of 5.20 with its call for surpassing righteousness. The term functions in the same way in v. 47 as it did in 5.20, showing that an abounding standard of love is required from community members. Thus Guelich perceptively sees that, "[i]n both 6:1 and 5:20 'righteousness' is at stake, and indeed it is here [5:47]."[139] Once again, Matthew is calling for a higher ethic for his recently constituted community, and their standard of righteousness is to surpass that of their opponents.

4.7.5 Verse 48

This verse both concludes both the sixth antithesis as well as the whole antithetical formulation of vv. 21-48. It also needs to be read in conjunction with 5.20, which set the agenda for Matthew's plea for a higher standard of righteousness within his own community. The command to be perfect in like manner to God's ethical perfection is, of course, an impossible demand. However, it is presented as the ideal to which the group is encouraged to strive to attain. The Lukan version of this saying with its call to be 'merciful', is more likely to be the original Q form of the saying, since it better fits the context of judging that follows in the source (Q 6.37). Thus, Matthew has intentionally made the switch to τέλειος, since it suits his discussion of heightened ethical values. Guelich comments on how the terms δικαιοσύνη and τέλειος function both in the antitheses and the macrostructure of the gospel. He observes, "Matt 5:20

---

[137] The idea of Jesus being the companion of tax collectors is brought out clearly in Matt 11.19, τελωνῶν φίλος καὶ ἁμαρτωλῶν. Although the creation of this verse may not be due to the first evangelist, as has been argued, retention of traditional material is an important indication of the attitudes of the gospel writers.

[138] Hummel, *Die Auseinandersetzung zwischen Kirche und Judentum im Matthäusevangelium*, 25.

[139] Guelich, *The Sermon on the Mount*, 233.

sets the demand for a 'greater righteousness' as the entrance requirement for the kingdom; 19:21 sets *wholeness* (τέλειος) as the requirement for eternal life. Therefore δικαιοσύνη (5:20) and τέλειος (5:48), opening and closing the Antitheses, hold the key to Matthew's understanding of Jesus' demand."[140]

This final imperative shows that Matthean ethics are in the truest sense theological ethics, for they are fundamentally grounded in the perfection of the one whom the community addresses as 'heavenly Father.' Yet, this new perspective is dependant upon the revelation brought by Jesus, as the one who interprets the law, either by redefining and radicalising its demands (as in the first three antitheses), or by rejecting and replacing its commands (as in the final three antitheses). Thus as Luz notes, when speaking in relation to the better righteousness,

> the evangelist points to the basic fact which makes the whole Sermon on the Mount possible and which he expresses in another way by putting the ethical demand of our chapter into the history of the path on which God has set out with his Son.[141]

So while the ethic is certainly a theological ethic, it is in some ways more a Christic ethic.[142] This focus does not stem simply from the fact that Jesus is the teacher of the Matthean community, in the same manner that the Teacher of Righteousness as pedagogue shaped the Qumran community's ethic. Instead, in the Matthean community Jesus' authority overrides that of Torah, and the ethical norms in the community stem ultimately from Jesus own behaviours and attitudes. Thus the antitheses reflect not only the social situation and theological understandings of the community, but at a fundamental level they are based upon the christological underpinnings that have led to the rejection of the group by its opponents and the development of its new theology. For, as is apparent from the antitheses, it is the authority claims that the community have made on behalf of Jesus, which have resulted in the group being ostracised and persecuted by their former synagogue partners, resulting in the struggle to redefine its own identity in the aftermath of that crisis.

---

[140] Guelich, *The Sermon on the Mount*, 234.

[141] Luz, *Matthew 1-7*, 347.

[142] Harrington argues that the purpose of the antitheses is to debate theological issues, and to demonstrate that Jesus is not a violator of Torah stipulations. He states, "[the] interpretation has focused on the theological framework in which the topics are presented by Matthew. The context is the debate within Judaism about the authoritative interpretation of the Torah. Matthew and other Jewish Christians viewed the Torah as divine revelation and the appropriate response to the God of the covenant, not as something obsolete and burdensome." (Harrington, *Matthew*, 92). Obviously the antitheses do focus on the issue of 'authoritative interpretation' however, it has been argued that the issue at stake for the Matthean community was where ultimate authority resided – in Jesus or in Torah.

4.7 Conclusions

Both 4QMMT and Matthew 5.21-48 use the form of antithetical halakhic argument to define the identity of their respective communities, in opposition to the respective forms of Judaism with which their groups are in conflict. Adopting halakhic positions that differed from the mainstream interpretation resulted in both the Qumran and Matthean groups being considered deviant by the opposing Jewish religious authorities. However, it cannot be assumed, as Saldarini argues, that nonconformity shows inclusion in the wider society. He states, "Deviance processes, far from driving a group out of society, often keep it in. Paradoxically, social theory has established that nonconformity, resistance to social structures, and deviance are always part of any functioning society."[143] While this is one possible outcome of social deviance, it does not automatically follow that such groups must continue to operate within the bounds of the society whose rules and values are brought into question. Rather than accept this theoretical position as *a priori* proof that Matthew's community had not broken decisively from its synagogue origins, it is more realistic to admit that social deviance may, or may not, lead to withdrawal (either voluntary or enforced) from the parent group.

The use of the antithetical formulations occurs at different periods in the relative histories of the Qumran and Matthean groups. For the Dead Sea sectarians their alternative halakhic positions are presented during the initial phase of the group's existence, and constitute one of the primary reasons for the split. Although there had been a geographical separation, there still remained at this stage a positive outlook towards the 'you-group', whom they hoped to reconcile by convincing them of the veracity of the understandings in 4QMMT. The acrimony between the Teacher of Righteousness and the Wicked Priest that is reflected in some of the scrolls (1QpHab, 4QpPs 37[a]) was a later development. As Eshel argues, "the author of 1QpHab was forced to account for the respectful tone of address in MMT by explaining the initial circumstances under which the Wicked Priest and Teacher of Righteousness had once been on reasonable terms."[144] By contrast, the Matthean antitheses, while also serving the function of boundary markers, in no way seek to conciliate the opposing party. Instead they are inwardly focused, seeking self-legitimation and advance exclusive authority claims for the community's foundational figure.

---

[143] Saldarini, 'The Gospel of Matthew and Jewish-Christian Conflict', 39.
[144] Eshel, '4QMMT and the History of the Hasmonean Period.'

In discussing the social processes known as 'rites of passage', whereby individuals and groups redefine their identity, Turner identifies three important phases; *separation, liminality and reaggregation.*[145] At the time of the composition of the Halakhic letter the Qumran party is best understood as being at the beginning of this progression, having withdrawn geographically but not yet considering themselves conceptually removed from Temple based Judaism. By comparison, the Matthean community is further down the path of redefinition of identity. This greater degree of withdrawal and separation is evidenced by the Matthean group's acceptance of its ostracised status, its vitriolic response to the Jewish faction with which it is in dispute, and its desire to reformulate its identity without reference to the previous authority standards. Kirk describes the liminal stage as, "Removal from normal social structure, accompanied by correlative destruction of status... This, however, creates the condition requisite for the instructional activities."[146] It would thus appear that Matthew's group is at that stage of transformation when, having accepted its permanent marginalized existence outside the synagogue, it now begins to redefine its status as an independent entity.

As part of this reaggregation process, the gospel, and in particular the antitheses, function as a transformative didactical tractate, which seeks to legitimise the social situation of the community. The basis of this redefinition stems from Jesus' own authority to reinterpret, redefine or even reject some aspects of Torah tradition. Thus, the antitheses implicitly make an authority claim for Jesus that distinguishes the Matthean community from the synagogue group, which held a more traditional understanding of the interpretation of the Torah. Fundamentally, this reaggregation stems from the Matthean community's decision to locate the highest level of authority within the group as stemming from the teachings of Jesus, rather than issuing out of Mosaic teaching as enshrined in Torah and its subsequent interpretations. Thus the relocation of the primary source of authority in the community's foundational figure, rather than in Torah, is one of the root cause of the tension between the Matthean communities and the synogogues, and eventually this tension led to heightened polemic, persecution and, finally, separation.

Moreover, as Carter perceives, the inclusive and egalitarian society that the evangelist promotes as the norm for his group stems from their acceptance of 'permanent liminality' outside of their formative parent body. He argue that this leads to an anti-hierarchical understanding of community,

---

[145] Turner, *Dramas, Fields and Metaphors*.
[146] Kirk, 'Crossing the Boundary: Liminality and Transformative Wisdom in Q', 3.

'Anti-structure' views the middle phase [i.e., liminality] and the experience of the *communitas* in contrast in contrast to the social experiences and structures which precede and follow it. The experience of an egalitarian existence contrasts with the hierarchical, differentiated society.[147]

It is therefore, out of this milieu of alienation and rejection that the community strives to redefine its own identity, to become more inclusive in its incorporation of Gentiles with the dominically inaugurated mission (Matt 28.16-20), and to transform itself onto a higher plane of righteousness by either transcending the rulings of their opponents, or even replacing their traditional halakhic values with a new ethic.

With the antitheses, the evangelist reveals what he understands by 'fulfilling the law' (Matt 5.17). It involves a new ethical programme, which emphasizes equality, mutuality and humility. It would be wrong, however, to assume that these values had been non-existent in the parent group. Yet, in order to present his community as superior, Matthew must of necessity play down the expression of these values in the synagogue setting, and instead characterize his opponents as hypocritical and duplicitous (cf. Matt 23). Thus the importance of traditional sources of authority is relativized for Matthew. As Stanton appreciates, "For Matthew the law and the prophets continue to be authoritative for Christians - with the proviso that they are interpreted in the light of the teaching of Jesus, especially the love command."[148]

Thus the composition of the antitheses (Matt 5.21-48) reflects both the social circumstances of the community as well as the creative manner in which Matthean presents his understanding of Jesus in order to address the pastoral needs of his community. To this end, he portrays Jesus not only as the supreme interpreter of Torah, but rather, as the ultimate source of authority within the community. Such a claim subverts the authority base of the synagogue party, and in turn defines a new ideology for the community based upon mutual love and egalitarian discipleship, but above all based upon the teachings of the central figure of the risen Jesus. Having been ostracised from the Jewish synagogues, those group members who constitute the circle of Matthean communities are encouraged to leave the past behind and to embrace the new existence sanctioned by their own divinely empowered foundational figure. Admittedly, embracing the group's values means a marginal existence in the present, but this is tempered by the promise of the transformation of status in the eschatological age. Thereby, Matthew assures his audience that it is only by accepting this redefined identity that they will be able to show forth abounding righteousness, and experience the true

---

[147] Carter, *Households and Discipleship*, 50.

[148] Stanton, *Gospel*, 49.

eschatological blessing of what it means to be 'sons' of their heavenly Father.[149]

---

[149] Barton notes that this not only results in the breaking of ties with synagogue based Judaism, but also creates a re-alignment in the understanding of family ties. He states that the subordination of family ties "gives Matthew's group a certain afamilial or suprafamilial ethos... In view of the coming of the kingdom and the Messiah, family ties do not matter in the way they once did." (Barton, *Discipleship and Family Ties*, 176).

Chapter 5

Matthew's Programmatic Statement on the Law (Matt 5.17-20)

5.1 Introduction

Few passages in the New Testament have occasioned as much scholarly debate as the verses in Matt 5.17-20, where Jesus is portrayed, at least in some sense, as declaring that his proclamation stands in continuity with the law. Opinions range from understanding these statements as providing a blanket affirmation of Torah and its ongoing validity for the Matthean community, to positions that assert that Jesus is claiming a prophetic or eschatological fulfilment of the law and hence is able to make supersessionary claims about its validity in relation to the new ethical understanding he announces.

Among proponents of the view that Matthew presents a conservative Jesus who taught that it was necessary to uphold every jot and tittle of the law, Bornkamm's work[1] deserves consideration not only because of its careful treatment, but more importantly because his study crystallized the earlier research in this area and shaped the debate for a later generation of exegetes. The ongoing validity of the law is seen as being the primary teaching of vv. 17-19, with the antitheses that follow understood as corroborating this perspective. It is worth quoting Bornkamm's interpretation at length in order to see both the assumptions it involves and to observe the logical structure of the argument. He states,

> Matthew gives to the words in 5.17-19, which obviously stem from the Jewish-Christian congregation and are directed against a tendency to abandon the law, a representative and programmatic meaning. Along with the unabridged validity of the Torah the interpretation of the scribes is also axiomatically binding for him. This is seen in the antitheses that follow, where, above all, there is no question of setting Torah and scribal interpretation over against each other, but what was said 'to them of old time' is at times quoted in the form which was self-evident to the Jew, namely that which tradition gave to the word of scripture.[2]

---

[1] Bornkamm, 'End-Expectation and Church in Matthew', 15-51.

[2] Bornkamm, 'End-Expectation and Church in Matthew', 24.

Firstly, the underlying premise that shapes Bornkamm's argument is the belief that the evangelist was reacting against a tendency to 'abandon the law'. This is part of his overall thesis that Matthew was 'fighting on two fronts', against such antinomians on the one hand, and also asserting the correctness of his community's stance in opposition to Jews who were not believers in Jesus. However, the party with lax attitudes towards Torah remain shadowy figures in Bornkamm's treatment, and no indication is given as to whether this group is part of Matthew's community or another branch of Christianity, external to the evangelist's adherents, but nevertheless, a faction with whom Mathew was in dispute.

The identification of this group is explored in greater detail by Barth. Basing the existence of this antinomian party on three pericopae (Matt 5.17-20; 7.15ff; 24.11ff), Barth rejects an equation between these supposed Matthean opponents and Paul, or a group of Paulinists. In contrast to the explicit use of πίστις terminology that occurs in the debate of Jas 2.14-26, where the dispute is seen as due to conflict with Paul or Christians who adhered to his teachings, no such link is seen in the first gospel. Thus, on this basis, it is asserted that,

> one can hardly see a Pauline group in the antinomians of Matthew, for in that case one would have to expect that they would make πίστις the basis of their attitude. There is, however, no trace of this; they do not appeal to πίστις, but to the fact that since the coming of Christ the validity of the law is at an end.[3]

Instead, having dismissed this option, Barth makes the bald assertion that "A group which represents the view that the law had no validity for the Church is unthinkable in the area of Judaism, in Jewish Christianity. It must concern Hellenistic Christians."[4] A number of points must be made in response to this position. For the sake of argument conceding the possibility of an antinomian party, Paul obviously is a demonstration of the potential for Jews to adopt a form of Christianity with a relaxed attitude to certain Torah stipulations. While this may not have been common, it does seem too much to claim that it is *a priori* 'unthinkable in the area of Judaism'. More importantly, however, it is debatable that the three pericopae cited by Barth do in fact constitute a firm basis for positing the existence of a party that rejected the law, and further seeing this group as a principal opponent of Matthean christianity. In fact, in the last two passages there is little to focus attention on the law as an issue of dispute, and even the references to ἀνομία in 7.23 and 24.12 do not appear to emphasize this aspect as the primary threat that the false prophets pose to the community. Although the reference to ἀνομία is highlighted by those

---

[3] Barth, 'Matthew's Understanding of the Law', 162.
[4] Barth, 'Matthew's Understanding of the Law', 162.

who argue for the existence of an antinomian group, the counterarguments appear conclusive. First rejecting a number of implausible minority positions, Hagner discusses the suggestion that these false prophets were Hellenistic libertines. He notes that this view assumes,

> that the false prophets are those referred to in vv 21-23 and places much emphasis on the ἀνομία, 'lawlessness', referred to in v 23. The passage in 24.11-12, which refers both to false prophets and ἀνομία. is taken up to confirm this hypothesis, and 5.17-20 is then understood to apply directly to the same group. D. Hill [*Bib* 57, (1976)], however, has argued strongly against this view, contending that vv 15-20 and 21-23 refer to different groups: the former to the Pharisees and the latter to charismatic Christians whose righteousness is insufficient.[5]

However, more questionable is Bornkamm's statement the antitheses represent the abiding validity of the law (see the earlier quotation). Actually, Bornkamm's subsequent comments in the same essay make it clear that he does not believe this to be true. He understands the evangelist to be ethicising the law in a creative manner in 5.21-48. Thus he suggests,

> Matthew obviously understands this radicalising of the divine demand, which, in fact, only means a sharpening of the law in the first, second and fourth antitheses, but in the third, fifth and sixth its abolition as a confirmation of the validity of the law down to the jot and tittle, without being aware of the inconsistency between these antitheses and the binding force of the 'letter' as stated in the Judaistic Jewish-Christian formulation of vv18f., which was firmly held down to the jot and tittle.[6]

Unless Matthew is extremely confused in his thinking, this reading has little to commend it. It is inconceivable, given the amount of redactional shaping that is present both in the statement on the law (5.17-20) and the antitheses that immediately follow (5.21-48), that the evangelist has simply juxtaposed these blocks, but, supposedly, failed to note the inconsistency. Moreover, the assertion that the fourth antithesis simply sharpens the law is also false. Here Bornkamm is too heavily dependent on the Bultmannian interpretation that views the first, second and fourth antitheses as traditional,[7] and therefore conservative in relation to their understanding of the law.[8]

---

[5] Hagner, *Matthew 1-13*, 182. Hagner, questions attempts to identify the reference to 'false prophets' to narrowly, although he sees a link in 7.21-23 between this group and charismatic enthusiasm. He states, "Confirmation that these enthusiasts of 7.21-23 can be considered 'false prophets' may be found in 24.24, where false prophets are associated with 'great signs and wonders,' even though that verse is a prophecy of the future." (183).

[6] Bornkamm, 'End-Expectation and Church in Matthew', 25.

[7] This widespread, and incorrect, assessment of which antitheses annul the law is still adopted by some scholars, despite the fact that Meier has already highlighted this error. He observes in relation to his own study, "our view of which antitheses revoke the letter of the Torah does not agree with Bultmann in his *Geschichte der synoptischen Tradition*.

The greatest weakness of Bornkamm's statement is the failure to explain how the 'abolition' of the law in the third, fifth and sixth antitheses[9] can in any way be taken "as a confirmation of the validity of the law down to the jot and tittle." This appears to be example of rhetorical gymnastics, which recognizes a tension between a number of the antitheses, but because of the overall model of a law observant community cannot cope with allowing the natural sense to stand. Thus, rather than modify the model, at this point Bornkamm modifies the evidence. As Meier notes, while *a priori* it is possible to suggest that "[t]he contrast could be understood in a mild sense: Jesus sharpens, radicalises, internalizes the Torah, going beyond the letter to the ultimate intention of the Torah,"[10] when one considers the actual declarations made in the antitheses it is no longer possible to sustain this position. Rather, there appears to be a combination of formulations, some which do merely radicalize Torah (first, second and sixth), while the remainder either revoke or annul the casuistic demands of the Mosaic legal system.

Yet, as is well known, although Bornkamm articulated this position in some detail and it is still adopted by scholars who wish to read these verses as a Matthean statement of strict Torah observance, Bornkamm, recognizing inconsistencies, moved away from this position. Summarizing the shift in his thought in regard to the social setting of the Matthean community Brooks describes the three different views that are provided in a series of three separate essays spanning a seventeen-year period.[11]

> The first of these, 'End Expectation and Church in Matthew,' proposes that Matthew's community exists within the Jewish synagogue. 'Der Auferstandene und der Irdische' depicts the community as showing signs of significant strain with the synagogue, while still maintaining its position within the synagogue. Finally, in 'Die

---

Unfortunately Bultmann's division has been taken over uncritically by many subsequent authors." (Meier, *Law and History in Matthew's Gospel*, 135).

[8] Source critically, Bultmann sees the first, second and fourth antitheses as pre-Matthean, but not in their present form authentic Jesus material. (Bultmann, *The History of the Synoptic Tradition*, 136).

[9] Again, this is following Bornkamm following Bultmann's scheme, which has been suggested to be an incorrect assessment of the antitheses that revoke the law.

[10] Meier, *Law and History in Matthew's Gospel*, 134-5.

[11] These essays, all originally printed in German, are 'Enderwartung und Kirche im Matthäusevangelium', in *Überlieferung und Auslegung im Matthäusevangelium*, but originally appeared in embryonic form as 'Matthäus als Interpret der Herrenworte' in *TLZ* 79, 1954, 341-6. Secondly, 'Der Auferstandene und der Irdische', in the Bultmann Festschrift, *Zeit und Geschichte*, Tübingen: Mohr, 1964, 171-91. Lastly, 'Die Binde- und Lösegewalt in der Kirche des Matthäus', in *Geschichte und Glaube*, Munich: Kaiser, 1971, 37-50.

Bilde- und Lösegewalt in der Kirche des Matthäus,' Bornkamm sees the Matthean community as separated from the Jewish synagogue.[12]

Focusing on the final article, Meier notes that this last position is more nuanced than simply understanding the community as having moved fully into the world of Gentile Christianity by the time of the composition of the first gospel. Instead, as he notes, "While presenting this new view, Bornkamm insists that he does not accept a simple shift form Jewish Christianity to Gentile Christianity. Rather, Mt is a complex phenomenon reflecting the coalescence of Jewish and Hellenistic elements."[13] It is interesting to note how the three positions that Bornkamm articulated, admittedly not in a fully developed manner and without the insights of social scientific criticism, reflect the three broad streams of thought regarding the location of the community that are currently debated. The initial position is perhaps closest to the work of Overman,[14] who argues that Matthew's group, although marginalized to some degree, nevertheless was still participating in the life of synagogue worship. The second position parallels Saldarini's thesis that the strain was pronounced between the Matthean group and formative Judaism,[15] but nonetheless they were still struggling to maintain participation in the synagogue. The final view Bornkamm expressed was that the church is aware that it is cut off from the synagogue, no longer gathers about Torah, but rather, meets in the name of Jesus and as such is assured of his presence.[16] While not exactly corresponding to Stanton's thesis, nonetheless, it has a number of similarities, especially in respect to the notion of a new orientation in the community focused on Jesus as the authoritative foundational figure.[17]

As has been noted above, Barth's dissertation is in many ways an unfolding of Bornkamm's initial position. This unpacking of his supervisor's thesis not only involves identifying the antinomian opponents, but also comprises investigation of the central role of the love command, the range of laws that remained valid in the community, the radical role of discipleship, and the relationship between law and Christology in Matthean theology. It is necessary to turn to these issues to understand how Barth arrives at a law observant Matthean community, and more specifically to appreciate how he sees Matt 5.17-20 functioning in the overall presentation as a statement about ongoing Torah validity.

---

[12] Brooks, *Matthew's Community, the Evidence of His Special Sayings Material*, 21.

[13] Meier, *Law and History in Matthew's Gospel*, 10.

[14] Overman, *Matthew's Gospel and Formative Judaism*.

[15] Saldarini, *Matthew's Christian-Jewish Community*.

[16] Bornkamm, 'Die Binde- und Lösegewalt in der Kirche des Matthäus', 40.

[17] Stanton, *A Gospel for a New People*.

Contrasting with the lax approach to the law, which Barth perceives to be under attack in the first gospel, he sees the repeated use of the love command to be directed against a second group that he labels as the 'Rabbinate'.[18] Initially, it must be noted that the usage of this term is not only undefined by Barth, but it is also highly anachronistic in the context in which it is utilised. As it is employed, it appears to denote an organized body or college of teachers of Torah with a fixed corpus of doctrine, against which Matthew could consciously define his own beliefs while being fully cognizant that the positions he articulated stood in opposition to the received norms of the Rabbinate.

Two statements illustrate the fact that Barth perceives the Rabbinate to be both a fixed and influential body at the time Matthew wrote his gospel in the last quarter of the first century C.E. Firstly, he states, "The evangelist, however, regards himself in opposition to the Rabbinate also with regard to the understanding of the law. The discussion of the schools about the greatest commandment has become with him a contention (22.34ff.)."[19] Presumably, although not cited, the major text from the rabbinic corpus to which Barth may be alluding is *Sifra* on Lev 19.18. As this text probably dates to the third or fourth centuries C.E. it is highly questionable whether one can assert that Matthew is interacting with a formalized scholastic debate at the time he wrote.[20] While later rabbinic texts show that questions about the greatest command or even summaries of the law were part of rabbinic instruction in the Yeshiva, all Matthew demonstrates is that such a question could be legitimately asked by a Jew during the first century C.E., but this in no way implies that in this period this type of question had already become part of a formalized rhetoric of

---

[18] Barth argues that despite the fact "that Matthew's understanding of the law is largely determined by his opposition to the antinomians this is by no means his only battle-front. Through the whole gospel there is likewise an opposition to Pharisaism and the Rabbinate." (Barth, 'Matthew's Understanding of the Law', 75-6).

[19] Barth, 'Matthew's Understanding of the Law', 76.

[20] As Neusner notes, the *Sifra* on Leviticus is a compilation and expansion of earlier rabbinic traditions, but is obviously later than the Mishnah. Discussing the combination of written and oral Torah he observes, "In a simple and fundamental sense, Sifra joins the two Torahs in a single statement, accomplishing a re-presentation of the written Torah in topic and in program and in the logic of cogent discourse, and within the rewriting of the written Torah, a re-presentation of the oral Torah in its paramount problematic and in many of its substantive propositions." (Neusner, *The Classics of Judaism*, 119-20). The derivative nature of Sifra in fully apparent, and illustrates the difficulty in claiming that its commentary on rulings in the Mishnah can be thought to reflect first century polemic between Matthew's group and emergent Judaism. Moreover, the assumption made be Barth that so soon after the destruction there was already an enfranchised Jewish leadership with whom the evangelist could construct diametrically opposed legal positions appears high problematic.

rabbinic education. The second significant statement that Barth makes which reflects the same lack of differentiation between the social setting of Matthew and the Rabbinate revolves around the tension between the rabbis making a summary of Torah in one or two commandments and the claim that there was no distinction between light and heavy injunctions. Barth states,

> In principle each command is as important as the rest; in fact, for the Rabbinical understanding of the law there can be no question of raising one commandment above the others in importance. The Rabbinate stated this many times. The danger that arises from this can been seen even by the Rabbinate, but according to the formal understanding of the law there is no possibility of avoiding it.[21]

To support the argument Barth cites a saying attributed to Johanan ben Zakkai, עלינו כתוב אוי לנו ששקל, (*b. Hag* 5a).[22] As this saying is found in a sixth century source, the Babylonian Talmud, the methodological problem of reading this text as reflecting a first century debate is obvious.

However, from this viewpoint, the love command which occurs repeatedly in Matthew (including within the context of the antitheses, 5.43),[23] is seen as reflecting an alternative Jewish way of upholding the law. Specifically this entails subordinating the law to a single dominant perspective, through which all the other ordinances are interpreted. Thus Barth comes to the conclusion that both the rabbinic and Matthean systems of thought seek to uphold the law. The former in a more traditional and conservative manner stating that all the injunctions of Torah are of equal weight, the latter in a more relative and liberal manner claiming that there exists a prioritized hierarchy of values that takes precedence over exact observance. Barth presents his understanding of the function of the love command as follows.

> With the meaning of the commandment of love as the essence of the law the contrast to the rabbinate is given. Matthew regards himself as separated from this not only by practice but also by teaching. He is linked with the Rabbinate in holding fast to the whole law; he parts from it in his interpretation. And not merely in the interpretation of particular questions, but this contrast goes already to fundamental depths and leads to a quite different understanding of the law.[24]

It is however, dubious whether observance and interpretation can be so cleanly dichotomised, for to uphold the law requires it to be upheld in a certain manner. Not only would emergent Judaism have rejected the

---

[21] Barth, 'Matthew's Understanding of the Law', 78.

[22] In English the quotation reads, 'Woe to us because the Scripture attaches the same weight to the easy as to the hard.' See Barth, 'Matthew's Understanding of the Law', 78, n. 1.

[23] The love commandment is cited at Matt 5.43; 7.12; 19.19; 22.39; 24.12.

[24] Barth, 'Matthew's Understanding of the Law', 85.

Matthean approach to Torah as valid observance, it also appears that the acceptance of Jesus' messianic claims would have be recognized by Matthean group-members as creating a subordination, and consequently a devaluation, of the law within this community of believers in Jesus that attributed authority to their foundational figure. This view seems to emerge from the analysis of 5.21-48, where Jesus is elevated by the first evangelist to a position of supreme authority in the community.

Moreover, the whole notion of Matthew creating distinctions between the heavy and light commandments, and subordinating certain laws in line with the hermeneutical interpretation of the love command, appears dubious in the light of the sayings in Matt 5.18-19.[25] For those for wish to maintain that Matthew has an ongoing allegiance to Torah the meaning of v. 18 is that even the smallest iota and pen-stroke in the law remains in force. However, even v. 18d itself seems to provide some temporal limitation to this view. Further, in line with the type of reading proposed by Barth, in v. 19 a distinction with less important commandments is clearly rejected. In fact, if Matthew is to be understood as an upholder of the ongoing validity of Torah then observance of the very least of the commandments is seen as having consequence for one's status in the kingdom. For whereas on the one hand failure to comply results in a position of subservience in the kingdom, ὃς ἐὰν οὖν λύσῃ μίαν τῶν ἐντολῶν τούτων τῶν ἐλαχίστων καὶ διδάξῃ οὕτως τοὺς ἀνθρώπους, ἐλάχιστος κληθήσεται ἐν τῇ βασιλείᾳ τῶν οὐρανῶν (5.19a), compliance results in exultation, ὃς δὲ ἂν ποιήσῃ καὶ διδάξῃ οὗτος μέγας κληθήσεται ἐν τῇ βασιλείᾳ τῶν οὐρανῶν (5.19b). However, Barth is incorrect in characterizing rabbinic Judaism as having an unnuanced understanding of the law. Although they could recognize a tension, the rabbis could both maintain the distinction between light and heavy ordinances,[26] while at the same time asserting that all commands were God-given and therefore, and were required to be observed with equal reverence and care. Luz comments upon the tension within rabbinic thought on this point, and the similarity with Matt 5.19. He observes,

---

[25] In *m.Abot* 2.1 it is suggested that all commandments should be kept, since it is impossible to know how much heavenly reward the observance of each command brings. This rabbinic discussion is not cited by Barth, but is extremely pertinent to countering the case he is trying to establish. For not only does it show that if the Matthean community is a law observant party that they view all commandments as having ongoing force, the reason for this statement is also seen to be the same, namely status or reward in the heavenly realm.

[26] Helpfully, the evidence is catalogued in Str-B I 901-5. Among the weighty commandments are injunctions concerning Sabbath, idolatry, honouring parents and shedding of blood. In comparison, laws pertaining to tabernacles, the bird mother (Deut 22.7) and the eating of blood were classified as light commandments (מצות קלות).

The rabbis distinguished between 'light' and 'weighty' commandments, a distinction that involves, on the one hand, the effort demanded of the believer, on the other hand, the reward for keeping it. Our logion agrees with them in the fact that it urges the keeping even of one of the least commandments, for in the last analysis one cannot -thus the rabbis- know how much reward each commandment brings.[27]

This illustrates the difficulty in trying to maintain Barth's argument, which asserts that while Matthew had a differentiated attitude to the individual ordinances in the Torah, the rabbis did not. Both parts of this argument appear flawed, and the failure to recognize this stems from a misreading of the rabbinic evidence and a desire to force Matthew into a model of an alternative, but equally valid form of ongoing Torah observance.

Barth is correct to emphasize that it is the central christological claims of the group that act as the catalyst for a different understanding of the role of the law, in comparison with the approach of formative Judaism. In turn, this Christology is seen as the basis for the patterns of discipleship that the evangelist is attempting to promote in the community, as well as ultimately shaping the interpretation of the law. Three 'traits',[28] or perhaps better trajectories, are followed to see the sequential influence of Christology on discipleship, which then shapes Torah interpretation. These are the Matthean prominence given to πραΰτης (Matt 5.3; 11.28-30; 19.13-15; 20.20-28; 23.8-12), the concept of δικαιοσύνη (esp. 5.10, 11, 20; 6.1), and the notion that judgment will be based upon relationship and attitude towards the Son of Man (12.36-7; 16.24-7; 25.31-46).[29] The first two

---

[27] Luz, *Matthew 1-7*, 267.

[28] Although 'trait' is the term Barth uses, in many ways 'trajectory' is to be preferred, since the influence is traced from Christology to discipleship and then into Torah interpretation. It is this fairly linear progression that Barth portrays, which makes the language of trajectories more appropriate. (Barth, 'Matthew's Understanding of the Law', 104).

[29] Although Matt 12.36-7 does not explicitly mention the Son of Man, Barth sees the other references as shaping the understanding that community members would have brought to this passage which speaks about judgment according to words. Thus he argues, "Originally 12.36f. had a broad ethical meaning, but Matthew refers to the words of the Pharisees who blaspheme against the Son of Man, or alternatively the Holy Spirit resting upon him. The judgment according to works is not carried out according to a broad ethical principle which is indifferent to the Christ-event. This is seen in 25.31-46 already, where the righteous have fed and clothed the Son of Man unknowingly, but above all in 16.24-7 where the disciples are judged in the judgment according to the imitation of Christ in suffering and their dedicated lives. When a man is judged in judgment 'according to his works' that means he is asked about his relationship to Jesus Christ, to whom his works bear witness." (105). This perspective is strengthened by the fact that the evangelist immediately follows the saying about judgment for careless words (12.36-37) with the Sign of Jonah pericope (12.39-42). In that judgment parable, not only is the Son of Man explicitly mentioned, but also judgment comes upon the evil

aspects are seen to generate a discipleship that is based on *imitatio Christi*, in the sense that the lowly and suffering Son of Man models behaviour to be replicated in the community even if this requires being persecuted for the sake of righteousness as Jesus himself suffered. However, the linking of judgment with response to Christological claims does assure the group that present suffering is to be reversed in the eschaton. Yet, in the present age, the evangelist requires a new ethical behaviour. This leads Barth to conclude that "in all these passages the influence of Christology upon ethics can be seen. The assumption seems therefore justified that it is Christology itself that has led Matthew to the interpretation of the law by the love-commandment and discipleship."[30] While it is claiming too much to assert that the love command has become the governing factor in terms of halakhic interpretation in the group, Barth successfully identifies the group's reflection on the person of Jesus as the defining identity forming concept amongst those who adhere to the community.

In relation to Matt 5.17-20 and the antitheses that follow, Barth posits a bifurcation in terms of its function in the gospel. He states that for the Matthean community,

> The Torah was thus received as part of the tradition and in its traditional meaning. It is plain that the antitheses are not directed primarily against the Old Testament itself, but against the interpretation of it in the Rabbinate. This is supported by the heading in 5.20, which is now directed against the Pharisees and the scribes, whereas previously 5.17-19 were directed against the antinomians.[31]

While from the perspective of source criticism it is correct to assert that the material in 5.17-20 did not originally form a unity, it appears problematic to assert that after the redactional reworking by the evangelist

---

generation being addresses because they have failed to recognize the greater wisdom in their presence. In terms of the social setting of the Matthean group an eschatological perspective is provided that again assures those who hold to the christological claims advanced on behalf of Jesus that at the judgment those who reject such claims will be judged on this basis alone. Edwards comments on the way in which Matthew has utilised the Sign of Jonah saying to advance authority claims for Jesus. He states, "the teacher is effective and to be heard because he is the one who died and rose. In a small way, the passion kerygma is combined with the 'authoritative teacher' message in this pericope, and Matthew is revealed as a theologian who has combined both strands of theological tradition in a single unified understanding of Jesus." (Edwards, *The Sign of Jonah*, 99). In a slightly different way Hagner also notes the themes of discipleship, christology and judgment coalescing in 12.37. He observes, "on the day of judgment one will either be justified (δικαιωθήσῃ, used again in Matthew only in 11.19) or condemned (καταδικασθήσῃ, used again in Matthew only in v 7) by the words one has spoken. Words, like deeds, are indicators of a persons discipleship to Jesus and relationship to the kingdom." (Hagner, *Matthew 1-13*, 351).

[30] Barth, 'Matthew's Understanding of the Law', 105.
[31] Barth, 'Matthew's Understanding of the Law', 93-4.

it is still possible to maintain a distinction between various groups of opponents under attack. In fact the formulaic λέγω γὰρ ὑμῖν emphasizes a continuity in thought with the preceding material in much the same manner as the almost identical formulation (ἀμὴν γὰρ λέγω ὑμῖν) creates the link between verses 17 and 18.[32] Furthermore, the reference to 'the kingdom of heaven,' either in terms of future status in the divine realm (v. 19) or participation in that eschatological state (v. 20), links the two verses far more closely than Barth allows. Davies and Allison recognize this link both in terms of language and logic. They state in relation to the two references to ἡ βασιλεία τῶν οὐρανῶν that "although the threat in 5.20 is the converse of the promise in 5.19, in both verses eschatology provides the motivation for proper behaviour."[33] From this perspective it appears possible to identify only one set of opponents in Matt 5.17-48, and that group is most naturally understood as being the form of synagogue based Judaism with which Matthew is contending.

This is confirmed by other references in the text where these people come clearly into focus, while the supposed antinomian adversaries are never explicitly mentioned but rather must be 'discovered' beneath obscure texts and allusions. Having demonstrated the weakness of the theory that Matthew is 'fighting on two fronts' it becomes possible to see the declaration μὴ νομίσητε ὅτι ἦλθον καταλῦσαι τὸν νόμον ἤ τοὺς προφήτας (5.17a) not as a polemical statement directed against opponents, instead it is a pastorally orientated assurance that seeks to legitimise the stance of the Matthean community in two ways. Firstly, the Matthean Jesus declares his intention is not destruction but fulfilment, and this saying may have been a community slogan or catchcry placed on the lips of the historical Jesus. Secondly, the antitheses seek to illustrate that the halakhic interpretation or redefinition of Torah can be seen as stemming from Jesus himself, who has become the ultimate source of authority for group members.[34] Since the gospel is more likely to be read by group members than by opponents, it is perhaps easier to sustain a pastoral intent for this writing.

---

[32] Analysing the grammatical structure of the argument Davies and Allison comment on the logical progression established between verses 17 and 18 in the following manner. "γὰρ follows 'amen' four times in the first gospel (5.18; 10.23; 13.17; 17.20; Mk: 0; Lk: 0). In the present clause the conjunction shows the conjunction shows that 5.18 establishes the basis for 5.17." (Davies and Allison, *Matthew*, vol 1, 489).

[33] Davies and Allison, *Matthew*, vol 1, 500.

[34] In the third of the four possible interpretations that Davies and Allison list as the primary approaches to the antitheses they note that in regard to Jesus' new pronouncements contained in his own declarations, that these "would seem to locate the authority of his declarations in his own person, so that although the Torah supplies him with a point of departure, it does no more than this." (*Matthew*, vol 1, 508).

Contrasting with the perspectives of Barth and the early Bornkamm, Meier approaches the question of the interpretation of the programmatic statement concerning the law only after mapping out a fairly rigid understanding of a Matthean salvation history scheme.[35] Focusing initially on the three mission statements in the narrative, which are all unique to the first gospel (Matt 10.5-6; 15.24; 28.16-20)[36], Meier notes that the first two sayings are,

> expressions of a very conscious attempt on Matthew's part to limit Jesus' public ministry to the territory and people of Israel. Jesus himself is sent only to the lost sheep of the house of Israel (15.24) and his missionary charge to his disciples during the Galilean ministry warns then not to go to the gentiles or Samaritans, but only to the lost sheep of the house of Israel.[37]

Obviously it is necessary for Meier to account for the material in these verses in a convincing manner, for these statements of a limited mission are cited as strong evidence by scholars who wish to present Matthew as a Torah observant Jew intent on bringing the message of Jesus to fellow Jews. Meier admits that both 10.5-6 and 15.24 present a limited mission and also that in Matthew's gospel they are "preserved in all their vigour, not to say harshness."[38] However, he seeks to account for this material in the setting of a community that was no longer part of Judaism. Meier finds the answer in the climatic charge of 28.16-20, which he reads as revoking the 'economical limitation' that existed before Jesus' death and resurrection.[39] In this sense the Easter events are understood as pivotal in

---

[35] In his introduction to the chapter dealing with salvation history in Matthew, Meier states his basic thesis as being that, "Mt tried to solve the problem of preserving yet reinterpreting stringent Jewish-Christian tradition by setting up his own schema of salvation-history." (Meier, *Law and History in Matthew's Gospel*, 23). He sees Matt 5.18 as an important verse in this debate since it contains two temporal clauses. These clauses give an insight into the Matthean notion of the periodization of time, while the content with its focus on the law shows how Torah belongs to one era, but its importance has become relativized in the post-resurrection period.

[36] Meier note that these verses are unique to the first gospel and even describes them as "belonging to the special material of Matthew." (Meier, *Law and History in Matthew's Gospel*, 27). However, it is uncertain whether Meier means by this that the statements are draw from M material, or represent the redactional handiwork of the evangelist. Perhaps the choice is ultimately not all that important, since regardless of whether these logia are source or redactional material the evangelist saw these statements as concurring with his overall perspective and thus integrated them into his reworking of the Markan account.

[37] Meier, *Law and History in Matthew's Gospel*, 27.

[38] Meier, *Law and History in Matthew's Gospel*, 27.

[39] As Stanton notes in his summary of Meier's position, "when the new age breaks in at the death-resurrection of Jesus (the culmination of the fulfilment of all prophecy), the letter will fall in favour of the prophetic, eschatological fulfilment of the Law which Jesus brings." ('The Origins and Purpose of Matthew's Gospel', 1937).

the Matthean *heilsgeschichte* scheme, for the resurrection heralds a new dispensation of the divine *modus operandi* with humanity. No longer is salvation mediated only to Jews who received the covenant by God's grace and maintain their status within the covenant by observing the law,[40] rather, the horizon has been broadened to include all people. While people still enter into relationship with God through grace, status is not preserved by Torah observance but by a higher form of righteousness. Meier describes the understanding of salvation as his first firm datum and represents it as follows. "Mt consciously arranges his data to fit a scheme of salvation-history which widens the geographical and national restrictions placed on Jesus' public ministry in favour of a universal mission after the death-resurrection."[41] This leads Meier to a second fact that he describes as "hardly disputable."[42]

The second datum is that "[i]n the missionary command of Mt 28.16-20, the author quite obviously sees the universal mission as dispensing with circumcision."[43] This second assertion may, however, not be quite as self-evident as Meier proposes. First, the text does not raise the circumcision issue so it seems perilous to advance this conclusion from silence,[44] and second, from Paul's epistles it is possible to see the existence

---

[40] Although Meier does not employ exactly Sanders' language of covenantal nomism it is interesting to see how his basic representation of salvation history prior to the death and resurrection of Jesus aligns with the perspective contained in *Paul and Palestinian Judaism*. Sanders defines his understanding of the pattern of Jewish religion as follows: "covenantal nomism is the view that one's place in God's plan is established on the basis of the covenant and that the covenant requires as the proper response of man his obedience to its commandments, while providing means of atonement for transgression....*obedience maintains one's position in the covenant, but it does not earn God's grace as such*....God's 'rewarding' the righteous because of his mercy – serves to assure that election and ultimately salvation can never be earned, but depend on God's grace. One can never be righteous enough to be worthy in God's sight of the ultimate gifts, which depend only on his mercy." (Sanders, *Paul and Palestinian Judaism*, 75, 420, 421-2). Similarly, Meier understands the observance of the law to be the condition by which status is maintained in the covenant prior to the resurrection. After the Easter events, it is argued that Matthew sees a new dispensation of salvation history which entails the end of Torah observance, but inaugurates Gentile mission and righteous living based on an internalised ethic. By contrast, Luomanen does seek to analyse Matthew in light of Sanders' categories, see *Entering the Kingdom of Heaven*.

[41] Meier, *Law and History in Matthew's Gospel*, 28.

[42] Meier, *Law and History in Matthew's Gospel*, 28.

[43] Meier, *Law and History in Matthew's Gospel*, 28.

[44] In fact, the whole of Matthew's gospel is silent on the issue of circumcision. Exactly what this means is probably impossible to determine with any objective checks or balances. Anything that is said about the Matthean attitude to circumcision is at best derivative on overall theories built up by scholars on the social location of the

of 'Judaizers' who engaged in missionary (or counter-missionary) activity among the gentiles but insisted on their circumcision (cf., Gal 5.3, 11-12; 6.12-13).[45] This pluriformity of practice should caution against too readily assuming the Matthean attitude to circumcision. Nonetheless, Meier having made this assumption proceeds to discuss the role of the law in Matthew's gospel and the tension that has been recognized in the divergent statements the evangelist has made. Meier portrays the issue in the following terms.

> How can we say that Mt conceives Jesus as one who gives the Mosaic Law a new interpretation, and that Matthew wishes the church to be faithful to the substance, or even the letter (5.18-19!) of the Mosaic Law, when he portrays the risen Lord as giving a mandate that strikes at the very heart of the Mosaic Law?[46]

It is this question that leads into the central concern of Meier's thesis, namely to discuss and account for the Matthean attitude to the law, as it is presented in Matt 5.17-48.

The strength of Meier's treatment of the material in 5.17-20 is that he seeks to make sense of these statements as a unified whole within the overall scheme of Matthew's gospel. Although seeing these verses as combining source and redactional material he nevertheless strives to read the editorial creation that emerges as saying something that accurately represents the theology of the evangelist in relationship to Torah. After briefly reviewing the placement of this programmatic statement concerning the law within the macronarrative of the gospel, and more specifically the Sermon on the Mount,[47] Meier launches into a detailed exegesis of these verses. However, prior to that analysis he makes the methodological decision not to treat the verses in the order presented, but instead to focus initially to investigate v. 18. While he concedes that this may not be the

---

community, but more often such statements are unsubstantiated assertions with no textual base.

[45] In relation to Gal 6.12-13, Martyn note that, "'the teachers' lack of complete success does not cause Paul to speak politely. In his description he...reduces their mission to the single act of circumcision." (Martyn, *Galatians*, 560).

[46] Meier, *Law and History in Matthew's Gospel*, 29.

[47] In terms of the structure of the Sermon on the Mount, Meier argues that 5.17-20 has a pivotal place. Although noting that the parables on salt and light (5.13-16) may have a slight undertone of warning, they primarily build upon the message of comfort, promise and exhortation contained in the beatitudes. By contrast, "The tone changes to one of firm warning (Μὴ νομίσητε), and the four verses of 5.17-20 speak of a new, hitherto untouched topic: Mosaic Law....This programmatic statement on the Law is then illustrated by six antitheses (5.21-48), which are introduced by 5.20 (and, in a broader sense, by the whole of 5.17-20). Mt 5.20 thus serves as a type of 'bridge' or transition between the statement of principle (5.17-19) and the applications or illustrations (5.21-48)." (Meier, *Law and History in Matthew's Gospel*, 29).

most natural way to approach the topic, he argues that it is legitimate in the
present case since only 5.18 has a parallel in any of the other gospels (Lk
16.17). He thus states,

> It seems advisable, therefore, to make an exception to the rule of following the given
> order, and to place 5.18 first in our treatment, since it offers the greatest possibilities
> for using objective 'controls' in discerning tradition and redaction. But besides
> having a Lukan parallel, Mt 5.18 is also of key exegetical importance because it
> seems to be the pericope's most stringent and uncompromising proclamation of the
> perduring value of the Mosaic Law (in apparent contradiction to the very antitheses it
> introduces).[48]

It appears, however, that decision has a further benefit for Meier, which he
does not state. It allows him to treat first the only verse in the pericope that
has a temporal reference and he then makes this the framework of
interpretation against which the other verses are understood. While the
present study has chosen to treat the antitheses prior to the statement on
the law in order to focus attention on Matthew's own commentary of his
programmatic statement, this does not correspond to Meier's approach. For
what Meier does in his approach is to break up the inner coherence of the
logical progression of a self-contained pericope. The 'control' that he
claims to have gained in terms of comparison between the verse (5.18) and
the source material it draws upon, is more than negated by the loss of the
'control' that the logic of the Matthean argument provides. Given these
reservations, it needs to be noted that at the end of his third chapter Meier
does restore the Matthean sequence and hence accounts for the logical
progression albeit in terms of the temporal indicators of 5.18.

Meier, starting with v. 17, notes that Jesus' pronouncement "warns
against thinking his activity concerning the Law and the prophets is purely
negative or destructive."[49] Instead it is argued that Jesus comes as an
eschatological fulfiller and that this is emphasized in 5.18, where with "the
solemnity of an apocalyptic prophet, Jesus assures his audience that, until
the eschatological passing away of heaven and earth which signals the new
age, not the slightest part of the law will pass, until all prophesied events
come to pass."[50] However, unlike apocalyptic expectations at Qumran, this
period is not inaugurated by some final decisive battle between the powers
of good and evil that unmistakably heralds in the new era (cf., 1QM).[51]

---

[48] Meier, *Law and History in Matthew's Gospel*, 45.

[49] Meier, *Law and History in Matthew's Gospel*, 123.

[50] Meier, *Law and History in Matthew's Gospel*, 123.

[51] The composite nature of the war scroll is well known, along with the different time
schemes it presents for the battle and the overthrow of the 'sons of darkness'. However,
there is a clear belief that this apocalyptic victory inaugurates an era of permanent and
undisputed divine reign. The battle is, therefore, the final encounter between good and
evil. 'This shall be a time of salvation for the people of God, an age of dominion for all

Rather, Meier suggests that it commences for Matthew, at least proleptically, with the death and resurrection of Jesus. Key to this interpretation is Meier's understanding that the earthquake, shattered rocks and the opening of the tombs of the dead with the reanimation of the corpses that they contained (Matt 27.51b-53) are a prefigurement of the eschaton. Since only Matthew presents these events, Meier concludes that they are *die Wende der Zeit*, and thus concludes he that "the death-resurrection of Jesus is the apocalyptic terminus prophesied in 5.18."[52] However, it is not only the rigidity of this salvation history framework that leads one to question whether the Matthean understanding was as fully developed as Meier proposes,[53] but also texts in Matthew's gospel that speak of eschatological fulfilment prior to the cataclysmic events. In particular, Matthew speaks of the arrival of the kingdom prior to the crucifixion, Matt 3.2; 4.11-17; 12.28. For Matthew, the eschatological era does not dawn with the death of Jesus, but has been breaking into history through his preaching and miracles. Meier, continuing with his sequential treatment of 5.17-20, sees v. 19 as presenting the corollary that prior to the new age "5.19 inculcates faithfulness to the Torah while the old aeon lasts."[54] Finally, 5.20 is both a transition to the antitheses that follow, but also stresses that righteousness is the new goal of life in Matthean community.

There are many strengths in Meier's detailed exegetical work. He clearly presents a unified understanding of Matt 5.17-48 in relation to the theology of the evangelist and also provides a possible insight into handling the apparently conflicting mission statements in Matthew. Nonetheless, his insistence that Matthew viewed the Easter events as marking the disjunction between two eras appears forced. It appears that a

---

members of His company, and for everlasting destruction of all the company of Satan....The dominion of the Kittim shall come to an end and iniquity shall be vanquished, leaving no remnant; [for the sons] of darkness there shall be no escape. {the sons of righteous]ness shall shine over the ends of the earth; they shall go on shining until all the seasons of darkness are consumed and, at the season appointed by God, His exalted greatness shall shine eternally to the peace, blessing, glory and joy and long light of all the sons of light.' (1QM 1.5-9). By comparison, the apocalyptic age, according to Meier's representation of Matthean eschatology, is inaugurated at least partially through the death and resurrection of Jesus.

[52] Meier, *Law and History in Matthew's Gospel*, 123.

[53] While in broad agreement with his exegetical conclusions in relation to 5.17-48, Stanton nonetheless questions the overall *heilsgeschichte* framework that Meier has imposed on the gospel. Thus Stanton cautions, "his salvation-historical schema seems to me to be too rigid: for Matthew, it is the birth and ministry of Jesus (see especially 4.12-17) as well as the death and resurrection of Jesus which mark the inauguration of the new aeon." (Stanton, 'The Origins and Purpose of Matthew's Gospel', 1937).

[54] Meier, *Law and History in Matthew's Gospel*, 123.

period of transition is envisaged by the evangelist, who sees the inclusion of the gentiles as part of the unfolding of the divine plan throughout the gospel and within the life of his own community. It is also dubious whether Matthew saw the resurrection as marking the close of the mission to Israel and the commencement of Gentile outreach in such clearly differentiated categories.[55] However, overall Meier's reading better accounts for the tensions within the Matthean narrative.

5.2 Context

Within the wider narrative of Matthew's gospel the programmatic statement dealing with the law (Matt 5.17-20) is placed in the context of Jesus' lengthy discourse set upon the mountain. Its link to the material that follows can be readily explained in terms of both structure and thematic content. Structurally, v. 20 provides a transition or bridge to the material in vv. 21-48. The formulaic opening in v. 20, λέγω γὰρ ὑμῖν (cf., 5.18), introduces a phrase reminiscent of the authoritative pronouncement that will be place on the lips of the Matthean Jesus throughout the antitheses as he declares his own interpretation of Torah, (Matt 5.22, 28, 32, 34, 39, 44).[56] The two differences in the formula used in the antitheses are the introduction of the grammatically necessary adversative δέ to formulate the contrast, and even greater stress being placed on the authority figure who utters the contrasting statement by employing the emphatic ἐγώ. Thematically, the reference to δικαιοσύνη in v. 20 links the antitheses to the preceding section by making them illustrations of the type of righteousness that is required for entrance into the kingdom.[57] In this vein,

---

[55] This view is more fully represented in Meier's slightly later paper, 'Nations or Gentiles in Matt 28:19', 94-102. As Saldarini notes, this perspective is based on a number of questionable assumptions. "The view that the mission to Israel is in the past and is now closed was commonly held. It is based on understanding ἔθνη in 28:19 as referring exclusively to non-Jews, on a periodization of chaps. 24-25 that associates the destruction of Jerusalem with the end of the Jewish mission, on a reading of chap. 10 that places the Jewish mission in the Palestinian past, and similar exegetical arguments." (Saldarini, 'The Gospel of Matthew and the Jewish-Christian Conflict', 43 n. 16).

[56] Hagner comments on the function of this authoritative speech marker as an important structural indicator. He states, "V 20 has the 'I say unto you' formula again, emphatically pointing to the righteousness in the following verses." (Hagner, *Matthew 1-13*, 104).

[57] This point is developed by both Guelich and Hagner. The former observes that "[an] ethical element is implicit in the comparison with the scribes and the Pharisees and is explicit in the evangelist's deliberate pairing of 5.20 with 5.19 as well as by his use of 5.20 to set the stage for the demands of 5.21-48....An even 'greater righteousness' was necessary. The following section of 5.21-48 indicates what the *righteousness that*

Hagner sees that "Jesus expects, as the antitheses to follow show, a new and higher kind of righteousness that rests upon the presence of the eschatological kingdom he brings and that finds its definition and content in his definitive and authoritative exposition of the law."[58] Furthermore, the use of the term righteousness forms a literary *inclusio* around the antitheses, 5.20 and 6.1. This not only highlights Jesus statements as declarations of the new righteousness that is being called for amongst community members, but also demonstrates that the material in 6.1ff., through a negative critique of inappropriate behaviour, illustrates the type of 'piety' that is not to be exhibited within the group. In this sense the link between 5.17-20 and the rest of the material that follows in the Sermon on the Mount is perhaps most plausibly understood as an exposition of the type of 'righteousness' that is called for in v20.

It is, however, much harder to account for the link between the statement on the law and the material that precedes those declarations. Immediately preceding 5.17-20 is the short section of exhortation in vv. 13-16 that uses the metaphors of salt and light to depict the distinctive prominence that should be apparent from a life of discipleship. Davies and Allison find it easier to account for the thematic links between this statement on discipleship and the material later in the Sermon on the Mount, than they do with the material that follows in vv. 17-20. Hence they state,

> The summary description of the disciples as salt and light, a description which fits those who live as 5.21-7.12 will detail, has the whole world (γῆ, κόσμος) as its backdrop. This implies that the Gentile mission is presupposed. The followers of Jesus are salt and light for all, for Jew and Gentile the world over. So Matthew's universalism is once more apparent.[59]

However, they fail to suggest a possible reason for the transition to the statements about Jesus' relationship to the law, which immediately follows on from the sayings on discipleship. Although not stated explicitly, Luz appears to see a disjunction between these two sequential blocks. He states, "Verses 17-20 introduce the main part of the Sermon on the Mount. Matthew 5.17 and 7.12 form an inclusion with the catchwords νόμος and προφῆται."[60] In fact, with the exception of Guelich, most commentators do

---

exceeds is by giving concrete examples of how that conduct in keeping with the will of God expresses itself." (Guelich, *The Sermon on the Mount*, 157-8).

[58] Hagner, *Matthew 1-13*, 109.

[59] Davies and Allison, *Matthew*, vol 1, 479.

[60] Luz, *Matthew 1-7*, 255. Again, in a similar vein to Davies and Allison, Luz sees a link between vv13-16 and the antitheses, but not with the programmatic statement concerning Torah. He sees the light which Christians bring into the world as being shown forth through their works and actions. Such appropriate actions are exemplified in the reorientation of behaviours and priorities that are described in the antitheses.

not even attempt to account for the transition between vv. 16 and 17, rather they see v. 17 both commencing a new topic and opening the central section of the sermon. In this sense the preceding material is seen more as a prologue, rather than a related topic. Yet the weakness of this position is that a number of the themes from 5.13-16 are taken up in subsequent sections of Matt 5-7.

As was noted above, Guelich has attempted to account for some degree of continuity between these two sections. He suggests both a forward and backward perspective are provided by 5.13-16. Initially reading v. 13 in connection with the beatitudes of persecution he sees the following link. "The warning of 5.13 cautions the disciples, the *salt of the earth*, about losing their effectiveness as disciples in mission. Whereas the beatitudes of 5.3, 10, 11-12 assure the afflicted of God's blessing, 5.13 admonishes one to beware of capitulating to the pressures of discipleship."[61] Then turning his attention to the material that follows he suggests the following relationship,

> [T]he nature of that mission (5.14-16) introduces the theme of 5.17-7.12. The light that shines (mission) is the *good deeds* that bring *glory to the Father* (5.16). The good deeds are synonymous with the 'greater righteousness' (5.20) and are defined in 5.21-7.12. These *good deeds*, as will be seen, bring glory to the Father because of their very nature as life and conduct commensurate with the restored relationship (*your Father*) between the disciple and others (5.21-48) and the disciple and God (6.1-7.12).[62]

However, although Guelich asserts that the sayings on discipleship introduce the theme of 5.17-7.12, he does not account for the material in 5.17-19. Perhaps he does better than most scholars, for not only does he manage to see a link with v. 20, but he also tries to link the whole section on the law with what precedes.

So can the material in 5.17-19 be related to the forgoing material in a plausible manner, or is it necessary to admit that Matthew has introduced an irreconcilable discontinuity into his narrative at this point?[63] First, it

---

[61] Guelich, *The Sermon on the Mount*, 130.

[62] Guelich, *The Sermon on the Mount*, 130.

[63] This second option is taken up by Green. Commenting on the extended beatitude on persecution (5.11-12), he notes the following structural relationship with the material that follows. "[T]he beatitude on the persecuted, is taken up, as we have seen, in the subsidiary beatitude at 5.11-12. Most scholars see the section as running on to 5.16, and the series of sayings at 5.13-16 is to be understood as an injunction to disciples not to keep their heads down, not to avoid persecution by being so inconspicuous that they have no example and no message for the world at large. 5.17-20, on the other hand, is not concerned with persecution as such, but with the 'greater righteousness' for which disciples must aim whether persecuted for it or not." (Green, *Matthew, Poet of the Beatitudes*, 258).

needs to be conceded that the difficulty that commentators have demonstrated in accounting for continuity at this point stems from a significant change in the form, theme and tone of the material in each section. However, this apparent *aporia* does not necessarily mean that the evangelist had envisaged these statements as a complete change of topic, with no connection to the sayings relating to discipleship. It is helpful to draw upon Davies and Allison's insight that the material in 5.17-20 is best classified as being a "*prokatalepsis*, that is an anticipation of objections."[64] Having just mapped out his generalized portrait of discipleship, the evangelist seeks to have Jesus apparently anticipate those charges that may be brought against his disciples. Contrary to what Torah observant Jews may think, such mission orientated discipleship,[65] with its focus on being salt and light in a rotten and dark world, does not constitute a rejection of the law. Thus, having presented the model for distinctive discipleship in vv. 13-16,[66] Matthew next addresses the fundamental criticism that was

---

[64] Davies and Allison, *Matthew*, vol 1, 481.

[65] Commenting on the references to 'earth' and 'world', Davies and Allison see quite naturally a mission orientation provided. They state, "Moreover, Jesus followers are not the salt and light of *Israel* (contrast T. Levi 14.3) but of the whole *world* (the passage thus presupposes the Gentile mission)." (Davies and Allison, *Matthew*, vol 1, 472). Cf. Green, *Matthew, Poet of the Beatitudes*, 249.

[66] These statements concerning discipleship are of course not entirely due to Matthean editorial creation, in fact a substantial core of the material is drawn from source material, and there is a reasonable probability that a number of these sayings may be traced back to the historical Jesus. Source critically, the parallels may be presented as follows:

5.13a	no parallel
5.13b	cf. Lk 14.34b (Q); Mk 9.50
5.13c	cf. Lk 14.35a (Q)
5.14a	no parallel
5.14b	cf. G. Thom 32; P. Oxy 1.7
5.15	cf. Lk 11.33 (Q); Mk 4.21; Lk 8.16; G. Thom 33b
5.16	no parallel

Thus, the two direct addresses to the audience are due to Matthean redaction (5.13a, 14a), showing that the pattern of discipleship being described is applicable to the hearers of the gospel. The Fellows of the Jesus Seminar have found an additional reason for seeing the two introductory sayings of 5.13a and 14a as Matthean. They state, "The first saying is Matthew's creation...As a parallel to 'You are the salt of the earth,' Matthew has created the saying in 5.14a: 'You are the light of the world.' Jesus himself rejected insider/outsider discriminations of this sort: he included outsiders such as sinners and toll collectors, along with other 'undesirables,' among his companions." (Funk, Hoover, *et al.*, *The Five Gospels*, 139). Likewise, the final imperative calls for community members to practice a type of discipleship that is qualitatively distinctive, of such an ethical standard that all observers will render praise to God. As Beare observes, the lives of Matthean disciples "are to be lived in such a way that they will be a constant testimony to

being levelled by Jews who did not accept Jesus' messianic claims: namely, that the life of discipleship required by the Matthean group was contrary to Torah, since it involved an abrogation of certain halakhic requirements. It is difficult to imagine why this charge would be levelled if the community had not deviated from the law in perceptible ways in the eyes of the synagoue based opponents.[67]

The response given in 5.17-20 seeks to legitimize the Matthean pattern of discipleship by demonstrating that it is a lifestyle of obedience to the divine ordinances. The charge of the opponents is rebutted in two ways. First, it is dismissed by having Jesus pronounce with decisive authority that, contrary to appearances, he in fact upholds the law. Second, in a typical game of brinkmanship common among opposing groups,[68] the evangelist calls into question the pattern of discipleship exhibited by scribes and Pharisees. Assessing their behaviour in terms of δικαιοσύνη, he asserts that the level of righteousness they practice is not sufficient to assure entry into the kingdom. On the contrary, only his group members can be assured of such a privilege provided that they conform to the pattern of discipleship he presents. Matthew continues this defence, which is in all likelihood has the pastoral function of consolidating the beliefs of group members rather than convincing adversaries, by presenting the examples contained in the antitheses. Their function is to illustrate how the group upholds the law, yet surpasses its literal observance in terms of the abounding righteousness that has become the Matthean catchcry.

---

others of the glory of the heavenly Father." (Beare, *The Gospel according to Matthew*, 138).

[67] By contrast, Sim states, "The evidence of the Gospel is clear that this Christian Jewish group both accepted without question the validity of the Torah and attempted to observe it in its entirety." (Sim, *The Gospel of Matthew and Christian Judaism*, 123). To hold this viewpoint together with the strident polemic against scribes and Pharisees, Sim see the hostility arising from a difference of opinion over how exactly to practice Torah, yet he does not clearly account for how such a law observant community as he presents the Matthean group, could be so punctilious in maintaining the law but also so far removed from emergent rabbinic Judaism. Sim's one suggestion appears to be drawn straight from the work of Bornkamm and Barth, namely that the concept of mercy and the love commandment prioritise the ordinances of the law (128). In the same vein, the antitheses intensify Torah, but do not abrogate or revoke it stipulations (130).

[68] Obviously, the Qumran group are an important contemporary Jewish example of this phenomenon. The competing rulings in 4QMMT is of course a case in point. Also, 11QT with its Temple based form of discipleship, advocates a more precise and exacting observance of the offering of sacrifices and libations (13-16; 18-24), the celebration of festival days (17; 25), and maintenance of purity laws (45-52).

5.3 Source and Redaction in Matt 5.17-20

Just about every possible combination and option has been proposed concerning the question of the origin of the material in the programmatic statement on the law. Also tied up with this discussion is the more difficult question of determining if any of these sayings can be traced back to the historical Jesus, and if so, in what form were they originally uttered and what did they mean in their original context? These issues cannot be ignored even when studying the Matthean intent behind incorporating such sayings into his narrative, for one way of dealing with sayings that appear to promote strict observance of Torah has been to describe them as inherited material (perhaps even dominical utterances) that Matthew took over into his account without necessarily fully agreeing with their meaning.

In relation to source criticism, there are few certain conclusions that can be drawn. However, it is apparent that Matt 5.18 does have a parallel in Lk 16.17, and it is also conceivable that the tradition behind Lk 16.16 may have shaped the first evangelist's formulation of Matt 5.17. The remaining two verses in the programmatic statement concerning the law (5.19-20) do not have parallels in the other canonical gospels, so it is harder to determine whether this material is due to redactional composition by the evangelist, or whether they stem from a pre-Matthean source (usually referred to as M).[69] This lack of a comparative source has led to

---

[69] Separation of M material from Matthean redaction is notoriously difficult, and even raises the more fundamental question of the existence of an M source. Brooks in his study of the Matthean community as reflected in the M material tries to set up a number of criteria for identifying and isolating tradition that constitutes this source. He suggests that aporias may reveal source material since "*a disjunction in the text that would not be expected from an author who is composing freely* will distinguish sayings that merit further investigation." (Brooks, *Matthew's Community, the Evidence of His Special Sayings Material*, 18). Having isolated a potential corpus of sayings, one next looks for redactional phrases to determine whether a particular saying may actually be redactional. "The criterion of vocabulary supports other criteria and helps to analyse aporiae." (19) Finally, one can ask if the content of a saying coheres with the evangelist's overall theology. Brooks does state that such a method will not reveal all of the sayings that belong to M, but he does feel that what is suggested is almost certainly authentic source material. He argues, "The method necessarily emphasizes somewhat one-sidedly the discontinuity and uniqueness of the sayings designated M. Matthew probably incorporates tradition into his Gospel that cannot be critically distinguished from his own style or interests, but our desire to be as certain as possible forces us to consider only what can be distinguished." (19) In many ways the criteria for distinguish content do not appear to have progressed much beyond the position postulated by Streeter. He suggests, "this tradition, corresponding to that element in Matthew which we have styled M, includes sayings of a strongly Judaistic character. The fact is one that has often been misconceived. It cannot be too emphatically insisted that this element in Matthew

diversity of opinion in understanding the material as either source or redaction. The issue is usually assessed by looking for distinctive Matthean vocabulary, and if found, the saying is usually classified as stemming from the evangelist. However, a number of times Matthew takes up a phrase found in his sources and replicates it in his own editorial sayings,[70] which means that although a repeated phrase is found this might not be due to redaction, but rather, it may be the seed from which the duplications have sprouted. Moreover, the lack of repeated phraseology does not ensure that a statement stems from a source, it could be an editorial creation, which due to the topic being treated requires terminology not replicated elsewhere in the gospel.

Turning to a sequential source analysis of the individual verses, it needs to be noted that Matt 5.17 does not have any close parallels in the canonical gospels, Thomas, nor is it utilised in the Didache.[71] Yet, although the saying in Q 16.16 is most clearly paralleled in Matt 11.13[72] it also appears that this tradition may have shaped the material in 5.17. Tuckett supports this possibility in his discussion of the original Q ordering of the material in Lk 16.16-18. He observes, "Matt 5.17 looks suspiciously like Matthew's rewriting of the saying in Lk 16.16. (Matthew's close parallel to Lk 16.16 comes elsewhere in Matt 11.12f.)'[73] Comparing the Lukan form of this Q saying, ὁ νόμος καὶ προφῆτας μέχρι Ἰωάννου· ἀπὸ τότε ἡ βασιλεία τοῦ θεοῦ εὐαγγελίζεται καὶ πᾶς εἰς αὐτὴν βιάζεται (Lk 16.16), it becomes apparent that if Matthew was dependent

---

reflects, not primitive Jewish Christianity, but a later Judaistic reaction against the Petro-Pauline liberalism in the matter of the Gentile Mission and the observance of the Law." (Streeter, *The Four Gospels*, 512). It needs to be observed that if this position is adopted, then it is *a priori* impossible that any M saying can be seen as stemming from a dominical origin.

[70] Examples of this are to be found in the phrase γεννήνατα ἐχιδνῶν (Matt 3.7; 12.34; 23.33). While the first reference has a Lukan parallel (Matt 3.7//Lk 3.7), the final two usages are due to the evangelist's duplication. Obviously, without Luke's gospel it might be incorrectly assumed that the repeated use meant all three examples were redactional. Similarly, the phrase ἐκεῖ ἔσται ὁ κλαυθμὸς καὶ ὁ βρυγμός τῶν ὀδόντων (Matt 8.12; 13.42, 50; 22.13; 24.51; 25.30), again the first usage is paralleled (Lk 13.28). Once again we see Matthew taking up a judgment phrase from Q and applying it in new contexts.

[71] The suggestion is not being advanced that the Didache is a possible source for Matthew's gospel, nor even that it may preserve Synoptic source material independently of the synoptic gospel. The Didache is best seen as a compilation and reworking of synoptic material and is most heavily dependent upon Matthew for the material it utilises. All that is being noted is that the material in 5.17-20 is not replicated in the Didache.

[72] It is not appropriate to tackle the vexed questions of the original form or meaning of the sayings in Lk 16.16-18. Here, only the possibility that Q 16.16 may have assisted in the evangelist's shaping of Matt 5.17 is noted.

[73] Tuckett, *Q and the History of Early Christianity*, 407.

upon this Q saying at 5.17, it was only in a minimal manner drawing on the phrase 'the law and the prophets'. While this is a stereotypical phrase, the fact that it occurs immediately preceding Q 16.17, means that it is not improbable that the same sequential relationship exhibited in Matt 5.17-18 is not due to chance. However, this leaves the large question of how one is to account for the majority of the rest of the material that comprises the logion of Matt 5.17.

In his redactional investigation of this verse Meier suggests that to a large degree that pre-Matthean tradition underlies this saying. Although Meier concedes that certainty is impossible because of the lack of a synoptic parallel, nonetheless he suggests that there are indicators that lend weight to the suggestion that Matthew has incorporated existing tradition at this point. He states, "Mt is a pure form of the ἦλθον-words, a *Gattung* which Mt did not create. Mt redactional activity seems rather to be the prefixing of μὴ νομίσητε to an ἦλθον -word he has received."[74] Second, Meier suggests that the reference to 'the prophets' is Matthean redaction since the notion of fulfilling the prophets is conceptually unclear. He presents his argument in the following terms,

> Once we understand Mt's general interest in prophecy and in particular his redaction of 5.18 (5.18d inserting the idea of prophetic fulfilment into what was merely a statement about Law, thus producing a 'Law-and-prophets' theme in 5.18 as well as in 5.17), to try and reduce προφῆτας to the meaning of 'the moral teaching of the prophets' would be forced. Yet to take προφῆτας at its full Matthean value causes difficulty in translating καταλύω. 'To declare the prophets unrealizable' is both an awkward idea and a doubtful translation of the verb.[75]

Third, it is argued that the notion of 'fulfilling the law' is unlikely to be original since it is absent from the LXX.[76] Thus replacing the infinitive πληρῶσαι with ποιεῖν, Meier comes up with the following reconstruction of

---

[74] Meier, *Law and History in Matthew's Gospel*, 83.

[75] Meier, *Law and History in Matthew's Gospel*, 84.

[76] Although Meier is correct concerning the absence from the LXX, he plays down the wider evidence of the NT in an unacceptable manner. He states that with respect to this phrase that, "In fact, it is unknown to the rest of the NT, with the exception of a few passages in Paul." (Meier, *Law and History in Matthew's Gospel*, 84). However, these Pauline passages are far more relevant than the Septuagintal evidence which may pre-date the Gospel of Matthew by over three hundred years. While the references from the epistles show that a Jewish contemporary from the second half of the first century could use this phrase and expect to be understood. The most significant Pauline texts are, Rom 8.4; 13.8 and Gal 5.14. In Rom 8.4 Paul conclude his description of God's action of sending forth his son in the likeness of sinful flesh with the following purposive clause: ἵνα τὸ δικαίωμα τοῦ νόμου πληρωθῇ ἐν ἡμῖν (8.4a). In Rom 13.8 Paul interprets the Golden rule as fulfilment of the law, ὁ γὰρ ἀγαπῶν τὸν ἕτερον νόμον πεπλήρωκεν. Similarly in Gal 5.14, Torah is seen as being fulfilled through love of neighbours, ὁ γὰρ πᾶς νόμος ἐν ἑνὶ λόγῳ πεπλήρωται, ἐν τῷ ἀγαπήσεις τὸν πλησίον σου ὡς σεαυτόν.

a traditional saying that he feels stands behind Matt 5.17: ἦλθον καταλῦσαι τὸν νόμον· οὐκ ἦλθον καταλῦσαι ἀλλὰ ποιεῖν.[77]

However, a number of points must be noted against Meier's reconstruction. First, simply because this saying partially parallels an existing form does not mean that Matthew was not responsible for reshaping the tradition, nor does the fact that this material may draw on a source imply that Matthew opposes the original meaning. It has already been noted that Matthew has a penchant for taking up forms or phrases from his tradition and duplicating their use in obviously redactional forms. The examples cited previously were of the phrases γεννήνατα ἐχιδνῶν (Matt 3.7; 12.34; 23.33) and ἐκεῖ ἔσται ὁ κλαυθμὸς καὶ ὁ βρυγμός τῶν ὀδόντων (Matt 8.12; 13.42, 50; 22.13; 24.51; 25.30), however, in the woes of Matt 23.13-33 the evangelist creates sayings of the same form, but which are unparalleled in Luke's gospel.[78] The second criticism against Meier's reconstruction is his dismissive attitude towards the reference to the prophets. As has been discussed, the phrase 'the law or the prophets'[79] is maybe the only part of v. 17 that has a synoptic parallel (cf., Lk 16.16a). Furthermore, and more significantly, Meier has failed to realize that within contemporary Judaism and other NT texts there is ample evidence for seeing the terminology 'the law and the prophets' as a stereotypical reference to Jewish sacred scriptural traditions.[80] Thus, the reference to not

---

[77] The final verb in this reconstruction is not certain according to Meier, and he offers at three possible alternatives: τηρεῖν, φυλασσεῖν, or πρασσεῖν, (cf., Meier, *Law and History in Matthew's Gospel*, 85).

[78] The woe against the proselytising activity of the scribes and Pharisees in Matt 23.15 has no synoptic parallel. The two woes contained in Matt 23.16 and 25 obviously are draw from Q sayings, but these were not originally cast as woes. Similarly, the woe in 23.14 draws upon Mark 12.40. This final example is particularly important, for although in all likelihood it was not part of the originally Matthean text (the verse is omitted in the following witnesses: ℵ B D L Z Θ f¹ 33. 892* pc a aur e ff¹ g¹ vg^{st.ww} sy^s sa mae bo^{pt}, the combined witness of some of the most significant uncial mss, a number of important minuscules and a wide spectrum of the versional evidence means that the case for Matt 23.14 not being part of the original gospel text is extremely strong), it demonstrates that even a post-Matthean scribe could create a saying that aligned with an existing form, and this does not necessarily mean that the saying must stem from an existing source.

[79] Contrary to Guelich (*The Sermon on the Mount*, 138), one should not give much significance to the fact that the Matthean phrase reads '*or* the prophets', rather than the more common combination 'the law *and* the prophets'. The conjunctive 'or' appears grammatically· preferable after the negative imperative μὴ νομίσητε for reasons of emphasis.

[80] Within the NT references to 'the law and the prophets' include Matt 7.12; Lk 16.16; Rom 3.21. There is also the significant reference in Lk 24.44-5 that may be an early witness to the emergence of a threefold canon within the Hebrew bible as well as the tendency to refer to this as scripture: '…everything written about me in the law of

abolishing the law and the prophets is simply a means of asserting that Jesus was not dispensing with the corpus of tradition contained in those writings. Finally Meier's attempt to replace πληρῶσαι with ποιεῖν is too speculative to command assent. Even Brooks, who is sympathetic to attempts to recover M tradition, cannot support Meier in describing 5.17 as demonstrably pre-Matthean. Summing up his disagreement with Meier, Brooks states,

> Matt 5.17 combined with 5.18a,d designates Jesus as the one who eschatologically fulfills the Law and the prophets. The evidence of Matthew's mode of expression in 11.13 reduces the weight of the supposed aporia in 5.17. A clear case for an underlying M saying cannot be demonstrated on the basis of this evidence.[81]

However, there still appears to be a firm basis for seeing the existence of a pre-Matthean saying behind v. 17,[82] especially because of the echo of the phrase 'the law and the prophets' from Q 16.16a.[83]

Moses and the prophets and the Psalms must be fulfilled. Then he opened their minds to understand the scriptures.' Within the DSS the following important example occurs: 'to you we have [written] that you may understand the book of Moses [and] the book[s of the p[rophets and of Davi[d...]' (4QMMT 91-95, 4Q397 14-21). Also in the introduction to the Community Rule the text refers to everything God 'by the hand of Moses and by the hand of his servants the prophets' (1QS 1.3). Other Jewish literature from around the turn of the eras demonstrates that this was not only a sectarian perspective. The text of 2 Maccabees reads 'Encouraging them from the law and the prophets...' (2 Macc 15.9a). In his *Contra Apionem* 1.37-43 Josephus describes the Jewish books as the five books of Moses, the prophetic writings and the four books of hymns. The prologue to Eccesiasticus opens with the statement 'Whereas many great teachings have been given to us in the law and the prophets...' (Ecclus). Later examples can be found in rabbinic literature *m. Yadaim* 3.5; *m. Megillah* 4.3; *y. Megillah* 73d; *t. Megillah* 4.20; and *b. Bava Batra* 14b-15a. Discussing the development of the Hebrew canon and the language used to refer to its components, Barton makes the following point. "Biblical books became accepted as authoritative at different times during the post-exilic period...by the age of the Maccabees the Torah had long been regarded as authoritative but not exclusively so, in the sense that it formed a closed body of material to which nothing could be added. By the end of the second century BC a similar conclusion had been reached about the prophets." (Barton, *Oracles of God: Perceptions of Ancient Prophecy in Israel after the Exile*, 29).

[81] Brooks, *Matthew's Community, the Evidence of His Special Sayings Material*, 27.

[82] Guelich asserts a position that is quite similar to Meier, but his arguments are not as clearly articulated. His reconstruction, which is somewhat misleadingly found in the section he entitles translation, reads as follows. "Do not think that I have come to annul the law; I have not come to set aside the Scriptures but rather to fulfill them." (134). He bases this reconstruction on the following points; "the presence of *or* in 5.17 betrays a Matthean redactional trait and implies (1) that 5.17 was indeed a pre-Matthean saying referring originally to the *Law* and (2) that Matthew inserted *or the Prophets* to complete his preferable phrase, *the Law and the Prophets*." (Guelich, *The Sermon on the Mount*, 138). However, there appears to be something lacking in the logic that Guelich puts forward. Even if the phrase 'or the prophets' is redactional, this does not automatically

Tuckett makes a number of important points that support understanding 5.17 as primarily due to redactional activity. First, he notes that any reworking by the evangelist cannot be limited to the odd phrase or word, rather there is a thoroughgoing Matthean feel to the entire logion. As he states, "The whole of verse 17 has clearly undergone some redaction: for the construction μὴ νομίσητε ὅτι ἦλθον... οὐκ ἦλθον ... ἀλλά cf. x.34, (diff. Lk. xii. 51); for 'law and prophets' cf. vii. 12; xxii. 40; for πληρῶσαι cf. the formula quotations."[84] The second significant point made by Tuckett involves consideration of v. 17 in respect to v. 18d, which is almost certainly Matthean redaction. He suggests,

> Possibly verse 18d should be taken in conjunction with verse 17: Matthew did think that 'all things' had come with Jesus, and so Jesus' teaching now fulfils the old law which, in its immutable character, has now by implication had its day. This therefore suggests that 18d is a redactional attempt to counter idea in the rest of verse 18.[85]

The observation is generally sound, for the redactional comment at the end of v. 18 does appear to moderate the preceding statement in that verse, and also bring it into line with the perspective of v. 17. This would lend weight to the conclusion that the similar outlook contained in 5.17, like v. 18, is due to the evangelist's redactional interests and if there was ever any traditional material behind v. 17 those traditions have been so heavily reworked to conform the saying to the Matthean perspective that they are no longer recoverable, or even identifiable. Luz comes to a similar conclusion about the prehistory of this verse. He states, "Much is redactional: πληπόω, νόμος/προφῆται, their connection with ἤ. How to judge the formal relationship with Mk 10.34 and whether the evangelist

---

preclude the rest of the verse from also being redactional, in fact it may well suggest the opposite.

[83] Banks, marshalling the evidence in a similar manner to Meier and Guelich, sees the saying as not only being pre-Matthean, but dominical. After cited the evidence in much the same form as we have described Meier's argument, Banks concludes, "All this suggests that rather than being a Matthean construction, or a creation of the early Palestinian church, the saying is substantially authentic." (Banks, *Jesus and the Law in the Synoptic Tradition*, 212). However, the jump Banks makes from pre-Matthean tradition to an authentic Jesuanic logion requires more support. He states that "Since Matthew alone preserves the saying, however, some account must be given for its omission from the other two gospels." (213). His solution is to argue that the saying was preserved in M, and hence was not accessible to the other evangelists. However, this view of M is far removed from Streeter's proposal that M was a later Judaistic source. (Streeter, *The Four Gospels*, 512).

[84] Tuckett, *The Revival of the Griesbach Hypothesis*, 152.

[85] Tuckett, *The Revival of the Griesbach Hypothesis*, 152.

has edited a traditional saying are disputed matters. But how it read we can scarcely now say."[86] Hence the approach of both Tuckett and Luz appears more cautious in regard to the claims it makes about the recoverability of underlying source material for Matt 5.17. Further, this approach ensures that perceived attitudes to Torah within the Matthean community are not constructed in terms of postulating the evangelist's negative reaction to a hypothetical source. Instead, it allows the statement of v. 17 to be assessed on its own merit as a Matthean redactional creation.

The tradition history of Matt 5.18 is easier to discern at one level, because of the existence of the Lukan parallel (Lk 16.17). However, the significant divergences between the two forms means that a careful analysis is required to determine the changes made by the evangelists from the Q form of the saying.[87] Initially it needs to be noted that the Lukan version presents a shorter, matched pairing of statements with a more absolute pronouncement. It reads as follows: εὐκοπώτερον δέ ἐστιν τὸν οὐρανὸν καὶ τὴν γῆν παρελθεῖν ἤ τοῦ νόμου μίαν κεραίαν πεσεῖν (Lk 16.17). Although he does not say in precisely what way, Fitzmyer asserts that, "In v. 17 Luke has simplified the inherited material for the sake of his Gentile readers."[88] It is thus unclear whether Fitzmyer sees the Matthean

---

[86] Luz, *Matthew 1-7*, 256. Luz goes on to draw two consequences from this observation. "1. It is rash to trace this saying back to Jesus and to make it the anchor of the interpretation of Jesus' understanding of the law. 2. It is hazardous to (re)construct from this saying an Aramaic original and to make such a (re)construction the foundation of an interpretation of the difficult word πληπόω. That would mean interpreting difficult material by totally hypothetical suggestions!" (256).

[87] Kloppenborg Verbin sees this verse (Q 16.17), along with only Q 4.1-13; 11.42c, as forming the final redactional touching added to the Q document, the siglum Q³ is used to denote these final minor editorial additions. He states, "Since all three units, 4.1-13; 11.42c; and 16.17, share a common perspective on the centrality of the Torah, they are best treated together. Within the larger compositional units of Q there is no evidence of a nomistic piety, and indeed, no special interest in the Torah at all. Only with the Temptation narrative does Torah observance become an issue and only in 11.42c and 16.17 is there an explicit statement embracing the validity of the Torah. It is logical to locate all these Torah-centered glosses at one redactional stage. Since each fits uncomfortably in its current setting, and is either positioned to function with regard to the whole collection-as is the case with 4.1-13-or to correct or qualify sayings from the main redaction (11.42c; 16.17), this stage must be a late one." (Kloppenborg Verbin, *Excavating Q*, 153). Moreover, Kloppenborg Verbin suggests an approximate date for these final glosses. Whereas the bulk of the document was completed in the late fifties or early sixties, he sees the three nomistic additions being incorporated about a decade later. "[S]ince the temptation story (Q 4.1-13) and the two glosses (11.43c [*sic!* 11.42c]; 16.17) are probably later additions, it would mean that Q did not achieve its final form until slightly after the events of 70 CE, even if the bulk of Q was redacted just before the first revolt." (87).

[88] Fitzmyer, *Luke*, 1115.

version of the saying as closer to the original Q form, or if he believes both forms have deviated from the primitive logion. Nolland is more descriptive in outlining the redactional work that he feels can be traced to the respective evangelists. The repetition of the temporal clause in the Matthean version is seen as redactional duplication, whereas Luke is considered to have deleted the one original ἕως ἄν clause that Nolland feels was part of the Q form, and in its place substituted the opening phrase, εὐκοπώτερον δέ ἐστιν.[89] He puts forward his understanding of the tradition history in the following manner.

> The awkwardness (in Matthew's form) of having two consecutive ἕως ἄν, 'until,' clauses is normally taken as implying one is original (and so Luke has restructured to give an 'it is easier…' form to the comparison, perhaps under the influence of the tradition that he reproduces in 18.25 [basing himself solely on the similarity with this text, Dewey (*Forum* 5.2 [1989] 109-20) has pronounced in favour of the Lukan form, but on this assumption it is hard to see how the development of the Matthean text can be explained]), and that the other is Matthean (or pre-Matthean editing).[90]

Despite the fact that Nolland compounds parenthetical remark on top of parenthetical remark, making the logic hard to follow, one is left wondering why there must have been an ἕως ἄν clause in the original saying.

Treating Matt 5.18 in detail, Meier first of all observes that in terms of its fourfold structure the initial and final clauses are almost beyond question due to MattR. He argues that the opening phrase appears to be an addition made by the evangelist not only because it is unparalleled in the Lukan version of the saying, but also because this introductory formula with its ἀμὴν λέγω form is a Matthean favourite, with some form of this expression being used 31 times in the first gospel.[91] Similarly, the final clause, ἕως ἄν πάντα γένηται, is almost uniformly regarded as due to Matthean redaction. Many reasons are suggested for this judgement, including the most obvious reason – the omission of this expression in the

---

[89] Although presented in a more compressed form, Marshall's earlier commentary comes to the same conclusions as those supported by Nolland. He states, "Luke's construction with εὐκοπώτερον (5.23; 18.25) and two accusative and infinitive phrases differs from Matthew's rather redundant use of 'until' clauses, and may represent a stylistic revision." (Marshall, *The Gospel of Luke*, 630).

[90] Nolland, *Luke 9:21-18:34*, 815.

[91] Word statistics show that this is disproportionately an expression favoured by Matthew. Some form of ἀμὴν λέγω appears 31 times in Matt, as opposed to 13 times in Mk and 6 times in Luke. Adding further weight to this expression being redactional, Meier notes, "only Mt uses the formula with γὰρ after ἀμὴν. Mk comes close to this usage, but only in one case, Mk 14.9: ἀμὴν δὲ λέγω ὑμῖν. Since γὰρ seems to be a Matthean stylistic peculiarity embedded in an introductory formula – an introductory formula lacking in the Lukan parallel – it seems best to assign the whole of 5.18a to Matthean redaction." (Meier, *Law and History in Matthew's Gospel*, 58).

Lukan parallel. While many of the suggestions have strong weight in their own right, the cumulative case is impressive. Hagner argues, "Matthew's final 'ἕως' ('until') clause, finding no parallel in the Lukan version, gives the strong appearance of having been added by the evangelist as an explanation and strengthening of his point."[92] Tuckett draws attention to a Matthean redaction phrase that parallels 5.18d, thereby lending weight to seeing that phrase also as an editorial addition. He states, "the final ἕως ἂν πάντα γένηται phrase in verse 18*d* fits very badly with the other temporal ἕως phrase in verse 18*b*; this, together with the fact that there is a close parallel to the phrase in Matt. xxiv. 34 (diff. Mk. xiii. 36) suggests that 18*d* is also a redactional addition."[93] Meier's argument is much the same as that proposed by Tuckett, except that he suggests a theological reason for such an addition. His reasoning is that,

> the Lukan parallel and, ..., Mt's imitation of the language of the eschatological discourse (Mt 24=Mk 13) argue instead [here Meier is refuting Lohmeyer (*Das Evangelium des Matthäus*, 108)] that Mt carefully added 18d for his own theological purpose...How is Mt to bring the time limit of 18b into harmony with his view of when the Law (at least in some important parts) passes away? He does this by adding 18d: ἕως ἂν πάντα γένηται.[94]

These arguments appear compelling in adjudging Matt 5.18d to be an editorial saying that modifies the preceding statements.

However, the reasons for taking the first ἕως ἂν clause in v. 18b as traditional, rather than redactional, are not necessarily as strong as sometimes asserted. Meier turns his 'working hypothesis' into an established result without proof or argument. He states, "As a working hypothesis, let us suppose that Mt 5.18bc, being the most stringent form of the statement we can isolate, and containing as it does a chiasm obscured by both Mt and Lk, reflects the most primitive form of the logion available to us."[95] Then in a somewhat vitriolic comment he confesses, "Strange to say, it is sometimes affirmed that Lk has the stringent affirmation of the Law's perduring validity."[96] Yet is it really the case that Matthew's 'Until heaven and earth pass away...' is really any more stringent than Luke's 'It is easier for heaven and earth to pass away...?'[97] This seems to be a very

---

[92] Hagner, *Matthew 1-13*, 103.

[93] Tuckett, *The Revival of the Griesbach Hypothesis*, 152.

[94] Meier, *Law and History in Matthew's Gospel*, 58, 61.

[95] Meier, *Law and History in Matthew's Gospel*, 59.

[96] Meier, *Law and History in Matthew's Gospel*, 59 n. 50.

[97] Interestingly, although Gundry agrees with Meier that Matthew's form is more intense, this does not result in him reaching the same conclusion about this version being the more primitive form. In fact he sees Matthew responsible for the increased stringency. He states, "Matthew escalates 'But it is easier' (Luke 16.17) to the emphatic negative οὐ μή, 'by no means'." (Gundry, *Matthew*, 78).

flimsy datum for determining stringency of attitude towards the law, and
hence on this basis to assert the relative primitivity of the Matthean form
in comparison to that contained in Luke.

Yet, it needs to be acknowledged that Meier is not alone in advancing
such a suggestion, but this appears to be a case where an argument has
gained popular currency due to repetition, instead of being based on the
perspicacity of its reasoning.[98] However, this argument is far from certain,
and Davies and Allison have effectively exposed various weaknesses.
Basing their argument on word statistics they note, "Luke almost certainly
preserves Q. Both ἕως as a conjunction (Mt: 20; Mk: 5; Lk 15) and ἕως
with ἄν (Mt: 9; Mk: 3; Lk: 3) are readily ascribed to Matthew while
εὐκοπώτερον (Mt: 2; Mk: 2; Lk: 3) cannot be said to be characteristically
Lukan."[99] In contrast to this observation which concludes that both the ἕως
clauses are due to MattR, Luz appears confused in his logic in regard to
5.18. Firstly, he agrees with Davies and Allison in his judgment that,
"There is in Luke 16.17 no Lukan redaction."[100] However, in what can
only be construed as a contradictory statement, he describes the second ἕως
clause as redaction, but the first as traditional. Drawing this comparison he
argues,

> an isolated logion with the temporal clause ἕως ἄν πάντα γένηται would be puzzling
> and would need a context. A traditional logion which contained the first ἕως ἄν
> clause (18b), on the contrary, would be understandable in itself. Besides, v. 18b as
> Matthean redaction would be very difficult to interpret.[101]

It appears impossible to hold these two statements together. If v. 18b is
indeed traditional then Luke's εὐκοπώτερον δέ ἐστιν (Lk 16.17a) must be
redactional, alternatively if Lk 16.17 has no Lukan redaction then Matthew
5.18b cannot be traditional. The only way to hold Luz's two statements
together would be to argue for different versions of the source material at
this point (i.e., Q^{Mt} and Q^{Lk}). However, this options is not necessary as the
tradition history can be adequately accounted for by seeing both of
Matthew's ἕως clauses as redactional and, concurring with both Luz and
Davies and Allison, that Lk 16.17 has no redactional elements.

---

[98] Cf. Guelich, *The Sermon on the Mount*, 144. "This phrase is the first of two
temporal clauses in 5.18: *before heaven and earth pass away* and *before all things come
to pass*. The presence of two ἕως clauses doubtless explains why the first occurs out of
normal order noted above. Since the vocabulary of this clause is also in Luke 16.17, this
phrase was the earlier traditional ἕως-clause relocated by the evangelist when he added
the second."

[99] Davies and Allison, *Matthew,* vol 1, 490.

[100] Luz, *Matthew 1-7*, 258.

[101] Luz, *Matthew 1-7*, 258.

The final element that needs to be considered in the discussion of the tradition behind Matt 5.18 is the longer reference to ἰῶτα ἓν ἢ μία κεραία, whereas the Lukan form only mentions the second element, μίαν κεραίαν. In his reconstruction of the underlying form, Tuckett presents the double reference in the Matthean version as the original Q form of the saying.[102] He gives no reason to support the inclusion of the reference to the iota in Matthew's source material. This first referent is, however, almost certainly redactional. Not only is the phrase absent in the Lukan version, but, moreover, it becomes almost impossible to suggest a convincing reason why Luke would delete this item that would be more recognizable by Gentile members of his readership,[103] while retaining μία κεραία, which requires some knowledge of semitic alphabetic script to understand the point that is being made. Banks suggests further reasons for seeing ἰῶτα ἓν as due to the evangelist's editorial work. He observes,

> Matthew's ἢ μία κεραία is sufficiently accounted for by his inclusion of ἰῶτα ἓν. The form of the first phrase is, as we have seen, typical of Matthean redaction. Further indication of an addition comes from a comparison of the rabbinic parallels where one or the other of these items appear but never both together, as well as the unlikelihood of Luke's omitting reference to ἰῶτα which also represented the smallest Greek letter.[104]

The case for ἰῶτα ἓν being Matthean redaction is strong. This leads to an important point being raised against those who wish characterize the Matthean group as self-consciously Jewish and even isolationist with respect to the Gentile world.[105] The inclusion of the phrase ἰῶτα ἓν appears to be another small piece of evidence that shows that Matthew's gospel does have an eye toward the Gentile world, and is attempting to make their

---

[102] The reconstruction Tuckett offers is of the logia in Q 16.16-17, as only the second verse is under discussion here, it alone is cited. Thus, the proposed source of Matt 5.18 is seen by Tuckett to have been, ἕως ἂν παρέλθῃ ὁ οὐρανὸς καὶ ἡ γῆ, ἰῶτα ἓν ἢ μία κεραία οὐ μὴ παρέλθῃ ἀπὸ τοῦ νόμου (Q 16.17).

[103] Gundry makes this same point. He writes, "Luke, who was very Hellenistic, would hardly have omitted 'one iota,' for iota was the smallest letter of the Greek alphabet. Matthew's adding it to 'one tittle,' not only produces a parallel with 'heaven and earth,' but also strengthens the denial of opposition to the law and the prophets and provides something understandable to Greek readers who might not know the Hebraic meaning of 'tittle'." (Gundry, *Matthew*, 80).

[104] Banks, *Jesus and the Law in the Synoptic Tradition*, 214, n. 1.

[105] Here the work of Sim is again shown to be lacking. See in particular his chap. 5 'The Matthean Community and the Gentile World.' He concludes by stating, "Like the other Jews of Antioch, they avoided contact with the Gentiles and viewed them with a mixture of fear and suspicion." (Sim, *The Gospel of Matthew and Christian Judaism*, 256). Yet, as with Sim's general tendency to ignore evidence contrary to his own position, he nowhere mentions the significance of Matthew's inclusion of ἰῶτα ἓν, a phrase best accounted for in terms of a Gentile audience.

Jesus kerygma more accessible to non-Jews, who are now being welcomed into the group.

So, in Matt 5.18, there is evidence to show that Matthew worked with an underlying tradition from Q, that the original form of this saying is best preserved in Lk 16.17,[106] but has been heavily redacted by Matthew in 5.18 to cohere with his overall perspective on the law. Specifically, the redactional changes that appear to have been introduced by Matthew include: (i) prefacing the introductory formulaic opening ἀμὴν γὰρ λέγω ὑμῖν; (ii) giving the central element a temporal perspective by commencing with the phrase ἕως ἄν; (iii) added the reference ἰῶτα ἕν, almost as translation equivalent to the existing μίαν κεραίαν; and (iv) appended the final temporal clause ἕως ἂν πάντα γένηται. The changes have been employed by Matthew not for stylistic purposes, but as shall be argued, to allow him to make claims about the law both in terms of his community's continuity with it, but also concerning the transcending authority of Jesus to interpret Torah in fresh ways.

The saying in Matt 5.19 has no parallels in the synoptic material. Also, in this verse there are a number of terms that appear to reflect preferred Matthean terminology. These two facts support taking this saying as redactional material, although the possibility exists that like v18, this verse may have an underlying tradition which has be edited in a thoroughgoing manner by the evangelist (if this is the case, it is doubtful whether the traditional is recoverable). Davies and Allison see the evidence pointing in the same direction. They observe both the presence of Matthean vocabulary and structure, but nonetheless admit the possibility of the existence of a pre-Matthean source.

> The vocabulary of this verse – a so called 'sentence of holy law', in which the human action in the prostasis correlates with a divine action in the apodosis – is largely Matthean, and the antithetical parallelism of 19a-b and 19c-d could also be

---

[106] While Luz states the source problem is ultimately unsolvable, "and there is nothing else to do except to interpret the verse as it stands", he does also observe that "[t]here is in Luke 16.17 no Lukan redaction", which is surely an indicator of the traditional nature of the Lukan logion (Luz, *Matthew 1-7*, 258). Davies and Allison have a more complex theory whereby they argue that the Lukan form accurately transmits the Q form, but Matthew's redaction reshapes this tradition to make it conform to the structure of a class of sayings often used by Jesus. They argue, "although the (ἀμὴν) λέγω ὑμῖν + οὐ μή + ἕως (ἄν) form was probably used by Jesus himself, its appearance itself does not guarantee a dominical birth. Lk 16.17 reads: 'It is easier for heaven and earth to pass away than for one jot of the law to become void'. Matthew has rewritten this sentence so as to give it a traditional form familiar to him from the Jesus tradition." (Davies and Allison, *Matthew*, vol 1, 488-9).

considered as characteristic of the redactor. But 5.19, which has no synoptic parallel, might nevertheless be a redactional version of a traditional line.[107]

However, some scholars suggest that they can trace the pre-history of this saying with more certainty. Although Brooks does not see the rest of Matt 5.17-20 stemming from the M source, he feels that the case for v19 is much stronger. He finds three principal arguments to support this conclusion: (i) an apparent aporia created by the use of the term τουτῶν; (2) the use of the 'rare' word in Matthew λύω, which he suggests is only used in M sayings in the first gospel; and (iii) the contents of 18b,c and v. 19 are conceptually disjunctive, thereby showing that these verses did not belong together in the tradition.[108]

Taking these points one at a time, firstly, the presence of the plural genitive pronoun τουτῶν is felt to create a disjointed logic in the overall flow of 5.17-20. Brooks frames the grammatical problem he feels to be present in the text in the following terms.

> In a Greek text two options for the reference of the pronoun exist: τουτῶν may either have an antecedent a plural would be expected by the Greek reader) in the immediately preceding context; or τουτῶν may refer forward. In the immediately preceding context of v. 18 no plural antecedent agrees grammatically with the τουτῶν of v. 19, nor can one be found in v. 17.[109]

In a strict sense this observation may be grammatically correct,[110] however, it is obvious that such canons of literary form were often broken especially in speech and popular literature. Brooks dismisses the suggestion made by some critics that the plural pronoun refers to the multiplicity of commandments that comprise Torah (i.e., νόμος in v. 17). However, he does concede that this understanding may account for the redactional incorporation of the saying into its present context, but still feels the break in the logic evidences an existing tradition. In this vein he suggests, "[a]lthough such an explanation may apply for Matthew's understanding of the text, the grammatical problem engendered by the lack of an antecedent for τουτῶν may be one indication that Matthew used an earlier tradition."[111] Yet Guelich, who like Brooks wishes to argue that v. 19 belongs to a pre-Matthean source, takes the presence of the pronoun τουτῶν as evidence that this statement was joined to the sayings in vv. 17-18 prior to the incorporation of this block of material into the gospel. Seeing both the grammar and the logic functioning differently to Brooks,

---

[107] Davies and Allison, *Matthew,* vol 1, 495.
[108] Brooks, *Matthew's Community, the Evidence of His Special Sayings Material,* 28-9.
[109] Brooks, *Matthew's Community, the Evidence of His Special Sayings Material,* 28.
[110] Cf., BDF, § 290, for relevant examples.
[111] Brooks, *Matthew's Community, the Evidence of His Special Sayings Material,* 28.

he argues, "the very construction *these commandments* necessarily implies the presence of an antecedent and precludes any independent existence for the saying."[112]

Also germane to his argument is the proposal regarding the original *Sitz im Leben* of v. 19, and the process by which it was attached to 5.17-18 in order to function as law observant interpretation of this older (perhaps even dominical) material.[113] Here he postulates the following setting and tradition history,

> Whereas 5.17, 18 may have distant roots in Jesus' ministry, 5.19 reflects the nomistic nuance of a strict Jewish-Christian community who may well have shaped the tradition of 5.17, 18 and added 5.19 as a commentary. This commentary would then round out the unit of 5.17, 18 by setting forth the practical implications of the keeping and teaching of the Law.[114]

Needless to say, the totally divergent understandings of the grammatical implication of the pronoun τουτῶν calls into question the process of building too heavy a case on this indecisive grammatical point. All that needs to be observed is that in its current context τουτῶν refers in some sense either to the law generally, or more specifically to the smallest iota or tittle of the law. This distinction is not that significant for understanding the overall trust of the Matthean logic, nor would determination of the correct option answer the larger problem, which is determining how Matthew holds both 5.17-18 and 5.19 together in terms of his perception of the function of the law within his own community.

---

[112] Guelich, *The Sermon on the Mount*, 151. Brooks would in all likelihood agree with Guelich that the pronoun does demand an antecedent, but he would argue that the grammatically required antecedent cannot be the found in the preceding verses. However, Guelich cites two further cases of Matthean usage of demonstratives to attempt to establish that the usage in this case is also grammatically possible. His examples are as follows. "In Matt 3:9, par. Luke 3:8, the broader context and in 25:40, 45 the logical context supply the antecedents for the demonstrative *these*, whose function in such instances is more adjectival than pronominal. The same function fits 5:18-19, since *one hook of the Law* could easily be the indirect antecedent for *one of the least of these commandments*." (152).

[113] It has already been noted in the discussion of vv. 17-18, contrary to Guelich and some other commentators, that it is both perilous and improvable to assert that these verses can be traced back to a dominical origin in anything remotely approximating their Matthean form. It may be true that in regard to Q 16.16-17 a much stronger case can be made for seeing a this material as stemming from the historical Jesus, but since the Matthean programmatic statement on the law shows so many signs of redaction and deviates so clearly from Lk 16.16 especially, but also Lk 16.17, it seems foolhardy to assert that these Matthean verses find their origin in the ministry and teaching of Jesus in anything more than the faintest of echoes.

[114] Guelich, *The Sermon on the Mount*, 152.

The second point Brooks suggests is that an indicator of the existence of pre-Matthean tradition is the use of the term λύω, which he depicts as being typical of the M source. Setting aside Matt 21.2 which is taken over from Mk 11.2, he focuses attention on the two other unparalleled uses of this term in the first gospel, Matt 16.19b and 18.18. Since Matthew nowhere inserts the term in Q or Markan contexts, Brooks draws the conclusion that "[t]he presence of the use in only unparalleled sayings may indicate that here [i.e., 5.19] Matthew uses an M saying."[115] However, Meier notes an important distinction between the usage of this term when he states, "we do not have here the set terminology of binding and loosing (Mt 16.19; 18.18)."[116] The important array of Mattheanisms in this verse are listed by Gundry as further support for seeing this saying in its current form as essentially a creation of the first evangelist.[117] In spite of the fact that much of this verse is linguistically Matthean, many commentators do not wish to give this evidence due force. Luz suggests a potential motivation for such reticence. "The judgment of many interpreters that the verse is completely traditional often comes from the fact that they dislike the thought of attributing such a legalistic logion to the evangelist."[118] So here this unparalleled saying is best understood as largely a Matthean creation, and while one must admit the possibility of there having been a traditional saying behind 5.19, the extent of redactional reworking means that one only has access to the final form of the saying as it occurs in its present context.

While the diversity of opinion concerning the traditions underlying the three sayings in Matt 5.17-19 has been amply demonstrated in the forgoing discussion, the opposite tendency is to be seen in regard to 5.20. Most major commentaries and monographs express the opinion that this verse is

---

[115] Brooks, *Matthew's Community, the Evidence of His Special Sayings Material*, 28.

[116] Meier, *Law and History in Matthew's Gospel*, 89.

[117] The list Gundry presents has each term followed by two bracketed numbers. The first number indicates the times Matthew inserts the term into paralleled passages, the second shows the number of times it is used in unparalleled passages. The list is ἐλαχίστων/-ος (2,3), διδάξῃ (3,3), οὕτως (18,5), ἀνθρώπους (35,17), κληθήσεται (8,8), βασιλείᾳ τῶν οὐρανῶν (25,7), ποιήσῃ (19,19), οὗτος in a resumptive usage (5,0), μέγας (11,1), γάρ (62-63, 15), λέγω ὑμῖν (27,7), περισσεύσῃ (3,0), δικαιοσύνη (5,2), πλεῖον (3,1), γραμματέων καὶ φαρισάων (9,0), and εἰσέλθητε εἰς τὴν βασιλείαν τῶν οὐρανῶν with a negative (5,0). Also Gundry makes the following points. "Matthew shows a greater or lesser tendency to interject all these expressions into shared traditions and to use them in unique passages. Often the total number of times he uses them exceeds that in Mark and Luke. Furthermore, the careful parallelism in v 19 typifies his style." (Gundry, *Matthew*, 82).

[118] Luz, *Matthew 1-7*, 258.

entirely due to the redactional activity of the evangelist.[119] The reasons for this judgment are both sound and easy to follow. At the level of source criticism the verse is not paralleled in the other synoptic gospels, in relation to vocabulary there are a number of distinctive Matthean expressions, and in terms of literary structure this verse functions as a carefully constructed transition between two significant blocks of redactionally fashioned material (Matt 5.17-19 and 21-48). The cumulative weight of these observations, especially with stress on the last point, has been seen as making a convincing case for v. 20 as having come exclusively from the hand of the evangelist. Even commentators who in the previous three verses press strongly for the presence of significant pre-Matthean tradition see that no case can be made for a similar claim in relation to v. 20. Meier perhaps does more to qualify his remarks than any other recent scholar, but in the end the weight of evidence forces him to concede that this verse must be attributed to Matthean authorship. The caveat he provides before stating his conclusion is "that we cannot completely disprove the existence of vs. 20 in some pre-Matthean tradition. But even if we had chosen to see vs. 20 as traditional, we would have to admit so much redactional activity on the part of Mt that it would be extremely difficult to regain the original logion."[120] At a theoretical level Meier is of course correct, one 'cannot complete disprove' that an existing saying stood behind Matt 5.20 without full access to all the written and oral material that comprised the Jesus tradition. However, this level of proof is hardly realistic. In the end he allows that v. 20 is best taken as being a redactional addition, and states, "Insofar as Matthew puts the verse into the mouth of Jesus during his public ministry, the evangelist can understand it as an expression of Jesus' fidelity to the Mosaic Law during his earthly life."[121]

Drawing together the conclusions of this investigation into the sources and redaction involved in the formation of Matt 5.17-20, it is necessary to emphasize that this is a unit that has been fashioned in its present form to a large extent by the evangelist and presents his own understanding of the validity, function and purpose of the law. It is not satisfactory to simply

---

[119] Representative of this outlook are Davies and Allison who state in relation to v20 that "[t]his redactional verse…is the transition between 5.17-19 and 5.21-48." (*Matthew*, vol 1, 498). Similarly, Hagner sees the verse as a redactional transition. "The reference to entering the kingdom of heaven binds this verse to the preceding one, so that it serves as a bridge between what precedes and what follows." (Hagner, *Matthew 1-13*, 104). Furthermore, Luz states, "*Verse 20* is redactional according to almost universal judgment, a saying that speaks of entering the kingdom of heaven, especially beloved of the evangelist." (Luz, *Matthew 1-7*, 258).

[120] Meier, *Law and History in Matthew's Gospel*, 119.

[121] Meier, *Law and History in Matthew's Gospel*, 119.

assert that pre-existing Matthean sayings are preserved that do not reflect the evangelist's own perspective on the law.[122] Even if it was the case that the evangelist had employed traditional material it would still be necessary to account for his use of material with which he fundamentally disagreed.[123] Although, Matthew may have been slightly influenced by Lk 16.16 in his reference to 'the law or the prophets' in 5.17, this verse is mainly an editorial creation. By comparison, v. 18 draws more extensively on the Q material (Q 16.17), but again, these traditions have been heavy reworked by Matthew. In studying v. 19, the possibility of an underlying tradition cannot be excluded, however, if this was the case it is also no longer susceptible to recovery. Thus it is best to interpret this verse in its present Matthean context without recourse to a hypothetical pre-history. Finally, v. 20 most clearly shows itself to be a redactional composition. It creates a highly significant link with the antitheses, showing that Matthew intended his comments on the law in vv. 17-19 to be read in light of the extended examples his provides in vv. 21-48, where he illustrates a number of Jesus' rulings.

5.4 Interpretation and Exegesis in the Matthean Context

The programmatic statement on the law (Matt 5.17-20), although drawing on some earlier sources and tradition, is largely a Matthean creation and deserves to be interpreted as such. It cannot be correctly understood in isolation from the wider narrative, especially the antitheses that immediately follow since they provide a form of commentary on what Matthew means by Jesus fulfilling Torah.[124] However, it also needs to be

---

[122] To a certain extent this is the position that Meier adopts in regard to 5.19. He asserts that, "In many ways, 5.19 is the most difficult verse to explain within the present Matthean context. It seems like an undigested morsel next to the carefully redacted 5.18. By arguing from converging probabilities, we suggested that 5.19 originally existed in Q and was linked to 5.18bc in a thesis-conclusion pattern. When Matthew took over 5.18bc, he kept the basic thesis-conclusion pattern, though he disturbed its clarity be inserting 5.18d. the concatenation of 5.18-19 in the tradition may show successive stages of Jewish-Christian attitudes on the Law. Vs. 5.18bc may reflect the severe view of stringent Jewish Christians, while 5.19 may be the corrective of more moderate Jewish Christians. This attempt at moderation has produced a curious piece (a low place in the Kingdom is a strange sanction), a kind of literary fossil now embedded in 5.19." (Meier, *Law and History in Matthew's Gospel*, 165-6).

[123] As has been noted earlier, Stanton has commented on the fallacy of only seeing distinctively redactional material as reflecting the evangelist's theological concerns. (Stanton, *A Gospel for a New People*, 41-2).

[124] This function of the antitheses as commentary, or illustration, is described by Allison who notes the formal relationship. He states, "Structurally, 5.21-48 consists of

remembered that vv. 17-20 follow on from a description of missionary orientated discipleship, as well as forming part of the evangelist's presentation of Jesus' teaching on the mountain.

5.4.1 Verse 17

Initially, the opening in v. 17 appears abrupt and unrelated to the forgoing description of ideal discipleship in the Matthean community. While Davies and Allison are correct in describing the negative aorist subjunctive imperative μὴ νομίσητε as being *prokataleptic*,[125] since it does indeed anticipate possible objections to the teaching Jesus is about to present as his interpretation of Torah, it is also related to the description of Matthean discipleship in vv. 13-16. The type of discipleship that Matthew demands is characterized by it being recognizably centred on Jesus, and distinctively public nature. The metaphors of flavoursome salt, city on a hill, and lamp on a stand, all depict the community members as being noticeable and able to attract others by these distinctive attributes. In essence, these symbols all reflect a missionary outlook. Gundry picks up on this element of mission, observing that, "We may therefore deduce that Matthew has composed the saying in v 14 around the figure of light, which comes from the tradition, and that he has done so for expansive reemphasis on the motif of worldwide evangelism (cf. v 13)."[126] Following on as they do from the final two beatitudes on persecution, the charge to remain committed to distinctive discipleship and not to lose one's savour was no empty concern for the Matthean community. Overman describes this experience of persecution for the Matthean community along with the evangelist's call for public discipleship in the face of such hostility and alienation. In relation to Matt 5.13-16 he argues,

> These verses, along with being beautifully crafted, also seem to say that Matthew plans to make his case in the public square....The disciples are to have a public presence and so should the Matthean community. As we shall see, it may be that by the time of the writing of the Gospel the Matthean church was losing much of that public face and was losing ground politically in terms of their reputation beyond the walls of their gathering place.[127]

---

six paragraphs, each illustrating the truth of 5.17-48." (Allison, *The New Moses*, 183). Here he sees each antithetical statement as informing the whole meaning of the tradition in 5.17-48. While this is certainly true, since a text derives its holistic meaning from all of its parts and the web of relationships which they form, nonetheless, the primary focus of the antithesis is to present, in a fairly linear progression, an explanation of the paragraph that precedes them.

[125] Davies and Allison, *Matthew*, vol 1, 481.

[126] Gundry, *Matthew*, 76.

[127] Overman, *Church and Community in Crisis*, 76.

While Overman may not be totally correct in seeing the group still within the confines of the synagogue, he correctly recognizes that Matthew calls upon his community to maintain its public presence despite the threat of persecution. It is likely that this persecution has arisen because of three factors that distinguish the group from its antecedent roots in Judaism: the authority claims made for Jesus; its engagement in Gentile mission; and its perceived lax attitude towards Jewish tradition – in particular Torah observance.

Thus, the μὴ νομίσητε that opens v. 17 does not only anticipate possible charges that may be brought against members of the group, but in a more concrete manner it responds to perhaps the most consistent and demoralizing accusation that was being levelled against Matthean disciples,[128] that was that they had apostacized in their attitude to the law. In this sense, the opening phrase and the explanation that follows does not respond to the opponents levelling the charge, but seeks to address concerns within the community. To nurture the confidence of this fledgling movement coming to terms with its separate existence, the evangelist calls for members to maintain their distinctively mission orientated discipleship. As part of his pastoral strategy he responds to the charge of 'destroying the law' by making the claim that the life of discipleship that he portrays as being taught by Jesus is not the abolition of the law, but is in fact the consummative fulfilment of Torah values.

In v. 17 the basic charge to which the Matthean Jesus proleptically responds is that of abrogating the law, ὅτι ἦλθον καταλῦσαι τὸν νόμον ἢ τοὺς προφήτας. As was noted in the discussion of source material the presence of the term ἦλθον has resulted in the suggestion that this saying belonged to a class of tradition logia designated as ἦλθον-words.[129] However, in the case of this unparalleled saying it is more probable that Matthew is responsible for its creation, although he may have conformed its structure to a known form of dominical utterance. Consequently, it is Matthew who has his Jesus deny the accusation that he had come for the purpose of καταλῦσαι. The various nuances that καταλῦσαι can take colours the interpretation of this verse, depending on which alternative is adopted. As Luz precisely summarises the problem, "The difficulties of interpretation are culminating in the two verbs καταλύω and πληρόω."[130]

---

[128] Luz also sees this negative imperative being spoken for the benefit of group members. "The introductory μὴ νομίσητε addresses the community directly." (Luz, *Matthew 1-7*, 260).

[129] This class of sayings was first identified as a possible authentic *Gattung* by Harnack, but he finds only eight such sayings in the synoptic tradition. (Harnack, ' "Ich bin gekommen." Die ausdrücklichen Selbstzeugnisse Jesu über den Zweck seiner Sendung und seines Kommens', 1-30).

[130] Luz, *Matthew 1-7*, 260.

Summarising the four fields of semantic meaning for καταλύω listed in
BAGD[131] illustrates this difficulty. The first alternative, 'to detach someth.
in a demolition process, *throw down*, detach' (cf. Matt 24.2; Mk 13.2; Lk
21.6), is clearly the literal meaning of the verb. Used primarily of the
demolition of buildings, and specifically of the temple in the gospel
passages cited, it denotes a violent dismantling of physical fabric. The
second class of meaning is defined as 'to cause the ruin of someth.,
destroy, demolish, dismantle'. This category is broken into two sub groups:
literal references to building (Matt 26.61; 27.40; Mk 14.58; 15.29; Ac
6.14, or figurative references where things that could still be conceived of
as constructions are destroyed ('the earthly tent' Gal 2.18; the Christian
congregation as the building of God (2 Cor 5.1, Rom 14.20). While these
first two categories of meaning do not align with the use in Matt 5.17, they
show that the term was used in contexts that required the denotation of
powerfully destructive acts that entailed an air of finality.

Moving from literal to metaphorical meanings, the third category is 'to
end the effect or validity of someth., *put to an end*'. Again this is split into
two sub groups the first of which contains Matt 5.17a as a listed
example,[132] however, the possible options are wider here than in the other
subcategories: 'abolish, annul, make invalid to do away with, repeal'.
However, a significant parallel exists in the fragmentary texts of Diod. S.
40, 2 dealing with Seleucid political intentions toward the Jewish religio-
cultural system. The text states that the Seleucids intended to καταλύειν
τοὺς πατρίους νόμους. This is significant not only because it links the term
καταλύειν with νόμος, but because we know, at least from the Jewish
perspective, the programme of enforced hellenization was seen as resulting
in the eradication of adherence to the ancestral law and traditions. The
second group in section three refers only to the NT in relation to Acts 5.38-
9 where the term denotes the 'ruin' or 'failure' of a plan. Similarly, Arrian
speaks of the of the 'ruin' or deposing of τυραννίδα (*Anab.* 4, 10, 3). The
final range of meanings encompasses 'to cease from what one is doing,
halt', or in the more specific sense of 'rest, find lodgings' (cf. Lk 9.12;
19.7).[133] Only the third of these options fits the context of Matt 5.17-20,
although the exact nuance is still difficult to determine. It is, however,
apparent that in its context in 5.17 the use of καταλῦσαι is a rejection of the

---

[131] *BAGD*, 3rd. ed., 521-2.

[132] The only other NT text listed in this group is Lk 23.2 however, this is textually
problematic. The relevant clause καί καταλύσοντα τὸν νόμον καὶ τοὺς προφήτας is only
witnessed in it[b, c, e, ff2, i, l, q] vg[mss]; Mcion[E]. It shows all the signs of being a scribal
addition.

[133] As Nolland notes of Luke, "Only he in the NT uses the verb found here to mean
'to stay/rest/find a place of lodging'." (Nolland, *Luke 1-9:20*, 441).

accusation that Jesus, and hence the Matthean community, can be seen as wishing to eradicate or completely destroy 'the law and the prophets'.[134] At this stage Matthew does not explain how this non-destructive attitude towards the law is demonstrated within the community. Rather, in an almost catechetical manner he simple asserts the inherent veracity of this statement. As Meier notes, Matt 5.17 discusses "the Law and the prophets, the center of OT faith, in their relation to Jesus, the center of Christian faith. Jesus immediately warns against thinking that his activity concerning Law and prophets is purely negative or destructive."[135]

Counterbalancing this negative assertion that rejects the charge that the Matthean Jesus sees as potentially levelled against him, is the positive affirmation, οὐκ ἦλθον καταλῦσαι ἀλλὰ πληρῶσαι (v. 17b), although the negative charge is initially repeated to emphasize the contrast. However, the meaning of this antithetical statement that dismisses the accusation that Jesus came to καταλῦσαι the law and the prophets can only be appreciated once the meaning of πληπῶσαι is determined. Yet this is no easy task in the present context.[136] Hagner divides the options into three groups, with the final group being split into three further subcategories. Citing his stemma of potential meanings results in the following list of options.

> (1) to do or obey the commandments of the OT; (2) a reference to Jesus' life and/or the accomplishment of the salvific acts of Jesus' death and resurrection ('fulfilment of prophecy'); (3) teaching the law in such a way as to (a) 'establish' or 'uphold' the law, (b) add to and thus 'complete' the law, or (c) bringing out the intended meaning through some definitive interpretation.[137]

Hagner himself opts for the final position that asserts that Jesus is upholding the law in ways that transcend the manner in which the opponents of the Matthean community claimed that the law should be maintained. This seems to be the most plausible interpretation, especially in light of the antitheses that follow. Those six statements show both that Jesus is attributed the authority to make pronouncements on the intent of the law, and that his interpretations deviate from those of his opponents. In

---

[134] It is not lexically possible to adopt Merx's proposal that καταλύειν simply denotes the rabbinic practice of "relaxing" the commandments. Neither the context, nor the meaning of the verb, allows this sense. (Merx, *Matthäus*, 73).

[135] Meier, *Law and History in Matthew"s Gospel*, 123.

[136] See the discussion of this term by Schulz, who suggests that Matthew is radically Christianizing the Jewish notion of Law. "'Erfüllung' kann hier [i.e. in Matt 5.17] also nur "verwirklichen" bedeuten. Der irdische Jesus verwirchlicht eschatologisch das ganze Gesetz, das will heissen: den grundsätzlichen und allein wesentlichen Gotteswillen, wie er in den zehn Geboten als den fundamentalen Geboten der Gottes- und Nächstenliebe und den Antithesen unverrückbar und bleibend zum Ausdruck gebracht ist." (Schulz, *Die Stunde der Botschaft*, 182).

[137] Hagner, *Matthew 1-13*, 105.

effect Matthew is saying to his adversaries, fulfilment yes, but not in the manner you expect Torah to be accomplished. While those outside the Matthean community would doubtless fail to be impressed by such reasoning, at a pastoral level it allows Matthew to claim that the ethnically Jewish members of his community do not need to have a crisis of confidence about being 'destroyers of Torah' for in fact adherence to Jesus is the ultimate way of 'fulfilling' the law. As Hagner states his conclusion, "In Matthew's view, the teaching of Jesus by definition amounts to the true meaning of Torah and is hence paradoxically an affirmation of Jesus' loyalty to the OT."[138]

Perhaps this interpretation does not even require any sharp dichotomy with Hagner's second possibility for the meaning of πληπῶσαι. While not wanting to take up Meier's rigid salvation history framework, because of its strict separation of the inbreaking eschatological age from the ministry of Jesus, the events of crucifixion and resurrection are for the evangelist a verification of the veracity of Jesus' teaching and authority to interpret the law. Furthermore, in the terms of the gospel, this authority becomes a delegated authority, which Jesus has passed on to his disciples and the community (Matt 16.18-19; 28.18-20). Interestingly, in the second passage such delegated authority is to be exercised in missionary activity. Thus, Jesus' resurrection legitimises the community's proclamation among Gentiles. Therefore, Guelich is correct in his judgment that "The redemptive historical motif so characteristic of Matthew is doubtless at work in 5.17 as well."[139] So reading 5.17 in the light of the antitheses which illustrate the fact that Jesus can interpret the Torah in fresh ways, and surveying the range of meanings for the important word pair καταλῦσαι/πληρῶσαι, leads to the following conclusion. Namely, that Matthew is refuting the charge that Jesus' teaching, as proclaimed by the community, can be seen as destroying the law, rather, it brings out the true purpose of the law. While this argument is not likely to have convinced those who were levelling this charge against group members, such was probably never its primary intention. Instead, it appears that Matthew's focus was pastoral, in that he was concerned to assure those who were wavering in their commitment both to the Matthean understanding of Torah and its implication for Gentile mission that not only was the group's position correct, but moreover, it was the understanding of the law and the course of action that Jesus had authorized and delegated group members to promote.[140]

---

[138] Hagner, *Matthew 1-13*, 106.

[139] Guelich, *The Sermon on the Mount*, 142.

[140] The interpretation being suggested for v17 is not dissimilar to Moule's thesis. He states, "Insofar as far as the Law bears witness to the will of God as an ideal yet to be achieved, and the Prophets hold out hope of a time coming when it shall be fulfilled, one

5.4.2 Verse 18

This verse comprises of four separate clauses: (i) a declaration of solemn speech; (ii) a temporal subjunctive statement concerning the cessation of the created realm; (iii) a declaration of the enduring validity of the smallest elements law while the created order remains; and, (iv) a conditional qualification that appears to reinforce the lasting validity of Torah only while the created order remains.[141] It has even been proposed by Berger that this fourfold structure reflects a NT form that can be characterized by the pattern, ἀμὴν λέγω ὑμῖν – οὐ μή + prophetic future + temporal clause with ἕως or μέχρις.[142] However, Luz has successfully called into question the applicability of such an underlying form being relevant to this heavily reworked verse. He states, "If Matthew used such a sentence [i.e., aligning with Berger's proposed form], then the first ἕως ἄν clause would have to be a Matthean addition. But an isolated logion with the temporal clause ἕως ἄν πάντα γένηται would be puzzling and would need a context."[143] Thus, the most appropriate manner to investigate this verse would be initially to treat each of the four components separately, but to understand that Matthew is responsible for both the resultant structure and meaning that emerges from his synthesis of redactional and traditional material.

The first clause, ἀμὴν γὰρ λέγω ὑμῖν, introduces a declaration that is solemn, profound and deserves the full attention of the audience. As Hagner appreciates, "these words stress the gravity of what follows."[144] The air of solemnity is created primarily through the use of the term ἀμήν, which is a transliteration of the Hebrew אָמֵן (but also carried over into

---

who perfectly fulfils the will of God confirms also the predictions of prophecy. Jesus is the one who brings to its perfect expression the ideal relationship between God and man expressed in the covenant-theme of the Torah and in the ideals of the great Prophets of Israel, and, in doing so, even through death to resurrection, fulfils all the Law stood for." (Moule, 'Fulfilment-Words in the New Testament', 316).

[141] This fourfold division is recognized by most commentators. See Davies and Allison's (Davies and Allison, *Matthew,* vol 1, 487-95). However, Guelich opts for the following threefold division. "Matt 5.18 consists of (a) an introductory formula (ἀμὴν λέγω ὑμῖν), (b) a subjunctive, and (c) a temporal clause (ἕως ἄν plus subjunctive)." (Guelich, *The Sermon on the Mount,* 143). In some respects this distinction is not highly significant, for the fourfold division simply recognizes the two parallel clauses in the underlying traditional saying, whereas Guelich simply collapses elements (ii) and (iii) from the fourfold schema into his part (b), thereby treating the traditional material as a unified component.

[142] For a full discussion see Berger, *Die Amen-Worte Jesu,* 73ff.

[143] Luz, *Matthew 1-7,* 258.

[144] Hagner, *Matthew 1-13,* 106.

Aramaic). This form of usage appears distinctively Christian since the "prefatory use of 'amen' is found neither in the OT[145] nor in rabbinic literature, where the word occurs consistently as a response to a preceding statement."[146] In this introductory position it is best understood as meaning 'truly', 'verily', 'assuredly' or some similar affirmation of certainty.[147] Of the fifty-one times ἀμήν occurs as a declaration of solemn speech in the synoptic gospels thirty-one of these instances are in Matthew,[148] (Mk: 14; Lk: 6). By comparison, in John the double amen formula is used consistently to introduce solemn speech either with the second person plural indirect pronoun (ἀμὴν ἀμὴν λέγω ὑμῖν, 20 times)[149] or less frequently with the first person plural indirect pronoun (ἀμὴν ἀμὴν λέγω σοι, 5 times).[150] Despite the fact that this form of announcing speech has strong claim to originate with the historical Jesus,[151] this does not mean that all the 'amen-sayings' have dominical origin. This memorable and distinctive locution was undoubtedly replicated, either as the preface to other authentic sayings, or attached to material that was the creation of the redactors. In fact, it appears that the four occurrences that combine the term with the conjunction γάρ (Matt 5.17, 10.23; 13.17; 17.20, i.e., ἀμὴν γὰρ λέγω ὑμῖν) are all redactional creations. Gundry supports this assessment in his discussion of Matt 5.17. "That the expression as a whole here comes from Matthew gains further support from the fact that only he ever uses the conjunction γάρ with the other words in it (10.23; 13.17;

---

[145] Although not in an introductory position, ἀμήν does occur seven or eight times in the LXX, see Hatch and Redpath.

[146] Hagner, *Matthew 1-13*, 106.

[147] In this sense *BAGD* (53) classifies ἀμήν as a strong affirmation of what is stated, 'asserverative particle, *truly*, always w. λέγω, beginning a solemn declaration but only used by Jesus (*I assure you that, I solemnly tell you that*).'

[148] Matt 5.18, 26; 6.2, 5, 16; 8.10; 10.15, 23, 42; 11.11; 13.17; 16.28; 17.20; 18.3, 13, 18, 19; 19.23, 28; 21.21, 31; 23.36; 24.2, 34, 47; 25.12, 40, 45; 26.13, 21, 34;

[149] Jn 1.51; 5.19, 24, 25; 6.26, 32, 47, 53; 8.34, 51, 58; 10.1, 7; 12.24; 13.16, 20, 21; 14.12; 16.20, 23.

[150] Jn 3.3, 5, 11 (to Nicodemus); 13.38 (to Simon Peter); 21.18 (to Simon Peter).

[151] Arguing for the origin of this form of saying with Jesus see Jeremias, *New Testament Theology*, 35-6. Here Jeremias observes, "A new use of the word ἀμήν emerges in the sayings of Jesus in the four gospels, which is without any parallel in the whole of Jewish literature and the New Testament....The retention of this alien word shows how strongly the tradition felt that the way of speaking was new and unusual....the ἀμὴν λέγω ὑμῖν that introduces the sayings of Jesus expresses his authority. The novelty of the usage, the way in which it is strictly confined to the sayings of Jesus, and the unanimous testimony be all strata of the tradition in the gospels show that here we have the creation of a new expression by Jesus." (35-6).

17.20)."[152] Matthew may therefore be seen as having prefaced this known authentic introduction to a saying that found its origin in the Jesus tradition (5.18bc) to stress the authority of the one making the utterance[153] and to call his audience to listen carefully to the pronouncement that follows. This is the first time Matthew uses the amen-formula in his narrative, and its impact would have been keenly felt by the original hearers of the gospel.

Having announced to the audience that a significant and authoritative statement is to follow, Matthew presents the heavily reworked saying to which he wishes his community to be attentive. The phrase ἕως ἂν παρέλθῃ ὁ οὐρανὸς καὶ ἡ γῆ (Matt 5.18b), differs from its Lukan counterpart in two significant ways, firstly instead of the opening εὐκοπώτερον δέ ἐστιν (Lk 16.17a) Matthew presents the first of his ἕως ἄν clauses, and secondly the subjective form παρέλθῃ occurs in the first gospel whereas Luke has the infinitive παρελθεῖν. There are also minor case changes as required by the different grammar in the two versions. Hill, citing Jewish parallels, takes this Matthean phrase as showing the immutability and permanence of the law. He says that the phrase means "for ever, until the end of the world. The eternity of the law is constantly asserted in the Jewish writings, cf. 4 Ezra 9.36f. and *Exod. R.* 1.6: 'Not a tittle shall be abolished from the Law for ever'."[154] This same perspective is asserted by Banks, "The central clause in v18 affirms the continuing validity of the Law and is not dissimilar to various rabbinic passages where the same theme is developed."[155] Some scholars have contested this understanding of the saying, and instead see it as providing a restriction to the validity of the law, that is marking its *terminus ad quem*.[156] Meier argues that the term ἕως, which he takes as traditional and not a Matthean addition in this first case, allows the possibility of termination of the law in the eschaton.[157] The meaning of ἕως is important in this context for resolving the meaning of the evangelist.

When ἕως occurs with the aorist subjunctive, as in this case, it is invariably followed, as the rule requires, by the particle ἄν. In this sense it functions as a conjunction denoting the end of a period of time and have

---

[152] Gundry, *Matthew*, 79.

[153] Jeremias, *New Testament Theology*, 36.

[154] Hill, *The Gospel of Matthew*, 118.

[155] Banks, *Jesus and the Law in the Synoptic Tradition*, 214.

[156] Among those who regard the phrase as restrictive in some sense are, Schlatter, *Matthäus*, 156; Lohmeyer, *Matthäus*, 109; Schniewind, *Matthäus*, 54; Filson, *Matthew*, 83; and, Wrege, *Bergpredigt*, 39-40.

[157] Meier then argues that the second ἕως clause, which he does see as Matthean, moves the meaning of this verse significantly towards understanding a sense of termination. (Meier, *Law and History in Matthew's Gospel*, 41-65).

the sense of 'till' or 'until'.[158] While some commentators classify v. 18b as a temporal clause[159] and others as a subjunctive clause,[160] no distinction should be made.[161] The conjunction ἕως is here a temporal term that is introducing a subjunctive condition as indicated by the presence of the particle ἄν. Davies and Allison correctly note that "'Until heaven and earth pass away' is not just hyperbole, the equivalent of "until mules bear offspring" (although note Philo, *Vit. Mos.* 2.14). Mt 5.18b, like 24.35 par., envisions the end of heaven and earth (without stating the manner of their passing)."[162] However, the larger debate concerns when this event can be seen as happening and what actually constitutes the end of the age.[163] Since the resolution of this question hangs on the interpretation of 18d, the treatment of that issue will be postponed until that phrase is studied. Suffice to note that in 18b a temporal subjunctive introduces a condition of the uncertain timing referring to the passing of the created order that will happen at some juncture in the future.

The next clause (18c) focuses attention on the enduring validity of even the most minute part of the Torah, as long as the prior condition of the continuance of heaven and earth holds force. Matthew, following Q in outline (Q 16.17), states that even the smallest penstroke in Torah remains

---

[158] See BAGD (422) for a full discussion of its various usages, and specifically section 1aβ for its function in Matt 5.18 as a temporal conjunction introducing a subjunctive condition, of as part of a sequence of events.

[159] Although not basing any exegetically weight on the labelling, Sim classifies both 18b and d as temporal clauses. As he states in passing, "The main area of dispute concerns the meaning of and the relationship between the two temporal phrases, 'until heaven and earth pass away' and 'until all is accomplished'." (Sim, *The Gospel of Matthew and Christian Judaism*, 124).

[160] Although Guelich simply classifies 18bc as a subjunctive clause in his tripartite division (143), later when referring just to 18b he describes it as a temporal phrase (144). (Guelich, *The Sermon on the Mount*, 143-4).

[161] Meier is quite accurate in his description of the function of ἕως. He states, "Here it is used as a temporal conjunction, to denote the end of a period of time: 'till, until'; it is employed here with ἄν and the aorist subjunctive to denote that the commencement of an event is dependent on circumstances." (Meier, *Law and History in Matthew's Gospel*, 48).

[162] Davies and Allison, *Matthew,* vol 1, 490.

[163] Pre-empting the discussion slightly, the debate revolves around the issue of when the eschaton may be seen as taking force. Is it to be understood from Matthew's perspective as being inaugurated only at the Parousia with the triumphant return of Jesus, or does his community already live in the eschatological age in which a new form of adherence and fulfilment of the law has taken sway. Allison has suggested that for Matthew the eschatological age has already dawned. He contends that "Matthew and his tradition associate the death and resurrection of Jesus with eschatological motifs; the end of Jesus is spoken off as if it had concurred with the end of the age." (Allison, *The End of the Ages has Come*, 49).

valid. His version of the tradition states, ἰῶτα ἕν ἤ μία κεραία οὐ μὴ παρέλθῃ ἀπὸ τοῦ νόμου (Matt 5.18c). Banks argues that "any attempt to circumvent the emphasis placed on even the most insignificant elements in the Law must be resisted."[164] Yet he immediately qualifies this statement by noting that Matthew himself tries to circumvent the natural force of these words. "In Matthew, however, this admission of the Law's continuing validity appears to be qualified by the two clauses that precede and follow the central element of the saying."[165] Banks is correct in this second observation, for Matthew does present a traditional saying, perhaps one that was well know among certain members of his community, and modifies it in order that its original or absolute force may be toned down. Hummel understood Matthew to be working with originally Jewish Christian material at this point, but by inserting it into his narrative and reinterpreting its original intent he effectively subverts its law abiding perspective.[166] While Stanton has strong arguments for rejecting Hummel's 'reinterpretation' thesis for Matt 10.5f. and 15.24, he does concede that "If Matt 5.18 represents a strict Jewish Christian attitude to the law, 5.17 and 5.18d (ἕως ἂν πάντα γένηται) make it clear that for the evangelist this view has been modified."[167]

Matthew does indeed state that the law is to be fulfilled, however, as the antitheses clearly illustrate, Jesus authority to redefine Torah demonstrates that for Matthew the law is in fact fulfilled in a new manner. While those who were not part of Matthew's group, but tried to uphold the law in more traditional ways, might object that this is not observance of the law, such people may not be his primary concern. Instead he writes for those who accept the authority of Jesus as the interpreter of Torah, and claims that by adhering to his teaching the law is more satisfactorily fulfilled even down to its smallest requirements. As Hagner describes the Matthean train of thought,

> We have here a deliberate hyperbole – an overstatement that is designed to drive home the main point that the law be fully preserved. Jesus' words stress that the law is to be preserved not as punctiliously observed by the Pharisees (although the words apart from this context could suggest such a perspective) but as definitely interpreted by Jesus the Messiah. That is, to follow the authoritative teaching of Jesus is to be faithful to the whole meaning of the law. Figuratively speaking, it is to uphold every 'jot and tittle.'[168]

---

[164] Banks, *Jesus and the Law in the Synoptic Tradition*, 214.
[165] Banks, *Jesus and the Law in the Synoptic Tradition*, 214-15.
[166] Hummel, *Auseinandersetzung*, 167.
[167] Stanton, *Gospel*, 330, n. 3.
[168] Hagner, *Matthew 1-13*, 106.

In a somewhat similar vein Guelich sees the original setting of this saying arising among Torah observant Jewish-Christians, whose perspective Matthew refutes. Yet he does this not through outright rejection of their claim, but by taking up their catchcry and saying that it was valid but in a radical way that Guelich claims more accurately reflects the teaching of the historical Jesus. "The evangelist, however, has modified 5.18 just as he did 5.17 in order to express more accurately Jesus' teaching regarding himself and the Law as well as to counter the strict Jewish-Christian influence felt within his own community. The evangelist modifies this statement by reworking it in terms of 5.18c."[169] However, the type of modification that ἕως ἂν πάντα γένηται (Guelich's 5.18c, but here designated 5.18d, in line with more common nomenclature) introduces requires closer study.

The second ἕως ἂν clause introduces the second aorist subjunctive condition that depicts future events, the precise timing of which is uncertain. It is then necessary to determine the events to which πάντα refers and to see if there is any indication as to their timing (the 'until they happen', γένηται). For Meier, γένηται refers to the occurrence of prophesied events.[170] However, his whole interpretation hinges upon the sense he attributes to πάντα. Utilising the evidence from the parallel in Matt 24.34c ἕως ἂν πάντα ταῦτα γένηται (which has become an important comparison in this debate), Meier first argues that the orientation is eschatological. From this insight he draws the conclusion that 5.18d,

> bears the idea of the fuilfillment of prophecy (in a apocalyptic context) as the time limit of the Law. The most insignificant part of the Law will not lose its binding force until all things prophesied come to pass in the eschatological event....The only prophecies mentioned up until ch. 5 are the OT prophecies which map out the 'life of Jesus'...A person reading Mt in the order in which it was written would naturally suppose that 5.18d referred to the OT prophecies which are fulfilled in the entire (*panta*) career of Jesus.[171]

Whether the leap Meier makes is quite as obvious or natural as he suggests is of course debatable. However, this allows him then to assert that the consummation of Jesus' life is his death and resurrection, and this in turn signals the culmination of the age of the law and the prophets. Meier find confirmation of his thesis that a new eschatological age has dawned with the 'happening' of the Easter event in the spectacular events that accompany Jesus death that are portrayed only in the first gospel,

---

[169] Guelich, *The Sermon on the Mount*, 145.

[170] For a rebuttal of other options see Meier, *Law and History in Matthew's Gospel*, 53-4, and for a summary of his own position see 57.

[171] Meier, *Law and History in Matthew's Gospel*, 63-4.

(Matt 27.51b-53).[172] Meier concludes his treatment of v. 18 with the following statement,

[T]he redactional form of Mt 5.18 is not a stringent affirmation of the perduring validity of the Mosaic Law for all time. Rather, by his redactional activity, Mt has adapted an originally stringent saying on the Law to his own 'economy' of salvation-history. The Mosaic Law as a whole and *qua* Mosaic lasts up until the apocalyptic event of the death-resurrection of Jesus. After this *Wende der Zeit*, the norm for the disciple is 'all whatsoever I commanded you' (Mt 28.19).[173]

Meier presents a strong case in terms of literary, form and redactional analysis for seeing that Matt 5.18 has been softened by the editorial additions of the evangelist. He also advances a highly plausible case to support his observation that in its present form the saying does not uphold the eternal validity of Torah. Nonetheless, despite the significant wider links that are found in the macronarrative for linking the death and resurrection of Jesus with eschatological events, it is somewhat detrimental to Meier's overall thesis that no similar link is found in the immediate context of Matt 5.17-20. Perhaps it could be argued (and this in fact is Meier's thesis) that the passing of heaven and earth is indeed apocalyptic, but this in itself does not establish the thesis that not only is the eschaton prefigured in the passion, but it also terminates the law in a way that would be readily recognized.

Davies and Allison object to interpretations that see a rapid revoking of Torah being implied by v. 18d. They state that notions that the inviolability of the law has come to an end either because of Jesus death, his obedience or the destruction of the temple are all unsound. "The natural objection to all three options is this: 'until heaven and earth pass away' most naturally suggests that there is still along period of time to elapse before the law passes away."[174] This perspective aligns with the sense of v. 18b, namely that the law is in force until the end of the created order arrives, but fails to account for the way Matthew qualifies that statement both in the rest of the verse and the discussion in 5.21-48. As the antitheses illustrate, the law being in force for Matthew does not necessitate its observance in traditional ways. The Torah is re-interpreted on the mountain by a new law-giver, its values are prioritised and some of its ordinances are set aside. Jesus' teaching and ministry do constitute a new order for Matthew,

---

[172] Describing these events Meier argues, "The earthquake is a well known theophanic and apocalyptic motif from the Old Testament, the apocrypha, and rabbinic literature. It symbolizes God's wrathful judgment on the old aeon and his powerful, irresistible intention to save His people and to bring in His rule and Kingdom....In bold apocalyptic terms, Mt depicts the resurrection of the dead as taking place proleptically at the death of Christ." (Meier, *Law and History in Matthew's Gospel*, 32-3).

[173] Meier, *Law and History in Matthew's Gospel*, 65.

[174] Davies and Allison, *Matthew*, vol 1, 474.

but he is not willing to admit that this means the 'end of the law' (cf. Rom 10.4), even if in practice within his community their actions certainly looked like a suspension of many of nomistic requirements. In some respects Thielman is correct in relation to the contrast he sees in Matt 24.35 between the eventual transience of the law and the permanence of Jesus' words. In relation to this tension he states,

> a contrast emerges between the Mosaic law and Jesus' words. Eventually, 5.18 implies, the Mosaic law will pass away; but according to 24.35 Jesus teaching in the gospel will not pass away, even when the end of the age has arrived. Jesus' words, then, are not an interpretation of the Mosaic law but a permanent and eschatologically oriented replacement for it.[175]

While Thielman may be correct in drawing out the implications of what the gospel's perspective on the law ultimately meant, it is questionable whether the Matthean community, or even the evangelist himself, fully recognized these implications. By trying to assert both Jesus' continuity with and authority over the law a tension had been created that could only be resolved by privileging one aspect of the equation over the other.

The two main options are summarised by A. Moses. He describes the options for the disputed ἕως ἂν πάντα γένηται phrase as follows. "(1) it has been taken as synonymous with the previous ἕως ἂν clause: 'till heaven and earth pass away'...(2) it has been noted that the second ἕως ἂν clause is more subtle, it is noted that (a) πάντα has no antecedent, and (b) that γένηται means literally 'happens' and is used of events (1.22; 21.4; 26.54-56), not of 'things being done' or obeying the law."[176] As has been argued the fact that 18d is a redactional addition leads most commentators to see some kind of modification of the underlying tradition. Thus Davies suggests that 5.18 in its Matthean form depicts the law remaining valid until what it looks forward to arrives, 'its destined end'.[177] In this sense the fulfilment or culmination, according to Matthew, is already happening in the ministry and teaching of Jesus.[178] It appears that in writing a pastorally sensitive gospel, for a community that has suffered persecution and the experience of disenfranchisement from synagogue origins, that Matthew is attempting to assure vacillating members that the charge brought against them of being anti-Torah was baseless. To this end he asserts continuity

---

[175] Thielman, *The Law and the New Testament*, 70.

[176] Moses, *Matthew's Transfiguration Story and Jewish Christian Controversy*, 180.

[177] Davies, *The Setting of the Sermon on the Mount*, 100.

[178] This view conflicts to a certain extent with that expressed from Davies and Allison's position in their commentary. This may not necessarily reflect a change in Davies view, but the fact that Allison may have had more input into that section of the commentary. In fact as the introduction to volume three indicates Allison did in fact take on more of the work as the work progressed especially in the exegetical sections. (Davies and Allison, *Matthew*, vol 3, ix).

with the law, but in a nuanced way, which still leaves Jesus' authority in the community beyond question. As the antitheses demonstrate, the right to interpret the law belongs to the community's foundational figure and he defines the new directions in which the group is to head.

5.4.3 Verse 19

In the discussion in the previous section it was noted that the material in this verse is not paralleled in the synoptic gospels, and although some have asserted that it stems from a pre-Matthean source, the presence of a number of distinctively Matthean terms makes it more plausible to see this verse as primarily a creation of the evangelist. The verse consists of two matched pairs that respectively describe sanctions or rewards either for 'loosing' or for 'doing and teaching' the commandments. After having marginalized the significance of 18d, Sim interprets vv. 18-19 as constituting strong evidence for portraying Matthew as a Torah observant Jew. He asserts, "[Matthew] was after all a Christian Jew who believed implicitly that not one jot or tittle had passed from the law with the coming of Christ (5.18), and that even the least of the Mosaic commandments must be observed and taught to others."[179] As an attempted counter to this type of thinking, Banks argued ἐντολῶν τούτων referred not to the ordinances of the Torah, but to Jesus' own commandments. Suggesting that there is an implicit christological reference similar to the more explicit self-references in Matt 18.6; 25.40; he sees the possibility that the same applies in 5.19. He asks, "is it too much to suggest that something similar has occurred in relation to 'the commandments' in 5.19? If so, the expression would refer not to the Mosaic legislation but to Christ's own instructions. Quite possibly, then, the original context of the saying behind 5.19, 5.19 itself being Matthew's reiteration of it, was also in the ministry of Jesus."[180] While this is a creative and in some ways attractive solution since it removes the exegetical problem, one can only answer Banks' own question by saying, yes it is too much to suggest that there is an implicit christological reference here. His methodology is faulty at this point. Even if the saying could be traced to the historical Jesus (hardly an assured conclusion of scholarship at this point), and even if it could be established that Jesus used the saying to refer to his own teaching (probably

---

[179] Sim, *The Gospel of Matthew and Christian Judaism*, 130. Sim erroneously sees this teaching agenda being mirrored in Matt 28.20 and specifically designating the teaching of the law. However, that verse makes clear that the content of the disciples instruction is to be all that Jesus taught them, not the Torah. While it could be argued that these are the same, this would produce a rather difficult and unsupported reading. (126).

[180] Banks, *Jesus and the Law in the Synoptic Tradition*, 223.

impossible to do without the saying being transmitted in its original context), the fact Matthew has inserted it into a cluster of sayings dealing with 'the law and the prophets' would show that the evangelist was using it in a discussion about this issue and his community's response to the charge of abrogating Torah. France also has objected to Banks' reasoning that ἐντολῶν τούτων does not refer to the law. He responds,

> Banks and others have tried to avoid this conclusion by proposing that 'these commandments' in 5.19 are those of Jesus, not of the Old Testament law, but this is to destroy the clear sequence of thought from verse 18 to verse 19, and also to ignore the regular use of ἐντόλη (commandment) in Matthew to refer to Old Testament laws.[181]

While the reference must certainly be to the commandments contained in the Mosaic law, the manner in which Matthew refers to the casuistry of his opponents at other points in the gospel and the way Jesus redefines the law in a number of the antitheses shows that this is no pedestrian or traditional Torah observance that the evangelist is promoting in this verse. For pastoral reasons Matthew assures his community that the law is still 'fulfilled' by their adherence to Jesus as Messiah. In fact, it is claimed, Torah requirements receive a higher level of fulfilment within the Matthean community than in the synagogue where Matthew's opponents seek to observe the law without Jesus as the true interpreter of the law (5.20).

Focusing directly on the text, v. 19a issues the first warning with a sanction, ὅς ἐὰν οὖν λύσῃ μίαν τῶν ἐντολῶν τούτων τῶν ἐλαχίστων καί διδάξῃ οὕτως τοὺς ἀνθρώπους ἐλάχιστος κληθήσεται ἐν τῇ βασιλείᾳ τῶν οὐρανῶν. In reference to the punishment of being called least in the kingdom, Meier states,

> Vs. 5.18bc may reflect the severe view of stringent Jewish Christians, while 5.19 may be the corrective of more moderate Jewish Christians. This attempt at moderation has produced a curious piece (a low place in the Kingdom is a strange sanction), a kind of literary fossil now embedded in 5.19.[182]

While he is correct that the sanction may appear a little strange, it certainly does not come across as a moderate statement for without doubt it calls for observance of the commandments. In the sense in which Matthew depicts the penalty, it is considered as high motivation for obedience.[183] Although, contrary to a possibility suggested by Luz, exclusion from the kingdom does not appear to be envisaged.[184] Perhaps what has been

---

[181] France, *Matthew*, 195.

[182] Meier, *Law and History in Matthew's Gospel*, 166.

[183] Hagner sees that the "ranking of persons…is directly related to the idea of rewards as a motivation for correct conduct." (Hagner, *Matthew 1-13*, 108-9).

[184] Luz, *Matthew 1-7*, 267-8.

previously neglected is that Matthew does set up a criterion for exclusion from the kingdom being based upon non-observance of the least of the commandments important as that is, but upon having a righteousness that surpasses that of the scribes and the Pharisees (v. 20). Yet it is questionable whether Gundry has the Matthean logic concerning exceeding righteousness correct in relation to v. 19b when he states, "if mere entrance requires so much, greatness requires even more, i.e., obedience to all the least commandments, too."[185] It appears that Matthew has in fact shown in v. 20 that there is something of greater importance for entrance into the kingdom than observing the least of the commandments, and that is righteousness. Nonetheless, he has taken up an accusation made by his opponents, one that in all likelihood was troubling more traditional members of his group, and answers the charge not by dismissing it, resulting in the alienation of certain individuals, but by agreeing that the law must be fulfilled. As Davies and Allison realize, through denying the suspicion that Jesus abrogated the law Matthew defends his community "from the accusation, no doubt made by non-Christian Jews, that they had dismissed the Torah."[186] Yet such fulfilment was not equivalent to that expected by his opponents, it achieved observance of even the least of the commandments through following the new way of righteousness. In this sense Matthew's ploy is a rhetorical strategy. He agrees with the words of his opponents, but gives them a new meaning that allows him to claim both fulfilment of the law and a new way of fulfilling it.

5.4.4 Verse 20

As was noted in the section on source and redaction, the vast majority of commentators view this verse as stemming from the hand of the evangelist.[187] The saying serves both as a link to the antitheses that follow, but also as Matthew's concluding answer to the charge that the teaching of Jesus annuls Torah. The polemical hard-edge of these words, and their relevance to the Matthean community are noted by Overman. "These are severe words and potent charges about the law. In employing such rhetoric and denouncing his opponents in such dramatic terms Matthew placed himself squarely within the conflicted setting of late-first-century

---

[185] Gundry, *Matthew*, 82.

[186] Davies and Allison, *Matthew*, vol 1, 500.

[187] The major dissenting voice in recent scholarship has been that of Banks (*Jesus and the Law in the Synoptic Tradition*, 224). He suggests that while there are obvious redactional traces in this verse, it is nonetheless basically a pre-existent saying that has been introduced from another context. For a refutation of this position see the earlier section on the redaction of v. 20.

Palestinian society."[188] So this redactional reflection is important for appreciating Matthew's attitude towards Torah observances and gaining insight into the manner by which the evangelist helped his liminal and ostracized group to find its identity through a life of surpassing righteousness.[189]

That this verse is to be taken as logically related to v. 19 can be seen from the open words, λέγω γὰρ ὑμῖν ὅτι. Guelich notes the manner in which v. 20 qualifies the preceding statement concerning fidelity to Torah. "In 5.19 the evangelist let stand *the least of these commandments* referring to the Law's commandments, but he qualified the phrase with a demand for a greater righteousness in 5.20."[190] However, the phrase also links back to the earlier statements of 5.17-18 both by grammar, so Guelich,[191] as well as by logic, so McNeile.[192] But grammatical arguments should not be read as literary evidence for a connection between vv. 17 and 20 as though the intervening material was a foreign body (contra McNeile), since as Davies and Allison note, "[t]he switch from the first person singular (in 5.19) to the second person plural (in 5.20) is to be put down to the stereotyped expression, 'I say to you'."[193] So v. 20 is introduced specifically as a qualification to the statements in v. 19, but also, more generally, as the conclusion to the whole discussion of the community's attitude to Torah that has been the focus of 5.17-19.

---

[188] Overman, *Church and Community in Crisis*, 80.

[189] Carter clearly perceives the formative function of the evangelist's narrative and the way in which it seeks to engage the audience in a commitment to new patterns of behaviour. As a socially marginalized group the audience required not only assurance but also some kind of 'theoretical' foundation for their belief that they constituted the people of God. In this sense Carter states, "Matthew's Gospel functions as an identity-forming action-interpreting narrative for the audience. Given the story's demand for allegiance to Jesus, it is *the* story in which the audience is to find itself. The audience that encounters Matthew's story is not left primarily with a list of characteristics (obey, serve, love, mission), but with an identity formulated in relation to the narrative of God's actions with Israel (1.1-17), in Jesus (1.18-25), and in the future (7.24-27; 24.3-41)." (Carter, *Households and Discipleship*, 32).

[190] Guelich, *The Sermon on the Mount*, 154.

[191] Grammatically, Guelich notes that v20 "resum[es] the second person plural of 5.17, 18." (*The Sermon on the Mount*, 154).

[192] In fact McNeile rejects a link between 5.20 and vv. 18-19, instead seeing only a logical link with v17. He states, "The γάρ forms a logical sequence with πληρῶσαι (v. 17), not with vv. 18, 19. Something more is needed than the ἐθελοπερισσοθρησκεία (Epiph.) of the Scribes and the Pharisees." (McNeile, *The Gospel according to St Matthew*, 60). While agreeing that there is a logical link, or progression of thought between vv. 17 and 20, this does not necessitating following McNeile in rejecting a link between vv. 18-19 and v. 20.

[193] Davies and Allison, *Matthew*, vol 1, 499.

The qualification that is called for is stated immediately after the introductory phrase and focuses on abounding righteousness. It is presented in the following terms, ἐὰν μὴ περισσεύσῃ ὑμῶν ἡ δικαιοσύνη πλεῖον τῶν γραμματέων καὶ Φαρισαίων. The term περισσεύσῃ is a quantitative reference, demanding a surpassing or abounding amount of some substance.[194] As Meier states, "The basic meaning of the verb in its intransitive use is: to be present in abundance, to be extremely rich or abundant, to be more than enough, to surpass, to abound, to exceed, to grow. The verb is used in the NT predominantly in a theological context, of spiritual abundance."[195] Being employed here in conjunction with the word πλεῖον the whole construction takes on a comparative force.[196] However, it is not possible to concur with Meier's perspective that,

> περισσεύσῃ often connotes (1) a fullness present and proclaimed in the age of salvation, as compared with the old aeon, or (2) a new standard that is required in the new age. To this extent, περισσεύσῃ is an eschatological catchword, and fits in with the eschatological ethic of the Sermon on the Mount and the eschatological colouring of 5.17-19.[197]

The desire to force περισσεύσῃ into an eschatological mould obviously stems from his desire to read the programmatic statement on the law as reflecting his *heilsgeschichte* scheme that already envisages the apocalyptic age as having dawned, thereby demonstrating that Torah observance is no longer required, since 'heaven and earth' have passed away, at least for his community. Any eschatological footprints that could be detected in 5.17-20 would help to support this thesis, but they are not to be found in the term περισσεύσῃ.[198] The term refers to a quantitative

---

[194] In relation to Matt 5.20 BAGD classifies περισσεύσῃ as intransitive, used in relation to things (not persons), and denoting a quantity that is *present in abundance*. Other passage that are seen as having similar grammatical usage are, Mk 12.44; Lk 12.15; 21.4; Rom 5.15; 2 Cor 1.5a, 5b; Phil 1.26. Also seen as paralleling Matt 5.20 is Maximus Tyr. 15,8d. (805).

[195] Meier, *Law and History in Matthew's Gospel*, 108.

[196] Discussing the grammatical of πλεῖον , Meier states, "πλεῖον might be considered redundant with περισσεύσῃ. But, since περισσεύσῃ need not always carry a comparative sense, πλεῖον serves a useful function." (Meier, *Law and History in Matthew's Gospel*, 109).

[197] Meier, *Law and History in Matthew's Gospel*, 109.

[198] In fact those places where περισσεύειν is seen as most closely paralleling Matt 5.20 have little eschatological reference. In Mk 12.44//Lk 21.4 the widow's mite is praised over the pretentious contributions of those who give from their abundance, περισσεύοντες; in Lk 12.15 Jesus refusing to arbitrate on a matter of family inheritance warns that life is not in abundance (περισσεύειν) of possessions; it could perhaps be argued that Rom 5.15 has an undertone of eschatology in that it describes the gift of grace that abounded (ἐπερίσσευσεν) in Christ, potentially reflecting a new era, but this is not the dominant theme; 2 Cor 1.5a, 5b, are pastorally oriented references to the

superiority, here in a comparative sense, but in no way can it be read as an eschatological catchword in the context of 5.20, nor are there any apparent apocalyptic overtones that are to be automatically associated with περισσεύσῃ.

The quantity that Matthew wishes his community to both possess and demonstrate in surpassing degree is δικαιοσύνη, 'righteousness'.[199] In his important study Przybylski argues that for Matthew righteousness is *not* a key term designating the conduct of disciples, rather the evangelist refers to δικαιοσύνη only in passages where dispute with opponents comes to the fore. He concludes, "It is, however, only in polemical contexts or in situations where the true followers of Jesus, i.e. the disciples, form only part of the larger group that the term δικαιοσύνη is used."[200] Contrasting Matt 5.20 with 7.21, Przybylski observes that whereas in the non-polemical context of 7.21 doing the will of God is set as the entrance requirement for the kingdom, this is not the case in 5.20. Rather,

> Mt 5.20 deals with an implied polemical situation. Jesus contrasts the disciples with the scribes and the Pharisees. In this polemical context righteousness is seen as the criterion for entrance into the kingdom of heaven. In 7.21, on the other hand, the immediate context does not refer to the religious leaders of the Jews, In this context doing 'the will of my Father who is in heaven' is seen as the criterion for entrance into the kingdom of heaven.[201]

While one may rightly question whether the notion of ποιῶν τὸ θέλημα τοῦ πατρός would not be considered as 'righteousness' in Matthean terms,

---

abundance of Christ's sufferings, which consequently is able to produce an abundance (περισσεύσει) of encouragement; and in Phil 1.26, Paul calls on the Philippians to make their boast abound in Christ, the reference to παρουσία is to Paul's return and carries no eschatological significance.

[199] Lexically BAGD divides the semantic range of the term δικαιοσύνη into three broad categories. The first is 'the quality, state, or practice of judicial responsibility w. focus on fairness, *justice, equitableness, fairness*'. This category contains the smallest group of biblical references (Mk 16.14; Ac 17.31; Rom 9.28; Heb 7.2; 11.33; Rev 19.11). The second category is the 'quality or state of juridical correctness with focus on redemptive action, *righteousness*'. Nearly all the references in this category come from the Pauline epistles or Hebrews (Rom 1.17; 3.5, 21f, 22, 25, 26; 4.3ff, 5, 9, 11, 13, 22; 5.17, 21; 6.13, 16, 18; 8.10; 9.30; 10. 3, 4, 6, 10; 1 Cor 1.30; 2 Cor 3.9; 5.21, 6.7; Gal 2.21; 3.6, 21; 5.5; Phil 3.9) It is noted that some have suggested that Matt 5.6 fits this category, however this is rejected by BAGD. The largest group comes under the general umbrella of 'the quality or characteristic of upright behaviour, *uprightness, righteousness*'. Matt 5.20 falls into a subcategory of this section, along with Matt 3.15; 6.1 in the sense 'of specific action *righteousness* in the sense of fulfilling divine expectation not specifically expressed in ordinances (Orig., C. Cels. 7, 18, 39, Did., Gen. 188, 27: οἱ κατα δ. ζῶντες) Mt 3.15=ISm 1.1; of a superior type Mt 5.20.' (247-8).

[200] Przybylski, *Righteousness in Matthew*, 114.

[201] Przybylski, *Righteousness in Matthew*, 114.

Przybylski helpfully notes the link between the explicit use of δικαιοσύνη terminology and polemical debates in some of the contexts where the term occurs. Therefore, through the use of δικαιοσύνη terminology Matthew calls into question the pattern of behaviour of his opponents, he criticizes their way of observing Torah, and promotes the portrait of his community as righteous and participating in the blessings of the kingdom. As Matt 5.10 emphasizes, persecution is experienced by community members because they adhere to the notion of 'righteousness' that is taught by the evangelist, but the concomitant reward is having a share in the kingdom of heaven (5.10b). Similarly, 7.21 emphasizes that entry into the kingdom can only come about for those who 'do the will of the Father', and simply confessing Jesus to be Lord is not a sufficient basis for entrance. Although Matthew does not explain what 'doing the will of the Father' means in the context of 7.21, when it is seen as an entrance requirement to the kingdom in the same way as δικαιοσύνη is in 5.10, it is reasonable to conclude that there is some overlap for Matthew between 'doing the will of the Father' and the practice of 'righteousness' by members of his community.

Matthew uses the term δικαιοσύνη on seven occasions (Matt 3.15; 5.6, 10, 20; 6.1, 33; 21.32). While Przybylski is correct in seeing in the majority of these cases a polemical overtone, this does not appear to hold for all references. Treating first those instances where a clear conflict or polemical situation can be observed, in Matt 5.10 not only are disciples persecuted for the sake of righteousness, but also their reward for this maltreatment is entrance into the kingdom. Davies and Allison note, "The perfect tense entails that persecution is a fact of the past and the present."[202] Also this verse implies that such acts of hostility are directly related to practising righteousness (ἕνεκεν), as it was understood by the Matthean community. Here then, the experience of persecution and the polemic it has generated can plausibly be seen as standing behind the use of δικαιοσύνη in this makarism. In the verse under consideration, 5.20, the whole context has been set up as responding to a charge, μὴ νομίσητε (5.17a).[203] Here also polemic stands behind righteousness terminology. Similarly, the discussion of prayer and giving alms in 6.1-6 refutes ostentatious public displays that seek popular acclaim. Sim helpfully draws attention to the fact that the issue at stake is the competitive claim that the evangelist's group has a higher standard of righteousness than their opponents, for even if their outward actions look similar his group alone has the correct inward piety. Thus Sim states,

---

[202] Davies and Allison, *Matthew*, vol 1, 459.

[203] As Guelich argues, the purpose of μὴ νομίσητε is "to counter false assumptions or misunderstandings about Jesus' coming in 5.17." (Guelich, *The Sermon on the Mount*, 136).

[I]t is clear from 6.1-18 that both the proponents of formative Judaism and the Matthean community share in common a number of religious practices, such as alms giving, praying and fasting. But Matthew draws a distinction between them at the level of motivation. While his opponents are denounced as hypocrite for parading these pious act in public to gain praise, the members of his group are encouraged to perform their acts of piety in private so that only God witnesses them.[204]

In this verse, the opening appeal 'Beware not to do your righteousness before men', (6.1) can again be seen to employ δικαιοσύνη terminology in a highly charged context of claim and counterclaim. Finally, the reference to John coming in the way of righteousness (21.32) forms the basis of a critique of Jewish leadership. As Hagner notes, "Their culpability is stressed...The Jewish authorities thus have no excuse."[205] So in the four passages discussed, Matt 5.10, 20; 6.1; 21.32, Przybylski is correct in his assessment that righteousness references occur in the context of confrontation and polemic.

There remain, however, three further references to δικαιοσύνη in the first gospel, (Matt 3.15; 5.6; 6.33). The first of these occurs in the context of the baptism narrative and serves as the basis of Jesus' appeal to John to permit his baptism, οὕτως γὰρ πρέπον ἐστιν ἡμῖν πληρῶσαι πᾶσιν δικαιοσύνη (3.15b). While there is an exchange between Jesus and John there is obviously nothing that can be described as polemical in this story, if anything it is clarification, certainly not polemic.[206] Here Przybylski makes a number of exegetical moves. Firstly he notes that δικαιοσύνη is used in both 3.15 and 21.32 in relation to John, and while it is not explicitly stated that the polemic of the latter passage informs the former, this seems to be an underlying possibility. Secondly, and more importantly, Przybylski suggests that apart from polemical contexts the term is used in setting of address to heterogeneous (and perhaps non-responsive) audiences. He states "the term δικαιοσύνη is reserved strictly for contexts in which Jesus is involved in polemical situations and/or is

---

[204] However, it is unnecessary to follow Sim in drawing the conclusion that competition over certain religious claims automatically implies that the Matthean group conceived itself as Jewish. (Sim, *The Gospel of Matthew and Christian Judaism*, 122).

[205] Hagner, *Matthew 14-28*, 614.

[206] While there may be no obvious polemic in the story, this explanatory or concessive clause may evidence an underlying disquiet in the early church about Jesus undergoing John's baptism that is explicitly stated as being for the remission of sins. Summarising this debate Taylor observes, "discomfort about the baptism of Jesus is found already in the gospel of Matthew (3.14-15). Jesus comes forward to be immersed, but John tries to prevent him and says, 'I need to be immersed by you, and you come to me?' Jesus calmly reassures him, 'Let it be so for now, for it is right for us in this way to fulfill all righteousness.' Jesus therefore does the decent thing, but he does not really need to do it." (Taylor, *The Immerser: John the Baptist within Second Temple Judaism*, 262).

dealing with non-disciples or audiences comprising both disciples and non-disciples."[207] The underlying assumption is that addressing mixed groups constitutes a setting for the use of non-insider terminology, and it is argued that in some sense John functions as a transition figure and not a full disciple.[208] Yet, none of these suggestions really provides strong evidence for seeing Matt 3.15 aligned with the use of δικαιοσύνη in the previously discussed conflict contexts.[209]

The second passage that defies straightforward designation as having a polemical background is Matt 5.6. This beatitude applauds those who pursue righteousness, μακάριοι οἱ πεινῶντες καὶ διψῶντες τὴν δικαιοσύνην. This verse is perhaps easier for Przybylski to handle, since obviously in the wider context of the beatitudes the theme of persecution arises (5.10; 11-12). He also makes the widely supported redactional observation that the term righteousness is Matthean (cf. Lk 6.21) and thus argues that its meaning is informed by the usages of the term elsewhere in the Sermon on the Mount.[210]

Finally in regard to 6.33, Przybylski once again advances the argument from context. As part of this mountain top sermon it is addressed once again to a mixed audience, and thus has polemical overtones. It may still be a critique of the 'hypocrites' mentioned in 6.2, 5f, since its "discussions concerning wealth and anxiety serve to illustrate the point that one's primary concern should be with future rather than present rewards."[211] In general, Przybylski has been seen to make important observations about the Matthean use of δικαιοσύνη in polemical contexts (Matt 5.10, 20; 6.1; 21.32, and perhaps 5.6), however he has pushed his thesis too far in arguing that it is equally applicable in Matt 3.15 and 6.33. Nonetheless, in relation to 5.20, he has convincingly demonstrated that an atmosphere of polemical conflict pervades the use of the term in opposition to the behaviour of adversaries.

The stereotypical Matthean opponents are οἱ γραμματεῖς καὶ Φαρισαῖοι. Without a lengthy excursus discussing the historical identity of

---

[207] Przybylski, *Righteousness in Matthew*, 116.

[208] Przybylski, *Righteousness in Matthew*, 117.

[209] In this context Przybylski sees δικαιοσύνη as referring to God's demand on man not denoting a divine gift. (Przybylski, *Righteousness in Matthew*, 94). He thus rejects Fiedler's view that, "Das 'Erfüllen aller Gerechtigkeit', das Jesus als die eine Forderung Gottes an ihn selbst und an den Taüfer Johannes erkennt, das er erkennt als die Forderung, die das gange Wollen Gottes über seinem Wege und also auch über seiner Taufe bezeichnet, ist nichts anderes als die besondere Aufgabe des Messias und seines 'Vorläufers'." (Fiedler, 'Der Begriff δικαιοσύνη im Matthäus-Evangelium, auf seine Grundlagen untersucht', part 1, 113).

[210] Przybylski, *Righteousness in Matthew*, 96-8.

[211] Przybylski, *Righteousness in Matthew*, 89.

these parties,[212] in the Matthean narrative they function at two levels: they are both the opponents of Jesus during his ministry; and are the enemies of the Matthean community.[213] The double reference contained in the phrase 'scribes and Pharisees' has occasioned discussion, in particular about the identification of the first named group, and its independence, or otherwise, from the Pharisees. Guelich describes the relationship and distinction between these two designations in the following manner.

> The phrase *scribes and Pharisees*, implying two separate groups in Judaism, lacks precision since they were not two distinct groups. Yet the phrase, occurring in all three Synoptic Gospels (e.g., Mark 7.1, 5; Luke 5.21), does maintain the dual concern of the Jewish religious leaders for the Law. The *scribes*, in particular, were the interpreters and instructors of the Law (teaching); the *Pharisees*, a broader category and referring to one of the Jewish religious groups and often including the former (cf. Mark 2.16; Luke 5.30), were zealous to keep the Law (doing).[214]

While Guelich helpfully emphasizes the overlap between the two parties in terms of membership,[215] the dichotomy between 'teaching' and 'doing' appears to be slightly forced. Not only does Matthew present 'doing and teaching' as one, in his presentation of the means of attaining greatness in the kingdom (Matt 5.19), but the OT, intertestamental writings, DSS and the rabbinic literature allow no such separation.

Returning to the immediate Matthean context of 5.17-20, Davies and Allison note an apparent tension with the introduction of the 'scribes and Pharisees' at this point in the narrative.

> The appearance of the scribes and the Pharisees in 5.20 creates tension with 5.17-19, for while this last seems to be directed against liberal or antinomian tendencies, 5.20 suddenly mentions the Jewish leaders...Probably we should think of Matthew as

---

[212] For a recent treatment of the Jewish parties at the time of Jesus, and beyond, see Stemberger, *Jewish Contemporaries of Jesus*. While he sounds an important warning (following Neusner) about reading Mishnaic traditions back into a pre 70 C.E. situation (142), it is questionable whether the degree of disjunction he creates between the Pharisaism prior to the destruction and the emergent rabbinic movement afterwards is valid. Obviously these groups were not equivalent (140-7), but the evidence of Matthew's gospel itself suggests at least enough continuity to warrant identifying the group's enemies with Jesus' Pharisaic opponents, thus creating a degree of identification spanning the events of 70 C.E.

[213] It is helpful to take note of Meier's caution. "Here we must distinguish carefully between history and theology. The phrase is practically a theologoumenon in Mt. Mt speaks of the 'scribes and the Pharisees' (in that order) nine times (5.20; 12:38; 23:2, 13, 15, 23, 25, 27, 29)." (Meier, *Law and History in Matthew's Gospel*, 111).

[214] Guelich, *The Sermon on the Mount*, 159.

[215] For a similar, but more detailed argument see, Rivkin, *A Hidden Revolution*; and idem, 'Scribes, Pharisees, Lawyers and Hypocrites: A Study in Synonymity', 135-42.

fighting on two fronts, against a Christian laxity towards the law on the one hand and against the rabbinic rejection of Christianity on the other.[216]

It is somewhat strange that having resisted the temptation to see Matthew 'fighting on two fronts',[217] now they take this as a solution to a problem that could be satisfactorily addressed otherwise. If, as is being suggested, Matt 5.17-18 is primarily a response to the critique of opponents, but written in such a manner to be pastorally sensitive to the concerns of group members who believe there may be some substance to the charge of 'annulling Torah', the introduction of the 'scribes and Pharisees' does not create a tension. Instead having defended the praxis of his community by asserting that, contrary to the charge, the evangelist's group in fact upholds the law, Matthew now turns from defensive to offensive mode. It is not his group that needs to be concerned with how they uphold the law, but his opponents. For, as the evangelist critiques his opponents in 6.1-6, even their apparent acts of righteousness are nothing more than an empty show of hypocritical conceit and showy displays of religions zeal. It is also this false piety that Matthew will present as jeopardising entrance into the kingdom (Matt 7.21-23).

The final phrase in v. 20, οὐ μὴ εἰσέλθητε εἰς τὴν βασιλείαν τῶν οὐρανῶν, is a Matthean favourite, as in shown by the presence of repeated redaction terminology. Not only is Matthew's replacement of θεός by οὐρανός in the phrase 'the kingdom of God' an indication of editorial activity,[218] but the whole expression 'entering into the kingdom of heaven'

---

[216] Davies and Allison, *Matthew,* vol 1, 500.

[217] See the discussion on this issue in the introduction to this chapter where the positions of Bornkamm and Barth were outlined in some detail, along with a refutation of the notion of the evangelist fighting against two groups of opponents.

[218] The switch from 'kingdom of God' as taken over from the source material to 'kingdom of heaven' is almost uniform. Matthew has the preferred form 'kingdom of heaven' thirty two times in the gospel (or less likely thirty three times; the reference in 19.24 is the more poorly attested variant reading), either altered from source material or reflecting his own creations, (Matt 3.2; 4.17; 5.3, 10, 19 (2x); 20; 7.21; 8.11; 10.7; 11.11, 12; 13.11, 24, 31, 33, 44, 45, 47, 52; 16.19; 18.1, 3, 4, 23; 19.12, 14, 23, 24; 20.1; 22.2; 23.13; 25.1). By contrast, the phrase 'kingdom of God' occurs only four times (Matt 12.28; 19.24; 21.31, 43). Attempts to explain the retention of 'kingdom of God' on these four occasions, only two of which stem from source material (Matt 12.28//Lk 11.20; Matt 19.24//Mk 10.25//Lk 18.25), usually fail to find a theological or literary purpose. Usually these are accounted for in terms of a lapse in the evangelist's concentration. The case would be strengthened if all four occurrences could be shown as occasions when the evangelist was copying source material. The actual parable of 21.28-31a (The Two Sons), may stem from source material, although it has been debated whether the reference to 'the kingdom of God' was part of the source or due to Matthean redaction. The reference to 'the kingdom of God' in 21.43 has even stronger claim to being a creation of the evangelist, since this saying is appended to a Markan parable and the logion is replete

is typical of the first evangelist.[219] The expression is used five times in the first gospel (Matt 5.20; 7.21; 18.3; 19.23-4; 23.13[220]). On all of these occasions the expression occurs in negative contexts, either saying to the audience emphatically by the double negative, οὐ μὴ εἰσέλθητε εἰς τὴν βασιλείαν τῶν οὐρανῶν (Matt 5.20; 18.3), or either outlining the difficulty (19.23-4), describing a prior condition that must be fulfilled (18.3), or correcting a false assumption about what is required (7.21) to enter into the kingdom. Davies and Allison note the close structural parallel between 5.20 and 18.3, although they are unsure about the direction of dependence. Discussing 18.3 they state, "Compare 5.20, whose structure seems (λέγω...ὑμῖν...ἐὰν μή...οὐ μὴ εἰσέλθητε εἰς τὴν βασιλείαν τῶν οὐρανῶν) seems to have influenced or been influenced by the present verse [i.e.,18.3]."[221] Matthew's use of this phrase reflects a number of complimentary editorial techniques at work concurrently. Firstly, the origin of the phrase pre-dates the first evangelist, and was found in his source material, although in the form 'entering the kingdom of God' (Matt 19.23-4//Mk 10.25//Lk 18.25).[222] Secondly, sometimes the evangelist chose to insert this expression into pre-existing negative sayings (Matt 7.21//Lk 6.46,[223] Matt 23.13//Lk 20.52[224]). Thirdly, a new saying referring to entrance into the kingdom is inserted into an existing context (Matt

---

with Matthean themes. Thus it seems less likely that Matthew would have lapsed into a non-Matthean form of the expression in a phrase he had created himself. However, he may have done so under the influence of 21.31, if the reference there was drawing on source material.

[219] See Gundry, *Matthew*, 82.

[220] The usage in 23.15 deviates somewhat from the other four sayings since the word order εἰσέλθητε εἰς τὴν βασιλείαν τῶν οὐρανῶν is not preserved. Rather, the reference to the kingdom of heaven occurs first then a discussion about 'entry', with the kingdom as the implied object. Οὐαὶ δὲ ὑμῖν, γραμματεῖς καὶ Φαρισαῖοι ὑποκριταί, ὅτι κλείετε τὴν βασιλείαν τῶν οὐρανῶν ἔμπροσθεν τῶν ἀνθρώπων· ὑμεῖς γὰρ οὐκ εἰσέρχεσθε οὐδὲ τοὺς εἰσερχομένους ἀφίετε εἰσελθεῖν.

[221] Davies and Allison, *Matthew*, vol 2, 756.

[222] As Hagner comments, "Matthew depends on Mark 10.23-27 for this pericope (cf. Luke 18.24-27). For the most part Matthew's changes consist of the usual omission of redundancy and the abridgment of Mark's text." (Hagner, *Matthew 14-28*, 560).

[223] Luz notes, "The Matthean thematic statement *v. 21* is the result of a redactional, new formulation of Q = Luke 6.46." (Luz, *Matthew 1-7*, 440). See also, Schulz, *Q – Die Spruchquelle die Evangelisten*, 427.

[224] Gundry suggests the following motivation for the Matthean changes. "'The kingdom of heaven' is a Mattheanism (25,7). Here it substitutes for 'the key of knowledge' and exhibits the lingering influence of 18.4. Typically, Matthew adds 'before men' (ἔμπροσθεν τῶν ἀνθρώπων - 3,1). This addition gives another echo of 6.1, a composition of his that recently influenced 5a [i.e., 18.5a]."

18.1-5, (but not v3)//Mk 9.33-37//Lk 9.46-48).[225] Fourthly, Matthew could both create a new saying (5.20), and the wider context in which it was to be included (5.17-20).

In relation to Matt 5.20, this saying reflects the evangelist's wider use whereby he warns his audience of the precautionary attitude that must be adopted by those seeking to enter into the kingdom. Thus as Beare notes in relation to the critique of the behaviour of the scribes and the Pharisees, "Even their high standards of conduct are not high enough for those who aspire to enter the kingdom of heaven."[226] In this sense Strecker is correct to notice that 'righteousness' is a different pattern of conduct to the ethical behaviour of the Matthean opponents, which does not lead to entry into the kingdom.[227] Meier helpfully draws attention to the OT background to the expression 'to enter the kingdom of heaven'. He suggests that two images lie behind the Matthean usage.

> The first image is the entrance of Israel into the promised land – either the historical entrance (Dt 4.1) or the entrance at the end time (Ps. Sol. 11.2-6)....The second and more proximate image involved in 5.20 is connected with requirements of cultic purity and ethical righteousness for entrance through the temple gates (cf. the temple liturgies giving *torot* of entrance Pss 15; 24; 118.19f) or the city gates of Jerusalem – raised to an apocalyptic image in Is 26.2f. The image has been projected here onto the apocalyptic screen of eschatological events, and so Mt 5.20 can take its place among the eschatological and apocalyptic logia of the gospels.[228]

While Meier again can be seen to be forcing material from 5.17-20 into an apocalyptic mould in a vain attempt to garner support for his thesis that the second temporal clause of 5.18 refers to the resurrection of Jesus as the eschaton, nonetheless, this does not invalidate the two sources of imagery as informing the Matthean understanding of entry into the kingdom. Both entry into the land and Zion imagery do connote ideas of being in the closer presence of God, but importantly, being in that realm also means that present marginal status is reversed because the kingship of God is apparent. There can be little doubt that for Matthew this entrance into the

---

[225] Davies and Allison offer the follow observations on the use of Matthean source material. "[Matthew] has shortened the narrative introduction (so that it has become much less colourful), dropped the declaration in Mk 9.35 ('If anybody wants to be first, let him be last of all and servant of all;' cf. 20.26-7=Mk 10.43-4; Mt 23.11), added the sayings in vv3 (from Mk 10.15, or more likely from M), and 4 (based probably upon the Q saying in 23.12=Lk 18.14), and omitted the end of Mk 9.37." (*Matthew*, vol 2, 752).

[226] Beare, *The Gospel according to Matthew*, 145.

[227] Strecker states in relationship to righteousness, "The term thus has an anthropological orientation. "Righteousness" is the comprehensive term for the right conduct of the disciples in general, and thus for the whole Christian community. Such righteousness must be different from that of the scribes and the Pharisees." (Strecker, *The Theology of the New Testament*, 382).

[228] Meier, *Law and History in Matthew's Gospel*, 113.

kingdom in 5.20 is seen as a future event. This is confirmed by the
beatitudes, which stand in close relation ship to 5.20, and offer
eschatological comfort in the kingdom of heaven. Beasley-Murray links
these Matthean blocks of material, "[The] beatitudes embody the Spirit of
the Sermon on the Mount and are in harmony on Jesus' teaching given
elsewhere on entry into the kingdom of God (see Matt 5.20 and 7.13-27;
Mark 10.13-27 and 12.28-34)."[229] Further, he rejects the notion that 5.20 is
concerned with a quantitative surpassing of Pharisaic righteousness,[230]
instead he sees it more in terms of a pattern of life that reflects the
imperatives of the new age that dawn not only in Jesus' death and
resurrection (contra Meier), but also in his teaching and ministry. Thus he
argues, "To respond wholeheartedly to the message of Jesus is to know
that 'eschatological superabundance' which issues in a righteousness
acceptable to God and entrance into the kingdom of God in the last day."[231]
Therefore, while there is a future aspect to entrance into the divine realm,
this cannot be construed as governing the whole outlook of 5.17-20.

In verse 20, Matthew is promoting a pattern of conduct among his
adherents that is noticeably distinct from that his opponents. Yet the
question remains as to whether this is a distinction in degree, or in kind. To
frame the contrast in an alternative set of terms, it needs to be resolved
with the righteousness of the Matthean ἐκκλησία is to be simply a
quantitative surpassing or rather a qualitative redefinition. For Segal,
portraying the Matthean group as still very much embedded within
emergent Judaism, the contrast is quantitative. He writes, "the use of
'righteousness' in Matt 5.20 indicates that Matthew understands entailing
the performance the commandments of Judaism. As he says, 'Unless your
righteousness exceeds that of the scribes and the Pharisees, you will never
enter the kingdom of heaven'."[232] However, the idea may be more than
simply exceeding the 'righteousness' of the opponents in some kind of
empirical, or measurable, sense. As Matthew exemplifies in 6.1-6, the
conduct of his opponents is wrong at its very core for its motivation is seen
as being for human recognition instead of divine acknowledgement.[233] Yet
this does not imply that Matthew is rejecting traditional acts of piety such

---

[229] Beasley-Murray, *Jesus and the Kingdom of God*, 165.

[230] Cf., Luz, *Matthew 1-7*, 270. "A quantitative comparison between the
righteousness of the disciples and the Pharisees and scribes lies in the text in any case."

[231] Beasley-Murray, *Jesus and the Kingdom of God*, 165.

[232] Segal, 'Matthew's Jewish Voice', 21.

[233] As Hagner presents the implication of the Matthean instruction, "Only deeds done
for God's glory will receive an eschatological reward. This stress is in keeping with
emphasis on the inner obedience to God in chap. 5. God is concerned with the heart, with
the motivation behind a person's deeds, as much as with the external deeds themselves."
(Hagner, *Matthew 1-13*, 141).

as almsgiving and prayer, but instead he is stating that there should be a qualitative difference in his community which functions as the basis for their righteousness. Guelich discusses the significance of this reorientation of motivation.

> The righteousness required in 5.20 stands in contrast to that of the scribes and Pharisees…Such 'righteousness' connotes a new relationship established by God with his people, a relationship that issues in conduct that is in keeping with the Father's will set forth in Jesus' teaching and ministry….the 'righteousness that exceeds' reflects a change in one's relationship with God (6.1-18) and with others (5.21-48). It is the 'good fruit' produced by the 'good tree' (7.16-20); it is doing the will of the Father (7.21-24). Put another way, 'the righteousness that exceeds' is the concomitant of true discipleship, the life-changing acknowledgment of Jesus as the one in whom the Father is at work.[234]

This understanding allows for the fundamental reorientation that has taken place within the group with its primary allegiance being to Jesus as the community's authority figure. The charge of hypocrisy that is levelled against the scribes and Pharisees implies that their practices are fundamentally flawed. Matthew does not allow the possibility that they are doing the right thing for the wrong reasons. This shows that the righteousness that Matthew expects in his community is not a difference of degree, but issues forth in a whole new pattern of discipleship which must be based on allegiance to Jesus and recognition of his status as the supreme source of authority within the community.

5.5 The Meaning and Function of Matt 5.17-20

The foregoing study of the programmatic statement on the law in terms of its sources, redactional reworking, exegesis of individual verses and its purpose within the wider context of the antitheses and the whole sermon, leads to the rejection of a number of earlier proposals. Firstly, the notion that Matthew was 'fighting on two fronts' as initially proposed by Bornkamm,[235] but given a more thoroughgoing treatment by Barth,[236] and moreover, that 5.17-20 represents the evangelist's attack upon the antinomians within his community, was seen as having little support in the text. Although not consistently following this understanding of a duality in the groups that the evangelist confronts, Davies and Allison do attempt to account for the mention of the scribes and Pharisees in v20 by drawing a

---

[234] Guelich, *The Sermon on the Mount*, 170-2.
[235] Bornkamm, 'End-Expectation and Church in Matthew', 15-51.
[236] Barth, 'Matthew's Understanding of the Law', 58-164.

contrast between the rejection of "liberal or antinomian tendencies"[237] and a strident attack on "the rabbinic rejection of Christianity."[238] It needs to be noted that this perspective does not govern Davies and Allison's exegesis of 5.17-20, and in many ways its appearance seems a little strange in the wider context of their discussion.

A second position that was seen as inadequate, despite numerous strengths and exegetical insights, was Meier's rigid *heilsgeschichte* scheme. Ultimately, his dependence on an implausible exegesis of Matthean salvation history, especially in relation to Matt 27.51b-53 as being the eschatological turning point that marked the 'passing away of heaven and earth' and the coming about of 'all things' spoken of in 5.18, severely limits the applicability of his overall theory. The importance of this eschatological scheme is reflected in Meier's statement that, "Inasmuch as the gospel is an extended form of paschal proclamation, we should approach Mt's teaching on the Law from the starting point which is Mt's own 'center own gravity,' the death-resurrection seen as the turning of the ages."[239] This perspective leads to the overall conclusion that,

> Jesus showed and inculcated fidelity to the Law during his public ministry; he announced that not one *yod* or stroke of the Law would fall until all events prophesied came to pass; the βασιλεία breaks into this aeon in a new, powerful way. It is in view of this new situation, with the Gentile mission it would involve, that the church abrogates some elements of the Mosaic Law in the antitheses. The rule of life for the Christian is thus an 'umbrella concept': 'all things whatsoever I commanded you' – be that *secundum, praeter,* or *contra* the Mosaic Law.[240]

While Matthew certainly operates with a two ages scheme,[241] it does not automatically mean that this is the key to the evangelist's understanding of the relationship between the communities for which he is writing and those synagogue based Jews in conflict with the Matthean adherents. It is the manner in which Meier seeks to find eschatological references in nearly every significant term in 5.17-20 that raises questions about the way Meier interprets this pericope, and leaves him open to the charge of importing a certain *heilsgeschichte* scheme in order to legitimise his reading.

---

[237] Davies and Allison, *Matthew,* vol 1, 500.

[238] Davies and Allison, *Matthew,* vol 1, 500.

[239] Meier, *Law and History in Matthew's Gospel,* 164.

[240] Meier, *Law and History in Matthew's Gospel,* 168.

[241] Allison recognizes that although there are eschatological motifs associated with the death of Jesus in Mark, these are certainly accentuated in the gospel of Matthew. Commenting on 27.51b-53, a passage unique to Matthew and of special importance for Meier's interpretation, Allison notes that "There is much to argue that the primitive Christian community believed that the new age was dawning in their time, that eschatological events had been and were unfolding before their eyes." (Allison, *The End of the Ages has Come,* 46).

Sim also argues against Meier's thesis that the death and resurrection of Jesus are viewed in 5.17-19 as the eschatological turning point of history that draws to a close the era of Torah obedience.[242] By contrast, Sim, while agreeing with Meier that the eschatological age signals the end of Torah, wishes to push that event forward until the time of the parousia.

> There is solid evidence in the Gospel that the evangelist believed that the eschatological age witnessed the destruction of the existing cosmic order (the passing away of heaven and earth) and its replacement by a new and eternal order (cf. 19.28). If this understanding of the phrase is correct, than the evangelist limits the law to the present age. Jesus did not come to abolish the Torah at the time of his ministry, but it will come to an end when all the eschatological events are accomplished (5.18*d*; cf. 24.34-35) with the passing away of the present world order (5.18*b*).[243]

However, Sim's thesis (like Meier's) attributes too rigid an eschatological framework to the first evangelist. It seems problematic to assert that the statement on the law, contained in 5.17-20, was really informed by a thoroughgoing apocalyptic schema. The apocalyptic language in these verses is not as central as has often been argued, and may simply reflect stereotypical language rather than a desire on the evangelist's part to develop an apocalyptic timetable. Moreover, the antitheses that follow are not interested in eschatology, but in Jesus' teaching and authority to issue declarations pertaining to the correct interpretation of the law for his disciples.

If then, the Matthean understanding of the law as contained in 5.17-20 is not to be taken as reflecting the perspective of a strictly Torah observant community (since Matthew immediately has Jesus redefine and at times rescind certain ordinances in 5.21-48), nor as representing a fight against two sets of opponent because of a paucity of evidence in the gospel for the existence of an antinomian party,[244] nor as determined by an eschatology realized in the events of the death and resurrection of Jesus, can a coherent reading of these verses be obtained? Part of the reason for the failure to

---

[242] Sim argues that the fault with Meier's interpretation is that "Such an interpretation must either play down or ignore the wealth of apocalyptic-eschatological material in the gospel which directly identifies the end of the present age with the parousia of Jesus and the final judgment." (Sim, *The Gospel of Matthew and Christian Judaism*, 125). Sim also cites his article, 'The Meaning of παλιγγενεσία in Matthew 19.28', *JSNT* 50, 1993, 9-11, as providing further corroboration for his argument against Meier.

[243] Sim, *The Gospel of Matthew and Christian Judaism*, 125-6.

[244] Discussing v17 as the introduction to this section, Luz likewise rejects any attack on antinomians. He states, "A direct polemic, perhaps against antinomians, cannot be proved; Matthew argues principles." (Luz, *Matthew 1-7*, 260). He continues by noting "It seems to me that it cannot be proved in 7.15-23 either that the opponents were theoretical theological antinomians." (Luz, *Matthew 1-7*, 260, n. 31).

come to terms with the Matthean meaning behind this material has stemmed from a tendency to only link vv. 17-20 with what follows, and not to consider the perspective of what precedes. Secondly, there has been too great a tendency to play redactional material off against source material, as if the two were not compatible in the Matthean account. The first tendency can be seen clearly in Davies and Allison's comments. They state in regard to the gospel narrative that, "[i]n denying the suspicion that Jesus abolished the Torah, 5.17-20 looks forward, not backward, for surely from what has gone before no suspicion could be generated."[245] Yet the pastorally oriented promises in the beatitudes and the encouragements to distinctive discipleship in 5.13-16 are not irrelevant for understanding the statements about the law. For the community undergoing the persecutions depicted in 5.10, 11-12,[246] silence, hiddenness or non-engagement with the world are not offered as possible options (Matt 5.13-16). In this sense, the opening injunction in v. 17 μὴ νομίσητε, is best understood an introducing and refuting the primary charge that has result in the persecution of the Matthean community by their Torah observant adversaries and led to a growing tendency for group members to become secretive about their allegiance, in some sense there may have been a tendency towards becoming crypto-Christians.

From this perspective 5.17-20 is not primarily hortatory, or polemical although both of these aspects are present to some degree. Rather, it needs to be understood as a pastorally pedagogical piece, that take up the accusations of opponents and the fears of certain group members in order to assure them that the charge of Jesus as law destroyer is patently false. To this end Matthew subverts the accusations of his interlocutors by turning the charge on its head.[247] He claims that Jesus does not destroy but fulfils Torah, probably taking up the very slogans of his opponents, which were also being reiterated by unsettled group members. He has Jesus state

---

[245] Davies and Allison, *Matthew,* vol 1, 501.

[246] Commenting on the beatitude in 5.11-12, Green notes, "Something of the nature of the persecution of which this beatitude speaks can be deduced from these allusions elsewhere in the Gospel: in addition to 5.11-12, 10.17-23 (much of it, strikingly, transposed in Matthew's redaction from its original apocalyptic context in Mark); 23.34-36; 24.9." (Green, *Matthew, Poet of the Beatitudes*, 247).

[247] Luz does not wish to take up the option of seeing this statement as interacting with a charge brought by Jewish adversaries. He argues, "Direct polemic against Jewish accusations that Jesus was an opponent of the law is improbable because the Matthean community stood no longer in direct discussion with the synagogue. Thus the sentence is best explained as a principal thesis." (Luz, *Matthew 1-7*, 260). While concurring that the community was not directly in debate with the synagogue any longer, Luz does not consider the possibility that synagogue-type accusations were being repeated by conservative group members, who had become unsure of their own beliefs and needed pastoral reassurance.

that even the smallest part of the law remains in force until heaven and earth pass (v. 18), again probably an assertion of his opponents. However, he glosses this claim in two significant ways. Firstly, the Matthean addition of ἰῶτα ἕν to the reference to one tittle, μία κεραία, shows that the evangelist is keen to make this charge clear to an audience that had members who only understood Greek.[248] The second highly significant gloss is contained in 5.18d (ἕως ἂν πάντα γένηται). While the precise meaning of this phrase has been endlessly debated, in some sense it qualifies the first subjunctive temporal clause in 5.18b. The qualification also appears to pick up the claim of fulfilling the 'law and the prophets' as stated in v. 17.

Fulfilment stands as a key Matthean concern not only in 5.17, but is also articulated in relation to a number of the scriptural citations throughout the gospel. Davies and Allison suggest one of the possible purposes of the formula quotations is that "the notion of promise and fulfilment may to some extent be an apologetic. Matthew may be supplying believers with scriptural ammunition with which to enter into debate with the synagogue."[249] France describes the possible basis of such formula quotations (Matt 1.22-23; 2.6, 15, 17-18, 23; 4.14-16; 8.17; 12.17-21; 13.14-15, 35; 21.4-5; 27.9-10), and the emotion they engender in the audience in the following terms. "A few Old Testament passages supply a possible model on which such a formula may have been based (1 Ki. 2.27; 2 Ch. 36.21-22=Ezra 1.1), and the wording has a rather formal, even archaic, sound which evokes in the reader a sense of awe at the outworking of the agelong purposes of God revealed long ago by divine declaration."[250] It is probably impossible to confirm or disprove the thesis whether such quotations may have formed part of a testimony book within the Matthean community.[251] Yet regardless of their origin, Matthew utilised these citations in his gospel to confirm that Jesus is the longed for divine messenger alluded to in the Old Testament. The scriptures find fulfilment in Jesus' life: in his birth (1.23; 2.6); places of residence (2.15, 23; 4.14-16); his entry into Jerusalem (21.4-5); and, the price paid for his betrayal (27.9-10); as well as in his ministry, in the healing of the infirm and demon possessed (8.17; 12.17-21); and the teaching in parables (13.14-15, 35[252]).

---

[248] See the discussion on the sources and redaction of v18 in section c. of this chapter.

[249] Davies and Allison, *Matthew,* vol 1, 213.

[250] France, *Matthew – Evangelist and Teacher*, 172.

[251] For a fuller discussion of the testimony book hypothesis see G.M. Soares Prabhu, *The Formula Quotations*, 67-73.

[252] Heil notes a progression in thought between 13.14-15 and 13.35. He states, "That the prophecy (προφητεία) of Isa. 6.9-10 is fulfilled (ἀναπληροῦται) for the non-

Stanton supports the notion that Matthew is using the statements of 5.17-20 to rebut Jewish accusations. Further, he sees this material as providing a higher authority for group members, namely, the teachings of Jesus.

> We know that Jewish opponents of Christianity frequently alleged that Jesus and his followers had abandoned the law, and we know that in several passages Matthew is responding to Jewish counter-propaganda....For Matthew the law and the prophets continue to be authoritative for Christians – with the proviso that they are interpreted in the light of the teachings of Jesus, especially the love command.[253]

The counter-polemic Stanton mentions is most clearly seen in Matt 28.11-15, which dismisses the story of the stolen body as a fabrication circulated among the Jews.[254] This use of the term Ἰουδαῖοι is highly significant,[255] for it shows a distinction between Matthew's communities and his opponents that is hard to account for if the evangelist and his adherents still considered themselves to be under Jewish synagogue authority.[256] As Gundry states, "Matthew mentions the wide circulation of the false rumor among the Jews not only to explain the unbelief of most of them, but also to bring them out of their unbelief by an exposé of the fraud it rested upon."[257] Yet, it is worth questioning whether Gundry is correct in understanding this Matthean response as seeking to bring Jews out of unbelief, or if it is not more plausible that he writes to prevent his own vacillating members from being lured back to the synagogue environment.[258] Perhaps both are possible purposes for the redactional

---

understanding crowds by Jesus speaking to them (vv 13-15) progresses to Jesus speaking to the crowds in parables (v 34) in order that what was said through the prophets (προφήτου) might be fulfilled (πληρωθῇ) (v 35a)." (Carter and Heil, *Matthew's Parables,* 82).

[253] Stanton, *A Gospel for a New People,* 49.

[254] Hagner notes in relation to the term 'the Jews' that, "Here for the first time the word is given a negative connotation , referring to those who do not accept the evidence for the resurrection of Jesus." (Hagner, *Matthew 14-28,* 877).

[255] However, see the discussion of Saldarini who tries to minimise the significance of this reference. (Saldarini, *Matthew's Christian-Jewish Community,* 34-7).

[256] Sim dismisses this as an insignificant piece of evidence since he notes that Josephus, a Jew, uses it in his own writings (although Sim cites no examples). However, Sim ignores the most important implication, which is not that Josephus himself was a Jew, but that his audience was Gentile. This too is the most plausible reconstruction of the relationship between author and audience in the first gospel: a writer of Jewish background, writing for an audience with a proportion of Gentiles in its midst. (See, Sim, *The Gospel of Matthew and Christian Judaism,* 148).

[257] Gundry, *Matthew,* 593.

[258] Admittedly there is not the Johannine concern with cryptic Christians (Jn 12.42), but the need to address the question of whether Jesus came to destroy the law for the

response of 28.11-15, however, since the readership is primarily already part of the Matthean circle the emphasis is more likely to be pastoral than polemical.

Similarly, in 5.17-20, Matthew writes for wavering believers whose faith was being weakened by the claim of emergent Judaism that following Jesus meant destroying or annulling the God-given law and covenant of the Old Testament. Matthew's pastoral strategy is both subtle and sophisticated. He does not directly attack his opponents claims, instead he takes them up and expresses his generally concurrence with their perspective. However, although he may even be using their slogans, he qualifies them, and subsumes them under the authority of Jesus, and the fulfilment of the law and the prophets that is seen to come to fruition in the ministry and teaching of Jesus. In essence this is a subversive strategy, for no longer is the focus on the issue of law observance, but rather on which pattern of law fulfilment one is to adopt. For Matthew the options are presented in a stark absolute antithesis, either one can continue with the tradition pattern and hence ignore the fulfilment of the law and the prophets which is to be seen in Jesus, or one can accept the divine disclosure and the authority of the community's foundational figure thereby embracing that 'all things have come to pass' in Jesus.

Obviously a partial eschatological fulfilment is involved here, although Matthew does not major on eschatological themes at this juncture. Instead his focus is ethical, playing off the higher righteousness (v. 20) demanded from his community members against the supposedly false motives of their opponents (cf. 6.1-18). Yet the implication of this new pattern of life, with a prioritised hierarchy of ethical imperatives, is presented in the antitheses (5.21-48).[259] While this does not necessarily entail a rejection of Torah at every point of its legislative agenda, when a tension emerges it is not resolved on the basis of Mosaic pronouncement, but in accord with the teaching of Jesus. So Matthew assures his community members that Jesus did not come 'to destroy the law or the prophets', yet his notion of fulfilment does not mean continuing in the same pattern as though Jesus' coming had no impact on Torah observance. For Matthew a new age had dawned, and he presents the implications of this new era to his group members.

---

benefit of community members does make vacillation and potential return to the synagogue at least a possibility.

[259] As Balch notes, such a rhetorical ploy was not uncommon in Hellenistic debate. "Matthew 5.17, just as a Hellenistic-Jewish audience would expect, makes the claim that Moses' law has not been 'abolished,' but in the same chapter, the antitheses do change some of them." (Balch, 'The Greek Political Topos περὶ νόμων and Matthew 5.17, 19, and 16.19', 76).

5.6 Conclusions

That Matthew's ideology was ultimately successful in providing the theoretical basis for understanding the relationship between Christianity and Judaism is not to be doubted. Not only did the church in the patristic period, and subsequently, claim to be the true Israel, and the upholder of the law and the prophets as it understood them to be fulfilled in Jesus, it also embraced the Matthean account as its first gospel in the canon of New Testament scripture and cited his comments with greater frequency than those of any other evangelist.[260] In this sense Matthew's pastoral agenda found its vindication in the assurance it gave to the early church and subsequent generations of Christians as providing an explanation of the relationship between Christianity and Judaism.

However, one may ask whether it had its desired purpose in Matthew's own community. If the highly speculative suggestion of Antiochean location of the community could be proved, the representation of Christianity in that city provided by Ignatius would perhaps suggest that Matthew's agenda was taken up by the descendents of Matthean Christianity.[261] Yet the weakness of such a reconstruction does not stem only from the uncertainty of Antioch being the home of the Matthean group, but from assuming that Ignatius' branch of Christianity represents a continuous link with all branches of Matthean Christianity.[262]

---

[260] On the use and reception of the Gospel of Matthew see Stanton, 'The Early Reception of Matthew's Gospel: New Evidence from Papyri?', 42-61.

[261] Gundry sees the importance of the Ignatian evidence in the following terms. "Ignatius militates against a Jewish sectarian definition of the Matthean community. Ignatius does not even seem to know alternative Jewish Christianity in Antioch or within hailing distance. So whether or not Ignatius knew and used Matthew, as John Meier argues, but all the more if Ignatius did know and use Matthew, how did the church in Antioch or thereabouts travel so far and fast from Jewish sectarianism?" (Gundry, 'A Responsive Evaluation of the Social History of the Matthean Community in Roman Syria', 62-3).

[262] Recent trends in the study of Ignatius of Antioch, have shown a questioning of the traditional dating of his epistles to the reign of Trajan. Instead, scholars like Hübner have argued that the textual traditions that are drawn upon in the Ignatian correspondence require a later date of composition than that usually supposed. Hübner suggests a date perhaps about half a century after the reign of Trajan as being more plausible. He states, "R.A. Lipsius hat Th. Zahn vorgehalten, er stelle, „um die Aechtheit der 7 ignatianischen Briefe zu retten, die ganze Kirchen- und Dogmengeschichte des 2. Jahrhunderts auf den Kopf". Vielleicht ist nach mehr als hundert Jahren die Zeit gekommen, sie wieder auf die Füße zu stellen." (R.M. Hübner, 'Thesen zur Echtheit und Datierung der sieben Briefe des Ignatius von Antiochien', 72.

While Sim is wrong about so much in his reconstruction, he is at least correct in noting the existence of references to Jewish-Christian groups in patristic literature.[263] Perhaps one of these was the product of alienated and disenfranchised Matthean Christians,[264] who, although not embracing an inclusive attitude towards Gentiles, did not give up their adherence to Jesus, instead they sought to establish a distinctively (and probably more primitive) Jewish Christianity. Obviously these options are mere speculations and with the evidence currently available the answer must remain unknown. However, there can be little doubt that Matthew saw the breach with the synagogue experienced by his community as having implications for understanding how the law was to be viewed and acting as an imperative for distinctive discipleship (5.13-16) and to encourage ongoing participation in the gentile mission (28.19). This was what was demanded by Jesus, the one to whom the community attributed ultimate authority, and whose teaching Matthew presented in a new way that his people might by a missionary orientated group characterized by surpassing righteousness[265] and fraternal love, with the promise of entering into the kingdom of heaven.

---

[263] For a helpful discussion of the pertinent references in the patristic literature see Sim, *The Gospel of Matthew and Christian Judaism*, 181-3. In this section Sim catalogues the references to three groups, the Nazarenes, Elkesaites, and Ebionites.

[264] It has not been uncommon to link some trajectory from the Matthean community with one of the groups standing behind the Jewish-Christian gospels mentioned in Patristic sources, (see note 262). It is, however, difficult to separate the polemical strategy of labelling opponents as 'Jewish', from the concrete reality of whether such named heretical parties were actually engaged in Jewish practices, and how this materialised itself in the respective groups that are criticised.

[265] While Przybylski is helpful in showing that righteousness is often used in the first gospel in polemical contexts its seems to much to assert that it was only a 'provisional' concept that was used because it would be understood by opponents. It is argued that the lack of significance of the term reflects the emergence of a new pattern of religion. Przybylski askes, "Were Matthew's contemporaries prepared for the shift from the righteous/righteousness terminology to that of disciple/will of God?" However, this strict dichotimization of these sets of terms is not required, Matthew alternates between these concepts as the context dictates. (Przybylski, *Righteousness in Matthew*, 122).

Chapter 6

Mission in Matthew's Gospel

6.1 Introduction

Determining an accurate and consistent picture of the Matthean attitude to mission, and then translating this to reconstruct the actual practice of the community behind the gospel has always been a vexed issue. Two factors make this endeavour particularly problematic. Firstly, the evidence of the gospel itself has been seen as contradictory, especially in relation to resolving whether Gentile mission was viewed as a legitimate activity, or if the community limited its proselytising exclusively to Jews. Secondly, it is difficult to know to what extent Matthew's gospel reflects current practice within the community in relation to this issue, or whether the evangelist perceived his task to be that of presenting a new direction to his audience, but nonetheless made it a mandate that came with the sanction of Jesus' own authority (Matt 28.16-20).

This tension has been recognized by numerous scholars. Hahn is particularly forthright in perceiving that the issue of mission in Matthew's gospel is highly significant for determining the reason why the early church become so missionary-focused, since Matthew's account established itself as the premier gospel in the Great Church of subsequent centuries. Hahn presents the tension in the following terms.

> [Matthew's gospel contains] many Jewish Christian elements, which makes possible a conclusion *a posteriori* on the particularist view of mission, and on the other hand it adopts (28.18-20) the unit of tradition that is fundamental for the Gentile mission of Hellenist Jewish Christianity. As can easily be seen, Matthew has allowed an important place both to the particularist expressions in his word of commission and to the missionary command at the end of his Gospel. But how did he himself understand the missionary task? How does he weld these two elements into a unity?[1]

While not wanting to follow all aspects of Hahn's argument, such as depicting 28.18-20 as a pre-existing unit of tradition,[2] nonetheless this

---

[1] Hahn, *Mission in the New Testament*, 120.

[2] Although Gundry advances the argument that Matt 28.9-20 reflects the lost ending of Mark, and therefore is traditional, this position is not adopted by the majority of commentators, (Gundry, *Matthew*, 590-1). More representative of the majority position Davies and Allison see the material in Matt 28.16-20 as a combination of Matthean

statement does reflect the fundamental tension that exists for all who try to determine the holistic meaning of Matthew's apparently divergent comments on mission, and either its limitations or universal applicability.[3]

The discussion of Matthew's attitude to mission has usually been conducted around a number of key texts (Matt 10.5-23; 15.21-28; 21.43; 24.14; 26.13; 28.16-20). This approach has the advantage of focusing the discussion, by concentrating on the most relevant sayings. However, it can also result in a loss of the overall emphasis that is conveyed by reading the gospel as a whole. Therefore, it is proposed here to concentrate on those texts that form the basis of the discussion, but also to look for their overall significance in the wider structure of the narrative.[4] Thus despite a seemingly initial limitation on the scope of the missionary activity for Jesus' disciples during the period of his ministry (10.5ff; 15.21-28), even these apparent constraints must be read against the overall attitude to Gentiles in the surrounding narrative, as this may assist in determining the evangelist's intent.[5]

Moreover, it is difficult to determine the actual shape of the activity that Matthew was encouraging his community to undertake. It is not necessarily the case that Matthew's perspective on mission should be understood in the same terms as the Pauline missionary journeys, which resulted in the establishment of new churches. However, it would perhaps be a mistake to think that such proselytising could only be conceived in terms of passively opening the doors of the Matthean community to non-Jewish members. While sociological theory may suggest that, in general, new religious movements tend to settle into a less active recruiting mode

---

redactional elements and underlying traditions, (Davies and Allison, *Matthew*, vol 3, 677-8).

[3] There is of course the possibility that Matthew's statements regarding mission are in fact not consistent. This view should perhaps only be adopted either if an obvious contradiction can be demonstrated within the gospel, or if attempts to find a unified, or overarching, train of thought are seen to fail.

[4] The significance of the gospel as a whole, for determining the Matthean attitude to Gentile mission, is also recognized by Luz. He states, "The Gentile mission is thus important to the Matthean community. The entire Gospel is designed to focus attention on it." (Luz, *The Theology of the Gospel of Matthew*, 16).

[5] Senior expresses a plea for balance in reading the supposedly exclusivist missionary texts in the gospel. He observes, "As is well known and often noted, during the Matthean Jesus' earthly ministry he restricted the community's mission to 'the lost sheep of the house of Israel' and forbade a mission to Gentiles and Samaritans. However, the appearance of several righteous Gentiles in the gospel who exhibit faith in Jesus, such as the magi, the centurion of Capernaum, and the Canaanite woman, signal that eventual mission. So, too, do texts in which Jesus confronts a lack of faith or responsiveness on the part of some Jews that is contrasted with 'other' – again, presumably Gentiles – who will be responsive (e.g., 11.20-24; 12.38-42; 21.43)." (Senior, 'Between Two Worlds', 6).

in their second or third generations,[6] this does not mean that the impetus to gain new converts had totally vanished in the Matthean group. In fact the imperative πορευθέντες that opens the charge in Matt 28.19 suggests that some form of outward looking activity that sought to enlist new members in a very direct manner was at least part of the evangelist's understanding of the challenge that is presented to the group.[7] Yet, it must be conceded, that the actual nature of the missionary activity promoted in the first gospel remains unknown. While it is possible that the model of Jesus' commissioning of the disciples was normative for the group (Matt 10.5ff.), it is equally plausible that Matthew has presented that narrative as part of his historicizing tendency[8] and therefore the actual details of the proselytising that Matthew is promoting must remain unknown to modern readers.

6.2 Individual Texts Relating to Mission

As was outlined above, the most widely discussed texts in relation to the Matthean missionary orientation are considered here. The first two passages (Matt 10.5-23; 15.21-28) present the most restricted attitude, however after chap. 15 there is almost without exception a positive attitude displayed to bringing Gentiles into the community. This is not of course to say that Matthew viewed all Gentiles without suspicion, and saw them as friendly to his group's cause. As Sim comments, Pilate and the Roman soldiers who crucified Jesus were Gentiles.[9] However, it is not necessary to follow the implication that Sim draws from this observation, namely that "[a]ll these negative Gentile figures [Pilate, executing soldiers and

---

[6] See Stark, *The Rise of Christianity: A Sociologist Reconsiders History*.

[7] In relation to itinerant preachers Theissen suggests, "Wandering charismatics were not a marginal phenomenon in the Jesus movement. They shaped the earliest traditions and provided the social background for a good deal of the synoptic tradition, especially the tradition of the words of Jesus." (Theissen, *Sociology of Early Palestinian Christianity*, 10). Whilst acknowledging that the situation of the Jesus Movement in Palestine and the more established Matthean community did not necessarily correspond in all sociological factors, the ethos of active missionary endeavour does appear to be preserved in the later proselytising work that centred on the group which adhered to the teachings of the first evangelist.

[8] As Strecker notes in relation to the missionary charge in chapter 10, "Erkennbar ist, daß Matthäus die Stellung der Jünger auf Jesus bezieht. So geht es schon aus der Komposition hervor, indem die summarische Aussage über die Tätigkeit Jesu (9, 35) dem Auftrag an die Jünger (10, 1ff.) vorangestellt ist. Im einzelnen: Jesu Verkündigung richtet sich an das Volk Israel (15, 24), so auch die der Jünger (10, 5f.)." (Strecker, *Der Weg der Gerechtigkeit*, 195).

[9] Sim, 'The Gospel of Matthew and the Gentiles', 23-4.

Gadarene demoniacs] in the Matthean story stand as a corrective to the standard view that Matthew always presents his Gentile figures positively"[10] and hence, "the missionary focus of this church had always been the Jews and not the Gentiles, and there is no real evidence that it considered abandoning its traditional missionary direction."[11] As the individual texts are studied in their wider context the implausibility of Sim's position will be clearly seen. It is to those texts that attention is now turned.

6.2.1 Matt 10.5-23

One of the difficult decisions in dealing with this cluster of sayings is to determine where to break the section. In some respects it would be fully justifiable to treat the whole of chap. 10 as a single unit dealing with the interlocking themes of discipleship and mission. The call of the twelve and the authority delegated to them in vv. 1-4 does not stand apart from the commission given in 10.5f, in fact the very act of choosing twelve disciples should be seen as an 'Israel-oriented' decision, reconstituting with numerological symbolism the tribes of Israel, and the sons of Jacob. However, to tackle the whole of chapter 10 would unnecessarily complicate the discussion by introducing a number of subsidiary issues, such as the relationship between disciple and teacher (10.24-25), the judgment and discord that arises from the proclamation of Jesus (10.34-39), and the debate surrounding the reception of wandering Christian teachers in early Christian communities (10.40-43).[12] Therefore a more appropriate decision might be only to tackle the material in 10.5-15. While this would focus the discussion quite specifically, it would, on the other hand, omit the closely related material on the persecution of missionaries (vv. 16-23). However, the greater weakness is that such a treatment would be open to the accusation that it had split off the section (vv. 16-23) that is often seen as supporting the notion of a mission limited to Israel. Moreover, at a literary level, there appears to be a structural *inclusio* between the two references to Ἰσραήλ in verses 6 and 23. For this reason the material in vv. 5-23 shall be the focus of the following discussion.

An initial issue that needs to be examined is the meaning of Matt 10.5b-6, and specifically what it prohibits. It has generally been assumed that the prohibition is forbidding any contact with Gentiles or Samaritans by the disciples while they are engaged in their missionary activities. Yet

---

[10] Sim, 'The Gospel of Matthew and the Gentiles', 24.

[11] Sim, 'The Gospel of Matthew and the Gentiles', 48.

[12] On this last issue see the reference in Did. 11.3-12.5, and the treatment in Theissen, 'Wanderradikalismus', 245-71.

the text is actually more specific in terms of the limitations it places on the disciples. What the text actually prohibits is going εἰς ὁδὸν ἐθνῶν or εἰς πόλιν Σαμαριτῶν. While the exact meaning of these two phrases may be disputed they are not the blanket rejection of contact with Gentiles or Samaritans that they are often claimed to be. Given the Matthean antipathy against towns[13] elsewhere in the gospel it is possible that the prohibitions have as much to do with ὁδός and πόλις, as they do with ἐθνῶν and Σαμαριτῶν.[14]

For Sim, the most obvious way to understand Jesus' injunction in Matt 10.5-6 is to view it as having continuing significance for the Matthean community. Thus he states,

> In this discourse the Matthean Jesus initiates a mission which is confined to the lost sheep of the house of Israel, the Jews, and from which the Gentiles and Samaritans are specifically excluded (vv. 5-6)...this mission, which begins during the time of Jesus, is to continue until the parousia.[15]

In support of this reading he presents two pieces of evidence. Firstly, he cites the Matthean omission of Mk 6.30, the return of the twelve, as proof that whereas Mark wished to limit the restricted mission to Jesus' lifetime Matthew specifically was undoing this implication. Secondly, he argues that the future Son of Man saying in 10.23 demonstrates that the restricted mission is in progress until the parousia.[16]

The first point is extremely weak. It is highly dubious to read Mk 6.30 as Mark's attempt to end the geographical restriction of the dimensions of the mission, and even if this was the case, it is more problematic to view this limitation as being the lifetime of Jesus. Surely it would have to be understood as having ended when the disciples returned, that is during the ministry of Jesus. Yet the truth is that Mk 6.30 in no sense undoes a restriction of an 'Israel only' mission, since the Markan text has no parallel to Matt 10.5b-6. Thus Guelich represents the majority of commentators on Mk 6.30 when he states, "Typical of Mark, however, the Twelve also report their ministry of "teaching" in keeping with the evangelist's accent on Jesus' ministry of "teaching"...Here again we see the essential relationship between the mission of the Twelve and Jesus' mission."[17] In this respect Sim is wrong to see the omission of Mk 6.30 by Matthew as

---

[13] Davies and Allison suggest that the first prohibition, εἰς ὁδὸν ἐθνῶν μὴ ἀπέλθητε, also relates to entering into a Gentile town. They state that "it probably refers to a road leading to a Gentile city." (Davies and Allison, *Matthew*, vol 2, 165).

[14] Negative attitudes toward cities are reflected in the following verses: Matt 4.5; 8.33-34; 10.14-15, 23; 11.20; 12.25; 21.17; 22.7; 23.34.

[15] Sim, *The Gospel of Matthew and Christian Judaism*, 158.

[16] Sim, *The Gospel of Matthew and Christian Judaism*, 158.

[17] Guelich, *Mark 1-8:26*, 338-9.

evidence that he was reversing the Markan attempt to bring a halt to the ethnic restriction of the mission to Israel. Mark knows nothing of such a restriction in his narrative, and Matthew certainly is not reversing this non-existing element by omission of Mk 6.30.

The second point, the inclusion of an unparalleled futuristic Son of Man saying, may initially appear to carry more weight since this is a positive addition the evangelist makes to his source.[18] This saying promises relief from persecution in terms of the imagery of not having exhausted all the cities to which one may flee in Israel prior to the return of the Son of Man. In typically Matthean terms the words of assurance are prefaced with an 'amen' saying that states, ἀμὴν γὰρ λέγω ὑμῖν, οὐ μὴ τελέσητε τὰς πόλεις τοῦ Ἰσραὴλ ἕως ἂν ἔλθῃ ὁ υἱὸς τοῦ ἀνθρώπου (10.23b). There seems little doubt that Matthew intended this saying to comfort those suffering rejection in their proselytising enterprises, by promising the not too distant return of the Son of Man. Answering their own question "why then the inclusion of 10.23?" Davies and Allison argue,

> Matthew was a member of a mixed community at the end of the first century, and he lived at a time when the success of the Gentile mission had come to overshadow the relative failure of the Jewish mission. It must have been a temptation for some missionaries to conclude that it was time to forget about preaching the gospel in the Jewish synagogues. 10.23, however, requires that the Jewish mission continue until the *parousia*.[19]

This perspective stands in opposition to the view articulated by Sim, namely that for the Matthean community only the Jewish mission was valid until the parousia. Rather, it appears that Matthew's historicizing tendency has again come to the fore (cf. 5.23-24). In order to make a point that is pastorally relevant to his own community while yet including it in his gospel account, he must make it fit the disciples' circumstances and leave his audience to extrapolate the application to their own situation. While it is possible that the saying had a different concern prior to its incorporation in the Matthean text,[20] after it had been taken up by the evangelist, although having a similar outlook, it was re-applied to the issue

---

[18] Gundry represents the viewpoint of the majority of scholars when he writes, "it appears that v23, like vv5-8, come from Matthew's pen rather than prior tradition." (Gundry, *Matthew*, 194).

[19] Davies and Allison, *Matthew*, vol 2, 192.

[20] Conzelmann's suggestions is that "Matt. 10.23 (Jesus' sending out of the disciples, special material) is an apocalyptic word of comfort in view of the persecution of the church, and therefore arose after Easter. Jesus is identical with the Son of Man" (Conzelmann, *Outline*, 135). If this is correct, then Matthew has correctly understood this saying and has re-applied it to the experience of persecution in his own community.

of mission to Israel.[21] Saldarini understands this saying in much the same way as Davies and Allison, and he detects no sense in which it rejects Jewish mission. He states, "Matthew's group most probably contained missionaries of some type and was involved in the attempt to persuade fellow Jews and also gentiles to accept the teachings of Jesus. The latter half of chap. 10, contains an exhortation to persevere in a Jewish mission."[22] Thus the injunction in v. 23 does not imply, contrary to Sim, that only a restricted mission to Israel continues until the return of the Son of Man, but rather, that the Jewish mission is not to be abandoned, albeit that it now occupies a minor focus in the Matthean community, until the events of the parousia transpire.

However, it is probably the statements of vv. 5-6 that create a more difficult problem than the two objections raised by Sim. Yet even this difficulty does not require one to posit an exclusively Israel orientated mission by the Matthean community. Loader helpfully summarises the issue in the following term.

> Within these instructions [i.e., 10:5-15] we find the striking prohibition, without parallel in Matthew's Markan source or Q, that the disciples are to avoid Gentile and Samaritan territory, and conduct their mission only in Israel. Within the overall context of Matthew's gospel this reflects the divine missionary strategy which applies equally to Jesus (15:24 'I have not been sent except to the lost sheep of the house of Israel').[23]

This prohibition raises the twin questions of why Matthew included it and what he expected his group members to understand by it. One possibility is to see this as yet another historicizing element in the Matthean text, or as a reflection of the evangelist's salvation history scheme.[24] While in the context of the gospel the limitation is strictly addressed to the Twelve, it is obvious in the material that follows that some of the instructions have wider applicability. Riches recognizes this inherent tension and presents it in the following terms. "There are, that is to say, features that suggest a

---

[21] Sim's thesis appears to struggle at this point. After confidently having asserted that the Matthean community was located in Syrian Antioch, he now sees 10.23 as promoting an Israel only mission that will precipitate the return of the Son of Man before the possibility of flight to cities in Israel is exhausted. It is difficult to see in what Judean cities offer safe haven for members of a persecuted group in Antioch.

[22] Saldarini, *Matthew's Christian-Jewish Community*, 107.

[23] Loader, *Jesus' Attitude to the Law*, 195.

[24] In relation to 10.5-6 (and 15.24), Meier suggests that Matthew " quite consciously orders an "economy" of salvation: to the Jews first and then to the Gentiles. The public ministry of the earthly Jesus stands under geographical and national limitations: the gospel is to be preached only to Israel, and only in the promised land. After the death and resurrection, however, this "economical" limitation falls at Jesus' all powerful command (Mt 28.16-20)." (Meier, *Law and History in Matthew's Gospel*, 27).

restrictive application to this exhortation to the Twelve for a limited period; there are other features which suggest that the implications of this charge extend beyond the Twelve are intended to be of lasting importance."[25]

For Luz this tension raise two questions, the first relates to the meaning of 5b-6 for Jesus' mission. Quite uncontroversially, Luz suggests that during the ministry of Jesus there was a limitation placed on the scope of the preaching activity.[26] The second issue is how 10.5-6 relates to the mission command of 28.19-20, and statements such as 24.14. The real problem that 10.5-6 creates within the macronarrative is how to hold together the injunction not to go to the Gentiles in 10.5 with statements that the gospel of the kingdom is to be proclaimed to the ends of the earth. The problem becomes more acute when the instructions of 10.5b-42 are all seen as having direct relevance to the Matthean community. In his treatment Schuyler Brown sees the discourse as both being a historicizing reflection on Jesus' ministry, but also having a secondary theological purpose in that it addresses the contemporary situation of the evangelist's group. Brown states,

> In Mt 9.35-11.1 the evangelist has Jesus address his community in the person of the twelve disciples, and in the point for point assimilation of their missionary functions with those of Jesus, who sends them out, the Matthean community must be able to see the delineation of its own missionary task.[27]

However, it is precisely this desire to see a perfect, or 'point for point', correspondence between the instructions of 10.5-42 given to the disciples and their function in the community of the first evangelist that can lead to denying the most natural reading of passages like Matt 24.14 and 28.18-20. Two possible solutions are suggested. The first involves interpreting "the mission to the ἔθνη as an *expansion* of their mission only to Israel."[28] This builds on the notion of continuity between the two missions. The other alternative creates a dissonance between Israel-only mission and the encompassing Gentile mission.

> A second possibility, however, is that we interpret the sending of the disciples to all ἔθνη as a *cancellation* of their exclusive mission to Israel. In this case Matthew

---

[25] Riches continues be stating the difficulty in maintaining these two competing perspectives. "It is difficult to see how to draw a coherent picture from this puzzling state of affairs. Matthew clearly addresses the charge to go to preach to Israel to the Twelve, but then extents the charge to include experiences which must have been common to many of Matthew's own community." (Riches, *Conflicting Mythologies*, 207).

[26] Luz, *Matthew 8-20*, 71-5.

[27] Brown, 'The Mission to Israel in Matthew's Central Section', 80.

[28] Luz, *Matthew 8-20*, 74.

would be advocating a substitutionary view. The Gentile church would replace Israel (cf. 21:43). Then ἔθνη would have to be translated as 'Gentiles.'[29]

While such a position creates the problem of accounting for the inclusion of vv. 5-6 in the gospel, Luz sees support for the notion of 'cancellation' within the text of the gospel. The evidence he adduces as support for the second position includes the apparent reversal the missionary charge of 28.19 announces in comparison to 10.5-6, which contains exclusive and particularistic language where the closing charge of the gospel is more inclusive and universal in orientation. Moreover, Luz suggests that these passages are intended to be read in the light of one another. He states, "the deliberate reference of 28.19 to 10.5-6 suggests that ἔθνη is to be interpreted the same way in both places. In our text, however, it is clear that ἔθνη means the Gentiles in contrast to Israel and not the nations including Israel."[30]

If this is indeed the correct way to interpret the significant of 10.5-6, it would imply that the mission to Israel was indeed inaugurated by Jesus in an exclusive sense during his earthly ministry. However, the lack of response and even the very persecution at the hand of synagogue opponents means that the primary focus is now to be seen in mission among the Gentiles. Yet, as Matt 10.23 makes clear, this mission to Israel has not ceased at least on the part of Matthew's community. They are still to accept their part in evangelizing Jews, even until the return of the Son of Man. Riches appears also to move strongly in this direction when he suggests

> while there is indeed evidence here for recruitment on the part of the community from other Jews at some point, this stage seems to have been superseded …The experience of expulsion from the synagogue has led the community to see itself as those whose primary task is to go to the Gentiles.[31]

Although this reconstruction may need to be nuanced slightly, perhaps to see that only certain members of the group had become convinced that the way forward was to see the principal missionary focus as being orientated towards Gentiles, nonetheless Riches and Luz seem to provide the most compelling understanding of 10.5-6 in terms of the overall stance of the gospel on the charge to go to the ἔθνη. It would therefore appear that Matthew is writing for a community that knew the words of 10.5-6 as part of its repository of dominical material, and moreover, had applied its limitation to some early phase of its activity of recruiting new members among Jews. However, the relative failure of that endeavour leads

---

[29] Luz, *Matthew 8-20*, 74.
[30] Luz, *Matthew 8-20*, 74-5.
[31] Riches, *Conflicting Mythologies*, 207-8.

Matthew to advocate a new way forward. An enterprise that was already bringing new members into the group, and also had a history of some decades as a successful endeavour (at least in the circle of Pauline churches), namely preaching primarily to the Gentiles. The Jewish ethnicity of the Matthean group is not denied, for 10.23 stipulates that their responsibility to proclaim their message to Jews is still valid,[32] but this appears now to take only a subordinate position in the group. Riches makes a similar point when he observes,

> This is not to say that they have thereby abandoned any claim to Jewishness; at the very least as brothers and sisters of Jesus, they are intimately tied to the Son of David and of Abraham. But their identity is established now, not by circumcision as a mark of participation in the Abrahamic covenant, but by baptism and receiving the teaching of Jesus (28:18-20).[33]

In effect, it appears that Matthew is treating the issue of mission in much the same manner as he approached the question of Torah observance. He is aware of the conservative elements in his group who wish to maintain strict adherence to an exclusive Israel mission. Rather than ostracise such people from a small and marginalized community, he attempts both to affirm the traditions they hold dear, but also to reshape them to demonstrate their limited validity.

6.2.2 Matt 15.21-28

The dialogue with the Canaanite woman in Matthew's gospel is often taken as primary evidence by those who wish to argue for an ongoing limited mission being exercised by the community for whom the evangelist wrote. Noting the redactional omission of the Markan statement 'let the children first be satisfied', Sim makes the following observation: "There is no indication here that the dogs, the Gentiles, deserve to be fed at a later point in time."[34] Further, Sim disallows the possibility that this parable could be advocating equality between Jews and Gentiles in the Matthean community. Commenting on the Matthean addition, οὐκ ἀπεστάλην εἰ μὴ εἰς τὰ πρόβατα τὰ ἀπολωλότα οἴκου 'Ισραήλ (15.24), Sim argues in relation to the Matthean Jesus that "[h]is focus remains firmly on the

---

[32] Hare argues for a much stronger notion of replacement in Matthew's theology of mission. The Church is seen as the exclusive replacement for Israel and this results in the "abandonment of the mission to Israel." (Hare, *The Theme of Jewish Persecution*, 171). While Matt 10.23 may not demonstrate that the mission was limited to Israel until the *parousia* (contrary to Sim), it does at least show that the mission to Israel is envisaged as continuing until the return of the Son of Man.

[33] Riches, *Conflicting Mythologies*, 208.

[34] Sim, *The Gospel of Matthew and Christian Judaism*, 224.

people of Israel (cf. v. 24), and there is no suggestion that Jew and Gentile are now placed on equal footing."[35] Although nowhere nearly as extreme in his position, Harrington does see this text as having relevance not only in depicting a limitation in the mission of the historical Jesus, but also speaking to the contemporary situation of the Matthean community.

> Relations between Jews and Gentiles were a very sensitive topic for the Matthean community. Though the majority of the community seems to have been Jewish by birth, some were Gentiles by birth. The conversation between Jesus and the Canaanite woman in Matt 21:21-28 would have functioned as a model or at least a causal explanation why Jews and Gentiles could exist together in the same Christian community.[36]

Thus while Harrington sees Matthew's programme in the writing of the gospel to be the preservation and continuation of Jewish tradition,[37] this does not preclude the inclusion of Gentiles within the community, nor calling that group a 'Christian community'. Strecker is willing to go even further by seeing the redactional addition of 15.24 as forming part of the initial debate about the legitimacy of including Gentiles. He states,

> Redaktionell eingefügt ist V. 24 (gegen Mk. 7, 25); in 10, 6 ist eine sekundäre Dublette bezeugt; danach scheint Matthäus das Logion als „frei tradiertes" vorgefunden zu haben. In seinem Ursprung verleugnet es einen partikularistischen Standpunkt nicht; es wird in den Debatten der Urgemeinde um die Heidenmission einen (der ersten?) „Sitz im Leben" gehabt haben.[38]

Yet it may be possible to take this incident as being more positive towards Gentiles than even Harrington allows, and within the narrative to see v. 24 not just as a historical reminder of the limitation of Jesus' earthly ministry. In his treatment of the Markan parallel to this pericope (Mk 7.24-30), Loader argues that, "The tradition preserved in Mk 7.24-31 reflects an understanding of Jesus which portrays him as beginning from a conservative stance in relation to issues of Law relating to boundaries."[39] However, for Loader this is not the end of the Markan story, for the narrative relates a change in Jesus' attitude. "The encounter with the Syrophoenician woman most clearly celebrates the crossing of a boundary and, within Mark, its removal."[40] Thus at least in its Markan context,[41] the

---

[35] Sim, *The Gospel of Matthew and Christian Judaism*, 224.

[36] Harrington, *The Gospel of Matthew*, 237-8.

[37] Harrington, *The Gospel of Matthew*, 16.

[38] Strecker, *Der Weg der Gerechtigkeit*, 107.

[39] Loader, 'Challenged at the Boundaries', 61.

[40] Loader, 'Challenged at the Boundaries', 60.

[41] Hooker argues that there must be at least a pre-Markan kernel behind this pericope. She states, "it seems unlikely that such a story would have been invented. If it was developed in the course of the Church's discussions about the admission of Gentiles

story is preserved because of the way it ends, not for its original rejection of the woman's request.

While Matthew has undoubtedly altered a number of the details of the Markan account, he does not reverse its outcome of the mother obtaining healing for her daughter, albeit that the request is granted because of faith, rather than a consequence of the mother's witty response. Here too, Matthew preserves the story not for its initial limited perspective on 'the house of Israel', but rather because even the Matthean Jesus who declares this boundary to be operative both in 10.6 and 15.24, is himself the one who removes this rejection of Gentiles by responding positively to the woman (not simply acquiescing), and moreover commends her on the basis of her faith. Although Davies and Allison see v. 28b as stemming from Matthean redaction,[42] they nonetheless argue that it is not a reversal of Jesus' own specifically Israel focused mission. They read the conclusion in the following manner, "Jesus, although he has not really changed his mind about anything – his mission is still only to the lost sheep of the house of Israel, and the priority of Israel in salvation remains uncontested – finally gives in to the woman."[43] However, to characterize Jesus' response as merely 'giving in' seems to miss the significance of the Matthean alteration to the Markan text. It is not the wit of the woman that presses Jesus to comply with her request, but rather the recognition of the requisite faith.[44] In this sense, Matthew portrays a Jesus who, because of the faith of the woman, does change his mind, and it is this alteration of perspective that that is celebrated in this pericope.

Moreover, the correspondence between faith and obtaining healing, or other requests, is significant in Matthew, especially in Matt 8.13; 9.21, 29; 21.22. The parallel between 15.28 and the first reference is striking. Apart from reference to faith or the act of believing, both verses involve a

---

to the Christian community, then it seems too vacillating to have lent much support to either side of the argument." (Hooker, *Mark*, 182).

[42] Davies and Allison dismiss the alternative viewpoint that v. 28b is derived from a non-Markan source in the following manner. "Although one might argue that our evangelist is here following a non-Markan source , especially as nowhere else in Matthew does μεγάλη qualify πίστις, it is to be noted that γίνομαι + the dative is characteristic of our gospel (Mt: 5; Mk: 2; Lk: 1); that Matthew's phrase recalls 8.13 (ὡς ἐπίστευσας γενηθήτω σοι - spoken by Jesus to a Gentile). As well as the redactional 9.29 (κατὰ τὴν πίστιν ὑμῶν γενηθήτω ὑμῖν); and the τοσαύτην πίστιν of 8.10 is the conceptual equivalent of 'great faith'. There is thus no reason not to assign v. 28b to Matthean redaction." (Davies and Allison, *Matthew,* vol 2, 556).

[43] Davies and Allison, *Matthew,* vol 2, 556.

[44] Hagner acknowledges this very point when he states, "The address, ὦ γύναι, 'O woman,' reveals the degree to which Jesus was moved by this gentile woman's faith." (Hagner, *Matthew 14-28*, 442).

curative act, a temporal reference to the immediacy of the miracle, designation to the minority of the one in relation to the person making the request, and although not explicitly stated the earlier material in each case emphasizes that these are healings made on behalf of Gentiles.[45] So it is possible to see that Matthew has already pre-empted the issue of Gentile inclusion on the basis of faith in 8.13, prior to introducing the limitations on Gentile mission that were preserved in the repository of the community's Jesus tradition and which more conservative group members wished to remain the norm. Matthew does not deny the existence of such tradition, but rather presents a Jesus who makes the same boundary-crossing journey in regard to non-Jews as the evangelist is trying to commend to his more conservative group members. Luz is fully attuned to the potential significance of this story for Matthew's audience. He writes,

> The Matthean community hears the message of the story also for itself....In addition, after 8:5-13 in the macrotext of the gospel this story means a further salvation-history 'signal' for the church that lives among the Gentiles with the task of proclaiming Jesus' message to them: Jesus has not confined God within the borders of Israel, but has let himself be moved by the faith of the gentile woman.[46]

Thus the faith of the Gentile woman produces an attitudinal change in Jesus,[47] and this re-orientation of perspective is presented to conservative community members as a new paradigm for them to adopt as the basis of the desired group perspective on mission.

---

[45] Davies and Allison list an impressive catalogue of parallels between Matt 8.5-13 and 15.21-29. (See Davies and Allison, *Matthew,* vol 2, 558-9). They suggest these similarities are due to two factors, assimilation in the oral tradition as well as redactional activity. Thus they state, "in the oral tradition, the two stories, because of their similar subjects, were to some extent assimilated to one another. But whatever the answer, Matthew himself, it is important to observe that Matthew himself has added to the catalogue of semblances." (558).

[46] Luz, *Matthew 8-20,* 341.

[47] Once again, it needs to be stressed that the attitudinal change is one that occurs in the literary creation, the Matthean Jesus, and this does not necessarily, or even plausibly, reflect the outlook of the historical Jesus. At the level of the historical Jesus, Porkorný is probably correct in his assessment that, "It is generally accepted that Jesus concentrated his activity on Israel, as in his saying: 'Go nowhere among the gentiles...go rather to the lost sheep of the house of Israel' (Matt 10.5; the second part is quoted also in the parallel to our pericope in Matt 15.24). This can be confirmed e.g. by the number of his twelve disciple who symbolize the renewed twelve tribes of Israel." However, he continues by noting, "This strategy did not in principle exclude the pagans from salvation. The eschatological (not necessarily radically apocalyptic) dimension implied in Jesus' image of the 'coming' of the Kingdom of God most probably included the expectation of a procession of pagan nations to Mount Zion at the end of time." (Porkorný, 'From a Puppy to the Child', 326).

6.2.3 Matt 21.43

This verse, which is unique to Matthew, presents a statement that is highly problematic for those scholars who seek to maintain that the first gospel was written for a community that identified itself as Jewish and rejected Gentile participation in the Jesus movement. Discussing this text, Sim introduces it by describing it as one of the Matthean statements that has "been appealed to as evidence that the Matthean community had broken definitively with Judaism."[48] However, in line with his thesis, this is of course an implication Sim is not willing to adopt. He calls this traditional interpretation into question in the following manner.

> The people who are given the kingdom of God, the new tenants and legitimate leaders of the Jewish people, are either the Matthean community alone or Christian Judaism in general. This pericope in no way suggests that the evangelist's community had broken with Judaism; rather, it details God's rejection of the Jewish leadership, and it demonstrates that Matthew's Christian Jewish group claimed (albeit unsuccessfully) a leadership role within the Jewish community and within the Jewish religion.[49]

Sim is correct to draw attention to the fact that the dispute is with the Jewish leadership. In 21.23 Jesus' opponents are named as οἱ ἀρχιερεῖς καὶ οἱ πρεσβύτεροι τοῦ λαοῦ, and this twin group of adversaries stays in focus at least to 22.23 when the Sadducees join the discussion, although there is a slight change of nomenclature in 21.45 where the two groups become οἱ ἀρχιερεῖς καὶ οἱ Φαρισαῖοι.[50] Nonetheless, this in itself does little to establish Sim's argument that the term ἔθνει in 21.43 denotes either the Matthean community as representatives of Christian Judaism, or that group in wider terms. In fact one is justified in asking how Sim is able to so confidently distinguish between the use of ἔθνει in this verse and the usages of ἔθνος elsewhere in Matthew (4.15;[51] 6.32; 10.5, 18; 12.18, 21;

---

[48] Apart from the references to 'their (your) synagogues' the other passage Sim takes as being used as standard evidence for arguing that the community was no longer within the bounds of Judaism is 28.15. (Sim, *The Gospel of Matthew and Christian Judaism*, 148).

[49] Sim, *The Gospel of Matthew and Christian Judaism*, 149.

[50] Hagner comments on this change in the following terms. "The last mention of the addressees was in vv 23-24, where the chief priests were linked with 'the elders of the people.' The reference to the Pharisees (only in Matthew) seems to have been added to intensify their culpability as the religious leaders of the Jewish people." (Hagner, *Matthew 14-28*, 623).

[51] In relation to 4.15-16, Sim rejects the standard interpretation Jesus is the light to the nations and that they will come to trust in him. Despite the original inclusive vision of the Isaianic text that is being cited (Is 8.23-9.1), Sim argues for Matthew this had now become a reference to the Jews who were dwelling in Galilee under Gentile oppression. This is the darkness that shrouds the Jews in that region, and Jesus is announced as the herald of light to the Jews alone. He states, "the evangelist is making the point that, prior

20.19, 25; 24.7, 9, 14; 25.32;[52] 28.19). Perhaps the only difference that may be significant is the fact that at 21.43 the term ἔθνει is in the singular, whereas the other references (apart from 24.7) are in the plural. While Harrington is partially correct that the reference to the kingdom being given to a nation bearing fruit need not be read as "applying to Gentiles or to the Church as a 'third race'",[53] the wider context of 21.28-22.14 supports the notion that a greater degree of replacement is envisaged than Harrington allows.

Turning to the context, 21.43 not only forms the Matthean conclusion to the parable of the rented vineyard (21.33-46), but also stands as the second of a triad of replacement parables, the first being the parable of the two sons (21.28-32) and the third being the parable of the wedding banquet (22.1-14). The relationship to the final parable is particularly instructive such it appears to unpack themes present in the first two parables in a more explicit manner. Matthew presents his own community as the legitimate replacements for the Jewish authorities, but that community is itself a mixed entity of members called from the margins of society. Specifically in relation to the parable of the Wedding feast, the demise of Jerusalem as the power base of the Jewish nation comes into focus.

> Not only in v. 7 does Matthew alone have the troops destroy the city of those who refuse the invitation (surely a post-70 CE reference to the destruction of Jerusalem, the stronghold of the religious leadership), but in v. 9 the narrative replaces the recalcitrant invitees with new guests who respond with gratitude.[54]

This viewpoint, present in the third of these parables, makes more likely the notion that Matthew envisaged more than his community being a substitute for the leaders of Judaism. Rather, it appears plausible that he saw his community as forming a new entity that in some sense supplanted existing Judaism, but his community also included those who previously

---

to the arrival of Jesus, these Jews have suffered and despaired because of their close proximity to their Gentile neighbours." (Sim, *The Gospel of Matthew and Christian Judaism*, 220). While disagreeing with Sim's interpretation, it is interesting that here he takes the reference as self-evidently denoting non-Jews.

[52] In Matt 24.32 the reference to πάντα τὰ ἔθνη all the nations is best understood as an all encompassing reference to the totality of humanity. However, Davies and Allison, while accepting this interpretation do catalogue five other possibilities. They note the following suggestions for the group designated: (i) All non-Jews; (ii) All non-Christians; (iii) All non-Jews who are non-Christians; (iv) All Christians; (v) Christians alive when Christ returns. They outline the difficulties presented by each of these alternatives. (Davies and Allison, *Matthew*, vol 3, 422-3).

[53] Harrington, *The Gospel of Matthew*, 303.

[54] Foster, 'A Tale of Two Sons', 36.

would not have been invited to the banquet.[55] Although not as accentuated, this same perspective of privileging the Matthean community at the expense of existing Judaism may also be present in the first parable describing the two sons. This becomes more obviously the case if the reading in Codex Vaticanus is in fact the original Matthean text.[56]

Dahl has argued that the meaning of the Passion Narrative can be understood through the statement made in Matt 21.43. While not wanting to concur with the anti-Jewish sentiments of the gospel, Dahl nonetheless takes such polemic seriously as historical evidence that reflects the strength of feeling displayed by the Matthean communities against their opponents. He finds the blood guilt with which the evangelist charges his adversaries in the passion narrative (Matt 27.8, 25; 28.15) to be anticipated in the earlier chapters of the gospel.

> That the assignation of guilt to the Jews is not a negligible aspect of the passion story for Matthew is confirmed by the preceding chapters of the Gospel. The parables in 21:28-22:14 and the speech in 23 are especially important in this connection. At its conclusion (23:35f.) we hear of the 'righteous blood' that shall come upon this generation. What one might call the theme of the passion narrative is stated in Matthew's conclusion to the parable of the vineyard: 'The Kingdom of God will be taken away from you and given to a nation producing the fruits of it' (21:43).[57]

The strength of this argument is that it takes note of the narratival flow in the gospel, and addresses its interpretation to those themes that recur in different ways. Similarly, Stanton comments on the importance of this verse. "This verse [i.e. 21.43] is certainly one of the most significant in the whole Gospel, for it confirms that Matthew's Christian community had parted company with Judaism."[58]

Luz addresses the issue of whether Matthew is presenting a fully developed rejection of Israel and its replacement by Gentiles. In his discussion, he notes that the use of the singular is not entirely making the substitution of 'Gentile nations' for Israel, and he answers his own rhetorical question as to whether Matthew sees the Gentile Churches as supplanting the nation of Israel with a nuanced 'yes and no' answer. The tension is presented in the following way.

---

[55] Hagner sees both the link with the preceding parable and the idea of replacement when he makes the following observation in relation to vv 8-9. "The open invitation serves in this parable as the counterpart to letting out the vineyard to other tenants in the preceding parable (21.41, 43). The result in both cases is the loss of Israel's privileged position, here as those who had been initially invited." (Hagner, *Matthew 14-28*, 630).

[56] For a defense of the Vaticanus text as the original Matthean form of the parable, see Foster, 'A Tale of Two Sons', 26-37.

[57] Dahl, 'The Passion Narrative in Matthew', 45.

[58] Stanton, 'Introduction: Matthew's Gospel in Recent Scholarship', 7.

No, because in this context he is quite clearly speaking to Israel's leaders and to no one else. No, because *ethnos* – that same Greek word for 'people' that means in the plural, 'nations' or 'Gentiles' – cannot simply be equated with 'church'. And yet, yes, because the image of the vineyard recalls Israel, and the mention of the persecuted prophets recalls its history. Yes, because the kingdom was promised to the entire people. Yes, because *ethnos* is used grammatically in opposition to God's kingdom, thereby kindling expectation of an opposing nation. Yes, because Matthew does not speak of the chosen or holy people *(laos)* but uses a term that recalls the Gentiles. Finally, yes, because Matthew's story is getting closer and closer to the final repudiation of Jesus by the entire people.[59]

Although, perhaps, not all of Luz's arguments carry equal weight, the affirmative case coupled with the contextual perspective of the parables of the two sons and the wedding banquet lends considerable support to arguing that Matthew at the very least had moved strongly in the direction of seeing Christian communities as the replacement for Israel as well as being the authentic inheritors of the Kingdom.[60] It is possible that Matthew has tailored his presentation in such a manner as to minimize offence to the more conservative long-term Jewish members of the group. Yet, nonetheless, his tractate is ultimately an attempt to move them from an Israel based adherence to a more Gentile orientated mission.

6.2.4 Matt 24.14

If the lack of the plural form of ἔθνει in 21.43 did cast any doubt about the meaning of that verse, the statements in 24.14 with the reference to ἔθνεσιν does not allow such a suggestion. The plural form can only plausibly be translated as either 'nations' or 'Gentiles'. Here, even Sim finds that he cannot deny that a mission to Gentiles is envisaged. Instead he tries to move the temporal horizon for that mission. He argues, "The most that can be safely concluded from 24.14 is that the evangelist saw the eschatological necessity for a universal mission to both Jew and Gentile; it exceeds the evidence to infer from this reference that the evangelist's community was actively involved in all aspects of this mission."[61] There are two fundamental errors in the way Sim construes the evidence. Firstly, it is dubious to see this exhortation to preach πᾶσιν τοῖς ἔθνεσιν as only

---

[59] Luz, *The Theology of the Gospel of Matthew*, 119-20.

[60] Strecker, however, argues that the replacement ἔθνει is not to be limited too narrowly either to the Matthean communities or the Church in general. Instead he argues, "Matthäus hat ihn durch konsequentere Durchfügung und durch die Einfügung von V. 43 (und schon V. 41b) besonders hervorgehoben. Gewiß umfaßt das neue Israel nicht ausschließlich Heidenchristen, aber die universale Ausdehnung steht jedenfalls im Vordergrund." (Strecker, *Der Weg der Gerechtigkeit*, 33).

[61] Sim, *The Gospel of Matthew and Christian Judaism*, 244.

having validity in the eschatological age, especially since the phrase τότε (24.14b) implies that the other events described in this verse are prior.[62] Secondly, Sim creates an exclusive dichotomy between the eschatological universal mission and the Matthean community engaging in *all* aspects of the Gentile mission. Nowhere else does Sim suggest that the group must be fully involved in all aspects of mission. Rather, he argues that the people for whom Matthew was writing had totally refuted the possibility of the inclusion of Gentiles in their community. Obviously, there exists a range of alternatives between the two possibilities offered by Sim, including the notion that the Gentile mission was a fairly recent innovation in the Matthean community and that Matthew was writing to convince hesitant group members to embrace the mission.

Referring to 24.14 Luz states, "judging from 24.9 and 24.14, the Gentile mission already seems to be underway in the present."[63] Obviously this perspective is diametrically opposed to the viewpoint of Sim. The strength of the position put forward by Luz is that it seems to represent most naturally the sense of the text. One cannot deny that there are eschatological motifs in Matt 24, however, the events depicted in vv. 9-14 are precursors to the end that reflect the present experience of the disciples and not the signs of the eschaton itself. As Loader recognizes, "24.14 includes an allusion to the expansion of the mission to include Gentiles, which Matthew reports in 28.18-20."[64] Moreover, Riches compellingly argues that both here and in 28.18-20 that there is a future dimension intended when, "At the end he [Jesus] will come and all shall see him; Christ will be revealed as judge and cosmocrator."[65] Yet the activity of transforming the present cosmological order into a remade sacred space does not wait to be initiated in the eschaton but is inaugurated in the present through the commission given to the disciples.

> As Joshua was commissioned to take possession of the land with its boundaries, so now the disciples are commissioned to preach the gospel 'throughout the whole world, as a testimony to all nations; and then the end will come' (24:14; cf. 25:32; 28:19).[66]

The most telling evidence against Sim's hypothesis that Matt 24.14 only envisages a Gentile mission in the final apocalyptic age comes in the final clause of that verse itself. After the depicting the need for the gospel to be preached throughout the world, this condition is then depicted as the precursor to the consummation of the age, καὶ τότε ἥξει τὸ τέλος (Matt

---

[62] See the discussion on the following page.
[63] Luz, *The Theology of the Gospel of Matthew*, 16.
[64] Loader, *Jesus' Attitude to the Law*, 248.
[65] Riches, *Conflicting Mythologies*, 256.
[66] Riches, *Conflicting Mythologies*, 257.

24.14b). In fact this Matthean addition to the Markan text makes the temporal sequence more explicit, and, if anything, rules out the possibility of seeing the Gentile mission as being postponed until the eschatological age.[67]

The real problem that 24.14 creates within the macronarrative is how to hold its clear command to preach the gospel of the kingdom to the ends of the earth together with the injunction not to go to the Gentiles in 10.5. Part of the problem arises when the instructions of 10.5-42 are taken as perfect descriptions of the categorical imperatives for the community but are divorced from the relevance they may have had at earlier stages of the tradition. Weavers argues that the danger implicit in determining an exact correspondence with the contemporary setting of the community is that the original historical setting is lost. Instead she suggests reading the gospel as a double exposure that depicts both the mission of the historical Jesus, but also addresses the contemporary situation of the community. This of course creates a tension between the two functions, but this is not a tension that is incompatible. She observes, "in the final analysis this approach virtually loses sight of the first half of the 'double exposure' in its emphasis on the second half."[68]

However, the majority of commentators would wish to resist such a reconstruction, since it both fails to account for the use of source material in Matt 10, and neglects the fact that some of the earliest source material does depict Jesus as limiting his mission to Israel.[69] In this sense, Matt 24.14 is best understood as an attempt by the evangelist to promote the necessity of Gentile mission. This is achieved by replacing the πρῶτον of Mark 13.10 with a reference to what must occur in the interim period prior to the *parousia*. The repeated use of τέλος parallels the usage of the same term in the previous verse, although the reference in v. 13 is taken over from Mark. What this illustrates is that like the call in 24.13 to 'remain steadfast until the end', the call to preach the gospel to all the nations is

---

[67] Here Gundry is incorrect in his assertion that this passage is included as polemic against antinomians within the Matthean group. He suggests, "the statement emphasizes the necessity of carrying out the great commission (28.18-20). The emphasis is due to the antinomians' withdrawal from the evangelistic enterprise. To escape persecution not only have they stopped living according to Christ's law before the world, they have also stopped preaching the gospel to the world." (Gundry, *Matthew*, 480). As has been discussed at some length, the possibility that Matthew was fighting on two fronts is hard to sustain since there is a paucity of evidence from which to reconstruct a developed party from the fleeting mentions of ανομία in the gospel.

[68] Weavers, *Matthew's Missionary Discourse*), 23.

[69] For a reasoned defence of the portrait of an initially conservative and Torah observant Jesus, see the significant article, Loader, 'Challenged at the Boundaries', 45-61.

likewise an activity that the community are to maintain until the end times arrive. This is no statement about postponement, rather it is a direct call for action in the present. The future aspect only relates to 'the end' coming about when the community has faithfully fulfilled the command to preach the gospel throughout the world.

6.2.5 Matt 26.13

This verse stands as both a mild rebuke to Jesus' disciples and a promise to this unnamed woman in the synoptic tradition that her act of anointing Jesus would not be forgotten. Here Matthew follows his source closely apart from minor grammatical alterations,[70] only one of which that may be theologically motivated. The only alteration that may reflect anything more than minor stylistic change is the addition of the demonstrative pronoun τοῦτο to the Markan reference to τὸ εὐαγγέλιον. Matthew may have simply preferred to consistently modify the Markan use of the absolute reference to 'the gospel', or perhaps there was a theological reason behind such a change. Strecker observes,

> Unlike Mark, Matthew never uses the term εὐαγγέλιον absolutely, but adds the genitive τῆς βασιλείας (4:23; 9:35; 24:14) or augments the term by the demonstrative pronoun τοῦτο (24:14; 26:13). Matthew appears to have found the term already in public use, and reflects the Greek Hellenistic usage.[71]

Therefore, Matthew has basically taken over a narrative from his Markan source and allowed it to stand in his own narrative. Specifically in relation to Matt 26.13//Mk 14.9, perhaps apart from the one case noted above, all the changes are due to stylistic rewriting.

Supposedly, the testimony given to the woman stating that her actions will be remembered wherever the gospel is preached throughout whole world (ὅπου ἐὰν κηρυχθῇ τὸ εὐαγγέλιον τοῦτο ἐν ὅλῳ τῷ κόσμῳ), is seen as providing an implicit perspective on Matthew's universalism, with

---

[70] The changes are the dropping of Mark's adversative δέ, the inclusion of the demonstrative pronoun τοῦτο to qualify the reference to the gospel, changing Mark's εἰς with accusative to ἐν with dative construction and bring Mark's λαληθήσεται to the head of the final clause.

[71] Strecker, *Theology of the New Testament*, 341. Strecker continues his discussion by noting Marxsen's argument that "the difference between the Markan and Matthean usage is explained by the fact that for Matthew εὐαγγέλιον does not mean the message of Jesus but 'speech complex'." Strecker goes on to criticize this perspective by noting, "Against this explanation is the fact that Matthew never uses the plural εὐαγγέλια. In addition the final example (26.13) does not stand in the context of a speech context but in the passion story and has a 'narrative' connotation." (341). See also, Marxsen, *Mark the Evangelist*, 124.

particular reference to the inclusion of the Gentiles in the people of God. As France states,

> The blessings of Israel are not for Israel alone. The mission of the disciples which Jesus had initially limited to Israel (10:5-6, 23) is soon to be 'preached throughout the whole world, as a testimony to all nations' (24:14), and the devotion of the woman who anoints Jesus' head before the passion will be remembered 'wherever this gospel is preached in the whole world' (26:13).[72]

Yet, although not disagreeing with France's overall thesis, one wonders whether Matt 26.13 specifically can be used as evidence for a Gentile mission and universal perspective in Matthew.[73] Admittedly, it does not conflict with such a perspective and may in fact corroborate other statements in the gospel, but there are difficulties using it as a prime piece of evidence.[74] First, it contains no direct reference to 'Gentiles', and second without reference to other material in the first gospel it could be understood as denoting the preaching of the gospel to diaspora Jews. Nonetheless, Sim is incorrect in the conclusion he draws when he takes this verse in collaboration with 24.14 and 28.19. Especially drawing on the insights of 24.14, he argues that 26.13 "specifies that just prior to the end of the age the gospel of the kingdom will be preached throughout the whole world as a testimony to all nations (cf. 26.13)."[75] To see such an eschatological scheme implied by 26.13 is truly bizarre. At most the verse offers a promise to the woman for her act of service to Jesus. The promise of course implies the spread of the gospel in the world, and Matthew happily takes this perspective over from Mark. However, it is equally dubious to assert that the verse has any independent value in either promoting Gentile mission, or that it reflects Sim's eschatological reading,

---

[72] France, *Matthew-Evangelist and Teacher*, 234.

[73] It is not the reality of an envisaged worldwide mission that is being questioned, but only whether it is possible to conclude from this verse that Gentiles can be clearly seen as part of that mission. Hagner supports the notion of worldwide mission being the clear intent in this verse. "Only a forced exegesis could conclude that this preaching is not the church's proclamation of the gospel (wrongly supposing that Jesus could not have envisioned a worldwide mission)." (Hagner, *Matthew 14-28*, 758).

[74] Gundry is more balanced in his view. In an aside he links this verse in a supportive manner to the overall thesis that Matthew was arguing for the continuance of an ongoing Gentile mission, but he gives this verse no independent weight as confirming that thesis. He simply states, "see the comments on 24.14 and 28.19-20 concerning the possibility of Jesus' foreseeing – indeed inaugurating – a worldwide mission." (Gundry, *Matthew*, 522).They state, "That the woman shall a have a memorial in the church's proclamation moves the reader beyond the upcoming passion to the vindicating resurrection and the time of the church."

[75] Sim, *The Gospel of Matthew and Christian Judaism*, 244.

namely that the gospel does not spread until there is "the eschatological necessity for a universal mission to both Jew and Gentile."[76]

Therefore, despite attempts to treat this verse as having significance for understanding the Matthean attitude to Gentile mission, it appears that the verse has little to contribute to a decision concerning the evangelist's attitude. At best it can corroborate the perspective of other material in the gospel, but it offers no independent perspective. One first has to decide upon the scope of the gospel going ἐν ὅλῳ τῷ κόσμῳ, before it can be asserted whether this verse is supporting Gentile mission. Because of this, it is best not to attempt to utilise the statements in this verse as though they clarified the issue. Rather, the verse should be given its full weight as a conclusion to the narrative dealing with the anointing of Jesus by the adoring woman.[77]

6.2.6 Matt 28.16-20

These verses form the climax to the gospel, and in line with ancient rhetorical practice[78] the main thrust of this literary work and its hortatory message are enshrined in its final charge.[79] These verses are largely a Matthean redactional complex and although not dependent on any of the other synoptic gospels, may potentially draw on other source material. However, the presence of many redactional terms and themes in these verses shows that Matthew has both reworked any underlying source material, and also that he agrees with the message of these statements especially in their rewritten form. [80] The carefully constructed charges that

---

[76] Sim, *The Gospel of Matthew and Christian Judaism*, 244.

[77] This is precisely what Davies and Allison do. (Davies and Allison, *Matthew*, vol 3, 448). However, there is nothing to suggest that it moves the reader into the eschatological age, nor does it clarify what the time of the church entails in regard to Gentiles and their inclusion in that church.

[78] An important comparison in terms of this thesis, and coming from a Jewish literary milieu is of course 4QMMT. The aim of the work is clearly stated in the climax of the letter, known as the hortatory epilogue. The writer addresses his audience directly, and informs them of the changes in their behaviour that he hopes the letter will bring about. Similarly, Matt 28.16-20 is perhaps one of the most direct addresses to the contemporary situation of the evangelist's adherents, and it too is seeking a change of attitude, in terms of embracing an inclusive mission to the Gentiles.

[79] The significance of Matt 28.16-20 for the overall understanding of the gospel is stressed by Michel. He states, "In a way the conclusion goes back to the start and teaches us to understand the whole gospel, the story of Jesus, 'from behind'. *Matt 28:18-20 is the key to understanding the whole book.*" (Michel's italics, see, Michel, 'The Conclusion of Matthew's Gospel', 45).

[80] Gundry sees the presence of redactional concerns in Matt 28.16-20 is the strongest evidence that this unit is the composition of the evangelist himself and does not derive from another source. He notes that, verses 16-20 "offer a compendium of important Matthean themes: Jesus as the greater Moses, the deity of Jesus, the authority

conclude Matthew's call to mission orientated discipleship are addressed to his own community as much as to the eleven. The going to Galilee is in obedience to what Jesus has commanded, the worship of some is contrasted with the doubt of others, the delegated authority that Jesus has received is to serve as the basis of the disciples' activities,[81] their mission is teaching orientated finding its content in Jesus' own instruction, and the promise motivating them is the ongoing presence of Jesus until the consummation of the age. This is very much an outward focused conversionalist agenda, but debate remains in regard to whom precisely were the targets of such activity. Without pre-empting the following discussion it is worth noting Stanton's comments, especially since they clarify the major issue involved. Referring to the joint article of Hare and Harrington he notes that they "insist that πάντα τὰ ἔθνη in 28.19 should be translated 'all the Gentiles'; Israel has been rejected finally and completely."[82] Although Stanton does not pretend that the evidence is straightforward, he does note the following objections.

> In a reply J.P. Meier argues, surely correctly, that in 21.43, the crucial Matthean redactional addition to Mark's parable, the ἔθνος to whom the Kingdom will be given includes both Jews and Gentiles. 24.14 also confirms that πάντα τὰ ἔθνη should be translated 'all nations'. I have myself insisted that 23.39 does not rule out the possibility that some individual Jews will become Christians: on the contrary, it expresses the confident hope that at the parousia some will say joyfully, 'Blessed is he who comes in the name of the Lord.'[83]

While the reference to πάντα τὰ ἔθνη is most plausibly understood as being universal in scope, not all scholars concur, so first an assessment will be given of those arguments used to dispute the universality of such missionary activity.

---

of his commands, the Trinitarian associations of baptism, the danger of doubt among the disciples, the danger of doubt among the disciples, the teaching ministry of the disciples, discipleship as keeping Jesus' law, the presence of Jesus with his disciples, and the directing of Christian hope to the consummation. Paramount among these themes, however, is the mission to all nations." (Gundry, *Matthew*, 593). However, it is dubious, given the inconclusive nature of such an analysis, whether one can assert with such certainty that this unit is purely redactional with no basis in the tradition.

[81] Overman reads the reference to authority in a similar manner, as denoted delegated authority that is transmitted to the Matthean community. "All authority resides with the anointed leader and divine agent of the Matthean community, Jesus. Jesus has passed this authority on to his followers in the community, who should now, in this post-resurrection period, act out this authority." (Overman, *Church and Community in Crisis*, 403).

[82] Stanton, *Gospel*, 137. See also Hare and Harrington, '"Make Disciples of all the Gentiles" (Mt. 28.19)', 359-69.

[83] Stanton, *Gospel*, 137-8.

For Overman the phrase πάντα τὰ ἔθνη should be rendered as 'all the world'.[84] This translation has the obvious grammatical problem of rendering the plural Greek phrase by what one must assume Overman takes to be some kind of collective singular in English, as well as rendering ἔθνη by the term 'world'. If Matthew had meant 'world' why did he not use κόσμος or οἰκουμένη, terms which he is happy to use elsewhere in his gospel?[85] However, the argument that Overman advances is not based on primarily on grammar. He states that the traditional translation 'all the nations' with overtones of turning from the Jews and embracing the Gentile world "owes a great deal to the predilections of twentieth-century biblical scholarship, particularly scholarship from the middle part of this century."[86] Despite Overman's contention, this translation is evidenced in English at least as early as the beginning of the seventeenth century.[87] Overman tries to link the traditional interpretation with Clark's argument that Matthew was a Gentile.[88] He then makes the following observation and conclusion,

> This view [Matthew being a Gentile] was followed by some Matthean scholars through the late 1980s, but the view is clearly now a small minority. But in the midpoint of the twentieth century many New Testament interpreters saw in verses like Matthew 28.19 an affirmation of what was being said in more popular and destructive terms in more than a few cultural and political venues, that is that the Jews had been rejected and the favour of God had turned towards the Gentiles – that is, the church. There God's people would flourish. This is an instance of scholarship following the more popular cultural currents of the period.[89]

Not only is this argument highly inaccurate, it also seeks to inflame scholarly debate by linking a possible interpretation of the Matthean phrase πάντα τὰ ἔθνη with the worse excess of anti-semitism. This is surely disingenuous, to say the least. A few points must be made in response. First, Clark's position has always been the minority viewpoint, [90]

---

[84] For this translation or his other possibility 'the rest of the world', see Overman, *Church and Community in Crisis*, 406.

[85] For κόσμος in Matt see 4.8; 5.14; 13.35, 38; 16.26; 18.7; 24.21; 25.34; 26.13. Although used only once, οἰκουμένη occurs at Matt 24.14.

[86] Overman, *Church and Community in Crisis*, 405.

[87] The Authorized version translates 28.18a as 'Go ye therefore, and teach all nations', while this of course does not mean it is the correct translation, it does illustrate that this translation is not simply a twentieth century fad. Similarly, the Vulgate appears to support a similar interpretation 'euntes ergo docete omnes gentes'. Of course, neither the Vulgate or the Authorized Version settle the question of whether 'gentiles' or 'nations' is intended in an inclusive or exclusive manner.

[88] Clark, 'The Gentile Bias in Matthew', 165-72.

[89] Overman, *Church and Community in Crisis*, 405.

[90] Among the leading scholars who have supported Clark are Strecker, *Der Weg der Gerechtigkeit*, and Meier, *Law and History in Matthew's Gospel*.

even among those who support the Matthean mission as being orientated towards the Gentiles. Second, regardless of whether Overman is correct that Matt 28.19 was taken up as a political proof-text (he offers no evidence), the antiquity of this translation decisively illustrates that scholars were not following popular cultural trends. Third, at a historical level, it is possible that Matthew was calling for a new direction in the community's missionary activity after the group's ostracism from the synagogue. Even if it was correct to label his negative statements about synagogue and Pharisaic leadership as anti-Jewish, the corrective to this is not deny Matthew's intolerance of his opponents, rather the situation should be described accurately (even if this involved Jewish hostility), but this does not mean that modern Christians need to own or adopt such an attitude and replicate these acts of intolerance and hostility. Finally, one wonders if Overman is not himself guilty of the charge he brings against those who hold to the traditional interpretation, namely of following popular cultural currents and attempting to make the biblical text appear more politically correct than may indeed be the case.

Unlike Overman, Sim does try and construct his argument from the text alone. Sim relativizes Matthew's call for a universal mission by linking such a mission with the eschatological age. Primarily, he makes the reference to ἕως τῆς συντελείας τοῦ αἰῶνος (28.20b) conform to the interpretation he has proposed for the final clause of 24.14, καὶ τότε ἥξει τὸ τέλος. This interpretation is that the Gentile mission is an eschatological event, and furthermore, this teleological focus is taken to mean that the Matthean community had no need to become involved with proselytising activities orientated towards non-Jews. He argues, "the Matthean community itself did not interpret 28.19 as a command to pursue a mission to the Gentile."[91] From this assertion, he continues by reconstructing the Matthean attitude to mission activity in the following ethnically delineated manner.

> In view of this, there is no necessity to attribute any role for Matthew's community in the Gentile mission which needed to take place before the arrival of the end (24:14). This church would continue to take responsibility for the Gospel to the Jews, while other Christian groups which had taken the responsibility for the Gentile mission would fulfil this role in the eschatological plan.[92]

Perhaps the first reaction one might have is to ask how can Sim know so much about the underlying motivations and ethnic attitudes of the Matthean group. Then, however, as one analyses the text it becomes apparent that even at those points when he allows the narrative itself to

---

[91] Sim, 'The Gospel of Matthew and the Gentiles', 42.
[92] Sim, 'The Gospel of Matthew and the Gentiles', 43.

govern the arguments that his interpretations are not the most natural. Focusing specifically on 28.20, it needs to be noted that the evangelist draws very little connection between the charge to 'make disciples of all nations' (28.19a) and the promise that Jesus is with his followers 'until the end of the age' (28.20b), at least not in the sense of the universal mission being temporally delayed until the eschaton. This would seem to be required if Sim's thesis was to be plausible. Obviously the promise of Jesus' presence is linked to the call for making disciples in as much as it serves as an assurance that they are not alone in this task. As Davies and Allison note the promise is not so much about presence as it is about assistance.[93] From this perspective, seeing the Matthean community as a marginalized and liminal entity, the promise is one of empowerment that equips the community for its expanded missionary horizon. Carter, who depicts the Matthean gospel as a counternarrative, states that this final promise serves to gives assurance to the powerless.

> The community does not struggle on its own in this mission task with the inevitable difficulties created by an environment of deceit and hostility (28:11-15) and by by faithless discipleship (chs. 26-27). Though Jesus is not physically present, his presence continues through the gospel's narrative of his words and actions, and based on 10:20, through the assisting role of the Spirit....The alternative, countercultural life of discipleship is lived in the time between Jesus' life, death and resurrection, and the end of the age...Until then, the present is a difficult time of tribulation (chs. 24-25) and mission.[94]

It is significant that Carter recognizes the role of mission in the contemporary situation of the Matthean groups both as being part of that countercultural lifestyle promoted among members, and also portrayed as a fundamental means by which the presence of Jesus is made real to the community of believers.

Although Sim's interpretation of 28.19 may not be the most straightforward, he argues that it is justified because of the eschatological schema represented in 24.14, the only other place in the gospel where Gentile mission is explicitly mentioned.[95] At this point it is worth quoting Sim's argument in full to see how he arrives at such a conclusion.

---

[93] As they state, "Here the dominant sense may not be so much that of divine promise as of divine assistance." (Davies and Allison, *Matthew,* vol 3, 687).

[94] Carter, *Matthew and the Margins*, 553.

[95] Sim identifies these two verses as the only possible places where one may derive support for a Gentile mission being supported in Matthew's gospel. He states, "There are in fact only two single verses which support the consensus position, Matt. 24.14 and 28.19." He then attempts to rob them of their significance by saying they form an narrow evidential base. "It is no exaggeration to say that one would be hard-pressed to find a comparable case where so much has been built on so little." (Sim, *The Gospel of Matthew and Christian Judaism*, 242-3). Then Sim proceeds to use these same verses to

Since Matt. 28:19 does not, as many scholars believe, necessarily point to an active Gentile mission on the part of Matthew's community, its involvement or otherwise in such a mission must be established by other evidence. Such evidence may be provided by 24:14. This verse concludes the evangelist's timetable of the end events in 24:4-14. It specifies that just prior to the end of the age the gospel of the kingdom will be preached throughout the whole world as a testimony to all nations (cf. 26:13).[96]

However, a straightforward reading of the text shows that it does not specify, as Sim claims, that only just prior to the eschaton will the gospel be proclaimed to all the nations. In fact that verse again provides an incentive to Matthew's audience to start the mission in their present situation, for it is only when they have completed taking the gospel to all nations that it is possible for the end to come. This is no plea for inaction among the Gentiles. On the contrary, Matthew implores those who hear his message to become fully involved in mission since it is seen as the very activity that will precipitate the arrival of the *parousia*.

Sim continues this argument by ruling out evidence that may corroborate a traditional understanding of 28.19 that may imply incorporation of Gentiles.[97] He then develops a reconstruction of late first century Christian mission that is a mixture of perceived anti-Gentile attitudes in Matthew's gospel, latent anti-Paulinism on the part of the first evangelist, and, a certain degree of speculation in filling the considerable historical gaps. He states that the Matthean community, while not actively involved in Gentile mission, believed in the validity of such activity, apparently now in their own contemporary situation, not in the eschatological future. Nonetheless, the evangelist repudiated the Pauline form of Gentile mission. As a consequence, such missionary work was being "conducted by missionaries from the Christian Jewish faction of the Christian movement. That such a law-observant mission to the Gentiles existed is not really open to dispute."[98] In support of this last statement Sim appeals to an article by Martyn.[99] While Martyn's essay is particularly

---

build his case that the mission is postponed until the eschaton. How can these two verses form an invalid base for building the case for involvement of the Matthean community in Gentile mission, but strangely at the same time they provide a strong enough base to assert that Gentile mission is an event that occurs only on the *parousia* horizon.

[96] Sim, *The Gospel of Matthew and Christian Judaism*, 244.

[97] For example, he excludes 22.8-10 in the following manner. "One cannot appeal to 22.8-10 in support, since the meaning of this material is rendered ambiguous by the very presence of 28.19 in the gospel." (Sim, *The Gospel of Matthew and Christian Judaism*, 245). However, it is only rendered ambiguous by Sim's reading of 28.19, a traditional reading makes for a coherent outlook between 22.8-10 and 28.19.

[98] Sim, *The Gospel of Matthew and Christian Judaism*, 246.

[99] See Martyn, 'A Law Observant Mission to the Gentiles: The Background of Galatians', 307-24.

cogent in illuminating the conflict that stood behind the epistle to the Galatians, it is highly dubious to assert without supporting evidence that the same groups were operative forty to fifty years later in a different part of the Roman empire.[100] It is of course more than likely that the momentum towards engaging in Gentile mission was not embraced by all nascent Christian communities at the same time,[101] but it is quite a different matter to assert that the precise history of the Matthean community can be mapped out, and that this involved an outright rejection of their own participation in such a mission, even though, according to Sim, they respected the attempts of other Christian-Jewish groups to engage in a law-obsevant Gentile mission.

In summary, Sim's argument that the groups that adhered to teaching of the first evangelist did not participate in missionary activity among the Gentiles is unsustainable for three reasons. Firstly, the eschatological scheme that Sim imposes upon the text cannot be supported by the statements made in the gospel. Even in the case of 24.14 the relationship between mission and *parousia* is not of the form Sim proposes. Mission to the nations is not to be delayed until the eschatological future, but must be actively engaged in to hasten the eschaton. Moreover, the statements made in 28.19-20 undermine this suggested eschatological schema, because they offer no support for such a delay in proselytising activity, instead they simply promise Jesus' presence with the group until the end of the age. Secondly, too much counter evidence is simply neglected or declared inadmissible. He neglects those passages where the faith of Gentiles is emphasized in contrast to that of Israel (8.10; 11.20-24; 12.38-42; 21.43), and misses the flow of the narrative as it becomes increasingly favourable to Gentile in the last third of the gospel.[102] Thirdly, Sim not only contradicts his own eschatological schema when he describes the Matthean community's 'in principle' support for Gentile mission in their contemporary setting, but more importantly it is highly questionable how he can find support to back up his proposal of a reactionary attitude to a Pauline type Gentile mission. On the whole, although Sim does not commit

---

[100] Obviously, Martyn himself makes no connection between the conflict in Galatia and the background to Matthew's gospel.

[101] For a more balanced approach to the data see Brown, 'The Matthean Community and the Gentile Mission', 193-221.

[102] In particular see Matt 20.1-16; 21.28-32 Codex B text form, (for details see Foster, 'A Tale of Two Sons'), 21.33-43; 22.1-14; 24.13; 25.31-46, 27.19, 54; 28.16-20. For a fuller list of texts throughout the gospel see Senior, 'Between Two Worlds', esp. 14-16. Of the eighteen passages that he notes he comments, "Of these eighteen texts, fourteen have no parallel in Mark, and twelve are found only in Matthew. Viewed cumulatively, these references to Gentiles are a substantial underlying motif of Matthew's Gospel" (16).

the excesses of Overman's approach, his suggestions remain totally implausible.

By contrast, Saldarini, although taking the mission orientated statements against the backdrop of a fundamentally Jewish community practising traditional Torah observance, nonetheless gives texts such as 28.19 and 24.14 their most natural sense. He makes the comment that, "In the final scene, the climax of the gospel, Jesus commands his followers to go and make disciples of the nations (28.19)."[103] He then continues by explaining that he understands this to mean that the evangelist is urging group members to widen their field of missionary endeavour.

> If the Matthean group is still predominantly Jewish, as is argued here, then these statements encourage the widening of the group's teaching mission, membership, and sense of self to include non-Jews. The nations to be won over to the teachings of Jesus certainly include non-Jews predominantly, but Jewish communities within the empire and within Israel and southern Syria may also be meant.[104]

There is little to disagree with here in relation to enlarged vision of mission that is set before the community. Saldarini is correct that making disciples of all nations does not entail a total curtailing of mission to Jews,[105] but he also emphasizes that the Matthean mission charge does appear to be giving a certain priority to Gentiles. Further, he sees the mission as not only based on teaching as a means of incorporating Gentiles into the Matthean group, but this is matched by the community's redefinition of itself in such a way that it can look positively on these new converts without the long term group members expressing resentment (cf. 18.6-11; 20.1-16; 23.8-12). Yet perhaps the one thing Saldarini does not manage to do effectively is to account for this change of perspective in the community.

According to Saldarini, the hostility that is expressed in Matthew's gospel is directed specifically at the leaders of Jewish society and the institutions they control. Thus the polemic is limited in its scope to the Jewish hierarchy, but wider Judaism is still embraced by the community and in this sense group members are still closely linked with other Jews in non-leadership position. The opposition contained in the first gospel is described in the following terms by Saldarini.

---

[103] Saldarini, *Matthew's Christian-Jewish Community*, 81.

[104] Saldarini, *Matthew's Christian-Jewish Community*, 81.

[105] This point is further reinforced by Saldarini when he writes, "the Jewish people are still recruitable, still not judged as beyond salvation or irrevocably condemned (as they are in later Christian literature). Thus, even as Matthew urges his group to undertake a gentile mission, he continues to appeal to fellow Jews." (Saldarini, *Matthew's Christian-Jewish Community*, 43).

Matthew...reserves his venom for hostile Jewish leaders and occasionally for people who have followed those leaders into a firm rejection of Jesus. Not only the leaders, but the institutions they control and they interpretations of Jewish law and custom they propose for Jewish society, are subject to constant and systematic attack.[106]

This conclusion, however, is based primarily on the material in chapters 21-23, with special emphasis being given to chapter 23. While Saldarini is correct that the 'all the people' of 27.25 should not be "burdened with salvation history weight",[107] it is nonetheless a text that calls his overall interpretation into question. However, one must be sensitive to the historical misuse of this text by recognizing the hostility that is expressed by Matthew does not mean, despite the evangelist's cursing of the τέκνα, that it is necessary for subsequent generations of Christians to replicate such vilification. All that is being pointed out is that the saying, καὶ ἀποκριθεὶς πᾶς ὁ λαὸς εἶπεν, τὸ αἷμα αὐτοῦ ἐφ' ἡμᾶς καὶ ἐπὶ τὰ τέκνα ἡμῶν, is not directed at the elders, nor at Jerusalem and the leadership as some representative class as Saldarini asserts. Rather, there appears to be far more distance between the Matthean community and synagogue based Judaism than Saldarini allows. It is claimed that references to 'their' or 'your synagogues' although they "suggest hostility prove that Matthew's group is in conflict with the Jewish community, [but] not totally separated from it."[108]

Yet, according to this theory, it would appear that hostility could never lead to separation (an obviously absurd corollary, which hence makes one question the validity of the theory itself).. While hostilities may wane with separation, it is likely that this would occur over a protracted period of time, and in the period immediately following a rift between two parties tension can remain acute and polemic is often still bitter. Moreover, following Saldarini's interpretation that the Matthean adherents are being encouraged to engage more actively in Gentile mission, such a realignment of priorities is perhaps more naturally seen as emerging in the aftermath of the group's ostracism from the synagogue environment, which had served as its first mission field. Despite such qualifications, Saldarini must be applauded for taking the mission charge of Matt 28.16-20 at face value and not claiming that it does not imply a call to become active in the Gentile sphere.

---

[106] Saldarini, *Matthew's Christian-Jewish Community*, 67.
[107] Saldarini, *Matthew's Christian-Jewish Community*, 33.
[108] Saldarini, *Matthew's Christian-Jewish Community*, 67.

6.3 Conclusions

Mission, or the spread of the gospel, is an important theme in Matthew's narrative and references to this topic increase in the final third of the gospel. Obviously the most restrictive reference occurs in 10.5-23, where the mission is limited to the house of Israel. The question arises as to whether Matthew understood this command as still applying to the situation of his own community.

Two factors suggest that the evangelist did not take the limitation to be normative for his contemporary situation. First, the number of texts throughout the later chapters of the gospel which promote mission to Gentiles, and second, indications within 10.5-23 that depict the community coming into contact with the Gentile world.[109] It has been argued that Matthew quoted this traditional saying to appease conservative elements in his group who wished to maintain strict adherence to an exclusive Israel mission. However, Matthew subverts such exclusivism by statements that are presented later in the gospel, particularly the final climactic charge of the risen Jesus to his disciples to engage in Gentile mission. That inclusion of non-Jewish elements in the community could have been an important issue after 70 C.E. is strongly supported by S. Brown. He sensibly notes that, "A considerable period of time may have elapsed before this process reached its term in total separation of the great Church from Judaism and the reduction of Jewish Christianity to an isolated Ebionite sect, cut off from both church and synagogue."[110] While Brown is probably too simplistic in his suggestion that the only remaining form of Jewish Christianity was Ebionism (probably he is thinking at some stage in the second century), his general point still remains valid. Namely, that the separation from Judaism was protracted and occurred at different times among different groups of believers in Jesus.

Furthermore, Brown is almost certainly correct that inclusion of the non-Jews was problematic precisely because Jesus during his earthly ministry had not instructed his disciples to actively take the message of the kingdom to Gentiles. As he cogently argues,

> The problem of the gentile mission in the post-Easter community arises from the fact that although Jesus shared in the belief that gentiles would have a share in the world to come, his initial expectation was that this would come about through the conversion of Israel, which would usher in the kingdom of God.[111]

---

[109] In particular Matt 10.18 reflects trials before governors and kings before whom disciples will make testimony *and to the nations* for Jesus' sake, καὶ ἐπὶ ἡγεμόνας δὲ καὶ βασιλεῖς ἀχθήσεσθε ἕνεκεν ἐμοῦ εἰς μαρτύριον αὐτοῖς καὶ τοῖς ἔθνεσιν.

[110] Brown, 'The Matthean Community and the Gentile Mission', 194.

[111] Brown, 'The Matthean Community and the Gentile Mission', 197.

Thus, although Jesus was not totally negative toward Gentiles, if they were to become participants in the kingdom it was through incorporation into Israel. By contrast, Brown sees Matthew promoting inclusive Gentile mission among a group of believers who in origin were primarily Jewish. Significantly, he sees the redactional passage Matt 13.36-43, the interpretation of the parable of the tares,[112] as containing a reference to universal mission. He states, "Matthew takes 'the field' to represent 'the world' (Mt xiii 38). In this reference to the post-Easter situation it is significant that the evangelist speaks of geographical not ethnic boundaries."[113]

In terms of Matthew's attempted redefinition of the missionary task, the post-Easter situation as he depicts it becomes normative for the contemporary life of his own community of disciples. It is not without significance that the complicit nature of 'the Jews' in attempting to falsify the facts of the resurrection (at least as Matthew understands them) is presented in Matt 28.15, immediately before the mission charge which most clearly speaks of the change of emphasis that is required by the group in terms of its proselytising activity. That this pejorative reference to the Jews *qua* Jews is the only use of this term in the gospel and occurs immediately before the climactic mission charge is part of Matthew's

---

[112] The parable of the Tares is attested in both Matthew and G.Thom 57. However, the interpretation 13.36-43 is contained only in Matthew and betrays redactional vocabulary and interests. Whether the parable (vv 24-30) itself can be traced back to the historical Jesus is debated. The Jesus Seminar assert that "The parable reflects the concern of a young Christian community attempting to define itself over and against an evil world, a concern not characteristic of Jesus." (Funk, Hoover, et. al., *The Five Gospels*, 194). Further, it is argued, "Although the version in Thomas lacks the appended allegorical interpretation, there is a distant echo of the final apocalyptic judgment made explicit in Matthew. This note is alien to Thomas, so it must have been introduced into the Christian tradition at an early date, probably be the first followers of Jesus who had been disciples of John the Baptist" (505). However, this assessment appears to be motivated by the programmatic concern of the Jesus seminar to de-eschatologize Jesus. On other grounds, Jülicher regarded the parable to have been composed by Matthew and not of dominical origin, (Jülicher, *Die Gleichnisreden Jesu*, vol 2, 555-63). However, Schweizer rightly questions the basis on which such decisions are made. He refutes the charge that the parable must be a creation of the early church to address the problem of evil in its midst. He states, "If the nucleus of the parable went back to Jesus, it would represent a strong protest against the tendency of the Pharisees, the Qumran community and the Zealots to delimit a sect of devout believers. Jesus rejected this practice and kept his circle open." (Schweizer, *The Good News according to Matthew*, 304). While it may be questioned whether one can determine so precisely that Jesus' opposition was directed against the practices of Qumran sectarians and Zealots, Schweizer does show that the saying can be read in the context of Jesus' practice of open commensality, something the Jesus Seminar are usually keen to promote.

[113] Brown, 'The Matthean Community and the Gentile Mission', 214.

argument for the compelling need to take the community's teaching to the Gentiles in a more determined fashion. This point is supported by Luz in his discussion supporting translating ἔθνη as 'Gentiles' in Matt 28.19.

> First, in the immediate context, a contrast arises with the conspicuous 'Jews' in verse 15. In a larger context, there is a clear allusion to 10:5-6, where Jesus forbade the disciples to go to the Gentiles. It is this very instruction which the risen Jesus now reverses....to Matthew's original readers 'now' referred to their own day, a time when the Gentile mission was apparently still a new or controversial task for the community. Having failed in Israel, the community has been assigned a new task by its Lord.[114]

This 'failure' in the Jewish mission need not imply an unwillingness to convert Jews, rather Matthew appears to be re-prioritizing the group's emphases. No longer would its focus be upon converting those synagogue Jews whom Matthew characterizes as falsifying the resurrection, ostracising members of his community, and imposing upon them the liminal status that they now experience. Rather, the community is encouraged to develop its partial contacts with Gentiles into its central missionary endeavour.[115]

A similar egalitarian perspective is provided by Matthean ecclesiology. The community members are not to obstruct the progress of the 'little ones' in the group (18.5f.),[116] rather there is to be an attitude of acceptance of support (18.4). Moreover, hierarchical structures are to be replaced by an attitude of humility and service (23.8-12). These statements show the

---

[114] Luz, *The Theology of the Gospel of Matthew*, 139-40.

[115] For von Dobbeler the Gentile mission in Matthew takes place only through a stricter application of Torah in a post 70 C.E. setting. This requires Gentile converts to conform to tradition legal interpretation in a fairly standard way. His position makes it hard to account for the exclusion of the Matthean group from the synagogue environment. In some ways it appears that the group are, in line with formative Judaism, following the trend to become more restrictive. He states, Matthew's gospel "reflektiert das MtEv in seiner Endfassung ein Judenchristentum der zweiten Generation, das durch eine strikte Orientierung am Gesetz (in der Auslegung Jesu) einerseits und durch ein messianisches Bewußtsein andererseits gekennzeichnet war, sich nach wie vor als Teil Israels sah, zu Israel gesandt, um die Niedergeschlagenen im Volk aufzurichten, und zugleich – als Teil seiner messianischen Sendung – seine Aufgabe darin sah, die Heiden unter die Herrschaft des einen Gottes zu bringen." (von Dobbeler, 'Die Restitution Israels und die Bekehrung der Heiden', 42).

[116] The identity of these 'little ones' is disputed. Obviously, as Davies and Allison recognize, the initial use (18.5) stands as a literal reference to the child introduced in verse 2. However, throughout vv 6-14 it would appear that this terminology is taken up as a metaphor for some subset of believers in the community. Suggestions have included catechumens, recent converts, lowly Christians, or those not in leadership positions. If Matthew, as is being argued here, is calling for the full acceptance of recent Gentile converts by long term group member then the reference could plausibly be understood as denoting such non-Jewish community members.

inclusive nature of the group cohesion that the evangelist is trying to promote. In his study on Matt 23.8-12 Hoet draws out the implications of this embracing fraternity that is presented as the hallmark of authentic community life.

> Les verset 8-12 de Mt 23 sont adressés à tous les disciples du Christ et non seulment aux de la communauté. Mais en mêtemps ils sont adressés à tous les hommes: non seulement aux 'foules' juives et aux païens qui se trouvaient sans doubte dans l'auditoire de Jésus, mais à tous peoples à qui l'Evangile est adressé, puisqu'il n'y a pas d'autre chemin vers la vie, qu'en vivant selon l'enseignement du Christ.[117]

However, Matthew does not idealize the Gentile mission as a relatively easy task in comparison to the Jewish mission. The material in 24.9-14, while appearing to reflect the fact that the Gentile mission is already underway in the Matthean community,[118] envisages the reality of rejection by the Gentile, καὶ ἔσεσθε μισούμενοι ὑπὸ πάντων τῶν ἐθνῶν διὰ τὸ ὄνομά μου, (Matt 24.9b). Furthermore, it is interesting that Matthew immediately moves from the description of the tribulations that arise from taking the gospel to all the nations, to a portrayal of dissent and division within the group. The twin uses of τέλος show that steadfastness resulting in salvation (24.13) and preaching the gospel to all the nations (24.14) are not unrelated concepts in the Matthean scheme. In a somewhat muted way Matthew does acknowledge that the decision to take the gospel to all the nations is a divisive issue in the life of the community (24.10).[119]

The picture that emerges from the relevant texts in the gospel in relation to mission is that of unqualified support by the evangelist for proselytising activity among the Gentiles to be undertaken by the community in its contemporary situation. Moreover, such mission activity appears already to be the practice of some group members,[120] although this apparently may have caused divisions and even acts of betrayal (at least from the perspective of those who promoted Gentile mission). In some ways, Matthew's promotion of the Gentile mission is undertaken in a partially conciliatory manner, for he acknowledges, as no doubt conservative group members were aware, that

---

[117] Hoet, *'Omnes Autem vos Fratres estis'*: *Etude du concept ecclésiologique des 'frères' selon Mt 23,8-12*, 213.

[118] See the earlier discussion on Matt 24.14.

[119] Hagner appears to appreciate this at least in part. He states, "the reference to the experience of persecution from 'all the Gentiles' here stands in poignant relationship to the same phrase in v 14, for it is just 'all the Gentiles' to whom the disciple are sent 'for a witness.' διὰ τὸ ὄνομά μου, 'because of my name' (cf. 10.22), means because of the disciples' identification with Jesus. But there will also be disloyalty and treachery among those who are Jesus' disciples." (Hagner, *Matthew 14-28*, 694).

[120] See Luz assessment that, "judging from 24.9 and 24.14, the Gentile mission already seems to be underway in the present." (Luz, *The Theology of the Gospel of Matthew*, 16).

Jesus himself commanded the disciples to limit their mission to 'the lost sheep of the house of Israel' (Matt 10.6). Yet he then engages in an exercise of conceptual redefinition. The Matthean Jesus proceeds, every time a reference to mission occurs or an inclusive parable is spoken, to emphasize the necessity of going to the Gentiles. This comes to a climax in the final commissioning words of 28.16-20. The evangelist having just castigated 'the Jews' for their duplicity in undermining the veracity of the community's resurrection beliefs, then has Jesus authorize his disciples to go to all the nations. This delegated authority is based upon passing on the teaching that is contained in Matthew's own tractate. Such a commission does of course not rule out the possibility of Jews being accepted into the community, it would be anachronistic to read the narrative in such a manner.

It does, nevertheless, call for a substantial change in emphasis, whereby the primary focus of proselytization is directed towards Gentiles who were to be accepted as full community participants, and traditional long-term group members were even warned of the potential danger of placing stumbling blocks before such new members (18.6-7). Whether this strategy proved effective is impossible to know at the level of the Matthean community, there is simply no evidence for that community after the writing of the gospel.[121] However, there is evidence for the reception of Matthew's gospel in the wider Church, even as the premier gospel. This shows that regardless of the outcome of Matthew's exercise of redefinition aimed at the traditional members of his group, this programme was recognized as a legitimate development and explanation of the Jesus tradition and the dominically inaugurated mission. Hence the gospel he wrote was seen, to a certain degree by the evangelist himself, as a celebration of Gentile participation in the Kingdom of Heaven.

---

[121] This should be freely acknowledged, and attempts to reconstruct the post-gospel history of the community should be seen for what they are, mere flights of fancy.

Chapter 7

Conclusions

7.1 Summary of Purpose

This thesis challenges an emerging consensus in Matthean studies,[1] namely, that the social setting of the Matthean community is best understood by seeing the gospel addressed to a Torah observant Jewish sect that limited its contact with Gentiles.[2] The development of this position was seen to have emerged since the mid 1980s onwards,[3] and has been closely linked with social-scientific approaches to the first gospel. However, as Stanton's studies have shown,[4] it is not *a priori* a necessary conclusion that application of social-scientific criticism in relation to the first gospel leads to seeing the community as still operating within the orbit of Judaism at the time of the composition of the gospel. Nonetheless, the dominant position has been, drawing on the sociological insight that intensity of polemic reflects proximity of relationship between opposing parties, that it is best to see the evangelist addressing a community that is still part of the synagogue environment shared with its Jewish opponents.

By contrast, this study supports an alternative scenario which suggests that although the Matthean community originated in the synagogue environment, at the time of the writing of the gospel the group had broken away from its former religious setting and was operating as an independent entity. This reconstruction is primarily based upon the evangelist's attitude towards both law and mission, as these topics are reflected in the gospel. Obviously information about these issues can only be gleaned from the group's one extant document, and such data must be privileged over general theories about the patterns of sectarianism or tendencies within new religious movements. This is not to say that insights from the social

---

[1] For a similar recent challenge, see Hare, 'How Jewish is the Gospel of Matthew?', 264-77.

[2] The main dialogue partners in this thesis who hold the view that Matthew's community was a Law observant Jewish group include Saldarini, Overman, Sim and Repschinski. While their positions have certain differences they share far more in common, and thus can fairly be seen as representing a new approach to the social location of the Matthean community.

[3] See chapter 2 of this thesis for an overview of the development of this position.

[4] Stanton, *Gospel*, esp. chaps. 4-7 and 10.

sciences are unimportant. In fact the opposite is the case. However, an approach that both reflects upon the particular data contained within the NT and then applies the insights of social-scientific criticism in a valid manner, without unsubstantiated extrapolations, must be given methodological priority.

7.2 Findings of this Study

It has been argued that Matthew's gospel, although telling the story of Jesus, offers a window through which one may understand the community behind the first gospel.[5] There are a number of texts that are most naturally understood as reflecting a specific situation or community outlook. Among these, probably the most significant are the following. First, there is the report of a conspiratorial agreement by Jewish opponents to falsify the facts of the resurrection (28.11-15). This is most naturally understood as reflecting part of the contemporary situation facing the group. This can be seen from the reference καὶ διεφημίσθη ὁ λόγος οὗτος παρὰ Ἰουδαίοις μέχρι τῆς σήμερον [ἡμέρας] which not only demonstrates that the pericope is included because of its contemporary significance for the Matthean audience, but also suggests that it is addressed to a situation where a number of Jews are using this argument against those who are members of the community of first evangelist. Next, the issue of the temple tax (Matt 17.24-27) is most plausibly seen as offering instruction to adherents of the Matthean community to continue paying the *fiscus Iudaicus* even though their primary loyalty can no longer be viewed as belonging to their Jewish heritage.[6] In this vein, Carter argues that this Matthean redactional

---

[5] This is in opposition to Bauckham's proposal that the gospels were written as universal documents, rather than being focused on a specific community, or cluster of groups, ('For Whom Were the Gospels Written?' in Bauckham (ed.) *The Gospel for All Christians*, 7-49). In fact, Bauckham's thesis raises two issues for those who support redaction criticism with its assumption that the individual evangelists were addressing the needs of their own communities. First, the explicit issue raised by Bauckham, whether in fact the gospels were addressed to small Christian communities, and second, even if they were group specific, is it possible to recover anything about those groups from the material contained in the gospels. It is argued here that although the gospels are not reflections of community situations in the same manner as, for instance, a Pauline epistle, nonetheless at some points they offer a partial window for viewing the community by addressing issues that were relevant to the evangelists' contemporary audiences, rather than raising concerns that were part of the agenda of the historical Jesus.

[6] For a treatment of the history of the *fiscus Iudaicus* and its role in the formation of Judaism as a religious rather than ethnic entity see Goodman, 'Nerva, the *Fiscus Judaicus* and Jewish Identity', 40-44.

pericope addresses specific political concerns about the validity of paying the post-70 Roman tax for the temple of Jupiter Capitolinus required of Jews, including Matthew's (largely) Christian-Jewish community.[7] Lastly, the references either to 'their' or 'your synagogues' (Matt 4.23; 9.35; 10.17; 12.9; 13.54; 23.34) must be given due weight as showing the boundary division that exists between the two competing communities.

Combined with these three specific examples of pericopae that reflect a narrowly focused readership one could also mention other less specific examples. These include the instruction concerning church order (Matt 18.1-10), the discussion relating to the teaching and status of the rabbis (Matt 23.1-7), the equality of status among Matthew's community members (23.8-12) as well as a host of smaller redactional changes that all are plausibly understood as the evangelist's attempt to make received traditions more relevant to his own specific situation.[8] Furthermore, it is argued in this study that the promotion of missionary activity is also a reflection of the contemporary situation of the Matthean community when the gospel was written. This is not to suggest that mission for Matthew was understood in the same sense of Pauline proselytising activity with its establishment of new churches throughout the eastern empire, but that Matthew was promoting the inclusion of Gentiles within his group and in fact saw them as the major source of new members.[9]

Having argued that the gospel reflects a specific communal situation, with some obvious tension between the evangelist's adherents and their synagogue based opponents, the thesis aimed to answer the specific question of whether the group now operated *intra muros* or *extra muros* in

---

[7] Carter argues that "[t]he central issue is the significance of paying the tax. It is argued that its payment, as paradoxical as it may seem, does not recognize Roman sovereignty but acknowledges God's reign. God displays sovereignty in providing the tax in the fish's mouth. Paying the tax contests and subverts Rome's claims and anticipates the establishment of God's reign in its fullness." Carter, 'Paying the Tax to Rome as Subversive Praxis: Matthew 17.24-27', 3-31.

[8] Here Sim is most helpful in his evaluation of Bauckham's argument. He notes, 'Bauckham provides no hard evidence that the gospels were open-ended texts intended for an unspecified readership. He merely assumes that this was the case because the gospels, unlike the Pauline epistles, provide no definitive indication of their intended readers. This explanation, however, is by no means the only one on offer. It is equally possible, perhaps more probable, that the lack of identification of the readers points to the proximity between the author and the Christian community for whom he was writing.' Sim, 'The Gospels for All Christians? A Response to Richard Bauckham', 17.

[9] Hare goes even further and suggests that the door had been closed to Jewish converts, thus he argues that the emphasis on Gentile mission stems from the relative failure of the mission among Jews. 'The invitation that Israel had refused so rudely is now to be offered exclusively to the Gentiles.' (Hare, *The Theme of Jewish Persecution*, 171).

regard to the synagogue environment. The most extreme version of the *intra muros* viewpoint can be seen in the works of Overman and Sim. The former sees the reception history of Matthew's gospel in the early church as a perversion of the evangelist's original intent. He argues,

> As G. Strecker demonstrated in his appendix to Bauer's *Orthodoxy and Heresy*, Matthew's type of Jesus-centered Judaism, or Matthean Judaism, by roughly the third century, save a few odd and isolated pockets, died out. Matthew's story became a text aligned with the church and very often set against Jews and Israel.
> Few things could be further from Matthew's message and original setting. Matthew's original intent was to instruct his congregation about the direction, nature, and identity of Israel in a time when many things were up for grabs.[10]

A few observations are required in response to Overman's comments. First, the citation of Strecker could not be more misleading. Not only did Strecker view the Matthean community as no longer operating within Judaism, rather he suggested that Matthew himself was a Gentile and, in line with Clark's thesis,[11] this accounted for the anti-Jewish bias in the gospel.[12] Moreover, Overman while correct in his assessment that in the post-destruction period Judaism was seeking to refashion itself and that there were competing forces operating in this quest for redefinition, he fails to see that this does not of itself prove that Matthew's community was on the inside of this process. Likewise, Sim wishes to argue for a picture of the Matthean community that views the group as a faction within emergent Judaism rather than as part of the wider Christian world. The group is seen as an isolationist sect in relation to other Christian groups, despite the fact that allegiance to Jesus is important within the community. Only in an extremely qualified manner does Sim allow the label 'Christianity' to be applied to the religion of those believers in Jesus who formed the adherents to the Matthean group. He asserts that,

> [T]he Matthean community was first and foremost a Jewish group of believers in Jesus. As faithful followers of Christ, they can properly be called Christians, but it is a mistake to label their religion 'Christianity'... By dispensing with the traditional laws which set the Jews apart from other peoples, Christianity (or Gentile Christianity) accepted no distinctions between Jew and Gentile. This religious tradition is not that of the Matthean community. The evangelist and his readers were

---

[10] Overman, *Church and Community in Crisis*, 414.

[11] Clark, 'The Gentile Bias in Matthew', 165-72.

[12] Strecker concludes his discussion on the identity of the evangelist in the following manner. 'Wenn es richtig ist, daß das judenchristenlich Element zum Anfangsstadium der Gemeinde gehört und daß der Evangelist dem Heidenchristentum zuzurechnen ist, so ist damit eine Entwicklung angedeutet. Eine neue, heidenchristliche Generation löst das Judenchristentum ab. Zwar wird das jüdische Gedankengut auch in Zukunft nicht ohne Einfluß sein, aber nur, indem es in den heidenchristlichen Lebenskreis eingeordnet ist.' Strecker, *Der Weg der Gerechtigkeit*, 35.

followers of the Christ who did not accept that the coming of the Christ had rendered null and void the precepts of Judaism. They observed the Jewish law in full according to the definitive interpretations of Jesus, and this included obedience to the laws of circumcision, tithing, purity and sabbath observance. The Matthean community was therefore Jewish.[13]

Not only does this reconstruction raise the methodological question in relation to how Sim knows the manner in which the community practiced the law (assuming that for the sake of argument that this is correct),[14] but moreover, it raises the question of the categories that Sim sets up. His alternatives appear to be either an antinomistic form of Gentile Christianity, or a rigorist Jewish group whose only deviation from emergent Jewish religion was an adherence to the belief that Jesus was the Messiah. However, there is a range of possibilities between these extremes, and it appears more plausible to argue that group was in a period of flux and redefinition seeking to enlarge its mission to Gentiles and promote a more egalitarian structure that would not alienate recent members.

It has been argued in this thesis that Matthew was not fighting on two fronts against both Jewish opponents and an antinomian faction.[15] Rather, that the tension arose from both a pastoral and pedagogical concern to hold together a community that was struggling with its new task of incorporating recent Gentile converts into its midst.[16] The Matthean

---

[13] Sim, *The Gospel of Matthew and Christian Judaism*, 299.

[14] Sim's claim that the community continued to require all male adherents to be circumcised, regardless of whether their background was Jewish or Gentile, simply cannot be proved. The gospel is silent on the issue of circumcision, and it remains invalid to draw any inference about the practice adopted by the group. It does, however, appear likely that if the group was integrating Gentiles into its meetings this issue must have been considered. Yet, the silence of the gospel on this matter means that there is no way of deciding whether circumcision was practiced or not. (Sim, 'The Gospel of Matthew and the Gentiles' 45). See also Levine, *Social and Ethnic Dimensions*, 178-85.

[15] This view, although perhaps originating in embryonic form with Bornkamm, should be attributed to Barth in a fully developed form, (Barth, 'Matthew's Understanding of the Law', 62-76). This position has been followed by Schweizer, 'Observance of the Law and Charismatic activity in Matthew', 213-30; Sand, 'Die Polemik gegen "Gesetzlosigkeit" im Evangelium nach Matthäus und bei Paulus', 112-25; Cothenet, 'Les prophets chrétiens', 300; Goulder, *Midrash and Lection in Matthew*.

[16] Although not developing the point, Luz sees this tension within the gospel. Framing the question 'Should the Matthean community, after the failure of its Israel mission, now set out on the 'road to the heathens' as many Christian communities had been doing in Syria since the days of Paul?' He answers in the following manner, 'It is highly possible that the feelings and perhaps even the practices of the community differed on this point. At this juncture the author of the Gospel of Matthew offered clear instructions in the name of the exalted Lord: Make all heathen (nations) my disciples (28.19).' Luz, *The Theology of the Gospel of Matthew*, 19-20.

attitude towards the law has shown that the evangelist did not advocate a wholesale rejection of Torah, but, as the antitheses demonstrate, he promoted a higher authority, namely Jesus as the legitimate interpreter and re-definer of Jewish traditions. This approach was aimed both pastorally and pedagogically at those long-term members who felt unease at incorporating Gentile converts into their community. The evangelist seeks to reassure such members of his group, whose heritage was in Judaism, that such a way forward does not abrogate their adherence to the law, but is in actuality the fulfilment of the law through a higher standard of righteousness. As Conzelmann noted,

> Matthew uses a logion from Q (Luke 16.17) about the abiding of the law. He makes this into a statement of principle about the law, righteousness and the way of salvation. Jesus has not come to destroy, but to fulfil, i.e., to assert as valid (in the sense of the 'exposition' that follows). Here Jesus seems to enter into competition with the rabbis: Christian exposition is set against that of the rabbis. In reality, however, Matthew does not think of a quantitatively definable number of regulations in the law which are to be carried out. He is concerned rather with exposition of the law as a whole through the commandment of love.[17]

It is this sense of competition, stemming ultimately from a different authority base that challenges Matthew to present the significance of the law in a fresh way. He asserts its continuity and ongoing validity in the community, thereby attempting to comfort members who are unsure about the position that the group is moving towards. However, this process also entails a creative redefinition, which subsumes the primary role of Torah in Judaism under the authority of the community's foundational figure. Obviously the logical consequence of this is the marginalisation of Torah observance within the group, and ultimately this results in a supersessionary attitude towards the status of the law within the community.

Matthew's programmatic statement on the law (5.17-20) is often employed as a proof text by those who wish to argue that the group still maintained strict Torah observance, and, if they did admit Gentile proselytes, they were required to embrace all the requirements of the law including circumcision.[18] The problem with this interpretation is that, in the antitheses that immediately follow, the Matthean Jesus does not uphold the law according to the contemporary traditional understanding, but modifies, redefines or even overturns its stipulations at a number of points. What then is intended by the apparent affirmation of the law in 5.17-20?

---

[17] Conzelmann, *An Outline of the Theology of the New Testament*, 145-6.

[18] See Saldarini, *Matthew's Christian-Jewish Community*, 157; White, 'Crisis Management and Boundary Maintenance', 242 n. 100; Mohrlang, *Matthew and Paul: A Comparison of Ethical Perspectives*, 44-5.

Hare argues that it 'must be taken as a general statement, not as a requirement of literal observance of all precepts, many of which had long since become dead letters or had been drastically reinterpreted.'[19] While Matthew may not have expressed his understanding of the function of the law in such terms, Hare's assessment presents the implication of what the evangelist says, and this interpretation appears to be supported by those antitheses that entail a significant reinterpretation of Torah.

Similarly, the attitude towards mission is characteristically at odds with traditional Jewish understandings.[20] Not only is mission foreign to Jewish practice, but the call for a specifically Gentile mission goes against Jewish avoidance of contact with Gentiles. The repeated refrain in the last third of the gospel that privileges a second group over a first group, talks of the kingdom being taken away from the traditional occupants (21.43), and, of course, the climactic commission at the end of the gospel projects an inclusive attitude toward Gentile converts. Whether Brown is strictly correct when he states, 'The sending to all nations here at the end revises the restricted sending to the lost sheep of the house of Israel and not to the Gentiles in the middle of the Gospel (10.5-6)'[21], he is at least right to note that the placement of this saying at the end of the gospel gives it a natural prominence. Matthew again locates Jesus on a mountain to instruct the community about the importance of mission. The pedagogical function of the gospel is perhaps most clearly seen when Jesus gives such mountain top orations, which provide the community with a new way forward sanctioned by its own authority figure.

7.3 Concluding Statement

Such creative redefinitions in regard to law and mission are best understood as occurring in a group that had made a recent and decisive break from its synagogue heritage, at the time of the writing of the first gospel. At that point, the animosity between the two group still ran high, at least as it can be gauged through Matthew's gospel. Yet the evangelist does more than engage in bitter polemic. Instead, addressing a newly formed autonomous community, which is struggling to come to terms with its own liminality, the gospel calls for an egalitarian structure (presumably a reaction to the Jewish leadership which was seen as the principal opponent). It also calls for an inclusive attitude toward Gentile converts,

---

[19] Hare, 'How Jewish is the Gospel of Matthew?', 270.

[20] See Goodman, *Mission and Conversion: Proselytizing in the Religious History of the Roman Empire*, for evidence of Jewish non-participation in Gentile mission.

[21] Brown, *An Introduction to the New Testament*, 203.

coupled with an active attempt to incorporate them into the group. Furthermore, there is a reprioritisation of the status of the law, which is now made subservient to Jesus' authoritative pronouncements. Such debates and struggles, as many recent treatments of the first gospel remind us, do suggest a Jewish background. However, the solutions and the vision for the future offered by Matthew do not reflect a group that was still inextricably tied to a Jewish heritage. Having already taken its first steps away from Judaism,[22] Matthew encourages community members to follow this path more actively. He claims that the incorporation of Gentiles into the group is not only the way forward,[23] but that to fail in this task is to fail to take up the direct challenge of the risen Jesus.

---

[22] In a recently published monograph on the role of the crowds in Matthew's gospel, Cousland comes to the same conclusion as this study in regard to the social location of the community. He sees the Matthean community as being outside of the synagogue environment, having been alienated by the Jewish leadership, but still open to winning converts from among the Jewish people. Thus he states, 'Matthew and the leadership of emergent Judaism have undergone an acrimonious divorce ... Thus, to answer the time-honoured question of whether Matthew's situation is *intra-* or *extra-muros*, one would have to reply that it is *extra-muros* but very much focussed on those who are still *intra-muros*.' (Cousland, *The Crowds in the Gospel of Matthew*, 394). Thus, Cousland's conclusions provide strong corroborative evidence for the discussion of the social location of the community argued for in this study. Perhaps the one major point of disagreement is whether Matthew's primary missionary concern is directed towards the Jewish people or the Gentiles. Cousland supports the former alternative whereas this study has advocated the latter position.

[23] This is not to suggest that such a course of action will be easy. As Stanton has noted 'The evangelist's firm commitment to a mission to the Gentiles is well known. But there is a string of other reference to Gentiles and the world in general which is often overlooked.' (Stanton, *Gospel*, 161). These other references reflect concern about Gentile attitudes and in this sense the group conceives of itself as being 'other' from both Judaism and the Gentile world.

Bibliography

Abegg, M.G. '4QMMT C 27, 31 and "Works Righteousness"', *DSD* 6 (1999) 139- 47.

Abogunrin, S.O. 'The Three Variant Accounts of Peter's Call: A Critical and Theological Examination of the Texts', *NTS* 31 (1985) 587-602.

Achtemeier, P.J. *The Quest for Unity in the New Testament Church* (Philadelphia: Fortress Press, 1987).

Alexander, L. *The Preface to Luke's Gospel: Literary Convention and Social Context in Luke 1.1-4 and Acts 1.1*, (SNTSMS 78; Cambridge: CUP, 1993).

Alexander, P.S. 'Jesus and the Golden Rule', in J.H. Charlesworth and L.L. Johns (eds.), *Hillel and Jesus: Comparative Studies of Two Major Religious Leaders* (Philadelphia: Fortress, 1997).

_____ · '"The Parting of the Ways" from the Perspective of Rabbinic Judaism', in J.D.G. Dunn (ed.), *Jews and Christians: The Parting of the Ways A.D. 70-135* (2nd. ed., Grand Rapids, Michigan: Eerdmans, 1999) 1-25.

Allen, W.C. *A Critical and Exegetical Commentary on the Gospel According to St. Matthew*, (ICC; 3rd ed; Edinburgh: T&T Clark, 1912).

Allison, D.C. *The End of the Ages has Come: An Early Interpretation of the Passion and Resurrection of Jesus* (Philadelphia: Fortress, 1985).

_____ · 'The Structure of the Sermon on the Mount', *JBL* 106 (1987) 423-55.

_____ · 'Divorce, Cellibacy and Joseph (Matt 1:18-25 and 19)', *JSNT* 49 (1993) 3-10.

_____ · *The New Moses: A Matthean Typology* (Minneapolis: Fortress, 1993).

Anderson, J.C. *Matthew's Narrative Web* (JSNTSS 91; Sheffield: Sheffield Academic Press, 1994).

Ashton, J. *Understanding the Fourth Gospel* (Oxford: OUP, 1991).

Aune D.E. (ed.), *The Gospel of Matthew in Current Study* (Grand Rapids, Michigan: Eerdmans, 2001).

Bacon, B.W. *Studies in Matthew* (London: Constable, 1930).

Bainbridge, W.S. *The Sociology of Religious Movements* (London: Routledge, 1997).

Balch, D.L. (ed.), *Social History of the Matthean Community: Cross-Disciplinary Approaches* (Minneapolis: Fortress, 1991).

Balch, D.L. 'The Greek Political Topos περὶ νόμων and Matthew 5:17, 19, and 16:19', in David. L. Balch (ed.), *Social History of the Matthean Community: Cross-Disciplinary Approaches* (Minneapolis: Fortress, 1991) 68-84.

Baltensweiler, H. 'Die Ehebuchsklauseln bei Matthäus. Zu Matth. 5,32; 19,9,' *TZ* 15, (1959) 340-56.

Banks, R.J. 'Matthew's Understanding of the Law: Authenticity and interpretation in Matthew 5:17-20', *JBL* 93 (1974) 226-42.

_____ · *Jesus and the Law in the Synoptic Tradition*, (SNTSMS 28; Cambridge: CUP, 1975).

Barclay, J.M.G. *Jews in the Mediterranean Diaspora: From Alexander to Trajan (323 BCE –117 CE)* (Edinburgh: T&T Clark, 1996).

Barrett, C.K. *The Gospel according to Saint John* (London: SPCK, 1955).

Barta, K.A. 'Mission in Matthew: the Second Discourse as Narrative', *SBLSP* (1988) 527-35.

Barth, G. 'Matthew's Understanding of the Law', in G. Bornkamm, G. Barth, and H.J. Held, *Tradition and Interpretation in Matthew*, (trans. Percy Scott, *Überlieferung und Auslegung im Matthäusevangelium*, Neukirken: 1960// London: SCM 1963) 58-164.

Barton, G.A. 'The Meaning of the "Royal Law," Matt. 5:21-48', *JBL* 37 (1918) 54-65.

Barton, J. *Oracles of God: Perceptions of Ancient Prophecy in Israel after the Exile* (London: Darton, Longman and Todd, 1986).

Barton, S.C. *Discipleship and Family Ties in Mark and Matthew* (SNTSMS 80; Cambridge: CUP, 1994).

Bauckham, R. (ed.), *The Gospels for all Christians: Rethinking the Gospel Audiences* (Edinburgh: T&T Clark, 1998).

Bauer, D.R., *The Structure of Matthew's Gospel. A Study in Literary Design* (Bible and Literature Series, 15; Sheffield: Almond Press 1988).

Bauer, D.R. and Powell M.A. *Treasures New and Old* (Atlanta: Scholars, 1996).

Bauer, W. *Orthodoxy and Heresy in Earliest Christianity* (Eng. trans.; London: SCM, 1972).

Bauman, C. *The Sermon on the Mount: The Modern Quest for its Meaning* (Macon, GA: Mercer University Press, 1985).

Baumgarten, A.I. *The Flourishing of Jewish Sects in the Maccabean Era: An Interpretation* (Supplements to the Journal for the Study of Judaism 55; Leiden: Brill, 1997).

Beare, F.W. *The Gospel according to Matthew* (Oxford: Basil Blackwell, 1981).

Beasley-Murray, G.R. *Jesus and the Kingdom of God* (Grand Rapids, Michigan: Eerdmans, 1986).

Beare, F.W. 'The Mission of the Disciples and the Mission Charge. Matthew 10 and Parallels', *JBL* (1970) 1-13.

Beaton, R. review of D.C. Sim, *The Gospel of Matthew and Christian Judaism. The History of the Social Setting of the Matthean Community*, *JTS* vol 51 (2000) 245-7.

Beavis, M.A. *Mark's Audience: The Literary and Social Setting of Mark 4.11-12* (JSNTSup 33; Sheffield: JSOT Press, 1989).

Becker, A.H. and Reed, A.Y. (eds.), *The Ways that Never Parted* (TSAJ 95, Tübingen: Mohr Siebeck, 2003).

Bellinzoni, A.J. *The Two-Source Hypothesis: A Critical Appraisal*, (Macon, Georgia: Mercer Univ. Press).

Berger, K. *Die Amen-Worte Jesu*, BZNW 39, (Berlin: De Gruyter, 1970).

―――― · *Die Gesetzesauslegung Jesu. Teil I: Markus und Parallelen* (WMANT 40; Neukirchen-Vluyn: Neukirchener, 1972).

Best, E. 'Matthew 5, 3', *NTS* 6 (1960-61) 255-58.

―――― .*Following Jesus: Discipleship in the Gospel of Mark* (JSNTSS 4; Sheffield: JSOT Press, 1986).

Betz, H.D. 'Die Markarismen der Bergpredigt (Matthäus 5, 3-12)', *ZTK* 75 (1978) 1-19.

―――― · *Essays on the Sermon on the Mount* (Philadelphia: Fortress, 1985).

―――― · 'The Sermon on the Mount and Q: Some Aspects of the Problem', in J.E. Goehring et al (eds.), *Gospel origins and Christian Beginnings: In Honor of James M. Robinson* (Sonoma, California: Polebridge Press, 1990) 19-34.

―――― · *The Sermon on the Mount (A Commentary on the Sermon on the Mount, including the Sermon on the Plain (Matthew 5:3-7:27) and Luke 6:20-49)* (Minneapolis: Fortress, 1995).

Blenkinsopp, J. 'Interpretation and the Tendency to Sectarianism: An Aspect of Second Temple History', in E.P. Sanders (ed.), *Jewish and Christian Self-Definition*, vol 2 – Aspects of Judaism in the Greco-Roman World (Philadelphia: Fortress, 1981) 1-15.

Bligh, J. *The Sermon on the Mount: A Discussion on Matthew 5-7* (Slough: St Paul Publications, 1975).

Böcher, O. 'Wölfe in Schafspelzen: Zum religionsgeschichtlichen Hintergrund von Mt 7,15', *TZ* 24 (1968) 405-26.

Bockmuehl, M. *Jewish Law in Gentile Churches: Halakah and the Beginning of Christian Public Ethics* (Edinburgh: T&T Clark, 2000).

Boismard, M.-É. *Synopse des quatre évangiles en français* (Tome 2, Commentaire; Paris: Les Éditions du Cerf, 1972).

―――― · 'The Multiple Stage Hypothesis', in *The Interrelations of the Gospels: A Symposium led by M.-É. Boismard – W.R. Farmer – F. Neirynck.* Jerusalem 1984. (BETL 95; Louvain: Louvain University Press and Peeters, 1990).

Booth, R.P. *Jesus and the Laws of Purity: Tradition History and Legal History in Mark 7* (JSNTSS 13; Sheffield: JSOT Press, 1986).

Boring, M.E. *Sayings of the Risen Jesus: Christian Prophecy in the Synoptic Tradition* (SNTSMS 46; Cambridge: CUP, 1982).

Bornkamm, G. 'End-Expectation and Church in Matthew', in G. Bornkamm, G. Barth, and H.J. Held, *Tradition and Interpretation in Matthew* (trans. Percy Scott, *Überlieferung und Auslegung im Matthäusevangelium*, Neukirchen: 1960// London: SCM, 1963) 15-51.

―――― · 'The Stilling of the Storm in Matthew', in G. Bornkamm, G. Barth, and H.J. Held, *Tradition and Interpretation in Matthew*, (trans. Percy Scott,

Überlieferung und Auslegung im Matthäusevangelium, Neukirchen: Kreis Moers, 1960//London: SCM, 1963) 52-7.

――― · Matthäus als Interpret der Herrenworte', *TLZ* 79 (1954) 341-6.

――― · 'Der Auferstandene und der Irdische', in Bultmann Festschrift, *Zeit und Geschichte* (Tübingen: Mohr, 1964) 171-91.

――― · 'The Authority to "Bind" and "Loose" in the Church in Matthew's Gospel: the Problem of Sources in Matthew's Gospel', in D.G. Miller (ed.), *Jesus and Man's Hope* (Pittsburg: Pittsburg Theological Seminary, 1970) 1:37-50.

――― · 'Die Binde- und Lösegewalt in der Kirche des Matthäus', in *Geschichte und Glaube* (Munich: Kaiser, 1971) 37-50.

Brant, J.A. 'Infelicitous Oaths in the Gospel of Matthew', *JSNT* 63 (1996) 1-20.

Brin, G. *Studies in Biblical Law: From the Hebrew Bible to the Dead Sea Scrolls* (JSOTSS 176; Sheffield: Sheffield Academic Press, 1994).

Broer, I. 'Die Antithesen und der Evangelist Matthäus', *BZ* (1975) 50-63.

――― · *Freiheit vom Gesetz und Radikalisierung des Gesetzes* (SBS 98; Stuttgart: Katholisches Bibelwerk, 1980).

Brooks, S.H. *Matthew's Community, the Evidence of His Special Sayings Material*, (JSNTSS 16; Sheffield: JSOT Press, 1987).

Brown, R.E. *The Gospel according to John I-XII* (Anchor Bible 29; New York: Doubleday, 1966).

――― · *The Churches the Apostles Left Behind* (New York: Paulist, 1984).

――― · *The Death of the Messiah* (2 vols.; New York: Doubleday, 1994).

Brown, R.E. and Meier, J.P. *Antioch and Rome* (New York: Paulist Press, 1983).

Brown, S. 'The Two-fold Representation of the Mission in Matthew's Gospel', *ST* 31 (1977) 21-32.

――― · 'The Mission to Israel in Matthew's Central Section Mt 9.35-11.1', *ZNW* 69 (1978) 73-90.

――― · 'The Matthean Apocalypse', *JSNT* 4 (1979) 2-27.

――― · 'The Matthean Community and the Gentile Mission', *NovT* XXII (1980) 193-221.

Bultmann, R. *History of the Synoptic Tradition* (Oxford: Basil Blackwell, 2nd ed. 1963).

Butler, B.C. *The Originality of St Matthew: A Critique of the Two Document Hypothesis* (Cambridge: CUP, 1951).

Byrskog, S. *Jesus the Only Teacher: Didactic Authority and Transmission in Ancient Israel, Ancient Judaism, and the Matthean Community* (CBNTS 24; Stockholm: Almqvist and Wiksell, 1994).

Cargal, T.B. '"His Blood be Upon Us and Upon our Children": A Matthean Double Entendre?', *NTS* 37 (1991) 101-12.

Carlston, C.E. 'Betz on the Sermon on the Mount – a Critique', *CBQ* 59 (1988) 47-57.

Carter, W. *Households and Discipleship: A Study of Matthew 19-20* (JSNTSS 103; Sheffield: Sheffield Academic Press, 1994).

———— · *Matthew: Storyteller, Interpreter, Evangelist* (Peabody, Massachusetts: Hendrickson, 1995).

———— · 'Paying the Tax to Rome as Subversive Praxis: Matthew 17.24-27', *JSNT* 76 (1999) 3-31.

———— · *Matthew and the Margins: A Socio-Political and Religious Reading*, (JSNTSS 204; Sheffield: Sheffield Academic Press, 2000).

Carter, W. and Heil, J.P. *Matthew's Parables, Audience-Orientated Perspectives*, CBQMS 30 (Washington: The Catholic Biblical Association of America, 1998).

Catchpole, D. *The Quest for Q*, (Edinburgh: T&T Clark, 1993).

Chancy, M.A. *The Myth of a Gentile Galilee* (SNTSMS 118; Cambridge: CUP, 2002).

Charlesworth, J.H. *The Beloved Disciple: Whose Witness Validates the Gospel of John?* (Valley Forge, Pennsylvania: Trinity Press International, 1995).

Chester, A. 'The Parting of the Ways: Eschatology and Messianic Hope', in J.D.G. Dunn (ed.), *Jews and Christians: The Parting of the Ways A.D. 70-135* (Grand Rapids, Michigan: Eerdmans, 2nd. ed. 1999) 239-313,

Clark, K.W. 'The Gentile Bias in Matthew', *JBL* 66 (1947) 165-72.

Cohen, S.J.D. *From the Maccabees to the Mishnah* (Library of Early Christianity; Philadelphia: Westminster Press, 1987).

———— · 'Crossing the Boundary and Becoming a Jew', *HTR* 82 (1989) 13-33.

———— · 'Was Judaism in Antiquity a Missionary Religion?', in M. Mor (ed.), *Jewish Assimilation, Acculturation and Accommodation: Past Traditions, Current Issues and Future Prospects* (Lanham, Nebraska: University Press of America, 1992) 14-21.

Collins, J.J. 'A Symbol of Otherness: Circumcision and Salvation in the First Century', in J. Neusner and E.S. Frerichs (eds.), *'To See Ourselves as Others See Us': Christians, Jews and 'Others' in Late Antiquity* (Chico: Scholars Press, 1985), 163-86.

Conzelmann, H. *An Outline of the Theology of the New Testament* (London: SCM, 1969).

Corwin, V., *St Ignatius and Christianity in Antioch* (New Haven: Yale University Press, 1960).

Coser, L. *The Functions of Social Conflict* (New York: Free Press, 1964).

Cothenet, E. 'Les prophètes chrétiennes dans l'Évangile selon saint Matthieu', in M. Didier, *Évangile selon Matthieu: Rédaction et théologie*, (BETL 29; Gembloux: Duculot, 1972), 281-308.

Cousland, J.R.C. *The Crowds in the Gospel of Matthew*, (NovTSup 102; Leiden: Brill, 2002).

Crosby, M.H. *House of Disciples: Church, Economics and Justice in Matthew* (Maryknoll: Orbis, 1988).

Cross, F.M. 'The Development of the Jewish Scripts', in *The Bible and the Ancient Near East* (New York: Doubleday 1966) 170-264.

Cullmann, O. *Peter: Disciple, Apostle Martyr*, trans. F.V. Filson (2nd ed.; Philadelphia: Westminster, 1962).

Dahl, N.A. 'The Passion Narrative in Matthew', in *Jesus in the Memory of the Early Church* (Minneapolis: Augsburg, 1976).

Daniel, C. '"Faux prophètes": Surnom des Esséniens dans le sermon sur le montagne', *RevQ* 7 (1969) 45-79.

Daniélou, J. *The Theology of Jewish Christianity* (London: Darton, Longman & Todd, 1964).

Darr, J.A. *On Character Building: The Reader and the Rhetoric of Characterization in Luke-Acts* (Louisville: Westminster/John Knox Press, 1992).

Daube, D. *The New Testament and Rabbinic Judaism*, (London: Athlone, 1956).

Davies, W.D. *Torah in the Messianic Age and/or the Age to Come* (JBLMS 7; Philadelphia: SBL 1952).

———— · 'Matthew 5:17, 18' in *Christian Origins and Judaism* (London: Darton, Longman and Todd, 1962), 31-66.

———— · *The Setting of the Sermon on the Mount* (Cambridge: CUP, 1966).

Davies, W.D. and Allison, D.C. *A Critical and Exegetical Commentary on the Gospel according to Saint Matthew* (3 vols; ICC; Edinburgh: T&T Clark, 1988, 1991, 1997).

Davison, J.E. '*Anomia* and the Question of an Antinomian Polemic in Matthew', *JBL* 104 (1985) 617-35.

Deutsch, C. *Hidden Wisdom and the Easy Yoke: Wisdom, Torah and Discipleship in Matthew 11.25-30* (JSNTSS 18; Sheffield: JSOT Press, 1987).

Dewey, J. *Markan Public Debate: Literary Technique, Concentric Structure, and Theology in Mark 2:1-3:6*, SBLDS 48, (Chico: Scholars Press, 1980).

Dobbeler, A. von 'Die Restitution Israels und die Bekehrung der Heiden: Das Verhältnis von Mt 10,5b.6 und Mt 28,18-20 unter dem Aspekt der Komplementarität. Erwägungen zum Standort des Matthäusevangeliums', *ZNW* 91 (2000) 18-44.

Dodd, C.H. 'The Beatitudes: A Form-critical Study', in *More New Testament Studies* (Grand Rapids, Michigan: Eerdmans, 1968).

Donaldson, T.L. *Jesus on the Mountain: A Study in Matthean Theology* (JSNTSS 8; Sheffield: JSOT Press, 1985).

———— · 'The Law That Hangs (Matt 22:40): Rabbinic Formulation and Matthean Social World', in D.J. Lull (ed.), *Society for Biblical Literature 1990 Seminar Papers* (Atlanta: Scholars Press, 1990) 14-33.

Duling, D.C. 'The Matthean Brotherhood and Marginal Scribal Leadership' in P.F. Esler (ed.), *Modelling Early Christianity: Social-scientific studies of the New Testament in its Context* (London: Routledge, 1995) 159-82.

Dungan, D.L. *A History of the Synoptic Problem: The Canon, the Text, the Composition, and the Interpretation of the Gospels*, (ABRL; New York: Doubleday, 1999).

Dunn, J.D.G. 'The Formal and Theological Coherence of Romans', in K.P. Donfried (ed.), *The Romans Debate* (revised and expanded ed.; Peabody, Mass.: Hendrickson, 1991) 245-250.

———— · '4QMMT and Galatians,' *NTS* 43 (1997) 147-53.

———— · *The Theology of the Apostle Paul*, (Edinburgh: T&T Clark, 1998).

———— · 'The Question of Anti-Semitism in New Testament Writings of the Period', in in J.D.G. Dunn (ed.), *Jews and Christians: The Parting of the Ways A.D. 70-135* (2nd. ed., Grand Rapids, Michigan: Eerdmans, 1999) 177-211.

Dupont, J. *Les béatitudes: Le problème litteraire. Les deux version du Sermon sur la Montangne et des Beatitudes* (2nd ed. Bruges: Abbaye de Saint-André, 1958).

Edwards, R.A. *The Sign of Jonah in the Theology of the Evangelists and Q*, SBT second series 18 (London: SCM, 1971).

Elam, Y. 'Some Remarks on 4QMMT and the Rabbinic Tradition: Or , When is a Parallel not a Parallel?' in John Kampen and Moshe J. Berstein (eds.), *4QMMT*, SBL Symposium Series 2 (Atlanta, Georgia: Scholars Press, 1996) 99-128.

Elliott, J.H. *Social-Scientific Criticism of the New Testament. An Introduction.* (London: SPCK, 1995). A British edition of *What is Social-Scientific Criticism?* (Minneapolis: Fortress, 1993).

Eshel, H. '4QMMT and the History of the Hasmonean Period', in John Kampen and Moshe J. Berstein (eds.), *4QMMT*, SBL Symposium Series 2 (Atlanta, Georgia: Scholars Press, 1996) 53-65.

Esler, P.F. *Community and Gospel in Luke-Acts: The Social and Political Motivations of Lucan Theology*, (SNTSMS 57; Cambridge: CUP, 1987).

———— · (ed.), *Modelling Early Christianity: Social-scientific studies of the New Testament in its Context* (London: Routledge, 1995).

Farrer, A. 'On Dispensing with Q', (in D. E. Nineham, ed., *Studies in the Gospels: Essays in Memory of R. H. Lightfoot* (Oxford: Blackwell, 1955), 55-88.

Fiedler, M.J. 'Der Begriff δικαιοσύνη im Matthäus-Evangelium, auf seine Grundlagen untersucht', vol 1, text; vol 2, notes (Diss. theol.; Martin-Luther-Universität, Halle-Wittenberg, 1957).

Fitzmyer, J.A. *The Gospel According to Luke I-IX* (Anchor Bible 28; New York: Doubleday, 1981).

———— · *To Advance the Gospel: New Testament Studies* (2nd ed., The Biblical Resource Series; Grand Rapids, Michigan: Eerdmans, 1994).

Filson, F.V. *The Gospel according to Saint Matthew*, BNTC, (London: A&C Black, 1977).

Fish, S. *Is There a Text in this Class? The Authority of Interpretative Communities* (Cambridge, MA: Harvard University Press, 1980).

Foster P. 'A Tale of Two Sons: But Which One Did the Far, Far Better Thing? A Study of Matt 21:28-32', *NTS* 47 (2001) 26-37.

———— · 'In Defence of the Study of Q', *ExpTim* 113 (2002) 295-300.

———— · 'Why Did Matthew Get the *Shema* Wrong? A Study of Matthew 22:37' *JBL* 122 (2003) 309-333.

———— · 'Is it Possible to Dispense with Q?' *NovT* 45 (2003) 313-337.

France, R.T. *Matthew – Evangelist and Teacher* (Exeter: Paternoster, 1989).

Frankemölle, H. *Jahwebund und Kirche Christi* (Münster: Aschendorff, 1974).

Freyne, S. *Galilee from Alexander the Great to Hadrian 323BCE to 135CE: A Study of Second Temple Judaism* (Edinburgh: T&T Clark, 1980).

_____ · 'Vilifying the Other and Defining the Self: Matthew's and John's Anti-Jewish Polemic in Focus', in J. Neusner and E.S. Frerichs (eds.), *'To See Ourselves as Others See Us': Christians, Jews and 'Others' in Late Antiquity* (Chico: Scholars Press, 1985), 117-44.

Fridrichsen, A. 'Exegetisches zum Neuen Testament', *SO* 13 (1934) 38-46.

Funk, R.W., Hoover, R.W., et al. *The Five Gospels: The Search for the Authentic Words of Jesus* (New York: Polebridge Press, 1993).

Gager, J.G. *Community and Kingdom: The Social World of Early Christians* (Englewood Cliffs: Prentiss, 1983).

Garland, D.E. *The Intention of Matthew 23* (NovT Supp 52; Leiden: Brill, 1979).

Goodacre, M. *The Synoptic Problem: A Way Through the Maze* (London: Sheffield Academic Press/Continuum, 2001).

_____ · *The Case Against Q: Studies in Markan Priority and the Synoptic Tradition* (Harrisburg, Pennsylvania: Trinity Press International, 2002).

Goodman, M.D. 'Nerva, the *Fiscus Judaicus* and Jewish Identity', *JRS* 79 (1989) 40-44.

_____ · *Mission and Conversion: Proselytizing in the Religious History of the Roman Empire* (Oxford: Claredon Press, 1994).

Goulder, M.D. *Midrash and Lection in Matthew's Gospel* (London: SPCK, 1974).

_____ · *Luke – A New Paradigm* (2 vols., JSNTSS 20; Sheffield: Sheffield Academic Press, 1989).

_____ · *A Tale of Two Missions* (London: SCM Press, 1994).

_____ · 'Is Q a Juggernaut?', *JBL* 115 (1996) 667-81.

Gourgues, M. 'Sur l'articulation des béatitudes matthéennes (Mt 5:3-12): une proposition', *NTS* 44 (1998) 340-356.

Green, H. B. *Matthew, Poet of the Beatitudes*, (JSNTSS 203; Sheffield: Sheffield Academic Press, 2001).

Gregory, A. *The Reception of Luke and Acts in the Period before Irenaeus* (II/169, Tübingen: Mohr Siebeck, 2003).

Guelich, R.A. 'The Antitheses of Matthew V. 21-48: Tradition and/or Redaction?' *NTS* 22 (1976) 444-57.

_____ · *The Sermon on the Mount: A Foundation for Understanding* (Waco, Texas: Word, 1982).

_____ · *Mark 1-8:26* (WBC 34A; Dallas, Texas: Word, 1989).

Gundry, R.H. *The Use of the Old Testament in St Matthew's Gospel* (NovTSupp 18; Leiden: Brill, 1967).

_____ · 'A Responsive Evaluation of the Social History of the Matthean Community in Roman Syria', in David. L. Balch (ed.), *Social History of the Matthean Community: Cross-Disciplinary Approaches* (Minneapolis: Fortress, 1991) 62-7.

_____ · *Matthew – A Commentary on His Handbook for a Mixed Church under Persecution* (Grand Rapids, Michigan: Eerdmans, 2nd ed. 1994).

_____ · 'In Defence of the Church in Matthew as a Corpus Mixtum', *ZNW* 91 (2000) 153-165.

Hagner, D.A. 'The *Sitz im Leben* of the Gospel of Matthew', in K.H. Richards (ed.), *Society for Biblical Literature 1985 Seminar Papers* (Atlanta, Georgia: Scholars Press, 1990) 243-69.

_____ · *Matthew* (2 vols; WBC 33A and 33B; Dallas, Texas: Word, 1993, 1995).

Hahn, F. *Mission in the New Testament*, trans. F. Clarke from *Das Verständnis der Mission im neuen Testament* (Wissenschaftliche Monographien zum Alten und Neuen Testament 13, Neukirchener Verlag, Neukirchen-Vluyn, 1963//London: SCM, 1965).

_____ · *The Titles of Jesus in Christology: Their History in early Christianity*, trans. H. Knight and G. Ogg (New York: World, 1969).

_____ · 'Mt 5,17 – Anmerkungen zum Erfüllungsgedanken bei Matthäus', in *Die Mitte des Neuen Testaments*, FS E. Schweizer, U. Luz and H. Weder (eds.), (Göttingen: Vandenhoeck & Ruprecht, 1983) 42-54.

Hamerton-Kelly, R.G. 'Attitudes to the Law in Matthew's Gospel: A Discussion of Matthew 5, 18', *BR* 17 (1972) 19-32.

Hann, R.R. 'Judaism and Christianity in Antioch: Charisma and Conflict in the First Century', *JRH* 14 (1987) 341-60.

Hare, D.R.A. *The Theme of Jewish Persecution of Christians in the Gospel according to St Matthew,* (SNTSMS 6; Cambridge: CUP, 1967).

_____ · 'How Jewish is the Gospel of Matthew?', *CBQ* 62 (2000) 264-77.

Hare, D.R.A. and D.J. Harrington, '"Make Disciples of all the Gentiles" (Mt 28.19)', *CBQ* 37 (1975) 359-69.

Harrington, D.J. *The Gospel of Matthew* (Sacra Pagina, vol 1; Collegeville: Liturgical Press, 1991).

Head, P.M. *Christology and the Synoptic Problem: An Argument for Markan Priority* (SNTSMS 94; Cambridge: CUP, 1997).

Hengel, M. *The Four Gospels and the One Gospel of Jesus Christ*, (London: SCM, 2000).

Hill, D. 'False Prophets and Charismatics: Structure and Interpretation in Matthew 7,15-23', *Bib* 57 (1976) 327-48.

_____ · *The Gospel of Matthew* (NCBC; London: Marshall, Morgan & Scott, 1972).

_____ · 'Son and Servant: An Essay on Matthean Christology', *JSNT* 6 (1980), 2-16.

Hoet, R. ' *"Omnes Autem vos Fratres estis"* ': Etude du concept ecclésiologique des "frères" selon Mt 23,8-12' (Rome: Università Gregoriana Editrice, 1982).

Hooker, M.D. *The Gospel according to St Mark* (BNTC, London: A&C Black, 1991).

Horbury, W. 'The benediction of the *Minim* and the Early Jewish-Christian Controversy', *JTS* (1982) 19-61.

_____ · *Jews and Christians in Contact and Controversy* (Edinburgh: T&T Clark, 1998).

Horsley, G.H.R. *New Documents Illustrating early Christianity: a review of the Greek inscriptions and papyri published in 1976*, vol 1 (of a series of now 9 vols) (North Ryde, N.S.W., Australia: Ancient History Documentary Research Centre, Macquarie University, 1981).

Hübner, H. *Das Gesetz in der synoptischen Tradition* (Witten: Luther, 1973).

Hübner, R.M. 'Thesen zur Echtheit und Datierung der sieben Briefe des Ignatius von Antiochien' *ZAC* 1 (1997) 44-72.

Hummel, R. *Die Auseinandersetzung zwischen Kirche und Judentum im Matthäusevangelium* (Munich: Kaiser, 1966).

Iser, W. *The Act of Reading*, (Baltimore, Maryland: John Hopkins University Press, 1978).

Jeremias, J. *Jesus' Promise to the Nations*, (SBT 24; London: SCM, 1958).

—————— · *The Sermon on the Mount* (Philadelphia: FBBS, 1963).

—————— · *New Testament Theology* (London, SCM, 1971).

Johnson, M.D. *The Purpose of Biblical Genealogies with Special Reference to the Setting of the Genealogies of Jesus* (SNTSMS 8; Cambridge: CUP, 1969).

—————— · 'Reflections on a Wisdom Approach to Matthew's Christology', *CBQ* 36 (1974) 44-64.

Jülicher, A. *Die Gleichnisreden Jesu*, (2nd.rev. ed.; Tübingen: Mohr, 1910).

Katz, S. 'Issues in the Separation of Judaism and Christianity after 70 C.E.: A Reconsideration', *JBL* 103 (1984) 49-75.

Keener, C.S. *A Commentary on the Gospel of Matthew* (Grand Rapids, Michigan: Eerdmans, 1999).

Kennard, J. 'The place of origin of Matthew's Gospel', *ATR* 31 (1949) 243-6.

Kiilunen, J. *Die Vollmacht im Widerstreit: Untersuchungen zum Werdegang von Mk 2,1-3,6* (Helsinki: Suomalainen Tiedeakatemia, 1985).

Kilpatrick, G. *The Origins of the Gospel According to St. Matthew* (Oxford: Claredon Press, 1946).

Kimelman, R. '*Birkath-Ha-Minim* and the Lack of Evidence for an Anti-Christian Jewish Prayer in Late Antiquity', in E.P. Sanders (ed.), *Jewish and Christian Self-Definition*, vol 2 – Aspects of Judaism in the Greco-Roman World (Philadelphia: Fortress, 1981) 226-44.

Kingsbury, J.D. *Matthew: Structure, Christology, Kingdom* (Philadelphia: Fortress Press, 1976).

—————— · 'The Figure of Peter in Matthew's Gospel as a Theological Problem', *JBL* 98 (1979) 67-83.

—————— · 'The Figure of Jesus in Matthew's Gospel: A Literary-Critical Probe', *JSNT* 21 (1984) 3-36.

—————— · 'The Developing Conflict between Jesus and the Jewish Leaders in Matthew's Gospel: a literary-critical study', *CBQ* 49 (1987) 57-83.

—————— · *Matthew as Story* (Philadelphia: Fortress Press, 2nd ed. 1988).

_____ · 'The Rhetoric of Comprehension in the Gospel of Matthew', *NTS* 41 (1995) 358-77.

Kirk, A. 'Crossing the Boundary: Liminality and Transformative Wisdom in Q', *NTS* 45 (1999) 1-18.

Kissinger, W.S. *The Sermon on the Mount: A History of Interpretation and Bibliography* (Metuchen, New Jersey: Scarecrow & ATLA, 1975).

Kloppenborg, J.S. *The Formation of Q: Trajectories in Ancient Wisdom Collections* (Philadelphia: Fortress, 1987).

Kloppenborg Verbin, J.S. *Excavating Q: The History and Setting of the Sayings Gospel* (Edinburgh: T&T Clark, 2000).

Klostermann, E. *Das Matthäusevangelium* (2nd ed, HNT; Tübingin: Mohr, 1927).

Kodjak, A. *A Structural Analysis of the Sermon on the Mount* (New York: de Gruyter, 1981).

Köhler, K. 'Zu Mt 5,22', *ZNW* 19 (1920) 91-95.

Lambrecht, J. *The Sermon on the Mount – Proclamation and Exhortation* (Wilmington, Delaware: Michael Glazier, 1985).

Lapide, P. *The Sermon on the Mount: Utopia or program for Action?* (trans. A. Swidler; Maryknoll, New York: Orbis 1986).

LaVerdiere E.A. and Thompson, W.G. 'New Testament Communities in Transition: A Study of Matthew and Luke', *TS* 37 (1976) 567-97

Lawrence, L.J. *An Ethnography of the Gospel of Matthew* (WUNT II/165, Tübingen: Mohr Siebeck, 2003).

Légasse, S. 'Les faux prophètes: Matthieu 7,15-20', *EF* 18 (1968) 205-18.

Lemcio, E.E. *The Past of Jesus in the Gospels* (SNTSMS 68; Cambridge: CUP, 1991).

Levine, A.-J. *The Social and Ethnic Dimensions of Matthean Salvation History: 'Go Nowhere Among the Gentiles ...' (Matt 10.5b)* (SBEC 14; Lewiston: Edwin Mellen, 1988).

Levison, J.R. 'A Better Righteousness: The Character and Purpose of Matthew 5.21-48', *Studia Biblica et Theologica* 12 (1982) 171-94.

Levison, J.R. 'Responsible Initiative in Matthew 5.21-48', ExpTim 98 (1987) 231-34.

Lieu, J. *Image and Reality: The Jews in the World of the Christians in the Second Century* (Edinburgh: T&T Clark, 1996).

Ljungman, H. *Das Gesetz erfüllen: Matth. 5,17ff. und 3,15 untersucht* (LUÅ n.s. 50.6; Lund: Gleerup, 1954).

Loader, W.R.G. 'Challenged at the Boundaries: A Conservative Jesus in Mark's Tradition', *JSNT* 63 (1996) 45-61.

_____ · *Jesus' Attitude Towards the Law: A Study of the Gospels* (WUNT II/97, Tübingen: Mohr Siebeck, 1997).

Lohmeyer, E. *Das Evangelium des Matthäus /nachgelassene Ausarbeitungen und Entwürfe zur Übersetzung und Erklärung von Ernst Lohmeyer; für den Druck erarbeitet und hrsg. von Werner Schmauch* (Kritisch-exegetischer Kommentar über das Neue Testament; Göttingen: Vandenhoeck & Ruprecht, 1956).

Luomanen, P. *Entering the Kingdom of Heaven : A Study on the Structure of Matthew's View of Salvation* (WUNT II/101, Tübingen : Mohr Siebeck, 1998).

Luz, U. 'Die Erfüllung des Gesetz bei Matthäus', *ZTK* 75 (1978) 398-435.

——— · *Matthew 1-7* (Continental Commentary; Minneapolis: Fortress, 1989).

——— · 'Der Antijudaismus in Matthäusevangelium als historisches und theologisches Problem: Ein Skizze', *EvT* 53 (1993) 310-27.

——— · *The Theology of the Gospel of Matthew* (Cambridge: CUP, 1995).

——— · 'The Disciples in the Gospel according to Matthew' in G.N. Stanton (ed.), *The Interpretation of Matthew* (SNTI; Edinburgh: T&T Clark, 2nd ed. 1995).

——— · *Matthew 8-20* (Minneapolis: Fortress, 2001).

Maddox, R., *The Purpose of Luke-Acts* (SNTW; Edinburgh: T&T Clark, 1982).

Malbon, E.S. 'Texts and Contexts: Interpreting the Disciples in Mark', Semeia 62 (1993), 81-102.

Malina, B.J. and Neyrey J.H. *Calling Jesus Names: the Social Value of Labels in Matthew* (Sonoma, California: Polebridge, 1988).

Manson, T.W. *The Sayings of Jesus* (London: SCM, 1937).

Marshall, I.H. *The Gospel of Luke: A Commentary on the Greek Text* (Exeter: Paternoster, 1978).

Martyn, J.L., *History and Theology in the Fourth Gospel* (rev. ed. Nashville: Abingdon, 1979).

——— · 'A Law-Observant Mission to Gentiles: The Background of Galatians', *SJT* 38 (1986) 307-24.

——— · *Galatians* (Anchor Bible 33A; New York: Doubleday, 1997).

Marxsen, W. *Mark the Evangelist: Studies on the Redaction History of the Gospel*, trans. J. Boyce *et al.* (Nashville: Abingdon, 1969).

Matera, F.J. 'The Ethics of the Kingdom in the Gospel of Matthew', *Listening* 24 (1989) 241-50.

McArthur, H.K. *Understanding the Sermon on the Mount* (New York: Harper, 1960).

McConnell, R. *Law and Prophecy in Matthew's Gospel*, (Basel: Reinhardt, 1969).

McEleney, N.J. 'Conversion, Circumcision and the Law', *NTS* 20 (1974) 319-41.

McNeile, A.H. *The Gospel according to St. Matthew* (London: Macmillan, 1915).

Meeks, W.A. *The First Urban Christians: The Social World of the Apostle Paul* (New Haven: Yale University Press, 1983).

Meier, J.P. 'Salvation History in Matthew: In Search of a starting Point', *CBQ* 37 (1975) 203-15.

——— · *Law and History in Matthew's Gospel: A Redactional Study of Mt 5:17-48*, Analecta Biblica 71 (Rome: Biblical Institute Press, 1976).

——— · 'Nations or Gentiles in Matt 28:19', *CBQ* 39 (1977) 94-102.

——— · *The Vision of Matthew* (New York: Paulist, 1980).

——— · *Matthew* (Wilmington: Glazier, 1980).

——— · 'John the Baptist in Matthew's Gospel', *JBL* 99 (1980) 383-405.

_____ · *A Marginal Jew: Rethinking the Historical Jesus*, vol 2: Mentor, Message and Miracles (ABRL; New York: Doubleday, 1994).

Mendels, D. *The Rise and Fall of Jewish Nationalism: Jewish and Christian Ethnicity in Ancient Palestine* (Grand Rapids, Michigan: Eerdmans, 1992).

Menninger, R.E. *Israel and the Church in the Gospel of Matthew* (New York: Lang, 1994).

Merx, A. *Das Evangelium Matthäus: Die vier kanonischen Evangelien nach ihrem ältesten bekannten*, Text (ii/1; Berlin: Reimer, 1902).

Metzger, B.M. *A Textual Commentary on the Greek New Testament* (2nd ed.; New York/Stuttgart: UBS/Deutsche Bibelgesellschaft, 1994).

Michel, O. 'The Conclusion of Matthew's Gospel: A Contribution to the History of the Easter Message' in G. Stanton (ed.), *The Interpretation of Matthew* (2nd ed.; Edinburgh: T&T Clark, 1995) 39-51.

Minear, P.S. *Matthew: The Teacher's Gospel* (London: Darton, Longmann & Todd, 1982).

Mohrlang, R. *Matthew and Paul: A Comparison of Ethical Perspectives* (SNTSMS 48; Cambridge: CUP, 1984).

Montefiore, H. 'Jesus and the Temple Tax', *NTS* 10 (1963-64) 60-71.

Moo, D.J. 'Jesus and the Authority of the Mosaic Law', *JSNT* 20 (1984) 3-49.

Moore, G.F. *Judaism in the First Centuries of the Christian Era*, 3 vols. (Cambridge: Harvard University Press, 1927-30).

Moses, A.D.A. *Matthew's Transfiguration Story and Jewish Christian Controversy*, (JSNTSS 122; Sheffield: Sheffield Academic Press, 1996).

Moule, C.D.F. 'St. Matthew's Gospel: Some Neglected Features', in *Studia Evangelica II* (TU 87; Berlin: Akademie-Verlag, 1964).

_____ · 'Fulfilment-Words in the New Testament', *NTS* 14 (1967-68) 293-320.

Müller, M. 'The Theological Interpretation of the Figure of Jesus in the Gospel of Matthew: Some Principal Features in Matthean Christology', *NTS* 44, (1999) 157-73.

Nau, A.J. *Peter in Matthew: Discipleship, Diplomacy and Dispraise* (GNS 36; Collegeville, Minn.: Liturgical Press, 1992).

Neusner, J. 'The Formation of Rabbinic Judaism: Yavneh from 70-100', in H. Temporini and W. Haase (eds.), *Aufstieg und Niedergang der Römischen Welt: Geschichte und Kultur Roms im Spiegel der Neueren Forschung* (II. 19.2, Berlin/New York: Walter de Gruyter, 1979) 3-42.

_____ · *The Classics of Judaism* (Louisville: Westminster John Knox Press, 1995).

_____ · 'Was Rabbinic Judaism Really "Ethnic"?', *CBQ* 57 (1995) 281-305.

Newport, K.G.C. *The Sources and Sitz im Leben of Matthew 23* (JSNTSS 117; Sheffield: Sheffield Academic Press, 1995).

Nissen, J. 'Community and Ethics in the Gospel of John', in Johannes Nissen and Sigred Pedersen (eds.), *New Readings in John: Literary and Theological Perspectives,*

Essays from the Scandinavian Conference on the Fourth Gospel - rhus 1997 (JSNTSS 182; Sheffield: Sheffield Academic Press, 1999).

Nolland, J. *Luke*, (3 vols, WBC 35A, 35B and 35C; Dallas: Word, 1989, 1993 and 1993).

Orton, D. *The Understanding Scribe: Matthew and the Apocalyptic Ideal* (JSNTSS 25; Sheffield: JSOT Press, 1989).

Overman, J.A. 'The God-Fearers: Some Neglected Features', *JSNT* 32 (1988) 17-26.

—————— · *Matthew's Gospel and Formative Judaism: The Social World of the Matthean Community* (Minneapolis: Fortress, 1990).

—————— · *Church and Community in Crisis*: *The Gospel according to Matthew* (Valley Forge, Pennsylvania: Trinity Press International, 1996).

Piper, J. *'Love Your Enemies': Jesus' Love Command in the Synoptic Gospels and the Early Christian Paraenesis* (SNTSMS 38; Cambridge: CUP, 1979).

Porkorný, P. 'From a Puppy to the Child: Problems of Contemporary Biblical Exegesis Demonstrated from Mark 7.24-30/Matt 15.21-8' *NTS* 41 (1995) 321-37.

Porter, S.E. 'Literary Approaches to the New Testament: From Formalism to Deconstruction and Back', in Stanley E. Porter and David Tombs (eds.), *Approaches to New Testament Study* (JSNTSS 120. Sheffield: Sheffield Academic Press, 1995) 77-128.

Powell, J.E. *The Evolution of the Gospel* (New Haven: Yale, 1994).

Powell, M.A. *God with Us: A Pastoral Theology of Matthew's Gospel* (Minneapolis: Augsberg/Fortress, 1995).

Przybylski, B. *Righteousness in Matthew and his World of Thought*, (SNTSMS 41; Cambridge: CUP, 1980).

—————— · 'The Setting of Matthew's Anti-Judaism', in P. Richardson and O. Granskou (eds.), *Anti-Judaism in Early Christianity*, vol. I (Waterloo: Wilfrid Laurier, 1988) 181-200.

Qimron, E. 'Miqsat Ma'ase Ha-Torah', in D.N. Freedman (ed.), *Anchor Bible Dictionary* (vol 4; New York: Doubleday, 1992).

Qimron, E. and Strugnell, J. (eds.), *Discoveries in the Judaean Desert X, Qumran Cave 4, V, Miqsat Ma'ase Ha-Torah* (Oxford: Claredon Press, 1994).

Rajak, T. 'The Jewish Community and its Boundaries', in J. Lieu, J. North and T. Rajak (eds.), *The Jews among Pagans and Christians* (London: Routledge, 1992) 9- 28.

Repschinski, B. *The Controversy Stories in the Gospel of Matthew. Their Redaction, Form and Relevence for the Relationship Between the Matthean Community and Formative Judaism* (FRLANT 189; Göttingen: Vandenhoeck & Ruprecht, 2000).

Riches, J.K. *Conflicting Mythologies: Identity Formation in the Gospels of Mark and Matthew* (Edinburgh: T&T Clark, 2000).

Riegel, S.K. 'Jewish Christianity: Definitions and Terminology', *NTS* 24 (1978) 410-15.

Riesenfeld, H. *The Gospel Tradition and Its Beginnings* (London: Mowbray, 1961).

Rivkin, E. *A Hidden Revolution* (Nashville: Abingdon, 1987).

—————— · 'Scribes, Pharisees, Lawyers and Hypocrites: A Study in Synonymity', *HUCA* 49 (1978) 135-42.

Robinson, B.P. 'Peter and his Successors: Tradition and Redaction in Matthew 16.17-19', *JSNT* 21 (1984) 85-104.

Robinson, J.A.T. *Jesus and His Coming* (2nd. ed.; Philadelphia: Westminster, 1979).

Rutgers, L.V. *The Jews in Late Ancient Rome: Evidence of Cultural Interaction in the Roman Diaspora* (Leiden: Brill, 1995)

Saldarini, A.J., *Pharisees, Scribes and Sadducees in Palestinian Society* (Edinburgh: T&T Clark, 1988).

———— · 'The Gospel of Matthew and Jewish-Christian Conflict', in D.L. Balch (ed.), *Social History of the Matthean Community: Cross-Disciplinary Approaches* (Minneapolis: Fortress Press, 1991) 37-61.

———— · 'Delegitimation of Leaders in Matthew 23', *CBQ* 54 (1992) 659-80.

———— · *Matthew's Christian-Jewish Community* (Chicago: University of Chicago Press, 1994).

Sand, A. *Das Gesetz und die Propheten* (Regensburg: F. Pustet, 1974).

Sanders, E.P. *The Tendencies of the Synoptic Tradition* (SNTSMS 9; Cambridge: CUP, 1969).

———— · *Paul and Palestinian Judaism* (London: SCM, 1977).

———— · *Jesus and Judaism* (London: SCM Press, 1985).

Sanders E.P. and Davies, M. *Studying the Synoptic Gospels* (London: SCM Press, 1989).

Schiffman, L.H. 'At the Crossroads: Tannaitic Perspectives on the Jewish-Christian Schism', in E.P. Sanders (ed.), *Jewish and Christian Self-Definition*, vol 2 – Aspects of Judaism in the Greco-Roman World (Philadelphia: Fortress, 1981) 115-56.

———— · 'The *Temple Scroll* and the Nature of its Law: The Status of the Question', in E. Ulrich & J. VanderKam (eds.), *The Community of the Renewed Covenant, The Notre Dame Symposium on the Dead Sea Scrolls* (Notre Dame, Indiana: University of Notre Dame Press, 1993).

———— · *Reclaiming the Dead Sea Scrolls* (ABRL, New York: Doubleday, 1994).

Schlatter, A. *Die Kirche des Matthäus* (BFCT 33/1; Gütersloh: Bertelsmann, 1929).

Schniewind, J. *Das Evangelium nach Matthäus* (Göttingen: Vandenhoeck & Ruprecht, 1962).

Schoedel, W.R. 'Ignatius and the Reception of Matthew in Antioch', in D.L. Balch (ed.), *Social History of the Matthean Community* (Minneapolis: Fortress, 1991) 129-177.

Schotroff, L. 'Non-Violence and the Love of One's Enemies', in *Essays on the Love Commandment*, trans. Reginald H. & Ilse Fuller (Philadelphia: Fortress 1978).

Schulz, S. *Die Stunde der Botschaft: Einführung in die Theologie der vier Evangelisten* (Hamburg: Furche, 1967).

———— · *Q – Die Spruchquelle der Evangelisten* (Zürich: Theologischer Verlag, 1971).

Schweizer, E. 'Matthäus 5,17-20: Anmerkungen zum Gesetzverständnis des Matthäus', *Neotestamentica* (Zurich: Zwingli, 1963) 399-406.

_____ · 'Observance of the Law and Charismatic Activity in Matthew', *NTS* 16 (1969-70) 213-30.

_____ · *Matthäus und seine Gemeinde* (SBS 71; Stuttgart: Katholisches Bibelwerk, 1974).

Scott, B.B. *Hear Then the Parable: A Commentary on the Parables of Jesus* (Minneapolis: Fortress, 1989).

Scroggs, R. 'The Earliest Christian Communities as Sectarian Movement', in J. Neusener (ed.), *Christianity, Judaism and Other Greco-Roman Cults: Studies for Morton Smith at Sixty* (SJLA 12/2; Leiden: Brill, 1975) 1-25.

Segal, A. F. 'Matthew's Jewish Voice', in D.L. Balch (ed.), *Social History of the Matthean Community: Cross-Disciplinary Approaches* (Minneapolis: Fortress, 1991) 3-37.

Seitz, O. 'Love Your Enemies', *NTS* 16 (1969/70) 39-54.

Senior, D. 'Between Two Worlds: Gentile and Jewish Christians in Matthew's Gospel', *CBQ* 61, (1999) 1-23.

Shellard, B. *New Light on Luke: Its Purpose, Sources and Literary Context*, (JSNTSS 215; London: Sheffield Academic Press/Continuum, 2002).

Sherif, M. *Group Conflict and Cooperation: Their Social Psychology* (London: Routledge, 1966).

Shiner, W.T. *Follow Me! Disciples in Markan Rhetoric* (SBLDS 145; Atlanta, Georgia: Scholars Press, 1995).

Sigal, P. *The Halakah of Jesus of Nazareth according to the Gospel of Matthew* (Lanham, Md.: University Press of America, 1986).

Sim, D.C. 'The Meaning of παλιγγενεσία in Matthew 19:28', *JSNT* 50 (1993) 3-12.

_____ · 'The Gospel of Matthew and the Gentiles', *JSNT* 57 (1995) 19-48.

_____ · *Apocalyptic Eschatology in the Gospel of Matthew*, (SNTSMS 88; Cambridge: CUP, 1996).

_____ · *The Gospel of Matthew and Christian Judaism: The History and Social Setting of the Matthean Community* (Edinburgh: T&T Clark, 1999).

_____ · 'The Gospels for All Christians? A Response to Richard Bauckham', *JSNT* 84 (2002) 3-27.

Smalley, S.S. 'Redaction Criticism', in I.H. Marshall (ed.), *New Testament Interpretation: Essays in Principles and Methods* (Exeter: Paternoster, 1977) 181-195.

Smith, D.M. *Johannine Christianity: Essays on its Setting, Sources and Theology* (Columbia: University of South Carolina Press, 1984).

Smith, I. 'A Rational Choice Model of the Book of Revelation', *JSNT* 85 (2002) 97-116.

Snodgrass, K. 'Matthew and the Law', *SBLSP* (1988) 536-54.

Soares-Prabhu, G.M. *The Formula Quotations in the Infancy Narrative of Matthew* (Rome: Biblical Institute Press, 1976).

Songer, H.S. 'The Sermon on the Mount and Its Jewish Foreground', *RevExp* *9 (1992) 165-77.

Squires, J.T. *The Plan of God in Luke-Acts* (SNTSMS 76; Cambridge: CUP, 1993).

Stanton, G.N. *Jesus of Nazareth in New Testament Preaching* (SNTSMS 27; Cambridge: CUP, 1974).

_____ · 'The Origin and Purpose of Matthew's Gospel: Matthean Scholarship from 1945-1980', in H. Temporini and W. Haase (eds.), *Aufstieg und Niedergang der römischen Welt* (II.25.3, Berlin: de Gruyter, 1983) 1889-1951.

_____ · 'The Origin and Purpose of Matthew's Sermon on the Mount', in G.F. Hawthorne and O. Betz (eds.), *Tradition and Interpretation in the New Testament*, FS E.E. Ellis (Grand Rapids/Tübingen: Eerdmans/Mohr, 1987), 181-92.

_____ · *A Gospel for a New People – Studies in Matthew* (Edinburgh: T&T Clark, 1992).

_____ · 'Revisiting Matthew's Communities', *SBLSP* (1994) (Atlanta, Georgia: Scholars Press, 1994) 9-23.

_____ · 'The Early Reception of Matthew's Gospel: New Evidence from Papyri?', in D.E. Aune (ed.), *The Gospel of Matthew in Current Study* (Grand Rapids, Michigan: Eerdmans, 2001) 42-61.

Stark, R. 'Antioch as the Social Situation for Matthew's Gospel' in David. L. Balch (ed.), *Social History of the Matthean Community: Cross-Disciplinary Approaches* (Minneapolis: Fortress, 1991) 189-210.

_____ · *The Rise of Christianity: A Sociologist Reconsiders History*, (Princeton, New Jersey: Princeton University Press, 1996).

Stark R. and Bainbridge, W.S. *A Theory of Religion* (New York: Lang 1987).

Stark R. and Glock, C.Y. *American Piety: The Nature of Religious Commitment* (Berkeley: University of California Press, 1968).

Stemburger, G. *Jewish Contempories of Jesus: Pharisees, Sadducees, Essenes* (Minneapolis: Fortress, 1995).

Stendahl, K. *The School of St. Matthew and Its Use of the Old Testament* (2nd. ed.; Philadelphia: Fortress, 1968).

Strecker, G. *Der Weg der Gerechtigkeit: Untersuchung zur Theologie des Matthäus*, dritte, durchgesehene und erweiterte Auflage (Göttingen: Vandenhoeck & Ruprecht, 1971).

_____ · 'Die Antithesen der Bergpredigt (Mt. 5.21-48 par.)', *ZNW* 69 (1978) 36-72.

_____ · *The Theology of the New Testament* (Berlin/Louisville: de Gruyter/ Westminster John Knox, 2000).

Streeter, B.H. *The Four Gospels* (London: Macmillian, 1924).

Strugnell, J. 'MMT: Second Thoughts on a Forthcoming Edition', in E. Ulrich & J. VanderKam (eds.), *The Community of the Renewed Covenant, The Notre Dame Symposium on the Dead Sea Scrolls* (Notre Dame, Indiana: University of Notre Dame Press, 1993).

Stuhlmacher, P. 'Jesu vollkommenes Gesetz der Freiheit: Zum Verständnis der Bergpredigt', *ZTK* 79 (1982) 283-322.

Suggs, J. 'The Antitheses as Redactional Products', in R.H. Fuller (ed.) *Essays on the Love Commandment* (Philadelphia: Fortress, 1978) 93-107.

Sussman, Y. 'Appendix 1, The History of the Halakha and the Dead Sea Scrolls, Preliminary Talmudic Observations on Miqsat Ma'ase Ha-Torah (4QMMT)', in E. Qimron, and J. Strugnell, (eds.), *Discoveries in the Judaean Desert X, Qumran Cave 4, V, Miqsat Ma'ase Ha-Torah* (Oxford: Claredon Press, 1994).

Syreeni, K. *The Making of the Sermon on the Mount: A Procedural Analysis of Matthew's Redactional Activity.* Part One: *Methodology and Compositional Analysis* (Annales Academiae Scientiarum Fennicae, Dissertation Humanarum Litterarum 44; Helsinki: Suomalainen Tiedeakatemia, 1987).

Taylor, J.E. *The Immerser: John the Baptist within Second Temple Judaism* (Grand Rapids, Michigan: Eerdmans, 1997).

Theissen, G. 'Wanderradikalismus. Literatursoziologische Aspekte der Überlieferung von Worten Jesu im Urchristentum' *ZThK* 70 (1973) 245-71.

_____ · *Sociology of Early Palestinian Christianity*, trans. J. Bowden (Philadelphia: Fortress, 1978).

Thielman, F. *The Law and the New Testament: The Question of Continuity* (New York: Herder & Herder, 1999).

Thompson, W.G. *Matthew's Advice to a Divided Community: Mt. 17,22-18,35* (AnBib 44; Rome: Biblical Institute, 1970).

Tilborg, S. van, *The Jewish Leaders in Matthew* (Leiden: Brill, 1972).

Trilling, W. *Das wahre Israel: Studien zur Theologie des Matthäus-Evangeliums* (EThSt 7; Leipzig: St. Benno-Verlag, 1959).

Trites, A.A. 'The Blessings and Warnings of the Kingdom (Matthew 5:3-12; 7:13-27)', *RevExp* 89 (1992) 179-96.

Trebilco, P. *Jewish Communities in Asia Minor* (SNTSMS 69; Cambridge: CUP, 1991).

Troeltsch, E. *The Social Teaching of the Christian Churches*, trans. O. Wyon (2 vols; London: George Allen and Unwin Ltd, 1931).

Tuckett, C.M. *The Revival of the Griesbach Hypothesis: An Analysis and Appraisal*, (SNTSMS 44; Cambridge: CUP, 1983).

_____ · 'The Beatitudes: A Source Critical Study: With a Reply by M.D. Goulder', *NovT* 25 (1983) 193-216.

_____ · *Q and the History of Early Christianity: Studies on Q* (Edinburgh: T&T Clark, 1996).

Turner, V. *Dramas, Fields and Metaphors* (Ithaca & London: Cornell University, 1974).

_____ · *The Ritual Processes* (New York: Cornell University Press, 1974).

Vaganay, L. *Le problème synoptique: une hypothèse de travail*, (Bibliothèque de théologie, série 3: Théologie biblique1; Tournai: Desclée, 1954).

VanderKam, J.C. *The Dead Sea Scrolls Today* (Grand Rapids, Michigan: Eerdmans, 1994).

Verseput, D. 'The role and meaning of the "Son of God" title in Matthew's Gospel', *NTS* 33 (1987) 532-56.

Wagner, G. (ed.), *An Exegetical Bibliography of the New Testament. Matthew and Mark* (Macon, Ga.: Mercer University Press, 1983).

Wansbrough H. (ed.), *Jesus and the Oral Gospel Tradition* (JSNTSS 64; Sheffield: JSOT, 1991).

Weavers, D. J. *Matthew's Missionary Discourse: A Literary Critical Analysis* (JSNTSS 38; Sheffield: JSOT Press, 1990).

Weeden, T.J. *Mark – Traditions in Conflict* (Philadelphia: Fortress Press, 1971).

Weber, M. *On the Methodology of the Social Sciences*, trans. E.A. Shils and H.A. Finch (Glencoe: The Free Press of Glencoe, 1949).

———— · *The Sociology of Religion* (trans. Ephrain Fischoff; Boston: Beacon Press, 1963).

Wenham, D. 'Jesus and the Law: An Exegesis on Matthew 5:17-20', *Themelios* 4 (1979) 92-96.

Westcott, B.W. *An Introduction to the Study of the Gospels* (London: Macmillan, 1875).

Westerholm, S. *Jesus and Scribal Authority* (CB NTS 10; Lund: CWK Gleerup, 1978).

White, L.M. 'Crisis Management and Boundary Maintainence: The Social Location of the Matthean Community', in D.L. Balch (ed.), *Social History of the Matthean Community* (Minneapolis: Fortress, 1991) 211-247.

White, R.E.O. *The Mind of Matthew* (Philadelphia: Westminster, 1979).

Wiefel, W. *Das Evangelium nach Matthäus* (Theologischer Handkommentar zum Neuen Testament; Leipzig: Evang. Verl.-Anst. 1998).

Wilkins, M.J. *The Concept of Disciple in Matthew's Gospel* (Leiden: Brill, 1988).

Wilson B.R. (ed.), *Patterns of Sectarianism: Organization and Ideology in Social and Religious Movements* (London: Heinemann, 1967).

———— · *Magic and the Millennium: A Sociological Study of Religious Movements of Protest among Tribal and Third-World Peoples* (London: Heinemann, 1973).

———— · *The Social Dimensions of Sectarianism: Sects and New Religious Movements in Contemporary Society* (Oxford: OUP, 1990).

Wink, W. *John the Baptist in the Gospel Tradition* (SNTSMS 7; Cambridge: CUP, 1968).

Wrede, W. *The Messianic Secret* (London and Cambridge, MA: Clarke; Greenwood, S. Carolina: Attic, 1977; German orig. 1901)

Wrege, H-T. *Die Überlieferungsgeschichte der Bergpredigt* (WUNT 9: Tübingen : Mohr, 1968).

Yadin, Y. *The Temple Scroll: The Hidden Law of the Dead Sea Sect* (London: Weidenfeld and Nicolson 1985).

Yang, Y.-E. *Jesus and the Sabbath in Matthew's Gospel* (JSNTSS 139; Sheffield: Sheffield Academic Press, 1997).

Yeung, M.W. *Faith in Jesus and Paul* (WUNT II/147, Tübingen: Mohr Siebeck, 2002).

Zetterholm, M. *The Formation of Christianity in Antioch: A Social-Scientific Approach to the Separation Between Judaism and Christianity* (Routledge Early Christian Monographs, London: Routledge, 2003).

Ziesler, J.A. *The Meaning of Righteousness in Paul* (SNTSMS 20; Cambridge: CUP, 1972).

Zumstein, J. *La condition du croyant dans l'évangele selon Matthieu* (Fribourg: Editions Universitaires, 1977; Göttingen: Vandenhoeck & Ruprecht).

Index of Authors

Index of References

Index of Subjects

Wissenschaftliche Untersuchungen zum Neuen Testament

Alphabetical Index of the First and Second Series

Bosman, Philip: Conscience in Philo and Paul. 2003. *Volume II/166.*

Bovon, François: Studies in Early Christianity. 2003. *Volume 161.*

Brocke, Christoph vom: Thessaloniki – Stadt des Kassander und Gemeinde des Paulus. 2001. *Volume II/125.*

Brunson, Andrew: Psalm 118 in the Gospel of John. 2003. *Volume II/158.*

Büchli, Jörg: Der Poimandres – ein paganisiertes Evangelium. 1987. *Volume II/27.*

Bühner, Jan A.: Der Gesandte und sein Weg im 4. Evangelium. 1977. *Volume II/2.*

Burchard, Christoph: Untersuchungen zu Joseph und Aseneth. 1965. *Volume 8.*

– Studien zur Theologie, Sprache und Umwelt des Neuen Testaments. Ed. von D. Sänger. 1998. *Volume 107.*

Burnett, Richard: Karl Barth's Theological Exegesis. 2001. *Volume II/145.*

Byron, John: Slavery Metaphors in Early Judaism and Pauline Christianity. 2003. *Volume II/162.*

Byrskog, Samuel: Story as History – History as Story. 2000. *Volume 123.*

Cancik, Hubert (Ed.): Markus-Philologie. 1984. *Volume 33.*

Capes, David B.: Old Testament Yaweh Texts in Paul's Christology. 1992. *Volume II/47.*

Caragounis, Chrys C.: The Son of Man. 1986. *Volume 38.*

– see *Fridrichsen, Anton.*

Carleton Paget, James: The Epistle of Barnabas. 1994. *Volume II/64.*

Carson, D.A., O'Brien, Peter T. and *Mark Seifrid* (Ed.): Justification and Variegated Nomism: A Fresh Appraisal of Paul and Second Temple Judaism. Volume 1: The Complexities of Second Temple Judaism. *Volume II/140.*

Ciampa, Roy E.: The Presence and Function of Scripture in Galatians 1 and 2. 1998. *Volume II/102.*

Classen, Carl Joachim: Rhetorical Criticsm of the New Testament. 2000. *Volume 128.*

Colpe, Carsten: Iranier – Aramäer – Hebräer – Hellenen. 2003. *Volume 154.*

Crump, David: Jesus the Intercessor. 1992. *Volume II/49.*

Dahl, Nils Alstrup: Studies in Ephesians. 2000. *Volume 131.*

Deines, Roland: Jüdische Steingefäße und pharisäische Frömmigkeit. 1993. *Volume II/52.*

– Die Pharisäer. 1997. *Volume 101.*

Dettwiler, Andreas and *Jean Zumstein (Ed.):* Kreuzestheologie im Neuen Testament. 2002. *Volume 151.*

Dickson, John P.: Mission-Commitment in Ancient Judaism and in the Pauline Communities. 2003. *Volume II/159.*

Dietzfelbinger, Christian: Der Abschied des Kommenden. 1997. *Volume 95.*

Dobbeler, Axel von: Glaube als Teilhabe. 1987. *Volume II/22.*

Du Toit, David S.: Theios Anthropos. 1997. *Volume II/91*

Dunn, James D.G. (Ed.): Jews and Christians. 1992. *Volume 66.*

– Paul and the Mosaic Law. 1996. *Volume 89.*

Dunn, James D.G., Hans Klein, Ulrich Luz and *Vasile Mihoc* (Ed.): Auslegung der Bibel in orthodoxer und westlicher Perspektive. 2000. *Volume 130.*

Ebel, Eva: Die Attraktivität früher christlicher Gemeinden. 2004. *Volume II/178.*

Ebertz, Michael N.: Das Charisma des Gekreuzigten. 1987. *Volume 45.*

Eckstein, Hans-Joachim: Der Begriff Syneidesis bei Paulus. 1983. *Volume II/10.*

– Verheißung und Gesetz. 1996. *Volume 86.*

Ego, Beate: Im Himmel wie auf Erden. 1989. *Volume II/34*

Ego, Beate and *Lange, Armin* with *Pilhofer, Peter (Ed.):* Gemeinde ohne Tempel – Community without Temple. 1999. *Volume 118.*

Eisen, Ute E.: see *Paulsen, Henning.*

Ellis, E. Earle: Prophecy and Hermeneutic in Early Christianity. 1978. *Volume 18.*

– The Old Testament in Early Christianity. 1991. *Volume 54.*

Endo, Masanobu: Creation and Christology. 2002. *Volume 149.*

Ennulat, Andreas: Die 'Minor Agreements'. 1994. *Volume II/62.*

Ensor, Peter W.: Jesus and His 'Works'. 1996. *Volume II/85.*

Eskola, Timo: Messiah and the Throne. 2001. *Volume II/142.*

– Theodicy and Predestination in Pauline Soteriology. 1998. *Volume II/100.*

Fatehi, Mehrdad: The Spirit's Relation to the Risen Lord in Paul. 2000. *Volume II/128.*

Feldmeier, Reinhard: Die Krisis des Gottessohnes. 1987. *Volume II/21.*

– Die Christen als Fremde. 1992. *Volume 64.*

Feldmeier, Reinhard and *Ulrich Heckel* (Ed.): Die Heiden. 1994. *Volume 70.*

Fletcher-Louis, Crispin H.T.: Luke-Acts: Angels, Christology and Soteriology. 1997. *Volume II/94.*

Förster, Niclas: Marcus Magus. 1999. *Volume 114.*

Forbes, Christopher Brian: Prophecy and Inspired Speech in Early Christianity and its Hellenistic Environment. 1995. *Volume II/75.*

Fornberg, Tord: see *Fridrichsen, Anton.*

Fossum, Jarl E.: The Name of God and the Angel of the Lord. 1985. *Volume 36.*

Foster, Paul: Community, Law and Mission in Matthew's Gospel. *Volume II/177.*

Fotopoulos, John: Food Offered to Idols in Roman Corinth. 2003. *Volume II/151.*

Frenschkowski, Marco: Offenbarung und Epiphanie. Volume 1 1995. *Volume II/79 –* Volume 2 1997. *Volume II/80.*

Frey, Jörg: Eugen Drewermann und die biblische Exegese. 1995. *Volume II/71.*

- Die johanneische Eschatologie. Volume I. 1997. *Volume 96.* – Volume II. 1998. *Volume 110.*

- Volume III. 2000. *Volume 117.*

Freyne, Sean: Galilee and Gospel. 2000. *Volume 125.*

Fridrichsen, Anton: Exegetical Writings. Edited by C.C. Caragounis and T. Fornberg. 1994. *Volume 76.*

Garlington, Don B.: 'The Obedience of Faith'. 1991. *Volume II/38.*

- Faith, Obedience, and Perseverance. 1994. *Volume 79.*

Garnet, Paul: Salvation and Atonement in the Qumran Scrolls. 1977. *Volume II/3.*

Gese, Michael: Das Vermächtnis des Apostels. 1997. *Volume II/99.*

Gheorghita, Radu: The Role of the Septuagint in Hebrews. 2003. *Volume II/160.*

Gräbe, Petrus J.: The Power of God in Paul's Letters. 2000. *Volume II/123.*

Gräßer, Erich: Der Alte Bund im Neuen. 1985. *Volume 35.*

- Forschungen zur Apostelgeschichte. 2001. *Volume 137.*

Green, Joel B.: The Death of Jesus. 1988. *Volume II/33.*

Gregory, Andrew: The Reception of Luke and Acts in the Period before Irenaeus. 2003. *Volume II/169.*

Gundry Volf, Judith M.: Paul and Perseverance. 1990. *Volume II/37.*

Hafemann, Scott J.: Suffering and the Spirit. 1986. *Volume II/19.*

- Paul, Moses, and the History of Israel. 1995. *Volume 81.*

Hahn, Johannes (Ed.): Zerstörungen des Jerusalemer Tempels. 2002. *Volume 147.*

Hannah, Darrel D.: Michael and Christ. 1999. *Volume II/109.*

Hamid-Khani, Saeed: Relevation and Concealment of Christ. 2000. *Volume II/120.*

Harrison; James R.: Paul's Language of Grace in Its Graeco-Roman Context. 2003. *Volume II/172.*

Hartman, Lars: Text-Centered New Testament Studies. Ed. von D. Hellholm. 1997. *Volume 102.*

Hartog, Paul: Polycarp and the New Testament. 2001. *Volume II/134.*

Heckel, Theo K.: Der Innere Mensch. 1993. *Volume II/53.*

- Vom Evangelium des Markus zum viergestaltigen Evangelium. 1999. *Volume 120.*

Heckel, Ulrich: Kraft in Schwachheit. 1993. *Volume II/56.*

- Der Segen im Neuen Testament. 2002. *Volume 150.*

- see *Feldmeier, Reinhard.*

- see *Hengel, Martin.*

Heiligenthal, Roman: Werke als Zeichen. 1983. *Volume II/9.*

Hellholm, D.: see *Hartman, Lars.*

Hemer, Colin J.: The Book of Acts in the Setting of Hellenistic History. 1989. *Volume 49.*

Hengel, Martin: Judentum und Hellenismus. 1969, ³1988. *Volume 10.*

- Die johanneische Frage. 1993. *Volume 67.*

- Judaica et Hellenistica. Kleine Schriften I. 1996. *Volume 90.*

- Judaica, Hellenistica et Christiana. Kleine Schriften II. 1999. *Volume 109.*

- Paulus und Jakobus. Kleine Schriften III. 2002. *Volume 141.*

Hengel, Martin and *Ulrich Heckel* (Ed.): Paulus und das antike Judentum. 1991. *Volume 58.*

Hengel, Martin and *Hermut Löhr* (Ed.): Schriftauslegung im antiken Judentum und im Urchristentum. 1994. *Volume 73.*

Hengel, Martin and *Anna Maria Schwemer:* Paulus zwischen Damaskus und Antiochien. 1998. *Volume 108.*

- Der messianische Anspruch Jesu und die Anfänge der Christologie. 2001. *Volume 138.*

Hengel, Martin and *Anna Maria Schwemer* (Ed.): Königsherrschaft Gottes und himmlischer Kult. 1991. *Volume 55.*

- Die Septuaginta. 1994. *Volume 72.*

Hengel, Martin; Siegfried Mittmann and *Anna Maria Schwemer* (Ed.): La Cité de Dieu / Die Stadt Gottes. 2000. *Volume 129.*

Herrenbrück, Fritz: Jesus und die Zöllner. 1990. *Volume II/41.*

Herzer, Jens: Paulus oder Petrus? 1998. *Volume 103.*

Hoegen-Rohls, Christina: Der nachösterliche Johannes. 1996. *Volume II/84.*

Hofius, Otfried: Katapausis. 1970. *Volume 11.*

– Der Vorhang vor dem Thron Gottes. 1972. *Volume 14.*

– Der Christushymnus Philipper 2,6-11. 1976, ²1991. *Volume 17.*

– Paulusstudien. 1989, ²1994. *Volume 51.*

– Neutestamentliche Studien. 2000. *Volume 132.*

– Paulusstudien II. 2002. *Volume 143.*

Hofius, Otfried and *Hans-Christian Kammler:* Johannesstudien. 1996. *Volume 88.*

Holtz, Traugott: Geschichte und Theologie des Urchristentums. 1991. *Volume 57.*

Hommel, Hildebrecht: Sebasmata. Volume 1 1983. *Volume 31* – Volume 2 1984. *Volume 32.*

Hvalvik, Reidar: The Struggle for Scripture and Covenant. 1996. *Volume II/82.*

Johns, Loren L.: The Lamb Christology of the Apocalypse of John. 2003. *Volume II/167.*

Joubert, Stephan: Paul as Benefactor. 2000. *Volume II/124.*

Jungbauer, Harry: „Ehre Vater und Mutter". 2002. *Volume II/146.*

Kähler, Christoph: Jesu Gleichnisse als Poesie und Therapie. 1995. *Volume 78.*

Kamlah, Ehrhard: Die Form der katalogischen Paränese im Neuen Testament. 1964. *Volume 7.*

Kammler, Hans-Christian: Christologie und Eschatologie. 2000. *Volume 126.*

– Kreuz und Weisheit. 2003. *Volume 159.*

– see *Hofius, Otfried.*

Kelhoffer, James A.: Miracle and Mission. 1999. *Volume II/112.*

Kieffer, René and *Jan Bergman (Ed.):* La Main de Dieu / Die Hand Gottes. 1997. *Volume 94.*

Kim, Seyoon: The Origin of Paul's Gospel. 1981, ²1984. *Volume II/4.*

– "The 'Son of Man'" as the Son of God. 1983. *Volume 30.*

Klauck, Hans-Josef: Religion und Gesellschaft im frühen Christentum. 2003. *Volume 152.*

Klein, Hans: see *Dunn, James D.G..*

Kleinknecht, Karl Th.: Der leidende Gerechtfertigte. 1984, ²1988. *Volume II/13.*

Klinghardt, Matthias: Gesetz und Volk Gottes. 1988. *Volume II/32.*

Koch, Stefan: Rechtliche Regelung von Konflikten im frühen Christentum. 2004. *Volume II/174.*

Köhler, Wolf-Dietrich: Rezeption des Matthäusevangeliums in der Zeit vor Irenäus. 1987. *Volume II/24.*

Kooten, George H. van: Cosmic Christology in Paul and the Pauline School. 2003. *Volume II/171.*

Korn, Manfred: Die Geschichte Jesu in veränderter Zeit. 1993. *Volume II/51.*

Koskenniemi, Erkki: Apollonios von Tyana in der neutestamentlichen Exegese. 1994. *Volume II/61.*

Kraus, Thomas J.: Sprache, Stil und historischer Ort des zweiten Petrusbriefes. 2001. *Volume II/136.*

Kraus, Wolfgang: Das Volk Gottes. 1996. *Volume 85.*

– and *Karl-Wilhelm Niebuhr* (Ed.): Frühjudentum und Neues Testament im Horizont Biblischer Theologie. 2003. *Volume 162.*

– see *Walter, Nikolaus.*

Kreplin, Matthias: Das Selbstverständnis Jesu. 2001. *Volume II/141.*

Kuhn, Karl G.: Achtzehngebet und Vaterunser und der Reim. 1950. *Volume 1.*

Kvalbein, Hans: see *Ådna, Jostein.*

Laansma, Jon: I Will Give You Rest. 1997. *Volume II/98.*

Labahn, Michael: Offenbarung in Zeichen und Wort. 2000. *Volume II/117.*

Lambers-Petry, Doris: see *Tomson, Peter J.*

Lange, Armin: see *Ego, Beate.*

Lampe, Peter: Die stadtrömischen Christen in den ersten beiden Jahrhunderten. 1987, ²1989. *Volume II/18.*

Landmesser, Christof: Wahrheit als Grundbegriff neutestamentlicher Wissenschaft. 1999. *Volume 113.*

– Jüngerberufung und Zuwendung zu Gott. 2000. *Volume 133.*

Lau, Andrew: Manifest in Flesh. 1996. *Volume II/86.*

Lawrence, Louise: An Ethnography of the Gospel of Matthew. 2003. *Volume II/165.*

Lee, Pilchan: The New Jerusalem in the Book of Relevation. 2000. *Volume II/129.*

Lichtenberger, Hermann: see *Avemarie, Friedrich.*

Lierman, John: The New Testament Moses. 2004. *Volume II/173.*

Lieu, Samuel N.C.: Manichaeism in the Later Roman Empire and Medieval China. ²1992. *Volume 63.*

Loader, William R.G.: Jesus' Attitude Towards the Law. 1997. *Volume II/97.*

Löhr, Gebhard: Verherrlichung Gottes durch Philosophie. 1997. *Volume 97.*

Löhr, Hermut: Studien zum frühchristlichen und frühjüdischen Gebet. 2003. *Volume 160.*

– : see *Hengel, Martin.*

Löhr, Winrich Alfried: Basilides und seine Schule. 1995. *Volume 83.*

Luomanen, Petri: Entering the Kingdom of Heaven. 1998. *Volume II/101.*

Luz, Ulrich: see *Dunn, James D.G.*

Maier, Gerhard: Mensch und freier Wille. 1971. *Volume 12.*

– Die Johannesoffenbarung und die Kirche. 1981. *Volume 25.*

Markschies, Christoph: Valentinus Gnosticus? 1992. *Volume 65.*

Marshall, Peter: Enmity in Corinth: Social Conventions in Paul's Relations with the Corinthians. 1987. *Volume II/23.*

Mayer, Annemarie: Sprache der Einheit im Epheserbrief und in der Ökumene. 2002. *Volume II/150.*

McDonough, Sean M.: YHWH at Patmos: Rev. 1:4 in its Hellenistic and Early Jewish Setting. 1999. *Volume II/107.*

McGlynn, Moyna: Divine Judgement and Divine Benevolence in the Book of Wisdom. 2001. *Volume II/139.*

Meade, David G.: Pseudonymity and Canon. 1986. *Volume 39.*

Meadors, Edward P.: Jesus the Messianic Herald of Salvation. 1995. *Volume II/72.*

Meißner, Stefan: Die Heimholung des Ketzers. 1996. *Volume II/87.*

Mell, Ulrich: Die „anderen“ Winzer. 1994. *Volume 77.*

Mengel, Berthold: Studien zum Philipperbrief. 1982. *Volume II/8.*

Merkel, Helmut: Die Widersprüche zwischen den Evangelien. 1971. *Volume 13.*

Merklein, Helmut: Studien zu Jesus und Paulus. Volume 1 1987. *Volume 43.* – Volume 2 1998. *Volume 105.*

Metzdorf, Christina: Die Tempelaktion Jesu. 2003. *Volume II/168.*

Metzler, Karin: Der griechische Begriff des Verzeihens. 1991. *Volume II/44.*

Metzner, Rainer: Die Rezeption des Matthäus- evangeliums im 1. Petrusbrief. 1995. *Volume II/74.*

– Das Verständnis der Sünde im Johannesevan- gelium. 2000. *Volume 122.*

Mihoc, Vasile: see *Dunn, James D.G.*.

Mineshige, Kiyoshi: Besitzverzicht und Almosen bei Lukas. 2003. *Volume II/163.*

Mittmann, Siegfried: see *Hengel, Martin.*

Mittmann-Richert, Ulrike: Magnifikat und Benediktus. *1996. Volume II/90.*

Mußner, Franz: Jesus von Nazareth im Umfeld Israels und der Urkirche. Ed. von M. Theobald. 1998. *Volume 111.*

Niebuhr, Karl-Wilhelm: Gesetz und Paränese. 1987. *Volume II/28.*

– Heidenapostel aus Israel. 1992. *Volume 62.*

– see *Kraus, Wolfgang*

Nielsen, Anders E.: "Until it is Fullfilled". 2000. *Volume II/126.*

Nissen, Andreas: Gott und der Nächste im antiken Judentum. 1974. *Volume 15.*

Noack, Christian: Gottesbewußtsein. 2000. *Volume II/116.*

Noormann, Rolf: Irenäus als Paulusinterpret. 1994. *Volume II/66.*

Novakovic, Lidija: Messiah, the Healer of the Sick. 2003. *Volume II/170.*

Obermann, Andreas: Die christologische Erfüllung der Schrift im Johannesevangeli- um. 1996. *Volume II/83.*

Öhler, Markus: Barnabas. 2003. *Volume 156.*

Okure, Teresa: The Johannine Approach to Mission. 1988. *Volume II/31.*

Oropeza, B. J.: Paul and Apostasy. 2000. *Volume II/115.*

Ostmeyer, Karl-Heinrich: Taufe und Typos. 2000. *Volume II/118.*

Paulsen, Henning: Studien zur Literatur und Geschichte des frühen Christentums. Ed. von Ute E. Eisen. 1997. *Volume 99.*

Pao, David W.: Acts and the Isaianic New Exodus. 2000. *Volume II/130.*

Park, Eung Chun: The Mission Discourse in Matthew's Interpretation. 1995. *Volume II/81.*

Park, Joseph S.: Conceptions of Afterlife in Jewish Insriptions. 2000. *Volume II/121.*

Pate, C. Marvin: The Reverse of the Curse. 2000. *Volume II/114.*

Peres, Imre: Griechische Grabinschriften und neutestamentliche Eschatologie. 2003. *Volume 157.*

Philonenko, Marc (Ed.): Le Trône de Dieu. 1993. *Volume 69.*

Pilhofer, Peter: Presbyteron Kreitton. 1990. *Volume II/39.*

– Philippi. Volume 1 1995. *Volume 87.* – Volume 2 2000. *Volume 119.*

– Die frühen Christen und ihre Welt. 2002. *Volume 145.*

– see *Ego, Beate.*

Pöhlmann, Wolfgang: Der Verlorene Sohn und das Haus. 1993. *Volume 68.*

Pokorný, Petr and *Josef B. Souček:* Bibelausle- gung als Theologie. 1997. *Volume 100.*

Pokorný, Petr and *Jan Roskovec* (Ed.): Philosophical Hermeneutics and Biblical Exegesis. 2002. *Volume 153.*

Porter, Stanley E.: The Paul of Acts. 1999. *Volume 115.*

Prieur, Alexander: Die Verkündigung der Gottesherrschaft. 1996. *Volume II/89.*

Probst, Hermann: Paulus und der Brief. 1991. *Volume II/45.*

Räisänen, Heikki: Paul and the Law. 1983, ²1987. *Volume 29.*

Rehkopf, Friedrich: Die lukanische Sonderquelle. 1959. *Volume 5.*

Rein, Matthias: Die Heilung des Blindgeborenen (Joh 9). 1995. *Volume II/73.*

Reinmuth, Eckart: Pseudo-Philo und Lukas. 1994. *Volume 74.*

Reiser, Marius: Syntax und Stil des Markusevangeliums. 1984. *Volume II/11.*

Richards, E. Randolph: The Secretary in the Letters of Paul. 1991. *Volume II/42.*

Riesner, Rainer: Jesus als Lehrer. 1981, ³1988. *Volume II/7.*

– Die Frühzeit des Apostels Paulus. 1994. *Volume 71.*

Rissi, Mathias: Die Theologie des Hebräerbriefs. 1987. *Volume 41.*

Roskovec, Jan: see *Pokorný, Petr.*

Röhser, Günter: Metaphorik und Personifikation der Sünde. 1987. *Volume II/25.*

Rose, Christian: Die Wolke der Zeugen. 1994. *Volume II/60.*

Rothschild, Clare K.: Luke Acts and the Rhetoric of History. 2004. *Volume II/175.*

Rüegger, Hans-Ulrich: Verstehen, was Markus erzählt. 2002. *Volume II/155.*

Rüger, Hans Peter: Die Weisheitsschrift aus der Kairoer Geniza. 1991. *Volume 53.*

Sänger, Dieter: Antikes Judentum und die Mysterien. 1980. *Volume II/5.*

– Die Verkündigung des Gekreuzigten und Israel. 1994. *Volume 75.*

– see *Burchard, Christoph*

Salzmann, Jorg Christian: Lehren und Ermahnen. 1994. *Volume II/59.*

Sandnes, Karl Olav: Paul – One of the Prophets? 1991. *Volume II/43.*

Sato, Migaku: Q und Prophetie. 1988. *Volume II/29.*

Schäfer, Ruth: Paulus bis zum Apostelkonzil. 2004. *Volume II/179.*

Schaper, Joachim: Eschatology in the Greek Psalter. 1995. *Volume II/76.*

Schimanowski, Gottfried: Die himmlische Liturgie in der Apokalypse des Johannes. 2002. *Volume II/154.*

– Weisheit und Messias. 1985. *Volume II/17.*

Schlichting, Günter: Ein jüdisches Leben Jesu. 1982. *Volume 24.*

Schnabel, Eckhard J.: Law and Wisdom from Ben Sira to Paul. 1985. *Volume II/16.*

Schutter, William L.: Hermeneutic and Composition in I Peter. 1989. *Volume II/30.*

Schwartz, Daniel R.: Studies in the Jewish Background of Christianity. 1992. *Volume 60.*

Schwemer, Anna Maria: see *Hengel, Martin*

Scott, James M.: Adoption as Sons of God. 1992. *Volume II/48.*

– Paul and the Nations. 1995. *Volume 84.*

Shum, Shiu-Lun: Paul's Use of Isaiah in Romans. 2002. *Volume II/156.*

Siegert, Folker: Drei hellenistisch-jüdische Predigten. Teil I 1980. *Volume 20* – Teil II 1992. *Volume 61.*

– Nag-Hammadi-Register. 1982. *Volume 26.*

– Argumentation bei Paulus. 1985. *Volume 34.*

– Philon von Alexandrien. 1988. *Volume 46.*

Simon, Marcel: Le christianisme antique et son contexte religieux I/II. 1981. *Volume 23.*

Snodgrass, Klyne: The Parable of the Wicked Tenants. 1983. *Volume 27.*

Söding, Thomas: Das Wort vom Kreuz. 1997. *Volume 93.*

– see *Thüsing, Wilhelm.*

Sommer, Urs: Die Passionsgeschichte des Markusevangeliums. 1993. *Volume II/58.*

Souček, Josef B.: see *Pokorný, Petr.*

Spangenberg, Volker: Herrlichkeit des Neuen Bundes. 1993. *Volume II/55.*

Spanje, T.E. van: Inconsistency in Paul? 1999. *Volume II/110.*

Speyer, Wolfgang: Frühes Christentum im antiken Strahlungsfeld. Volume I: 1989. *Volume 50.*

– Volume II: 1999. *Volume 116.*

Stadelmann, Helge: Ben Sira als Schriftgelehrter. 1980. *Volume II/6.*

Stenschke, Christoph W.: Luke's Portrait of Gentiles Prior to Their Coming to Faith. *Volume II/108.*

Stettler, Christian: Der Kolosserhymnus. 2000. *Volume II/131.*

Stettler, Hanna: Die Christologie der Pastoralbriefe. 1998. *Volume II/105.*

Stökl Ben Ezra, Daniel: The Impact of Yom Kippur on Early Christianity. 2003. *Volume 163.*

Strobel, August: Die Stunde der Wahrheit. 1980. *Volume 21.*

Stroumsa, Guy G.: Barbarian Philosophy. 1999. *Volume 112.*

Stuckenbruck, Loren T.: Angel Veneration and Christology. 1995. *Volume II/70.*

Stuhlmacher, Peter (Ed.): Das Evangelium und die Evangelien. 1983. *Volume 28.*

– Biblische Theologie und Evangelium. 2002.
Volume 146.

Sung, Chong-Hyon: Vergebung der Sünden.
1993. *Volume II/57.*

Tajra, Harry W.: The Trial of St. Paul. 1989.
Volume II/35.

– The Martyrdom of St.Paul. 1994.
Volume II/67.

Theißen, Gerd: Studien zur Soziologie des
Urchristentums. 1979, ³1989. *Volume 19.*

Theobald, Michael: Studien zum Römerbrief.
2001. *Volume 136.*

Theobald, Michael: see *Mußner, Franz.*

Thornton, Claus-Jürgen: Der Zeuge des
Zeugen. 1991. *Volume 56.*

Thüsing, Wilhelm: Studien zur neutestamentlichen Theologie. Ed. von Thomas Söding.
1995. *Volume 82.*

Thurén, Lauri: Derhethorizing Paul. 2000.
Volume 124.

Tomson, Peter J. and *Doris Lambers-Petry*
(Ed.): The Image of the Judaeo-Christians in
Ancient Jewish and Christian Literature.
2003. *Volume 158.*

Treloar, Geoffrey R.: Lightfoot the Historian.
1998. *Volume II/103.*

Tsuji, Manabu: Glaube zwischen Vollkommen-
heit und Verweltlichung. 1997. *Volume II/93*

Twelftree, Graham H.: Jesus the Exorcist. 1993.
Volume II/54.

Urban, Christina: Das Menschenbild nach dem
Johannesevangelium. 2001. *Volume II/137.*

Visotzky, Burton L.: Fathers of the World. 1995.
Volume 80.

Vollenweider, Samuel: Horizonte neutestamentlicher Christologie. 2002. *Volume 144.*

Vos, Johan S.: Die Kunst der Argumentation bei
Paulus. 2002. *Volume 149.*

Wagener, Ulrike: Die Ordnung des „Hauses
Gottes". 1994. *Volume II/65.*

Walker, Donald D.: Paul's Offer of Leniency
(2 Cor 10:1). 2002. *Volume II/152.*

Walter, Nikolaus: Praeparatio Evangelica. Ed.
von Wolfgang Kraus und Florian Wilk.
1997. *Volume 98.*

Wander, Bernd: Gottesfürchtige und Sympathi-
santen. 1998. *Volume 104.*

Watts, Rikki: Isaiah's New Exodus and Mark.
1997. *Volume II/88.*

Wedderburn, A.J.M.: Baptism and Resurrection.
1987. *Volume 44.*

Wegner, Uwe: Der Hauptmann von Kafarnaum.
1985. *Volume II/14.*

Weissenrieder, Annette: Images of Illness in the
Gospel of Luke. 2003. Volume II/164.

Welck, Christian: Erzählte ‚Zeichen'. 1994.
Volume II/69.

Wiarda, Timothy: Peter in the Gospels . 2000.
Volume II/127.

Wilk, Florian: see *Walter, Nikolaus.*

Williams, Catrin H.: I am He. 2000.
Volume II/113.

Wilson, Walter T.: Love without Pretense. 1991.
Volume II/46.

Wisdom, Jeffrey: Blessing for the Nations and
the Curse of the Law. 2001. *Volume II/133.*

Wucherpfennig, Ansgar: Heracleon Philologus.
2002. *Volume 142.*

Yeung, Maureen: Faith in Jesus and Paul. 2002.
Volume II/147.

Zimmermann, Alfred E.: Die urchristlichen
Lehrer. 1984, ²1988. *Volume II/12.*

Zimmermann, Johannes: Messianische Texte
aus Qumran. 1998. *Volume II/104.*

Zimmermann, Ruben: Geschlechtermetaphorik
und Gottesverhältnis. 2001. *Volume II/122.*

Zumstein, Jean: see *Dettwiler, Andreas*

For a complete catalogue please write to the publisher
Mohr Siebeck • P.O. Box 2030 • D–72010 Tübingen/Germany
Up-to-date information on the internet at www.mohr.de